C000133917

APPROXIMATION

In our era of 'fake news', Stella Bruzzi examines the dynamism that results from reusing and reconfiguring raw documentary data (documents, archive, news etc.) in creative ways.

Through a series of individual case studies, this book offers an innovative framework for understanding how, in our century, film and media texts frequently represent reality and negotiate the instabilities of 'truth' by 'approximating' factual events rather than merely representing them, through juxtaposing disparate, often colliding, perspectives of history and factual events. Covering areas such as true crime, politics and media, the book analyses the fluidity and instability of truth, arguing that 'approximation' is more prevalent now in our digital age, and that its conception is a result of viewers' accidental or unconscious connections and interventions.

Original and thought-provoking, *Approximation* provides students and researchers of media, film and cultural studies a deeper insight into our understanding and acceptance of what truth really means today.

Stella Bruzzi is Dean of the Faculty of Arts and Humanities at University College London (UCL) and Fellow of the British Academy. She has published widely in the areas of documentary, costume and masculinity in Hollywood. Her publications include *Undressing Cinema: Clothing and Identity in the Movies*, *New Documentary* and *Men's Cinema*. *Approximation* is an output from a Leverhulme Major Research Fellowship.

APPROXIMATION

Documentary, History and the Staging of Reality

Stella Bruzzi

Routledge
Taylor & Francis Group

LONDON AND NEW YORK

First published 2020
by Routledge
2 Park Square, Milton Park, Abingdon, Oxon OX14 4RN

and by Routledge
52 Vanderbilt Avenue, New York, NY 10017

Routledge is an imprint of the Taylor & Francis Group, an informa business

© 2020 Stella Bruzzi

The right of Stella Bruzzi to be identified as author of this work has been
asserted by her in accordance with sections 77 and 78 of the Copyright,
Designs and Patents Act 1988.

All rights reserved. No part of this book may be reprinted or reproduced or
utilised in any form or by any electronic, mechanical, or other means, now
known or hereafter invented, including photocopying and recording, or in
any information storage or retrieval system, without permission in writing
from the publishers.

Trademark notice: Product or corporate names may be trademarks or
registered trademarks, and are used only for identification and explanation
without intent to infringe.

British Library Cataloguing-in-Publication Data
A catalogue record for this book is available from the British Library

Library of Congress Cataloging-in-Publication Data
Names: Bruzzi, Stella, 1962– author.
Title: Approximation : documentary, history and staging reality / Stella Bruzzi.
Description: London ; New York : Routledge, 2020. | Includes
    bibliographical references and index.
Identifiers: LCCN 2019056710 (print) | LCCN 2019056711 (ebook)
Subjects: LCSH: Documentary mass media. | Truthfulness and falsehood. |
    Representation (Philosophy) | Mass media—Psychological aspects. |
    Mass media—Philosophy.
Classification: LCC P96.D62 B78 2020 (print) | LCC P96.D62 (ebook) |
    DDC 070.1—dc23
LC record available at https://lccn.loc.gov/2019056710
LC ebook record available at https://lccn.loc.gov/2019056711

ISBN: 978-0-415-68832-1 (hbk)
ISBN: 978-0-415-68835-2 (pbk)
ISBN: 978-0-203-12948-7 (ebk)

Typeset in Bembo
by Apex CoVantage, LLC

CONTENTS

ACKNOWLEDGEMENTS

Approximation has been with me for a number of years, from the chilly morning at the end of a tiring Autumn Term at Warwick, when I opened the letter from the Leverhulme Trust congratulating me on being one of that year's crop of Major Research Fellows (one of four in that round won by Warwick, of which I – as Chair of Faculty at the time – was immeasurably proud, although much credit goes to Liese Perrin, our outstanding research development manager). I am hugely grateful to the Leverhulme Trust for giving me two years' research leave to formulate *Approximation*, to finally visit Dealey Plaza in Dallas which, since my conspiratorial teenage years, had been an imaginative obsession; to visit Washington DC and Boston – and to write. As part of the review process I was undoubtedly helped by the kind assessments of my two reviewers, John Corner and John Izod, to whom I owe sincere and belated thanks for their enthusiasm and for their constructive and perspicacious comments. Thank you also to Routledge, and in particular my editor, Natalie Foster, not only for her patience but also for her unwavering support; my debt over the years to her and to Routledge is considerable – the publicity poster for *Undressing Cinema* still hangs on my office wall!

This book started life during my ten years as a member of Warwick's Department of Film and Television Studies. Thank you to Charlotte Brunsdon, my wise next door neighbour, to Tracey McVey, who kept us all sane, to my heads of department Jon Burrows, Catherine Constable and Alastair Phillips and to all my other brilliant colleagues. Thanks also to the Leverhulme Trust for bringing us Karl Schoonover to cover my absence, not only an outstanding scholar but now a dear friend. It was also such a pleasure to teach the topics of documentary re-enactment, representations of history and other areas covered in the pages that follow. My research is always incalculably enriched by my teaching, so I am immensely grateful to the classes of 2014, 2015 and 2016, especially my Third Year classes on Re-enactment – your enthusiastic voices are in this book.

In 2017, I became Dean of Arts and Humanities at UCL, which halted progress until I became an absentee landlady and carved out a term's sabbatical. I've since learnt that a concerned colleague in Mechanical Engineering saw me on the bus in Oxford and wondered if I'd been issued with my P45; I am eternally grateful to UCL for not letting me go, but instead letting me go off and write, and I'd like to thank all my colleagues, especially the faculty staff who did so much more than merely keep the show on the road while I assumed my post in the Bodleian Library: John Mullan, interim Dean *sans pareil*, Dania Herrera, Katie Canada, Julie Smith, Arne Hofmann and everybody else who supported them. I'm also indebted to Anthony Smith, the most supportive of 'line managers', and to our President and Provost Michael Arthur.

An academic's life can be charted through their books – and the relationships that made them possible. I extend warmest thanks to all my friends with whom I've shared fun and scholarship, but especially to those who helped me get over the finish line with *Approximation*: Daniela Berghahn, who read a draft of my Introduction and asked me all the right questions; Ingrid de Smet, also one of 'my' Leverhulme Major Research Fellowship round; Pamela Church Gibson, who will now tempt me back to costume and décor; Jackie Jarvis, who endearingly refers to my summer of writing as my 'time off'; and, last but not least, to Beth Millward, my theatre-going companion of some 30 years!

I am grateful too to the filmmakers who shared their work with me: to Jasper Rigole, for giving me a DVD of *Paradise Recollected* and supplying stills from the film; to Milo Rau, Carey Young and Marc Isaacs for granting me access to their documentaries via Vimeo. And thanks to John Keane for granting Routledge permission to use 'Comedy Ballistics' on the cover. And thanks to Denise Hansen for her work on the Index.

Gratitude too to those who have invited me to give papers on *Approximation* in Bristol, Liverpool, Ghent, Delhi, Santiago de Chile, Brno, Monash, Chapman, Navarra and KCL at the BFI Southbank, to name but a few. Although much changed, earlier versions of some chapters appeared in other publications. Some of what appears here in the chapter on political mimicry was tested out in '"It Won't Be Iraq They'll Remember Me For, Will It?": Tony Blair and the War on Terror', for Stephen Lacey and Derek Paget's *The War on Terror: Post-9/11 Television Drama, Docudrama and Documentary* (2014); two earlier stabs at the true crime documentary section appeared in *Documentary Across Disciplines* (editors Erika Balsom and Hila Peleg, MIT Press, 2016) and in Vol. 10, Issue 2, 2016 of *Law and Humanities*; work on *The Eternal Frame* and *Report* appeared in *The Moving Image Review and Art Journal* (*MIRAJ*) in Vol. 2, Issue 1, 2013, and in 'The Pink Suit' in *Fashion Cultures* Revisited, which I co-edited with Pamela Church Gibson (Routledge, 2013).[1]

As ever, my biggest debt of gratitude is to my family, to my husband Mick Conefrey for making everything possible, my father Stefano and my brother Josh. Nothing about these relationships is approximate, and this book is dedicated with love to my children, Frank and Phyllis.

Note

1 Parts of 'The Pink Suit' research informed Chapter 3, *Mad Men* and the incidental events of the 1960s.

INTRODUCTION

Approximation

Imagine a montage sequence in which the extracts from the following are played and repeated in random order:

- Abraham Zapruder's 8mm home movie footage.
- Mary Norman being interviewed on television 22 November 1963 about the polaroid photograph she had taken earlier that day of the presidential motorcade.
- Footage from the FBI's (Federal Bureau of Investigation) 1964 re-enactment of Lee Harvey Oswald's (alleged) feat of firing all three bullets from the 6th Floor of the Texas School Book Depository.
- Bruce Conner's found footage compilation film *Report* (1967).
- Emile de Antonio and Mark Lane's documentary *Rush to Judgement* (1966).
- A film about a fictional political conspiracy and assassination – maybe *Executive Action* (David Miller, 1973).
- The video game *JFK Reloaded* (2004).
- The drama-documentary *The Kennedys* (2011).

Interspersed with reproductions of:

- Robert Rauschenberg's *Retroactive* (1963).
- One of Andy Warhol's *Jackies* (1963–4).
- One of John Keane's series 'Truth, Lies and Super-8' (1997).
- A Jackie Kennedy Onassis cut-out fashion doll dressed in a pink suit and pill-box hat.

FIGURE I.1 Jackie Kennedy in *Report*, Bruce Conner 1967

Lacking either the illogicality of the archival sequences in a film such as Ed Wood's *Glen or Glenda?* or the insidious freneticism of the comparable sequence in *The Parallax View*, any putative montage constructed from the images above has a focus: the assassination of President John F. Kennedy in Dealey Plaza, Dallas on 22 November 1963. As images endlessly repeat, they comment upon and collide with each other differently and create alternative meanings and mini histories; each sequence, however, still possessing some form of narrative or sub-narrative logic. Many will be familiar with novelist and critic E.M. Forster's classic maxim: "'The king died and then the queen died" is a story. "The king died, and then the queen died of grief" is a plot' (1927: 87). While some edits would, in Forster's binary opposition, sit under 'story', others would have their elements arranged in such a way as to conform to his notion of 'plot'. But in conjunction with each other – whatever the local plot or story focus (and different sequences might throw up alternative narratives) – all are likely to congregate around the assassination, regardless of the fact that not all of the individual components, prior to such contextualisation, will be 'legible' to the same degree. Regardless of any prior awareness of the JFK context or 'plot', a scene from *The Kennedys* would, courtesy of its inherent plotting and narrative development, remain intelligible as a story about a large, wealthy, political, Roman Catholic family beset by tragedy whether or not the viewer had any prior knowledge about who John Kennedy was or how he died. Conversely, the extract from the mute and unedited video compilation of the FBI marksmen's attempts from the point of view of a rifle trained on a male figure in the back seat of an open-topped limousine (re-enactments that date to the FBI and Secret Service visit to Dallas, Texas on 24 May 1964 'to simulate the conditions that existed at the assassination scene on November 22')[1] would not be 'readable' by the same viewer except as a series of repetitions of approximately the same actions: the male figure sitting upright, upright with his arms raised or slumped to the left, poses that would resonate with those familiar with other referents, notably the Zapruder film.

Now, by contrast, recall a single image: a black and white photograph used in James Marsh's documentary *Man on Wire* (2008) of Philippe Petit tightrope walking between the twin towers of the World Trade Center. In 1974, the subject had been the (barely visible) figure of Petit on his wire; the passenger jet is accidental. And yet now, if the photograph carries additional meaning at all, it will evoke events to which this image is not related from 27 years later, namely '9/11' and specifically the attacks on the World Trade Center when al-Qaeda terrorists flew two passenger planes into the towers on the morning of 11 September 2001.

Both the catalogue of images that collect around a core theme and the single picture fall into the category of what I am terming 'approximation': a process whereby a subject, event or act is evoked through bringing together contrasting versions and interlocking points of view, even if it is not straightforwardly represented. Through 'approximation' associations are made between multiple, often conflicting and tangential points of view, data is re-ordered, and meaningful connections established between frequently disparate and unconnected elements, bringing about an, often complex, consolidation of diverse allusions, influences and inferences. Triggers within texts set off 'approximation', indicating (as in the examples above) the fluidity and instability of truth – that it remains open to reinterpretation and change. The layered thinking that underpins 'approximation', I argue, suggests two things: that 'approximation' is, if not absolutely a 21st century phenomenon, then much more prevalent now than it was (no doubt fuelled and facilitated by advancements in digital technology); that it is centred on the moment of reception and comes into being as a result of the viewer making connections and interventions, some of which (as with the 1974 photograph) may be entirely accidental or unconscious.

'Approximation' is performative in that it is generated and comes into being as its multiple elements connect and collide; a prerequisite is the active interaction with facts and history and the equally active engagement of a receptive audience; consequently, if it is to intervene or function as commentary, 'approximation' will only work if it is 'readable', if it can be decipherable. Generic and temporal relations are key, as 'approximation' works across time by seeing and making connections between the past and the present and across genres, by acknowledging that the routes to understanding factual events are multifarious, and draw together a diversity of perspectives and even extend to fiction. The images in the JFK montage (from actuality to drama) are not a hierarchical sequence of concentric circles with a stable 'truth' at their epicentre and at their periphery the most fictionalised representations. The centrality of fiction to this project remained important throughout, and one starting point for my thinking on 'approximation' was, perhaps inevitably, the attacks of 11 September 2001, not just because of their traumatic momentousness but because of the way in which cultural critics (such as Susan Sontag, Jean

Baudrillard, Slavoj Žižek and filmmaker Robert Altman) wrote about the extent to which those terrorist acts (in particular the destruction of the twin towers) resembled Hollywood fictions.

In making allusions beyond the superficialities of any given text or narrative, works that exemplify 'approximation' are literally or intellectually fragmentary; they rupture the surface of representation, and in so doing question the very notion of a fixed and identifiable 'truth' by perpetually opening up a fact or a historical moment to reassessment and reinvestigation. The clashes between points of view might be implicit and embedded (as in the 'based on a true story' drama-documentary), or explicit, as when archival and dramatized material is edited together in a film such as *Detroit* (Bigelow, 2017) in its recounting of the riots that followed the deaths of black teenagers at the hands of police at the city's Algiers Motel in June 1967. Alongside the internal juxtaposition between archive and fiction (announced by a switch in screen ratio) the events are also informed by contemporary events; firstly, there was the unhappy coincidence between the film's release in the US and the violent clashes between white supremacists and counter-protestors in Charlottesville, Virginia; secondly, there was, more broadly, the systemic and institutional racism exemplified by President Trump's response to that violence when he declared there to be 'blame on both sides'. The triggers that enable and inform 'approximation', as here, can be accidental; they might be elliptical and shadowy presences, a sequence of tectonic plates that nudge, shunt, overlap; they might be more overt and definite references that irrevocably change each other. 'Approximation' is essentially a democratic process, not limiting, prescribed or didactic as a 'closed' expositional 'based on a true story' film might be.

Concomitantly, 'approximation' is also characterised by turbulence and unpredictability, the result of an excitable flirtation with how to show and perform facts and evidence, with mixing genres and switching cultural arenas. Just as 'approximation's' consumer, the viewer, needs to be able to engage with and 'read' a text, so an important element of that engagement is that the same viewer also comes to *feel* 'approximation'. As options and perspectives multiply, so 'approximation's' sensory dimension emerges with the *frisson* that comes with recognition (however transitory or oblique) of a film or text's point of reference, as occurs with many of the images referenced at the outset of this Introduction. 'Approximation' becomes somewhat fixated on the moment of transition from one state (of innocence, of not knowing) to another (of experience and knowledge), as the process of watching metamorphoses into one of conjoining facts and interpretations, of detecting the unresolved presence of one within the other, or the oscillation between them. The shudder of this affective acknowledgement marks the impact of the textual fissure and becomes the current we sense when an ephemeral, shady allusion to a previous reality, a previous moment, sets off a chain reaction across time, images and genres. These responses serve as reminders that the most potent and enduring examples of 'approximation' contain relevance to the contemporary, the 'now', but a 'now' that, just like its counterpart 'the past', is neither closed nor sealed, but rather an ever-shifting present, constantly multiplying and superseding itself.

Thinking of broader structures now, as a conceptual framework 'approxima-tion' offers the *mise-en-scène* or staging of fact and history: a place where what is known about a historical event, a factual occurrence or a real person is inserted into a narrative, not in order to be collapsed into fiction, but to co-exist in colli-sion with it. Elizabeth Cowie argued (in relation to psychoanalysis and Hollywood film) that 'the opposition real/not real is wholly inappropriate to a consideration of fantasy' as fantasy, usually 'characterised as a series of wishes presented through imaginary happenings', is also 'a structure: fantasy as the *mise-en-scène* of desire, the putting into a scene, a staging, of desire' (1992: 149). Approximations are similarly both figurative and imaginary structures, the stagings of evidence and fact, re-enactments of the pooled resources of filmmakers, spectators, historians and other collators of evidence. In addition, recent technological advances enable 'approximation' and facilitate, alongside film and television, the dissemination of satirical photomontages of collage artists such as 'Cold War Steve', whose John Heartfield-esque *Time* magazine cover, 'Brexit Britain',[2] showed an 'out of ser-vice' red bus sinking into the Thames (with royals and politicians on board), or earlier, works such as 'Photo Op' by KennardPhillips, in which Tony Blair grins into his phone taking a selfie as behind him the black smoke and flames of an oil field explosion billow.

The chapters that follow are arranged between discussions of what are effec-tively the twin pillars of this project: archive and re-enactment. After Michel Fou-cault, who made the case for fetishism as the 'model' perversion, the 'guiding thread for analysing all the other deviations' (1990: 154), I argue for re-enactment as the 'model' 'approximation'. Re-enactment is the quintessential embodiment of this project, as 'approximation' always, in a fundamental sense, has re-enactment at its core. Conversely, the use of archive enacts most clearly how 'approximation' works on the level of form and style. Very rarely do works examined in this book have no archive in them at all, for the simple reason that actuality footage possesses the crucial trace of the real that underpins 'approximation'. As a result, even when authentic archive is missing, as in Roman Polanski's adaptation of Robert Harris's novel, *The Ghost* (2007), quasi-archival fictional images take its place, which often explicitly recall real and/or familiar newsreel or actuality footage. Archive and re-enactment thereby offer the purest, most explicit expressions of the moment of collision between images and versions of events that characterises 'approximation'. Having started to develop this notion of 'approximation', I recalled André Bazin's far less positive use of the word in *What is Cinema?* as he dismissed anything other than the presumed purity of photographic image as 'a *mere approximation*' (Bazin, 1967: 14; my italics). Seeking to establish an alternative usage and premise for the term, the status of fiction as a component of 'approximation' became key. For Bazin, like so many others since, the photographic image and fiction sit in binary opposi-tion; although they will never, in some Baudrillardian mélange, be the same, con-fused and/or interchangeable, what if the two were (as represented in the piece of archive and the re-enactment) potentially equal mechanisms for unlocking reality? 'Approximation' grants fictionalisation this power.

In one crucial sense, of course, Bazin is right: nothing can ever supplant the charge of recognition generated by the piece of archival 'ocular proof'. When, for instance, in Rithy Panh's *The Missing Picture* (2013), over a re-enactment using clay figurines of a scene from Panh's Cambodian childhood, the whir of helicopter blades becomes audible, for many this will be all that is required to convey the encroachment of the Cambodian War in advance of the archive footage that follows. In the quite different context of the first episode of Russell T. Davies's dystopian, counter-factual drama, *Years and Years* (2019), the insertion into a fictional news bulletin of genuine headlines from the day before (such as the announcement of the death of Doris Day) instantly make us recalibrate our responses to the surrounding hypothetical fiction. These are triggers, not explanations, however; something that 'approximation' also brings is realism about the indexical image's limitations – what it can definitively *explain* as oppose to 'merely' *evoke* about the events it portrays. In wanting to broaden the discussion beyond the nonfictional image, this book extends many of the discussions in *New Documentary* (Bruzzi, 2006), in which I argued that all factual representation is performative and that images discussed as 'real' or 'authentic', just like their copies, only ever speak to the 'truth' of the moment of encounter between reality and its representation. The representation of reality is never the same as the reality of a moment as it would have transpired had the camera not arrived to capture it; filming is always an incision, an intrusion. As a result, the 'truth' in any piece of film is only ever a representation, the result of a complex negotiation between reality on the one hand and interpretation on the other. 'Approximation' enacts the tensions of this realisation with, at its root, realities that remain unseen; breaks are exposed as opposed to camouflaged behind continuity editing or other mechanisms for averting our gaze from the issue of representation.

Which brings me back to 'approximation's' 'readability'. Judith Butler's extended discussion of 'realness' and 'reading' in *Bodies That Matter* speaks to the elastic complexities of 'approximation' but also to the limitations of an attachment to 'realness'. (She, like Bazin, makes use of the term 'approximation'). Butler's object of discussion is *Paris is Burning* (Jennie Livingston, 1990), a documentary about the Harlem drag balls of the late 1980s. The drag performers (or 'walkers') aspire to 'realness', to authentic replication; though 'not exactly a category in which one competes', Butler writes, it becomes 'a standard that is used to judge any given performance' (Butler, 1993: 88). To attain such a consummate level of authenticity that their performance goes unnoticed would, in turn, ensure that the performance is not 'readable'. 'Reading', as interviewees explain, is to take a performance apart, to discern and expose 'what fails to work' (88). 'For a performance to work', Butler sums up, 'means that a reading is no longer possible ... the impossibility of reading means that the artifice works, the approximation of realness appears to be achieved, the body performing and the ideal performed appear indistinguishable' (88). Yet as the very setting of the drag balls gives each performance away, as it were, I question Butler's conclusion that a performance has failed if it is identifiable as a performance.

The question of 'realness' has obvious ramifications for the nonfictional image, and as with the drag balls, context as opposed to actual performance often supplies the disruption of the 'real'. In *24 City* (2008) Jia Zhangke's documentary about a former weapons factory in Chengdu (called Factory 240), fictionalised interviews with actors Joan Chen, Lü Liping, Chen Jianbin and Zhao Tao are inserted among 'genuine' interviews with former Factory 240 workers. No additional information is supplied to signal that these are different or fake – they are filmed in comparable settings and, as for their 'real' counterparts, the characters' names are supplied at the start of their interviews, along with the dates of their employment. However, as critics noted,[3] with Joan Chen's appearance comes an explicitly performative signpost, as Chen, one of China's globally recognised screen actors, plays a worker nick-named 'Little Flower' as a result of her resemblance to . . . Joan Chen in her first film, *Little Flower* (1979). Her fluid status is further gestured by one specific element of the interview's *mise-en-scène*, namely a mirror positioned behind Chen (who is interviewed in a dilapidated hairdresser's shop) that, by giving us two Joan Chens, continually reminds us of her dual status.

These discreet, covert signs that puncture the 'realness' of Chen's performance differ from the accurate lip-synching by actors of interviewees' voices in Clio Barnard's *The Arbor* (2010). Although once again there is little trace of the performative artifice involved, at the outset of *The Arbor* on-screen text announces the lip-synching, so the staged interviews are both 'real' (in that the disparity between image and voice is hard to detect) and 'readable', as we are apprised of the rules of the game. Likewise, the radical synchrony of some performances during the 1988 British Broadcast Ban (when the voices of spokespeople from Sinn Féin and other Irish political organisations were banned from UK television and radio) could be, in Butler's terms, judged as having succeeded, as actors such as Stephen Rea became so proficient at re-voicing politicians such as Gerry Adams that 'to all intents and purposes . . . the words you were hearing were coming from his lips'.[4] Their 'realness', however, was still always 'readable' through context (news bulletins during 'the troubles') and often through on-screen labelling.

'Reading' is essential to 'approximation', a realisation I was reminded of when, having watched Quentin Tarantino's *Once Upon a Time . . . in Hollywood* (2019), I overheard an exasperated young adult in the foyer of the cinema only learning about the Sharon Tate murders *after* having seen the film. This fellow cinemagoer and I attended the same screening but enjoyed fundamentally different movies. That *Once Upon a Time . . . in Hollywood* is alternate history is crucial to its 'readability' – unless, of course, you are unaware of the facts being countered; 'realness' is not sought by any work (nonfiction or fiction) that seeks to comment on reality. So, in response to Butler, I would argue that to be 'readable' as 'approximation' is, is not an indication of failure but instead a constructive opening up of a film or performance to multiple perspectives and interpretations, which in turn are the embodiment of the inherent fracturedness of reality and the performative instability of 'realness'.

These multiple perspectives extend from actuality footage to re-enactment, both of which can lead us back to the 'truth' it is concerned with but is unable to authentically replicate. Errol Morris, who, with *The Thin Blue Line* (1988), introduced the hyper-stylised re-enactment to documentary, has written eloquently on the value and purpose of re-enactment as a mechanism 'to better understand what really happened' (Morris, 2008) – notwithstanding that, with a re-enactment such as the much-cited chocolate milkshake looping slowly through the air in *The Thin Blue Line*, his images had travelled so far from the indexical moment they recalled that the re-enactment could not possibly be mistaken for it. Likewise, the sub-genre of documentary animation provides further illustration, with films such as *Persepolis* (Marjane Satrapi and Vincent Paronnaud, 2007) and *Waltz With Bashir* (Ari Forman, 2008), of the effective use of superficially inauthentic representational detachment as a response to traumatic memory. These documentaries (which arguably twenty years ago might not have been thought of as documentaries) counter the indexical historical image with animation and contribute to the post-millennial rejection of straightforwardly representational images as the primary means of accessing 'truth' by offering a radical, creative reassessment of how reality can be represented. The 'truth' is not contingent on proximity, and it is worth remembering that all the visual excess and stylisation of its re-enactments did not prevent *The Thin Blue Line* from intervening in reality by helping to get a wrongly convicted man off 'death row'.

As already intimated, the idea behind 'approximation' is to propose that there is a proliferation of ways to capture 'realness', thereby rejecting the belief that 'realness' resides only at the most indexical end of a hypothetical continuum of representation. One key issue for 'approximation' is the relative value of proximity and distance, and the possibility that critique and analysis often more readily follow on from more detached versions of events. The passage from one approximate layer to another is charted literally in films such as *The Deal* (2003) and *The Queen* (2006) in which several sequences are constructed using television archive, dramatisations which, through the quality of the image, framing and use of camera, are made to look like archive but are not, and fully-fledged dramatised sequences that have left all vestiges of nonfiction behind. Two common assumptions underpin responses to sequences such as these: firstly, that more indexical and proximate images reveal more about reality; secondly, that fictionalisations of factual events are to be viewed as 'uncanny' versions of those recognisable, real occurrences – that is, to be eerily defined by them. 'Approximation' acknowledges and promotes a less hierarchical and more fluid relationship between reality, the indexical image and fiction. An important notion, for instance, which I developed with while developing 'approximation' and its democratisation of the relationship between nonfiction and fiction as routes to arriving at the truth of 'what really happened', was that of a 'reverse uncanny'. Soaking in the weirdness of Dallas's Dealey Plaza, the scene of President Kennedy's assassination, I had the 'unhomely' sense that I had been there before – but in fiction and other images rather than in reality. The 'reverse uncanny' (applied as a concept at various times throughout this book) took shape as a way of understanding the return to a reality familiar from fiction and other forms of fantasy; the 'real' in this instance will never be able to shake off its uncanny resemblance to those imaginary embodiments and will instead become tainted or changed by them. The Kennedy assassination has been re-enacted so many times that Dealey Plaza will forever feel like a movie set – just as Blair (the most dramatized prime minister in British history) will feel like an uncanny impersonation of Michael Sheen or the 1974 photograph of Philippe Petit an allusion to '9/11'.

At the epicentre of the satirical series *The Thick of It* (2005–2012) resides the fictional government's Alastair Campbell-esque foul-mouthed director of communications, Malcolm Tucker. *The Thick of It*'s 'reverse uncanniness' comes to the fore as Tucker, during the UK's 2010 General Election, became a 'real' presence in 'real' print and social media commenting directly on events such as Gordon Brown's calamitous 'bigotgate'.[5] In 'Malcolm Tucker's Election Briefing' (which ran in the *Guardian* newspaper throughout the campaign), Tucker declared 'bigotgate' to be 'unspinnable',[6] while on Twitter, he was even blunter: 'Jesus Christ. This is like watching Bambi get fucked by a giant bastard moose. FUCK. #ge 10' (quoted in Wallace, 2018: 131). In a supreme 'reverse uncanny' manoeuvre, the only-just-fictional Tucker comments on real politics, and it is less than one giant leap from satirical 'reverse uncanny' to 'fake news' and the invention of entirely new realities. 'Approximation' explores that area of representation that both transcribes information and factual events and transgresses the frequently crudely delineated boundaries between 'fact' and 'fiction'. Propelled by the resulting dynamism of the relationship between raw documentary data (documents, archive, news etc.) and their re-use and reconfiguration, 'approximation' marks and enacts the *jouissance* of recognition: of knowing a work's point of reference, but also being able to recognise that the reconstruction and the point of reference are not equivalents. It is into this gap that we insert out desires, convictions and opinions.

A brief note on chapters

This book (though it makes reference occasionally to earlier work) is a book about contemporary, post-millennium film and media. 'Approximation' is commonly about looking back; but it remains also about looking outwards to the present, a collision between temporal perspectives that informs, in different ways, all six chapters. Each chapter comprises an individual case study linked back to the underlying notion of 'approximation'. Chapter 1, Archive and the Power of Actuality, looks at the use and the role of archive in documentary and fiction films. Archive carries the direct imprint of reality, but is it always – or ever – incontrovertible evidence of something having happened? Among others, my main examples of archive-based works are Belgian artist Jasper Rigole's *Paradise Recollected* (2008), Pablo Larraín's idiosyncratic biopic *Jackie* (2016) and two recent Adam Curtis's documentaries, *Bitter Lake* (2015) and *Hypernormalization* (2016). Chapter 2, '9/11' as 'Not 9/11':

United 93 and *Man on Wire*, examines some alternatives to the dominant narratives that built up around the terrorist attacks of 11 September 2001 through detailed discussions of Paul Greengrass's feature film, *United 93* (2006), and James Marsh's documentary, *Man on Wire*. Alongside these, Ken Loach's section of *11'09"01, September 11* (2002), focused the 'other 9/11' – the overthrow of Salvador Allende's democratically elected government of Chile – is also discussed and informed by the writings of Sontag, Butler and others who challenged the received 'official' '9/11' narratives that started to form remarkably swiftly. Chapter 3, *Mad Men* and the Incidental Events of the 1960s, looks at Matthew Weiner's long-running series in terms of how it both fixates on the 'big history' of the 1960s and yet 'incidentalises' it in relation to its own dominant fictional narrative. The first part of the chapter discusses the series as a whole; the second focuses on a single episode from Season 3, 'The Grown Ups', which covers the Kennedy assassination. Chapter 4, Documentary and the Law: True Crime and Observation, is likewise split between a discussion of the recent exponential rise of true crime documentaries (both series and one-off films) and a study of a trio of less mainstream observational documentaries: Raymond Depardon's *The 10th District Court: Moments of Trials* (2005), Marc Isaacs's *Outside the Court* (2011) and Carey Young's *Palais de Justice* (2017), which emphasise the law's essential fragmentariness, mutability and lack of finality. In Chapter 5, Political Mimicry: From Mimesis to Alternate History, different forms of post-millennial political mimicry are examined through very different portrayals of former British Prime Minister, Tony Blair, from the mimicry of *The Queen*, to the hypothetical satirical comedy of *The Trial of Tony Blair* (2007) to, finally, the full-blown alternate history of the cinematic adaption of *The Ghost*, in which thriller and genuine politics collide. The recent more cartoonish satirical tradition of political mimicry is represented by *A Very English Scandal* (2018). The final instalment is Chapter 6, Documentary Re-enactment: The 'Model' Approximation; as previously argued, re-enactment is framed as the 'model' 'approximation' because all are, to a degree, re-enactments – copies or echoes of prior acts and events. Here, documentaries discussed include Clio Barnard's *The Arbor*, Milo Rau's *The Last Days of the Ceausescus* (2009), Errol Morris's *Standard Operating Procedure* (2008), Rithy Panh's *S-21: The Khmer Rouge Killing Machine* (2003) and *The Act of Killing* (2012), which all focus specifically on trauma and re-enactment and Jeremy Deller's *The Battle of Orgreave* (2001), an example of 'living history'.

Notes

1 Files: 065.JFK.007-REEL 1–2; 065.JFK.018-REEL 1–2; Cf. 'Chapter 3: The Shots from the Texas School Book Depository – the Trajectory Film and Tests', *Report of the President's Commission on the Assassination of President Kennedy*. www.archives.gov/research/jfk/warren-commission-report/chapter-3.html. Accessed 10 August 2019.

2 17 June 2019 cover. Cf. https://time.com/5602103/cold-war-steve-time-cover-brexit/. Accessed 12 October 2019.

3 Cf. Peter Bradshaw, '24City', *The Guardian*, 29 April 2010. www.theguardian.com/film/2010/apr/29/24-city-review. Accessed 13 July 2019.

4 BBC Producer Peter Taylor speaking in *Speak No Evil: The Story of the Sinn Fein Broadcast Ban* (BBC, 2005). www.youtube.com/watch?v=-yqXeIYmtsc. Accessed 29 September 2019.

5 During the 2010 UK General Election Gordon Brown had a televised conversation with a voter, Gillian Duffy. In the apparent sanctity of the car, but not realising that his microphone is still switched on, Brown has a disastrous exchange with his aide in which he refers to Mrs Duffy as a 'bigoted woman'. The gaffe went viral and was played back to the Prime Minister soon after on Jeremy Vine's radio show.

6 www.theguardian.com/commentisfree/2010/may/01/malcolm-tuckers-election-briefing. Accessed 4 October 2019.

1

ARCHIVE AND THE POWER OF ACTUALITY

In *The Missing Picture* Rithy Panh recounts the history of the Cambodian War and the destruction of his family using clay figurines. For a few minutes, the idyll of his pre-war life – relatives coming to visit bearing guava and jack fruit, children enjoying their lessons – survives. 'I remember how sweet life was', muses the voiceover, as the pulsing of helicopter blades encroaches on the sweet strains of a Cambodian song, before the image catches up and cuts to black and white archival montage of a blazing palm forest, soldiers rounding up villagers, a woman pleading for her life and people weeping over a line of bodies in body bags on stretchers. Over the last of these, the voiceover muses: 'so many pictures that go by again and again in the world. We think we own them because we've seen them'; these, he concludes, are the memories 'that are not missing'.

Using only archive and clay figurines, Panh's re-enactment of the crimes perpetrated by the Khmer Rouge between 1975 and 1979 is an 'approximation', the juxtaposition with its factual basis – the war – enacted explicitly in the sequence that follows as red-scarfed puppets of Khmer soldiers cluster in front of a background of monochrome archive of bombings and military violence. As Sontag writes, 'real wars are not metaphors'; 'A picture, as everyone knows, is worth a thousand words. We will relive the event' (2007: 119). In *The Missing Picture* this is both true and not: the 'reality' of the Cambodian War intrudes upon and destroys the pastoral serenity of the opening minutes, but Panh's idiosyncratic retelling of the war extends, complicates and goes beyond the thousand-word picture as multiple personal and temporal perspectives converge, collide and inform each other. Very often tracing the paths of an 'approximation' and its potentially endless referents opens up the central 'picture' to such an extent that we find ourselves a long way from it and its familiar, tangible reality. So, every picture tells and does not tell a story.

For many documentary filmmakers, the archival image is an incontrovertible, verifiable record of and link to a no longer present moment. Emile de Antonio's anti-Vietnam collage documentary, *In the Year of the Pig* (1969) contains a piece of archive from the French colonialist era of two Frenchmen in white hats and suits being pulled in rickshaws by Vietnamese servants, who are then summarily shooed away when they tentatively request payment for having delivered the men to a café. De Antonio maintained that this 1930s scene 'encapsulates the whole colonial empire' and is 'the equivalent of a couple of chapters of dense writing about the means of colonialism' (Crowdus and Georgakas, 1988: 167). A single piece of archive might lack nuance and detail, but it bears the direct imprint of reality; although de Antonio overextends archive's capabilities, he neverthe-less touches on what marks it out from other documentary elements, namely the emotive potency of its indexicality. If (as, after Foucault, I argue in Chapter 6) re-enactment is the 'model' 'approximation', the one that defines this project intellectually, the archive-based compilation film is its practical embodiment. The recycling and juxtaposition of archival images are key components of 'approxima-tion', acts of yoking together that bring different representations into construc-tive collision, alongside alternative perspectives, temporal planes and arguments. Archive is also contained within another 'approximate' space: *the* archive, the ever-growing repository, whether physical or virtual, wherein sits the 'grubby, infi-nite heap of *things*' a researcher will wade through knowing they will not finish (Steedman, 2001: 18).

Archive has the allure of imperfect, incomplete authenticity; it rings with the resonance of having *been there*, of having borne witness to a moment that is now passed. For all its limitations (and one of the characteristics of archive is its perpetu-ally unfinished state, its residual inability to offer a full interpretation of the event it represents) the archival fragment brings back a moment of raw reality with which, as Emile de Antonio suggests, no written word can ever quite compete. Intensely familiar images – footage of the liberation of Auschwitz in 1945 by the Red Army, Nick Ut's photo of North Vietnamese children fleeing a US napalm attack in 1972, the second plane striking the World Trade Center in 2001 – can seemingly cut through or condense layers of amassed information and knowledge, but they also possess an unexpected frailty, vulnerable to misinterpretation or manipulation, as occurred with the video footage of Rodney King being beaten by members of the LAPD in 1991. The 'thereness' of actuality footage is therefore compelling and immediate, but archive is also unstable, not merely because it embodies temporal dissonance as it re-evokes the presentness of when it came into being, but through the fact that it is, by its very nature, an expression of reflectiveness and historicity. In archival form the event is always something returned to and so, although it was once 'there', it, the image, is no longer actuality. The collage or compilation film is inherently dialectical, it constructs through the juxtaposition of eclectic fragments (a process of collisions, not sutures) a multiplication of presents, it can interrogate, reflect on, oppose as well as simply show.

The use of archive material is a crucial act of 'approximation'. Archival material embodies and connotes a sense of discovery and appropriation, as well as the 'foundness' pastiched in found footage films; but it also resonates with the idea of temporal distance, of a past that was once the present and is now one in a multiplicity of presents – the present of the original archive, the present of the new film into which the archive has been re-appropriated and then the 'present' in which the archive is watched at different moments. 'Archive' is frequently identified as both authentic and *authenticating*, as both illustrative and evidentiary, which is how library and stock images are often used in the traditional archive-based documentary. Spence and Navarro, for example, under the sub-heading 'Uses of Evidence', discuss Alain Resnais's juxtaposition of 'archival footage and contemporary shots' in his 1955 documentary *Nuit et brouillard* (*Night and Fog*) as helping 'to give meaning to the *evidential material* by suggesting we compare the past with the present' (2010: 40; my italics). The archive of the Nazi camp atrocities is characterised as 'raw', the most basic form of documentary 'evidence', as somehow *unadulterated* or *pure*, although the naïve idealism of this belief in 'evidence' is swiftly signalled by Spence and Navarro with references to the not so incontrovertible 'evidence' of King's beating or the inconclusiveness of the Zapruder footage of Kennedy's assassination. As will be discussed in greater detail when it comes to documentary trials in Chapter 4, the entire issue of the still or moving photographic image as 'evidence' that can trump other forms of recollection about an event (personal testimony, artists' impressions, letters) is intrinsically problematic. Archive does not (or cannot) lie, but it can remain unreadable. Likewise, the documenting camera does not necessarily know what it is looking at; it might be blank and anonymous, or it might be wielded selectively. Of course, it is not the apparatus, the inanimate camera, that possesses intention, but rather the people behind it, and that intention alters as the archive is generated, used, edited, recycled and reedited.

So, a single segment of archive footage, though constitutively simple, is inherently stratified, and the act of watching even an isolated piece of archive or actuality comparably layered. The archival fragment perennially carries with it the strength of its potent link to the events it records, as well as the flimsier vestiges of what has been irretrievably lost in that transfer from original event to its representation (a tacit recognition that the act of 'being there' can be echoed but never wholly reproduced). In watching archive, we notice its aesthetic qualities and what these speak to (its age, its format, its deterioration, or whether it is shot on film or video), what it is about, what responses it might set off (emotional, psychological, intellectual, nostalgic), how it interconnects with other formal elements such as narration, music or fictionalisation, and where it leads us or what it prompts us to think about. The fragment of archive never just *is*; it is powerfully indexical, which lends it a sense of permanence, although it is also perversely incomplete, as it needs other elements, narratives and contexts to make fuller sense of it. It is of its time and time*less*. Each time a piece of footage is reused, altered or created anew. So, archive is both stable and remarkably insecure.

And this is only to really consider the original audiovisual fragments. Other elements of the repackaging or recycling of archive also confirm its approximate status and modify or compromise the way it is viewed and understood: voiceover or on-screen text can indicate how the archive is to be understood; narrative can impose linearity on an otherwise fragmented world; editing can dictate and reconfigure intellectual responses; music and non-diegetic sound can add sentiment, emotion, perspective. Archive film and video can also be modified through, for instance, the multi-planing of photographs as in Brett Morgen's *The Kid Stays in the Picture* (2002) or the animation of a still image in James Marsh's *Man on Wire*. All these guide, compromise or circumscribe spectator responses to the original archive in its raw state. Alongside the multiple textual relations, there is also the relationship of the image to the implied off-screen space, most importantly that between what is caught on camera or microphone and what happened either side of those images and sounds. The outtake is classically appealing to compilation filmmakers such as Adam Curtis, for it captures the moment of delicate negotiation and selection that creates more official or *archived* archival footage. Most commonly, the cross-camera dialogue is excised, which makes such marginalised fragments especially allegorically pregnant, but also eloquent on the subject of archive's malleable and mutable fragility; that it is as much defined by what is *not* there as by what *is*.

Part of this split status stems from an acknowledgement that archive footage in a documentary carries with it the connotation of having been edited. All film and television is edit-based, an edit – a cut, a splice – is always a fissure, a rift, a filmic moment of rupture that is both imperceptible and definite, that marks the transition from one image to another while not always drawing attention to itself or altering meaning. The re-use of archival material is linked directly to the dialectical core of any historical inquiry (fiction- or documentary-based), and the cutting together of recycled images that were not intended to go together entails the construction of new meanings and consequently invites their content to be viewed and questioned afresh. The edit is a primary means of putting 'approximation' into action, of ensuring it becomes more than an intellectual idea about the unfinished or un-finite nature of history and factual enquiry.

In *Experimental Ethnography*, Catherine Russell describes 'Found-footage film-making, otherwise known as collage, montage or archival film practice' as 'an aesthetic of ruins', for its 'intertextuality is always also an allegory of history, a montage of memory traces, by which the filmmaker engages with the past through recall, retrieval, and recycling' (Russell, 1999: 238). 'Archive' as a term probably conjures up imperfect monochrome stock footage depicting a more often than not grim past inserted into earnest historical documentaries – films such Esfir Shub's *The Fall of the Romanovs* (1927), for which she pillaged the Romanov archives and newsreel footage, Resnais' *Nuit et Brouillard*, made to commemorate the 10th anniversary of the liberation of the Nazi death camps or maybe *Atomic Café* (Rafferty, Loader and Rafferty, 1982), a film made at the height of the Reagan-era Cold War about the nuclear build-up of the 1950s. Thinking of UK television for a moment and the rise of popular factual television (of which 'documentary' is only one, now small, component), it certainly seems as if 'archive' is out of favour; the archive-based historical documentary of a filmmaker such as Laurence Rees has waned in popularity, giving way to 'constructed reality', introduced as a BAFTA (British Academy of Film and Television Arts) category in 2012 to honour shows, such as *The Only Way is Essex* and *Made in Chelsea*, in which participants are 'put into environments or formats, then observed interacting in situations devised by the producers' (BBC News, 2011). As television audiences and executives (at least in Britain) have turned against imperfect newsreel and actuality footage, has the inexorable rise of scripted reality concomitantly made us distrustful of anything – such as found footage – that might lay claim to greater authenticity, to having witnessed an unrehearsed event as it actually happened? In fact, the very different uses of archive in the examples examined below are not necessarily about trust or distrust, as they exemplify 'approximation' by juxtaposing textual elements that embody the schisms and tensions not just of historical representation but of 21st century fact-based entertainment. But what to call the primary element of this particular 'approximation'? I have already used two terms – 'archive' and 'found footage' (although the latter has been appropriated by Russell and others and also carries the quite distinct definition of film or video presented as if it has been discovered, as in *The Blair Witch Project* [1999] or *Cloverfield* [2008]) – but there are others. Jay Leyda, for example, prefers the term 'compilation', Emile de Antonio 'collage junk', Jaimie Baron 'appropriation', while 'found footage' is commonly reserved for art films.[1]

To return to Russell's 'aesthetic of ruins': the archive-based film salvages and reassembles; out of the ruins can come narrative, causality or logic. The archival film is resonant with temporal disjuncture and formal 'approximation'; it is a kaleidoscopic piecing together of unfinished bits of 'past' and 'present', fact and fiction, the public and the personal. The fragment – film, video, photograph, piece of sound – around which any archival film is constructed, whether documentary or not, is the moment when the documentation of a historical event intermeshes with, rubs up against, collides with the filmic present. It is at once frequently easy to identify and tricky to define. Mary Ann Doane, for example, in her examination of early cinema's ability to capture actuality, starts by remarking:

> Within physics, biology, statistics, psychoanalysis, and physiology, there is an epistemological shift towards the weighting of a legible contingency. The significance of cinema, in this context, lies in its apparent capacity to perfectly *represent* the contingent, to provide a pure record of time. And this effort is particularly legible in the most dominant genre of early cinema – the actuality, which appears to capture a moment.
>
> *(Doane, 2002: 22)*

Doane here emphasises cinema's apparent purity and legibility, its indexical credibility, before going on to problematize such faith in the moving picture's capacity for fidelity when she posits that the 'unrelenting forward movement' of film 'appears as the incarnation of the thermodynamic law of irreversibility', so that film 'seems to respond to the dilemma of the representability of time with an easy affirmation' (23). Although the archive/compilation/collage film's perceived strength is that the factual fragments at its core bring with them a trace of an indisputable 'real', the 'goal of pure inscription or recording', according to Doane, 'was, from the first, self-defeating' (23) – although her residual attraction to that potential for purity remains tangible.

So, at the heart of the 'archive film' is *archive*, the 'ruins' of a past captured on film, video or in still photography, which, as historian Raphael Samuels detects, are trusted and treated 'as transparent reflections of fact' by historians 'normally so pernickety about the evidential status of their documents' (quoted in Sjöberg, 2001: 45). In the digital age, these trusted image-ruins form part of the 'vast image bank, an archive from which images can be taken and re-contextualized at will', identified Peter Wollen (1989: 29). Wollen here draws attention to another meaning of 'archive': *the* archive, the physical repository or institution in which are indexed and catalogued collated documents – the 'selected and consciously chosen documentation from the past' (Steedman, 2001: 68), the dust-gathering folders, tinned old film and worn videos the historian and/or researcher can consult and which bring with them a tangible authenticity, a reminder of having 'been there' when the events they represent and relay happened. The archive, of course, can now also be virtual but, whatever form it takes, it stores the artefacts and detritus of history – 'History as *stuff*' (Steedman, 2001: 67) – it does not mediate or interpret it (except inasmuch as it is highly selective and not 'made up of *everything*, as is human memory' [68]). The pleasure, as evoked so eloquently by Carolyn Steedman in *Dust*, lies in entering a domain that is both familiar, when one goes in search of some-*thing* in particular, and unknown, as it becomes where one discovers the unexpected.

Some time ago I spent several days in the British Library's old newspaper archive at Colindale leafing through copies of *McCall's* magazine from the late 1940s and 1950s in search of stories about GI fathers returning to the US. Though I unearthed some 'useful' *stuff*, what I discovered and found myself irresistibly drawn to was the regular stream of recipes for garishly coloured, ornately shaped milk- and jelly-based post-war puddings. We might google a book if we know in advance what we are looking for, but it is the deliciously random encounter that characterises the archive which, though methodically assembled, can still surprise. Alongside archive, the found footage itself, and *the* archive, therefore, there is also the action *to* archive: the act of, purposefully or accidentally (as Abraham Zapruder did on 22 November 1963), *archiving* events for posterity. *To archive* events carries with it the suggestion that the events depicted, whether public or personal, are inherently worth preserving, remembering, revisiting. Archives have always housed both official and unofficial materials, although to differing degrees, depending on the archive. Jaimie Baron makes the distinction between the term 'document' which can refer to 'both material and virtual objects' and the alternative 'archival materials', which, she argues, 'emphasizes the physical materiality of the archival object' (2014: 10). In an era in which the digitization of paper and analogue archives is becoming increasingly commonplace, it is arguably no longer the case that the most meaningful distinction is between physical and virtual spaces.

To return to the action of *archiving*, what the digitization process has amply drawn attention to is the cohabitation of official and unofficial documents or materials, as one finds, for instance, in the online institutional archives such as those of the BBC, the Imperial War Museum or British Pathé. On a visit to the online archive of the last of these, one would find under a menu of categories – from (when I visited the site) 'War and Revolution' to 'Science and Technology' to 'Lifestyle and Culture' – quirky scraps of footage that give a little nostalgic insight into a rapidly fading past.[2] To revert, for a minute, to the quest for 1950s culinary inspiration, the Pathé site is full of morsels such as the one entitled 'Cooking Hints AKA Cooking Tips' from 1957, in which early UK celebrity chefs Fanny and John Craddock transform the 'much maligned hard-boiled egg' into a 'romantic' swan with the aid of a pipe cleaner and some duchesse potatoes. Such a snippet of film is the audiovisual equivalent of Steedman's 'tiny flotsam that's ended up in the record office you are working in' (2001: 18); that one no longer needs to travel to the physical archive to view it does not diminish the material's indexical trustworthiness or the fact that it retains a strongly tangible historical trace. The advent of the digital archive has disrupted the physical relationship between researcher and actual object, yet the archival fragment retains the vestiges of its previous physical presence and still brings with it a piece of concrete reality. Even in the digital age, it reminds us of its analogue antecedent, of the fact that somebody had been present to record the moment depicted, even if it is no longer 'their dust that I breathed in' (Steedman, 2001: 19).

For film scholars the issue of indexicality has been troublesome, although Doane makes a plea for not simply rejecting it as much film theory has done, not to link it merely to realism, but instead to understand that

> indexicality is a function that is essentially without content – in language, it is allied with the pure denotation of 'this' or 'here it is'. . . . In the cinema, it is the guarantee that anything and everything is filmable.
>
> *(2002: 25)*

This decoupling of indexicality and content raises the affiliated question, equally significant and just as troublesome for an examination of archive, of authorship. Doane's suggestion that indexicality is 'a function essentially *without content*', carries with it the awkward inference that, despite the archival document being the result of someone having 'been there', actuality footage is not, in a conventional sense, 'authored'. Archival material is often thought to be authorless, exemplified by the filmmaker's or the film researcher's act of visiting *the* archive in order to purloin *archival material* and transport it to an entirely different film. *Point of Order* remains 'an Emile de Antonio film' despite the fact that it does not contain any sequence filmed by de Antonio himself, and was, in fact, rejected by the New York Film Festival because (being a collage of 'anonymous' live television coverage) 'it was not a film' (Waugh, 1976). An archival fragment is comparable to Michel Foucault's 'statement' – a much more basic unit lacking the 'structural criteria' of more complex linguistic forms such as the sentence, the proposition, or the speech act. (2002: 86–87). As Foucault then identifies later in 'The Statement and the Archive': 'For a series of signs to exist there must – in accordance with the system of causality – be an "author" or a transmitting authority. But this "author" is not identical with the subject of the statement' (92). A peculiarity of how archival footage is understood is that authorial agency is frequently transferred to the appropriating filmmaker (Emile de Antonio, Adam Curtis, Asif Kapadia) or to the interpreting researcher-viewer.

In the same way that the archives are great levellers, minimisers of the differences between 'important' official documents and ostensibly more trivial found footage, 'anonymous' archival footage embodies fluidity and the idea of being perpetually open to interpretation and reconfiguration. Just as a clip such as the Craddock master class in food presentation sits alongside 'Churchill the Man, Reel 2' in which (to the portentous strains of Beethoven's *Fifth Symphony*) General Montgomery signs the acceptance of Germany's surrender before proceeding to Churchill's announcement in London, so the 'collage junk' films of de Antonio or Curtis do not lose the capacity to convey the democratic leanings of either the archival space or their respective *auteurs*, an intrinsic non-didacticism that is heightened by the archive's accessibility via a digital platform.

The past, as Hayden White has observed, is not just another country where things are done differently, but a place of fantasy. Similarly, the same piece of archive footage can, in different formal or narrative contexts, acquire quite different meanings, not determined by original intention or authorship. De Antonio, like Shub before him or the directors of *Atomic Café* after him, made 'collage junk' films from archive whose original meaning or intention he frequently suppressed or undermined. Likewise, Alain Resnais controversially inserted images from Leni Riefenstahl's Nazi propaganda documentary, *Triumph of the Will*, into *Nuit et brouillard*. The perpetual paradox of archive footage is that it is, firstly, by virtue of its indexicality, the authenticating link to an event, its verification; but secondly, is perennially vulnerable to reconfiguration, distortion, alteration and manipulation. Archive is therefore simultaneously secure and insecure, a locus of remembering as well as its opposite: forgetting. In a similar way, *the* archive, as Steedman identifies, is both 'a prosaic space where the written and fragmentary traces of the past are put in boxes and folders, bound up, stored, catalogued. . . . And . . . a place of dreams' (2001: 69). Compilation/archive/found footage films offer exemplary 'approximations' that embody temporal disjuncture, mutability and generic instability. In an attempt to capture and analyse some of the ambivalences and complexities of 21st century screen media's use of archive and found footage, I will discuss some quite distinct case studies from across the generic spectrum, from Jasper Rigole's *Paradise Recollected*, to Pablo Larraín's Hollywood movie *Jackie*, to Adam Curtis's *Bitter Lake* and *Hypernormalization*.

Rigole's idiosyncratic half-hour film (available to view on Vimeo) centres on a *faux* archival project: the collection of the International Institute for the Conservation, Archiving and Distribution of Other People's Memories, shortened to its acronym, IICADOM. *Paradise Recollected* charts acts of surreal 'scavenging'; it assembles *authentic* fragments of found footage (which Rigole bought second hand) into a *fictional* archive. There are several moments in *Paradise Recollected* when viewers familiar with the generic boundaries between fiction and nonfiction film might fret about whether or not they have quite 'got' the film's tone. As, for example, when, following on from a silent opening credit sequence of white typed letters on a grainy grey background, the blandly authoritative 'Received Pronunciation' male voice (a stock feature of so many mid to late 20th century documentaries) begins: 'While some people collect stones, stamps or coins, IICADOM collects memories', the reassuringly didactic narrator explains, over images of semi-precious gems, stamp collectors, coins and . . . busy street markets. The slavish proximity of 'stones', 'stamps' and 'coins' to the corresponding illustrative images might be anticipated, but the sequence's predictability is soon disrupted as the notion of collecting the more abstract 'memories' is illustrated by a montage of colourful shots of smiling women weaving through vintage flower and food stalls. If the link between collecting the memories in found footage and street stalls is opaque, then the voiceover's assertion that IICADOM is the '*market* leader in memory preservation' clarifies things (somewhat). Echoing the playfully surrealist image associations in the similarly imagistically complex non-narrative films of Dziga Vertov and Alberto Cavalcanti, the convergence of 'market' and 'market' initially mocks the notion of collecting memories at all, let alone for 'future use' by a spurious archive. However, Rigole rapidly switches tonal register when the same dispassionate, tempered narration ruminates on how 'at a certain point in time, these memories were important enough to be capture and preserved . . . cherished by their rightful owners'. Over images of especially vibrant market floral displays, the pathos of the insight that so much found footage is inevitably tinged with the act of forgetting emerges.

Artist Robert Rauschenberg observed 'A picture is more like the real work when it's made out of the real world',[3] an ethos he carried over most notably into his Combines: collage works that made use of discarded materials the artist had found on the streets. As William C. Wees argued in *Recycled Images: The Art and Politics of Found Footage Films* (1993), 'perfect films' were those that used found objects in the most basic sense of that word – amidst rubbish, in the attic, on the forgotten shelf of the archive, in the flea pit *et al* – objects that thereafter, as Patrik Sjöberg, in response to Wees, glosses, are 'presented as they were found' (2001: 16). Wees's examples from the 1970s and 1980s include Ken Jacobs's *Urban Peasants* (1975) and Alain Berliner's *Family Album* (1986). 'Found footage' in this context is accidental archive: bumped into as opposed to sought out. It is in this sense that Wees argues for its 'perfection', especially when used in unedited form. The found-ness of found footage makes for a fundamentally different relationship between archival images and the films in which they are embedded than occurs in more conventional 'compilation' films discussed later in this chapter. Whereas *Paradise Recollected* is constructed around, dictated by and directly responsive to the footage Rigole has found in markets and car boot sales, in 'archive films' such as Asif Kapadia's *Senna* (2010),

FIGURE 1.1   Jasper Rigole's *Paradise Recollected* (2008)

historical footage – however creatively used or edited – serves an illustrative narrative function, the visual evidence for the story or argument already *in situ*.

Although to the unattuned eye of the proverbial Martian, a film such as *Paradise Recollected* might superficially resemble the political collage documentaries of Adam Curtis or even more conventional archive/voiceover documentaries such as Laurence Rees's *The Nazis: A Warning from History* (1997), the divergence between these examples and Rigole's work stems from the inverted hierarchy between footage and argument on which *Paradise Recollected* is founded. The film's enforced dislocation between images and sound makes for a quite different and *un*-documentary viewing experience, more akin to that exemplified by Patrick Keiller's *Robinson* films, in which actuality and documentary film material likewise exists in juxtaposition to the films' fictional narrative premise and voiceover narration. As Sjöberg states, 'Without film archives and photo archives no compilation film could be produced' (2001: 39). This is an obvious but crucial observation, for, as Jay Leyda observed, the temporal disjunction is the *sine qua non* on which every compilation film is predicated, for although it '*begins* on the cutting room table' it also 'has to indicate that the film used originated at some point in the past' (quoted in Sjöberg, 2001: 22). Rigole foregrounds the significance of the archive (the store of images and materials) and embeds an awareness of the *archive's* physicality into the construction of the fictional archive IICADOM. The majority of 'compilation films' which use archive illustratively leave behind the notion of the physical archive, just as they purloin and copy materials from it and set about constructing another film out of the spoils of their scavenging.

Found footage has an ever-looser relationship to its past, firstly because it has been *fortuitously* stumbled upon: its relationship to past events might well be opaque, even unknown, and so the logical causality of 'archive' in the mainstream documentary that Rigole's narration emulates and mocks is likewise lost. The traditional male voiceover of *Paradise Recollected* putatively 'explains' the images it is set alongside, but not so we know who these people who collect stamps and stones are, where the markets are etc. That the market stallholders are selling flowers not home movie footage are symptoms of a fractured, illogical relationship between archive and argument. And yet, the 'purity' of the found footage material that has lost its evidentiary moorings also serves to emphasise the simplicity of the film's archival mission. *Paradise Recollected* resembles *the* archive in crucial and fundamental ways, its bank of images has been amassed around the 'pleasure' Steedman identifies 'in finding something that the writer did not know was there' (2001: 10). The 'reader' in the written archive enters a process of discovery which, in *Paradise Recollected*, Rigole mimics. His film actively problematizes and disrupts the conventional relationship between found footage, memory and time: accidental footage forms accidental narratives.

A few minutes in, the fictive narrator of *Paradise Recollected* ponders the relationship between collective memory and time and determines – over a superficially quite random set of images of a tortoise, a group of girls looking into the camera, a man holding a snake – that 'chronology is an irrelevant notion, since every fragment exists simultaneously'. The collation (as opposed to the more deliberate *collection*) of images is characterised by randomness; the found footage can fortuitously reveal a narrative, but this too is unplanned. Rigole compels us to contemplate these images without recourse to temporal logic, not in order to make sense of them, but rather to deliberately enjoy *not* making sense of them in the way one might comparable pieces of illustrative archive. Footage in *Senna* of the Formula One driver's horrific crash at Imola in 1994 adds to the discussion of – and is causally linked to – how and why he died. Conversely, it is pointless but liberating to speculate what the logic of Rigole's sandwiching of smiling girls between two reptiles might be; the logic is arbitrary not profound – and speculation can lead to naïve *mis*recognition or false conclusions. In another sequence, Rigole's anonymous voiceover – over a short montage of labourers – remarks on how unusual it is for found footage to depict labour, that although collected memories comprise memories that actively want to be remembered, *collated* memories frequently construct false histories in which there was little labour, politics or education and 'no class struggle'. Over a little boy dancing in fancy dress for the manifest benefit of a camera, Rigole's voiceover surmises: 'in fact, there's no sign of historical events or their consequences', after which there's another inconsequential edit to a bizarre scene of a dog standing on its hind legs and displaying its belly on a window sill to camera as a man (its owner?) looks on from the front porch. Just as the debate rumbles on about how Instagram and other social media outlets project lives of contentment and happiness, ignoring the depression, chaos and difficulties that also colour our individual existences, so others' found footage, *Paradise Recollected* suggests, articulates the 'paradoxical relationship between memory and history' because, above all, 'people want to remember their own lives, activities friends – they write their own history', although these same memories and histories are eventually forgotten and discarded. Thus, a delusional idyll emerges from the scraps of unclaimed archive of *Paradise Recollected*, and in that rewriting of history inevitably lurks revisionism and the acknowledgement that revisionism can potentially tinge *any* or *all* archival material, that images from a public archive or an institutional memory bank can likewise be *mis*recognised or the causality that putatively defines them be a false construction.

Mary Ann Doane's analysis of actuality in early cinema and the fidelity it inspired is again pertinent, as comparable assumptions about 'the technological assurance of actuality' are frequently made about archival images. The first cinema of the mechanical age, Doane argues, ostensibly 'produced continual evidence of the drive to fix and make repeatable the ephemeral', to the extent that 'film was perceived as the imprint of time itself' (2002: 22). Film theory has long since abandoned this naïve faith in all film's indexicality, but 'archive' still retains a special hold (which is also, if not to the same degree, naïve). Archive is commonly perceived not to have been adulterated by subjectivity in the form, for example, of authorial intent behind the camera or performance in front of it; archive footage is defined by, even collapsed into, the event(s) it depicts. Rigole's playful recycling of discarded found footage fragments queries such loaded assumptions about what archive can or does represent. He is acutely aware, for one thing, that his once treasured (and authored) found footage has been abandoned, one result of which is that archive material resonates as much with the act of forgetting as the act of remembering. But is not archive footage – like any record or preservation of the past – *perennially* defined by the ability to forget as well as the compulsion to remember, the pathos of which imbues the images throughout *Paradise Recollected*? As Steedman recognised, only a miniscule portion of what could be remembered (her 'tiny flotsam' [2001:18]) ever finds its way into an archive; archive material is therefore only ever a selection, and so it follows that selectivity has inevitably been forced upon found footage from the very point of its coming into being. Found and archival footage is only in part about presence – confirmation that what it depicts happened, it is also always marked by the presence of absence – of what has been abandoned, lost and omitted from it.

Hayden White's witty distinction between the annals, chronicle and 'history proper' (White, 1980: 9) in 'The Value of Narrativity in the Representation of Reality' memorably draws attention to the role of absence in the narrativising of history. Annals, according to White, 'represent historical reality *as if* real events did not display the form of story' (9). When he comes to a brief analysis of the *Annals of St Gall*, he sets out the events as recorded for the period 709–734. All the recorded events, as White observes, are 'extreme' (11), whether this be the devastation of the Saxon by Charles in 718, the 'hard year' which left 710 'deficient in crops' or the death in 731 of the 'Blessed Bead' (11). The recorded events are marked, as White discerns, by 'the fact that they were recorded' (12); why or by whom we do not know. And what to make of the blank years, White subsequently asks, 'those years in which "nothing happened"' (14)? Like Rigole's unsystematically acquired found footage, the annals do not come armed with a narrative, even a rationale; they are wilfully disordered and fragmentary. White the historian appreciates order; Rigole the artist is more accepting of disorder. Arguably White's real problem is that no historical account – rudimentary like the annals, intermediate like the chronicle or more narratively complex like 'history proper' – is ever complete, it is merely that the gaps become progressively less obvious, because what is narrative if not a sophisticated means of papering over the cracks, of masking the elisions that the Annals expose? Later, White asks:

> Does the world really present itself to perception in the form of well-made stories, with central subjects, proper beginnings, middles, and ends, and a coherence that permits us to see 'the end' in every beginning? Or does it present itself more in the forms that the annals and chronicle suggest, either as mere sequence without beginning or end or as sequences of beginnings that only terminate and never conclude?
>
> *(White, 1980: 24)*

History never presents itself as fully formed, as its narrative can only ever be shaped retrospectively; rather, it is moulded – much as Victor Frankenstein did his monster – in order to be made sense of. White's obsession with the issue of whether or not the world 'ever really comes to us narrativized' (24) and what historians borrow from fiction in order to make history intelligible, suppresses awareness that history is dictated by absence and forgetting almost as much as it is by presence and remembering. *Paradise Recollected* underscores found footage's innate lack of causality, logic or pre-existing narrative by performing – or indeed narrativizing – the very act of lending cogency and causality to the fragments of memory or history. Rigole's film persistently acknowledges not only the duality of history (that the past happened but will for the most part go unrecorded) but also the inevitable limitations of archive: that, notwithstanding its blatant indexicality, it cannot ever capture *everything*; that it will only ever be drifting splinters of flotsam.

Rigole can be likened to the chronicler: he orders other people's memories and yet stops short of rearranging them into a 'proper history'; images are spliced together much as the parts of the body are in a game of 'consequences': they are linked, but only at the level of image-association. Thus, a man performing an expressive dance outside a house dressed only in pair of white boxer shorts is followed by some equally fuzzy home movie material capturing a group of women in colourful 1950s summer dresses (and one bare-chested man) dancing freely until a hose starts to shower them, at which point they disperse. There are associations here, evidently – the two bare-torsoed men, the carefree dancing – but none that the voiceover signals directly. Instead, the narrator, after a pregnant-seeming pause, ponders the fact that 'as the days grow longer and spring is in the air, we go out into the open. Leisure times and holidays ask for remembrance. Doors of memory are cleansed by sunlight. What happens inside seems too obscure to be remembered'. Although the last sentence is read over images of dingy interiors lit only with the ineffectual light of candles and a table lamp, this observation (like so many throughout *Paradise Recollected*) remains serenely unverifiable except in the most pedantically literal sense. Forming a surreal self-fulfilling prophecy, the only form of corroboration for this or any other statement remains the image itself. And so, over images of boys having a snowball fight with their father, the unflappable narrator of *Paradise Recollected* interjects sardonically, 'But winter *does* occur. In the collected memory, wintertime lasts one day, which is characterised by its heavy snowfall'. Although the following line, 'A day like this is something on which to reflect', is unnecessary and illustrative of Rigole's residual tendency to over-egg a point, the initially absurd observation that winter lasts one day is actually inspired. In home movies – as now on social media – winter is distilled down to the one day of snowfall. At first glance it is as if this is the proverbial Martian again, having been co-opted into narrating this quintessentially terrestrial film, now attempting to forge a logical path through this ragbag tombola stall of found images. However, the voiceover is also archly reflexive – as when, just after the one image of wintertime and over a montage of babies trying to walk, the narrator ponders how 'strangely enough this selective memory seems to lead to generalisations. Many people have similar memories and many look exchangeable'. As babies continue to be helped along by eager parents, the narrator concludes that these 'archetypical memories' serve as 'models for archiving similar memories'. The inference here, of course, is that home movie-makers film certain moments because other people's memory archives have deemed such moments as a baby taking its first steps or siblings joshing in fluffy snow to be worth recording; they are both 'filmable' (Doane postulates that the 'common denominator' shared by 'hundreds of films in the Lumières' catalogue' is that 'they are filmable' [2002: 22]) and generically popular. Embedded in Doane's slightly opaque notion of the 'filmable' is both the chance and luck factors that characterise actuality and its staged, reflexive *alter ego*. Cumbersome, old technology dictated that a filmmaker and their film movie camera did not just stumble across a dog standing upright displaying its tummy, but rather that this action is a re-iteration of an already familiar past action being performed again for the benefit of that camera. Likewise, the Lumières did not just fortuitously happen upon the workers leaving the factory in serendipitous synchronicity but rather rehearsed and choreographed the end of the working day action until it both flowed and appeared smoothly spontaneous. *Workers Leaving the Lumière Factory in Lyon* (1895) was not a fictional rendition of an actual historical event in the manner of Sergei Eisenstein's 'storming of the Winter Palace' sequence for *October* (1927) which, in the absence of copies of the 1920 mass spectacle reconstruction, came to be used as an archival record, and yet it demonstrates a similar performativity.

Just as *Paradise Recollected* is a *faux* documentary, so it is showcasing IICADOM's *faux* archival project. The *faux* inflects even the more philosophically profound moments in the film, for example when the narrator earnestly ruminates on the relationship between collected memories and history. The 'now', the narrator states at one-point midway through the film is entirely absent from the 'collected memory', and so such images lack 'any form of historicity as history can only emerge from looking back from the now at the past'. Such potentially stretching philosophical interventions are problematised, however, by being positioned alongside blurry, chaotic images of a costumed jousting display, which descends at one point into puerile medieval fisticuffs.

Paradise Recollected, in the vein of Peter Greenaway's early documentaries or the not-quite-documentaries of Patrick Keiller, is a heady combination of the profound and the profoundly anarchic, exemplified by the moment when the unchanging voiceover raises the question of 'active memory management' as the camera of a home movie excerpt pans down from the face to the bare thighs of a woman sitting having a drink on a patio bathed in early evening, golden-hour sunlight. The particularly amateurish crudity of this filming – the excessively jerky pan across to the woman she is talking to, then back to the original subject as she adjusts the bag shielding her crotch, before the camera zooms in a little closer on her thighs as she unsuccessfully attempts to pull her skirt down over her exposed flesh – punctures the seriousness still further. What is one supposed to be taking in here? Certainly, the mute tussle between subject and an intrusive camera at the mercy of its thigh-obsessed operator is more engrossing than the narrator's ponderings about 'what will be remembered and what will be forgotten', but the two elements are, as is often the case with 'approximations', linked. Elsewhere, the dovetailing of images and narration draws attention to rather than simply detracting from the latter, such as when the voiceover remarks how, 'if one is registering, this means one is excluded from the action', over a pan across a swimming pool encircled by empty sun loungers, the pathos of which in turn underscores Rigole's detachment from his subject matter. 'Time comes to a halt', the narrator then goes on to state, 'by focusing on the act of remembering itself'. Much the same could be said of both Rigole's act of assemblage and re-cutting – the act of splicing up a roll of film necessarily detaches fragments of found footage from their context and brings with it a sense of timeless, just as the superimposition of a quasi-philosophical voiceover onto a protracted sequence of a pair of grandparents and a camera-resentful granddaughter trying to get the pose just right for a primitive proto-selfie, draws attention to the scrappy banality of the 'act of remembering itself'.

The inherent, often unsettling voyeurism of taking the act of remembering out of itself and making it public recalls Steedman's description of the historian in the archive: forever 'the unintended reader' always reading 'what was never intended for his or her eyes', other people's stories, 'the fragmented traces of *something else*' (2001, 75). *Paradise Recollected* makes us uneasy about this fetishization of 'authentic' documents and found footage: amidst the thrill of experiencing the authenticity of the moment nestles the residual guilt of feeling we are voyeurs, trespassers who should not be there, as well as the confusion that comes with not quite knowing the status of what we are looking at. Late on in *Paradise Recollected* there is some sepia-tinged film of (another) bare-chested man impersonating the animated gesticulations, salutes, moustache and swastika armband of Hitler. Sensitive to our discomfort, the accompanying narration declares that 'all of a sudden, reality does slip in; still, it's a theatrical inversion rather than the real thing'. The performativity of this private/ public moment magnifies the feeling that we are not the intended viewers of this film. *Paradise Recollected* concludes with on-screen text confirming that 'Any resemblance to existing people is pure coincidence'. On the one hand, this is patently absurd, one last jest about the authenticity of the abandoned archive, while on the other, its silliness draws attention poignantly and acutely to our growing awareness that each segment of this discarded found footage, unshackled as it is from its historical moorings, is still 'the real thing' depicting real people – just a reality that has been forgotten. The man with the swastika armband and Hitler moustache might have assumed that memories, once forgotten and discarded, would be rendered unreal, but he had not bargained for future car boot sale scavengers. *Paradise Recollected* enacts the process of accidental discovery at the heart of the found footage project, the importance of chancing upon forgotten images that, as his narrator remarks, 'somehow didn't make it into the canon of so called history' – until, that is, they were reassembled by Rigole into *Paradise Recollected*.

Paradise Recollected reminds us that history and memory are only tenuously related. Formal written history, as Steedman posits, 'has provided a way of thinking about what is in a particular place – a place which for the moment shall simply be called Memory' (2001: 67); it is an account – not so much '*stuff*' as '*process*'; history, like narrative, 'has shaped memory' (67), helped us to order, make sense of the chaos of a disorderly domain. Whereas Rigole's IICADOM (at the same time as it repackages it) appreciates the unruly freedom of 'other people's memories' and so fabricates an alternative archive not linked causally to official 'history', the mainstream historical film and television drama that incorporates archive footage generally seeks to tame or 'process' the raw data of the past just as Steedman suggests, as a means of shaping it into a coherent narrative. Of course, narrative cohesion is in part an ideological endeavour, not merely the means of offering an underpinning structural rationale for mainstream fictional entertainment, as closure and the tying up of loose ends more often than not helps maintain the status quo and gets in the way of re-evaluation. In this context, archive footage – often a moment of tension or fissure – is divested of contrary, radical potential and often becomes subsumed into the overarching predetermined narrative.

The course of the relationship between archive and narrative never did run smooth. Archive is constitutively – even constitutionally – independent of a narrative in which it may find itself; it predates the fiction film that has reappropriated it and into which it has been subsumed and has, most likely, been re-edited in form and maybe altered in content. It is this independence that, as previously alluded to, leads to the assumption that archival material is indexical, that, like the document a historian consults in '*the* archive', it has a direct link to the factual occurrences it captures, to possess a causal link to the events it represents and to have innate and fixed meaning. As already intimated, the same archival images can be used to vastly different ends when used in different narrative contexts. Charles A. Ridley of the Ministry of Information, for instance, satirises the Nazis in *Schichlegruber – Doing the Lambeth Walk* (1941), by playing around with footage of Hitler and Nazi troops on parade taken from Leni Riefenstahl's *The Triumph of the Will*. Re-edited to the popular British dance tune 'The Lambeth Walk', the original Nazi propaganda is transformed into comical counter-propaganda. However, the very fact that the same piece of archive can remain intelligible in different contexts mitigates against the notion of archive's innate solidity, raising instead the spectre of the realisation that, in its chameleon-like reflectivity, actuality footage is not intrinsically more of a guarantor of 'truth' than other representations of fact and history. Documentary filmmakers who construct archive-based films (from Shub and Ridley to Adam Curtis), commonly do so in order to formulate counter-narratives, to critique the establishment not defend it; reedited archive footage in the hands of Emile de Antonio, for example, the most consistently eloquent agitational voice in US documentary of the 1960s and 1970s, became a political tool, even if the found (often buried) footage was not inherently radical. The juxtaposition between the archive's original ideology and de Antonio's contrasting ideological imperative brought an important dialectical dimension to his 'collage junk' documentaries and exemplified his approach that 'it's wrong to explain everything to audiences. The material is there, and interpretations can be made' (quoted in Waugh, 1976). Archive can carry two even diametrically opposed meanings simultaneously.

In the context of how, in writing and culture, narrative makes sense of the past Hayden White's interventions are crucial (as previously intimated) because, at the very least, they offer the opportunity to see narrative as a *positive* as opposed to negative when it comes to historical representation. Putting history on the screen is always a challenge. As Robert Rosenstone articulates:

> No matter how serious or honest the filmmakers, and no matter how deeply committed they are to rendering the subject faithfully, the history that finally appears on the screen can never fully satisfy the historian as historian (although it may satisfy the historian as filmgoer).
>
> *(Rosenstone, 1988: 1173)*

As Rosenstone continues, 'inevitably, something happens on the way from the page to the screen that changes the meaning of the past as it is understood by those of us who work in words' (1173). In the same journal edition, White, in direct response to Rosenstone, writes that his essay

> raises at least two questions that should be of eminent concern to professional historians . . . the relative adequacy of what we might call "historio*photy*" (the representation of history and our thought about it in visual images and filmic discourse) to the criteria of truth and accuracy presumed to govern the professional practice of historio*graphy* (the representation of history in verbal images and written discourse).
>
> *(White, 1988: 1193; italics in original)*

Whereas cinema and video are 'better suited', White concedes, to certain forms of historical representation ('landscape, scene, atmosphere, complex events such as wars, battles, crowds and emotions' [1193]) the residual question of film's capacity to represent nuanced documentary argument remains. But, it can be argued, archive footage, like the document on which written history is based, contains a similarly strong trace of authenticity of which White might approve. For all the arguments mounted through this book of the comparability between very different types of 'approximations', the residual attraction of archive footage to narrative cinema is that it has not metamorphosed into something 'trivial' like narrative but has retained its sobriety, thereby granting the film in which it appears not just a grounding in actuality but reflective *gravitas*. The relationship between actuality footage and fictionalisation, even if frequently ideologically simplifying, is equally frequently formally complex, as exemplified by Steven Spielberg's *Munich* (2005), about the secret Israeli retaliations following the murder of 11 of their national athletes and their coach at the 1972 Munich Olympics.

After the athletes have been taken hostage by members of the Palestinian terrorist group, Black September, news of the attack is swiftly conveyed around the world. The dramatization of the raid on the athletes' rooms in the Olympic Village is intercut with footage of ABC's news anchorman, Jim McKay, speaking live from the channel's studio just outside Munich about how the peace of the so-called 'serene Olympics' had been 'shattered'. There ensues an edit to a fictional scene in an Israeli bar as men converge on the small television set to watch a different news report detailing the kidnappers' demands for the release of 200 political Arab prisoners in return for the hostages' safe release. On the small diegetic screen, as McKay reads the kidnappers' call for 'revolutionaries of the world unite', there is (to some viewers familiar) black and white footage of the balcony outside the rooms where the hostages are being held. Over a further dramatized scene, this time in a pro-Palestinian Arab location, McKay's voice continues the story as the visuals include a further fleeting glimpse of Israeli-subtitled coverage of the balcony footage. As McKay starts to idiosyncratically describe the event's most iconic image – the 'man with a stocking mask over his head, weird; what's going on inside that head and that mind?' – the image cuts from the crowd watching the Israeli news broadcast outdoors to inside the hostage room. Here, the screen is effectively (but not actually) split between another diegetic television set, screen left, showing this iconic image of the disguised kidnapper emerging onto the balcony and, screen right, a simultaneous colour dramatization of the same terrorist exiting from the room towards the balcony. This crucially suggestive juxtaposition encapsulates the limitations as well as the expressiveness of archive in the fictionalised setting: that its view of events, however authentic, is full-frontal and two-dimensional, able to convey *what* happened, but not necessarily *why* (which is the reason for archive's attractiveness to agitational filmmakers who can interpret it). In response, this diegetically split screen economically evokes what drama can achieve, namely that it can, however speculatively, go beyond that public-facing image and take us (in this instance, literally) behind the archive. Narrative, *Munich* suggests, can complement archive, not merely compromise or distort it. Archive offers authenticating ballast in a slip-pery fictionalised world.

Later in 'Historiography and Historiophoty', Hayden White concurs with Rosenstone that 'the historical film need not necessarily feature narrative at the expense of analytical interests' and that, 'Like the historical novel, the historical film draws attention to the extent to which it is a constructed . . . representation of a reality we historians would prefer to consider to be the "found" in the events them-selves' (1988: 1195). With its split diegetic space, the sequence in *Munich* is mani-festly 'constructed' and able to 'shape' the representation of reality. White remains reluctant to concede that the historical narrative film is capable of historical archae-ology (of discovering 'the "found" in the events themselves') or of analysis, and yet this sequence in *Munich* offers a deftly economical response to the newsreader McKay's questioning of the 'weird' man with the stocking over his head.

Unlike in *Paradise Recollected*, the (albeit diverse) ways in which mainstream nar-rative film and drama inserts and deploys archival images has an explicit and linear relationship to history and collective memory. First and foremost, a film such as *Munich* references 'big history', that is, events that had widespread ramifications and with which many audience members would have already been familiar. Its fictionalisation takes place, therefore, against a backdrop of verifiable authenticity, whereas perversely Rigole's genuine found footage displaces public, collective his-tory by focusing on forgotten personal memories and ignoring 'big history'. The mainstream drama is maybe overly preoccupied with proving its proximity to 'big history' and the years in which much happened, though narrative films use and adapt archival footage in a multiplicity of ways. Newsreel or actuality footage is not commonly used unadulterated or unedited, and it often appears at the beginning or the end of a film, maybe in the form of a compilation montage. It is generally cut down and/or intercut with either other archival or fictionalised sequences, or maybe incorporated into the overarching fictional narrative by being overlaid with non-diegetic music or having actors matted into it; frequently archive shots, once established, give way to full-blown dramatized re-enactments: a way of saying, 'we can take it from here'. Archival images function as 'evidence of past events' and offer us an *experience* of pastness, an experience that no written word can match' (Baron, 2014: 1); their importance to the 'based on a true story' film stems from their direct affiliation with the 'big history' it depicts.

Ben Affleck's *Argo* (2012), which recounts a dramatic episode within the Iran hostage crisis when 52 US diplomats and citizens were held hostage for 444 days from November 1979 to January 1981, starts by giving a truncated and selective potted history of Iran.[4] This opening sequence, in which storyboard-like cartoon images,[5] photographs, newsreel and an explanatory voiceover are stitched together in a familiar history film tapestry, is thin on detailed hard fact as it canters through the 1953 *coup d'état* which brought Pahlavi to power, his brutal methods for hold-ing onto that power and the unrest that led to his deposition and eventual flight to the US. In the tradition inaugurated by Shub's recycling of Romanov family home movie footage, photographs of the Shah skiing or dining in a tuxedo and bow tie on food, according to the narrator, 'flown in from Paris', are used contrapuntally to signal the opposite of their original intention, especially when in juxtaposition with images of starving Iranians huddled in the street. In fact, this dialectical realignment of archive is synergistical as opposed to analytical, as throughout this three-minute-long sequence a tight collusion is maintained between archive, voiceover and narrative, as they all back each other up. Unlike in *The Fall of the Romanovs*, the space between textual strata is closed down rather than prized opened; so, for example, as the voiceover recounts how the 'Shah kept power through his ruthless internal police', the image sequence shows a storyboard drawing of a subservient man kneeling down and kissing Pahlavi's foot, which morphs into a photograph of the same before an edit to moving newsreel of a row of police saluting as they march along. The only plausible inference of this otherwise formally elaborate sequence is that the Shah held onto power ruthlessly, an inference that establishes the 'big history' narrative behind the film's micro narrative.

The anti-Shah narration which establishes *Argo*'s ideological position is swiftly folded into another, equally but less overtly ideological narrative, namely that *Argo*'s version of truth is authentic and factually accurate, as 'proven' by the sequence that follows the potted history in which newsreel and dramatic reconstruction (of angry crowds outside the US Embassy in Tehran) are intermingled, the latter a close and complementary approximation of the former. The two forms of film material remain identifiably separate by shifts in aspect ratio from widescreen (for the dramatisations) to squarer for the archive, but narratively they segue into rather than collide with each other. The twin trajectories converge in a majestic crane shot that swoops over the throng of protestors outside the Embassy and over the gates, before cutting to a nervous female character inside on the telephone. Coming at the start of a film, an archive-driven sequence such as this lays down a marker for the credibility of what follows, however far the subsequent narrative deviates from the facts (and *Argo*, with its frenetic, tense final chase sequence, sorely tests Hayden White's rule of thumb that 'narrative, when applied with moderation, does not alter the perception of the facts' [quoted in Sjöberg, 2001: 146]).

The implications of putting a significant archival sequence at the end of a narrative film can be quite different. *Argo* also concludes with archival images as, to accompany its end credits, photographs of the actual protagonists of the hostage crisis are directly compared to the actors who have just played them. Apart from Affleck himself who looks nothing like CIA agent Tony Mendez, the others (aided by vintage spectacles and costumes and retro haircuts) offer accurate visual caricatures of their prototypes. But what, if anything, does this look-alike-ness prove, and why does it matter? Firstly, it 'matters' because *Argo* is a paean to Hollywood and cinematic invention, for the way the featured hostages escaped Iran was under the guise of being involved in preparatory work for a studio science fiction movie. Secondly, there is the expectation that, where 'big history' is concerned, the resemblance between actors and their real, frequently familiar (from archive), counterparts is necessary for audience immersion, and seals a film's claim to represent the true story on which it is based. Resemblance retains for the narrative film vestiges of reality, a historical imperative underscored in the concluding moments of *Argo* by the insertion, alongside the portrait shots, of flashbacks to archival moments replicated at the start of the film, such as US flag being set alight from the embassy's balcony or the figure of a man hanged from a crane. Finally, there is the use of President Jimmy Carter's voice over the last few images, retrospectively explaining the importance of Mendez's actions to getting every hostage home 'safe and sound' while managing to uphold 'the integrity of our country . . . peacefully'. Carter's emphasis on 'peacefully' carries a contemporary perspective and is, we can presume, a not so indirect criticism of George W Bush's far more aggressive response to '9/11'.

Argo represents the Hollywood model, the first category of films analysed by Jean-Luc Comolli and Paul Narboni in their seminal post-May 1968 *Cahiers du Cinéma* editorial, 'Cinema/Ideology/Criticism', which 'are imbued through and through with the dominant ideology in pure and unadulterated form, and give no indication that their makers were even aware of the fact' (1971: 31). Quite different is the use of archive in Marco Bellocchio's *Buongiorno, notte* (2003), a part factual, part fictionalised account of the kidnapping of Italian politician Aldo Moro, the former Prime Minister and then President of the leading Christian Democrats Party who was seized on 16 March 1978 in broad daylight by Red Brigade terrorists and detained for 54 days before his crumpled corpse was discovered in the boot of the Renault 4 on 9 May 1978. Made by a director who, born in 1939, had experienced directly Italy's years of lead, the 'approximation' at work in *Buongiorno, notte* is that it exists as one of a cluster of post-millennial films that looked back at an earlier period of international terrorism against the (not explicitly referenced) backdrop of the '9/11' al Qaeda attacks. As Alan O'Leary comments, 'The Moro kidnapping demonstrates that events cannot exist as "facts" independently of the context of their interpretation' (2011: 31). Archival footage is used through the film sparingly but symbolically; there will be few Italian spectators who do not recall, when it is re-enacted, the iconic photograph of the captive Moro, a look of wry resignation on his face, under the Red Brigade's banner. Although some archival images (both fictional – such as the clips from Roberto Rossellini's *Paisà* – and factual – such as Pope Paul VI's late plea to the Red Brigades to 'free [Moro] without conditions') appear full screen, television and news footage is generally peripheral and incidental and appears in the background on the terrorists' diegetic television set.

That is, until the film's finale, which plays, at far greater length, news footage of Moro's state funeral/memorial. Just prior to this closing sequence, there is a fantasy, from the perspective of the female terrorist, Chiara (Maya Sansa), who has begun to have misgivings about the kidnapping. Drugged by Chiara, his captors sleep as Moro (Roberto Herlitzka) emerges from his tiny cell, dons a coat and leaves the apartment unchallenged.[6] He emerges free into a drizzly grey Rome street and looks about him as he walks away from the camera and towards the Roman suburb of EUR. After a fade to black and a switch in music from whimsical strings to the harsher electronic guitar-led strains of Pink Floyd's 1975 'Shine On You Crazy Diamond' that will continue loudly over footage of the ceremony, there is a cut back to the apartment, this time to re-enact what really happened as a blindfolded Moro, following the terrorists' kangaroo court's ruling, is led away to be executed. Video footage of Moro's public funeral begins, as the camera tracks along the sombre-suited, stony-faced leaders of the Christian Democrat Party. The unappealing video-ness of the magnified archive and the insistent crescendo of the Pink Floyd track stand for and echo the criticism that underpins the archive. 'Moro was the subject of a "double funeral"', as John Foot explains, this 'pompous' Vatican affair presided over by Pope Paul VI (in his final public appearance and carried into church on a chair) and the 'small private funeral' on 10 May 1978 (Foot, 2009: 201). It is the '*fake* funeral – thanks largely to the mass media – that has become part of the collective memory', Foot continues, and whose 'ambiguity is repeated in the final scene of *Buongiorno, notte*' (201) as, after the mass, there comes one final brief resumption of the fantasy of Moro walking free.

Bellocchio is a formerly active member of the Italian Communist Party, and the funeral footage is used reflectively, underscoring his resignation to the fact that this is how the kidnapping ended. The sequence is lengthy, largely unedited, and accompanied by the blare of intrusive and insistent music that resonates with a desire to cut through the lies and cover-ups, to recall the unverifiable belief that Moro's death could have been averted, had the political establishment desired it. The cut to muted archive after the closing titles is an act of aggrieved grief emphasised by the sequence's visual plainness (aesthetically and politically) and the internalised, visceral tension of the oscillation between archive and fantasy. That the film ends with the fantasy not the reality gives voice to the awareness that archive material can never, however authentic and unadulterated, tell a completed story; that part of what drama or narrative are able to do is tap some of its gaps, join up its dots. Narrativisation can also, as here, proffer an alternative political perspective or reopen familiar history. Unlike the end of *Rush* (or, thinking of more compara- bly political subject material, Ron Howard and Peter Morgan's earlier film, *Frost/ Nixon*), Bellocchio's archive-fuelled conclusion to *Buongiorno, notte* does not bring closure to the Moro story but, more democratically and less didactically, affords spectators insight into the reasons to doubt the official conclusion. The death of Moro will remain 'approximate' and open; Bellocchio is due to return to it in his next project, challenging Leonarda Sciascia's characterisation of 'the Moro Affair' as an already 'completed literary work, already existed in all its unbearable perfection' (2002: 24).

One feature of *Buongiorno, notte* is that the television set is on much of the time.[7] A kind of archival 'white noise', the diegetic television in the background is a common universal trope in realist film and television, including examples such as the Chilean series *Los 80* (Boris Quercia, 2008–2014) that recounts the story of a fictional Santiago-based family living through the years of military dictator- ship, *Mad Men* (Matthew Weiner, 2007–2015)[8] or *Jackie*. The use of television in this way fits Richard Abel's idea of the '*bricolage model*' – the early cinema prac- tice of 'joining actualité footage to contemporary fiction scenes' (Sjöberg, 2001: 194).[9] This basic *bricolage* technique continued to be widely used in both cinema and television drama with the insertion of stock footage and newsreel depicting events (such as battles for war films) that could not otherwise be filmed. The bricolage model adopted by modern archive-based mainstream drama is more complex, as actuality footage is not cut and pasted in merely to plug a narrative hole. The mainstream historical drama adopts a bricolage model of narrative construction of which diegetically inserted archive is a generically familiar element; the television news broadcasts throughout *Buongiorno, notte* serve both a symbolic function and an epistemological one: they vivify the historical subject matter by making it part of the fiction's presentness, and underscore the fiction's basis in truth. Sjöberg worries about the 'possible *contamination* of the footage' when set alongside fiction (2001: 194; italics in original) and asks if the status of 'fictive material' is 'transformed . . . when presented in the context of documentary', or if the reverse is possibly true – that it is maybe documentary or actuality footage that becomes 'fictionalized when presented in a fictional context' (194). Dramatisations 'based on a true story' permit their audiences to disavow and displace the direct actuality moment and the presence, direct or indirect, of *the moment* itself fractures its smooth surface and will always bring into play wider historical questions that reference the factual history on which the drama is based.

As exemplified by Jasper Rigole's discarded found footage, forgetting exists in symbiotic relation to memorialising; before the advent of the (still or moving) camera – and even more so before printing, people had to actively strive, in the absence of technology that could do this for them, to *not-forget* events deemed worthy of being committed to memory. The dramatization of true stories in mainstream narrative film and television *without* the use of archive replaces *the moment* with *the performance*, a paradoxical act of amnesiac remembrance, of fictionalising factual events in order to create out of and around them an alternative memory. The original meaning of a document or archival fragment, though, as previously discussed, always open to reassessment, re-appropriation and even manipulation, can never be entirely disavowed; context can alter its meaning, but it cannot entirely annul it – unless, that is, archive is absent altogether. Archive is, as Baron attests, 'the point of access to what counts as evidence of past events' (2014: 10), before going on to paraphrase Philip Rosen's assessment that what occurs to the document within the documentary is 'the conversion of primary materials to a secondary, historicized understanding' of them (10). Without any trace of the 'document', this 'conversion' runs the risk of being replaced by the document's elision.

An instance in which forgetting can never entirely supplant remembering, even in the most superficially amnesiac, actuality-free fiction, is when the subject matter is an iconic event that is and of itself 'a major temporal break in history' (Baron, 2014: 40). The holocaust as imagery or a point of reference is absent from Oliver Hirschbiegel's *Downfall* (2013), but as we watch the fictional rendition of Hitler's last days, we hardly forget that it occurred as in these cases, subliminal archive achieves something provocative and interesting. When used in documentaries, archive of, for example, the Kennedy assassination can make us fixate on *the moment* itself to the extent that what we forget is that this 'temporal break' in fact did not (as discussed in Chapter 3 in relation to *Mad Men*) make time stop, in spite of the fact that, in the majority of narrative contexts in which it appears, the death of Kennedy is the climactic narrative moment. Even the most notable and accidental artefact in the JFK archive – Zapruder's 8mm home movie film of the assassination – follows a natural narrative arc, which begins with the motorcade turning the corner into Elm Street and ending, after the shots have been fired, as the presidential motorcade speeds under the Stemmons Freeway Bridge. Considering the Kennedy assassination narrative arc, there are many fewer extant images of the following three and a half-mile journey from the Stemmons Freeway to Parkland Hospital where doctors tried in vain to save the president's life; this hiatus between the scenes of assassination and official death is, in terms of the official annals of the day, the minutes when, to appropriate Hayden White, 'nothing much happened'. The focus on these extraneous minutes is one of the things that marks out Pablo Larraín's *Jackie* from many other fictionalised renditions of the assassination. In close-up a camera focuses on Jackie's (Natalie Portman's) anguished face and frozen stare as the presidential limousine races towards the hospital; as it does so, Larraín invites speculation on not only what transpired in the speeding car after it left the abundantly archived site of Dealey Plaza, but what it felt like to be in it, to be the First Lady cradling her husband's blasted head, the injured Governor Connally or his wife. In *Jackie*, Larraín inhabits both the iconic archive and the cracks between such archival moments as it constructs various alternate and fresh points of view of these overly familiar events.

The framing device for *Jackie* is not the assassination *per se*, but the interview Jackie Kennedy granted journalist Theodore White for the 4 December 1963 commemorative edition of *Life Magazine*. In 'For President Kennedy: An Epilogue', White quotes the former First Lady's comment: 'There'll be other great Presidents again – and the Johnsons are wonderful, they've been wonderful to me – but there'll never be another Camelot again' (White, 1963). With this allusion to her husband's favourite musical, the real Mrs Kennedy determined the script of her first husband's presidency. With the benefit of hindsight that now includes access not just the sanitised *Life Magazine* version of White's interview but also to his typed transcript and scrawled notes,[10] Larraín signals the importance of scripted and orchestrated history to the creation and perpetuation of the Kennedy myth. Legacy and the contemplation of history were, from the first raw days after the assassination, already important to Jackie. In the published commemorative piece, Jackie recalls how 'history made Jack what he was' and worries about the President's memorial (White, 1963); during the first interview sequence in Larraín's film, Portman asks Teddy White (Billy Crudup), 'When something gets written down, does that make it true?' Thinking back to the debate between Rosenstone and Hayden White, history, *Jackie* posits, results from the collision between written or archived history, private or repressed memory and speculative or hypothetical drama. The film overturns normative history by focusing away from *the moment* and positioning the mythic figure of 'JFK' as marginal though omnipresent; it presents the assassination as the reverse shot or the alternate, other history, not the point of departure and conclusion. In *Jackie* the death of Kennedy is both an excessively archived *iconic* event and a *lived* one. As a film constructed around the two not always compatible versions of Mrs Kennedy's account of her husband's death – Theodore White's notes (not made public until 1995, a year after her death) and the shorter official 'epilogue' published in *Life Magazine* – it also crucially questions its own status as a fictionalised, yet historically informed contribution to the historicising of a story so shot through with gaps and unknowns. The fictionalisation of the assassination is an important component of its archive. A multitude of images exist of that day which all seem overly familiar. By focusing on the First Lady, *Jackie* neatly both augments and captures the deficiencies of that bulging archive: that we still do not know definitively what happened that day, for example, reverberates through its non-archival sequences, especially the private (non-archived) moments omitted from official versions, such as the Presidential widow's return to the White House in the middle of the night, when Portman finally undresses and, after holding the blood-stained pink suit at arm's length, enters the shower to wash the blood from her body and hair. This oddly unmoving, clinical dissection of Jackie Kennedy finds the transition from verifiable and archived past to fictionalisation endlessly fascinating, as if striving to unearth where the difference between the two comes from and what it means. Elision as well as elusiveness has played a key role in the formation of the persona 'Jacqueline Kennedy', from the public denial of her chain-smoking (something else that features prominently in Larraín's film) to the omissions in White's published 'Camelot' piece. We know now from the full transcript of the interview that Mrs Kennedy did describe how her husband's 'blood and his brains were in my lap',[11] although such graphic details are excised from the original printed version.

Larraín's fixation on the moment of transition from archive to fictional haunting studies how the re-enactment both expands upon and supplants the original. 'A Tour of the White House with Mrs John F. Kennedy' (first transmitted 14 February 1962) features prominently throughout *Jackie*, and in this case a common trope is to begin a sequence with a long-shot from the original, which then gives way to a black and white mid-shot mocked up to look like archive with Portman mimicking Jackie, which in turn segues into a full-blown, modern-looking re-enactment. This verbatim and repeated layering within a single shot sequence complements the fragmentariness of *Jackie*'s overall narrative which does not follow chronology and instead moves between arrival in Dallas and the assassination, the 1962 White House tour documentary, the Teddy White interview and high points of the Camelot years such as Pablo Casals' concert at the White House. However fragmented, Larraín's biopic does not, for instance, emulate the conspiratorial assassination mash-up in Oliver Stone's *JFK* (1991), which caused consternation for drawing 'no limits to what could legitimately be said about it' and 'placing in abeyance . . . the distinction between the real and imaginary' (White, 1996: 19).

In the archetypal 'postmodernist docu-drama or historical metafiction', Hayden White asserts, everything is presented 'as if it were of the same ontological order' (19). Conversely, Larraín's much later biopic does not conform to this model and, as there is with other works discussed in this book, a temporal claim can be made for it as a post-'9/11', post-truth, post-constructed reality film more alert to the dangers of making ontological distinctions secondary to the construction of controversial historical argument. Unlike *JFK, Jackie* distinguishes between fact and fiction – not necessarily in order to assert their erasable difference, but to signal their equivalence in terms of their ability to comment upon historical events. The real and the imaginary do not offer up alternative versions of history; instead, their juxtaposition within one narrative functions as a metaphor for the inherent fracturedness of history, that it is not confined to the archive and what is 'written down', but exists just as validly at the junction with narrative, imagination and fantasy. *Jackie* is therefore one film that offers a 'third way', a route that does not hold as sacred the binary opposition between fiction and archive, but rather identifies them as occupying different points along a continuum. *Jackie* signals this, as Oliver Stone and Clint Eastwood had done before Larraín, by focusing on a secondary story of the assassination, namely its impact on Jackie,[12] with her dead iconic husband ironically becoming the 'empty vessel' Norman Mailer found Kennedy the man to be, the palimpsest that offered his generation 'a mirror of ourselves' (Mailer, 1967: 69–70), and the assassination resonating far beyond the immortalised brutality of its archival presence.

Doane arrives at the conclusion, regarding early cinema's ability to capture actuality, that 'it is important to emphasize that notions of film as record and films as performance/display are not necessarily contradictory or incompatible', that despite cinema's 'central role as entertainment', it is still 'linked to the accumulation of knowledge' (2002: 24). It is useful to think of film as archive and archive in cinema – but also to see cinema in its totality as *an* archival depository. The archive of historical events on film includes fiction, for the fictionalisation of true stories is part of how those true stories are remembered. The generic status of a film or drama does not restrict its significance to and as archive; although the context of archival footage alters depending on generic context, fictionalised versions of factual events can still be part of the repository that comprises *the archive*. In analysing the distinction between the statement and the sentence, Foucault provides one way into understanding the importance of context *to* archive and countenancing the possibility of fiction *as* archive. Like Foucault's statement, the piece of archival material 'is not in itself a unit, but a function that cuts across a domain of structures and possible unities' (2002: 98). The archive, like the statement, is rendered intelligible by context – but that context can be factual or fictional. Fictional contextualisation does not disavow the factual footing of actuality, or dispute its indexical link, but it does add a new dimension – the foundation for the third way – which is the notion that fiction can become archive, can acquire the status of evidence as well as narrative.

British documentary filmmaker Adam Curtis practices a particular type of recycling of images, plundering *the archive* for fictional as well as documentary material with which he constructs his polemical treatises on modern global politics. Very different, therefore, to Asif Kapadia's celebrity-portrait documentaries – *Senna, Amy* (2015) and *Diego Maradona* (2019) – in which causal narratives are told exclusively via the assemblage of nonfictional archive matter matched to the voices of interviewees. Although less politically motivated than Emile de Antonio, Kapadia permits his compiled footage to tell its own story, whereas Curtis (with his insistent *auteurist* voiceover) is far more openly didactic. For Curtis the act of collage film-making is frequently one of *erasure*, as archival fragments are emptied of significa-tion and made to mean something else through radical recontextualisation. Earlier in his career Curtis's films were not exclusively archive-based and were less didactic, but over the decades his style has become increasingly focused on the re-appro-priation of eclectic, frequently esoteric found footage, a technique that conforms to Lévi Strauss's classic model of *bricolage*, which, like 'mythical thought', 'expresses itself by means of a heterogeneous repertoire' (1962: 11). Via *bricolage*, Lévi Strauss continues, 'mythical reflection can reach brilliant unforeseen results' (1962: 12), and Curtis utilises a 'heterogeneous repertoire' of, in his case, eclectic archival frag-ments and reaches, much as Lévi Strauss might have envisaged, 'brilliant unforeseen results' by yoking such disparate elements with violence together.[13] Curtis is docu-mentary's exemplary 'bricoleur', the natural heir to earlier documentary archivists but extending their ideologically-motivated art of compilation (especially resonant is de Antonio's idea of 'radical scavenging')[14] into a less causal, less systematically dialectical form of *bricolage* that responds to and exploits the inherent 'unruliness of archival objects' (Baron, 2014: 4) and is altogether more feverish in its formal construction. Having said this, a distinctive feature of Curtis's documentaries is his pervasive and didactic voiceover; de Antonio, for one, did not believe in narration, wanting to make the process of watching his films more democratic and less deter-mined. Curtis's films have an essay-like quality lacking in *In the Year of the Pig* or the de Antonio-influenced *The Atomic Café*; arguably, their 'authoredness' is more hon-est. One aspect of Curtis's recent radicalism is that, since *It Felt Like a Kiss* (2009), which premiered at the Manchester International Festival and was then available (film only) online,[15] he has only once (with the 3-part series *All Watched Over by Machines of Loving Grace* in 2011) chosen to broadcast his work via a mainstream television channel. Curtis's archive-centred work is distinctive and influential; tak-ing as examples two recent full-length works, *Bitter Lake* and *Hypernormalization*, this discussion will focus on the principal elements of his signature *auteurist* style in relation to *bricolage*, 'junk' recycling and the polemics of contrapuntal archiving.

Bitter Lake and *Hypernormalization* exemplify Curtis's post-'9/11' style and obses-sions; both also demonstrate the ambivalent status of archive footage when it comes to 'explaining' the world. In a more journalistic, less irreverent way than an artist such as Jasper Rigole, Curtis's collages disrupt archive's status as indexical evidence, and yet his documentaries are fixated upon trying to make sense of a chaotic world. *Bitter Lake* opens with the director's familiar voice declaring: 'Increasingly, we live in a world in which nothing makes any sense', in which 'those in power tell stories to help us make sense of the complexity of reality, but those stories are increasingly unconvincing and hollow'. Over a (trademark Curtis) barrage of disjointed images, *Hypernormalization* commences with the similar narration that this time suggests: 'We live in a strange time; extraordinary events keep happening that undermine the stability of the world', an observation illustrated by a bewilderingly eclectic assem-bly of clips of Muhammad Ali, a capsizing boat of immigrants, Arab television and a pre-2016 election Donald Trump. The classic Adam Curtis's bombardment of seemingly random images exists alongside the premise of most of his documentaries, namely that we live amidst chaos which those in power only pretend to have any control over: 'no one in the West had any idea of how to change the world', Curtis surmises at the outset of *Hypernormalization* over images of Gordon Brown and Barack Obama; 'no one knew what was true, and what was fake any longer', he continues, this time linked to images of Vladimir Putin. Over the actress Jane Fonda in gaudy Lycra leading one of her 1980s 'feel the burn' exercise classes, Curtis (in *Hypernormalisation*) gripes that 'Trying to change the world was just too complicated'. This is a common refrain in his later work; maybe, rather than it being the world that is 'just too complicated', it is that trying to *explain* the world is just too complicated, although this is precisely – if paradoxically – what each Adam Curtis's documentary sets out, in ambitiously but infinitely parody-able fashion, to do.[16]

A little over a third of the way through *Hypernormalisation*, Curtis embarks on a long, intricate sequence centred on allegations that through the mid-1980s and early 1990s, the US government, in order to mask their weapons programme, spread rumours that the unknown objects in the skies were UFOs and used people to spread the rumours of alien invasions. Fake documents were produced – 'a blur of fact and fiction' which the government called 'perception management'. The sequence culminates in a classic piece of voiceover that concludes by stating that the aim had been 'to tell dramatic stories that grabbed the public imagination . . . it didn't matter if the stories were true or not, provided they distracted them, and the politicians, from having to deal with the intractable complexities of the modern world'. Could we possibly infer that the same is true of Adam Curtis's films? The rationale for his hugely complex, frenetically feverish films is remarkably similar, as he too constructs narratives out of confusingly and distractingly eclectic archival detritus that grab his audiences' collective imagination and help them deal with the world's 'intractable complexities'.

In 'Archive Fever', Jacques Derrida sets out the idea that the archive is a shelter, but that the shelter also 'forgets' (1995: 9). '*Every* archive', Derrida writes, 'is at once *institutive* and *conservative*. Revolutionary and traditional' (12). Pursuing the inherent duality of *the archive*, archive material could also be argued simultaneously to offer two states of history – set in aspic 'traditional' and unchangeable 'big history' (of leaders and wars) and the 'revolutionary', interventionist one, that changes perceptions on the narrativising of 'big history', frequently by using unexpected and untraditional archival images to advance its argument. The conventional means by which documentary on the whole arrives at 'big history' is via the compilation of frequently familiar images from the main archive repositories of 'big' events, such as Soviet-filmed footage of the liberation of Auschwitz, January to February of 1945, used repeatedly in documentaries since. Curtis juxtaposes frequently familiar 'big historical images' (the war in Afghanistan; Osama bin Laden; the twin towers of New York's World Trade Center) with the flotsam of marginalised history and fragments appropriated from ostensibly irrelevant and generically wide-ranging fiction films (*Pillow Talk; Stalker; Solaris; Carry On Up The Khyber*). The narratives that subsequently emerge are commonly idiosyncratic, unexpected, even perverse, querying the normative informational function of conventional found footage; and yet, they are also doggedly causal.

Laura Mulvey in 'Visual Pleasure and Narrative Cinema' argued stridently: 'It is said that analysing pleasure, or beauty, destroys it. That is the intention of this article' (1975: 8). 'Visual Pleasure' was a polemic, and Adam Curtis's films, in a comparably agitational, polemical manner, set out to destroy the pleasures of causal, logical archive-rich documentary history. If a landmark series such as *The World at War* is the 'well-made play' of archival documentary, Curtis's unsettling, extrovert and extreme post-'9/11' works embrace and extend the notion of 'radical scavenging'. His documentaries, echoing Derrida's archive 'fever', are built on an 'internal contradiction' between commemoration and finality on the one hand, and overlooking and disregarding on the other; for Derrida the contrariness of the archive is that it encompasses both states, so 'There would be no archive desire without the radical finitude, without the possibility of a forgetfulness which does not limit itself to repression' (1995: 19). Curtis's attitude is to 'forget' received versions of events or repress them in favour of more radical critiques or counter-arguments that formulate intellectual theses for 'why we live in a world in which nothing makes sense'. The archive is where past and present brush up against each other, and archive footage the representation of that encounter. The past, films such as *Bitter Lake* imply, did not make sense as it was being lived because, without hindsight, we collectively lacked sufficient sense of where it was headed; as played out in Curtis's films, the past is explained through being put in dynamic juxtaposition with the present, so the encounter is more of a collision than a communion. Similarly, Derrida talks of the archive not as 'a concept of dealing with the past', but as 'a question of the future . . . of a promise and of a responsibility for tomorrow' only fully understood 'in the times to come' (1995: 27). This is a crucially suggestive observation for many audiovisual texts, not just Curtis's documentaries. In many more conventional circumstances, the 'past' as seen in archive is lost or finished with (or 'forgotten' through being misrecognised); however forcefully a piece of found footage articulates its proximity to the subject it represents, the 'why' and the 'how' of that subject is not fixed in time but alters as later information is brought to bear on it. The past, his films generally imply, needs Adam Curtis to make sense of it, as the documentaries mix democratic inquiry (delving into the archives and using others' perspectives and images) with didactic narration and narrative. And with this tactic, a significant shift has occurred, as archive is no longer shackled, in anything other than in the most rudimentary sense, to the context or story behind the events it depicts; it exists to be made sense of 'in the times to come'.

Derrida detects both 'desire' and 'disorder' in the archive (1995: 52), and the allure of archival chaos resonates throughout Curtis's work, as he works with found footage in a variety of ways. Most straightforwardly, Adam Curtis employs archive material *synergistically*, as being closely aligned to and illustrative of his argument – that is, as closely parqueting with the commentary, the visual components to an illustrated lecture. Cutting an explanatory path through the historical forces that led to the terrorist attacks of 11 September 2001 is a common underlying motive and motif of Curtis's recent documentaries and frequently the impetus behind his synergistic employment of archive and complementary narration. For example, in *Bitter Lake*, the director's voice warns of the arrival of a 'dark and apocalyptic Jihadism' and the 'coming battle between good and evil' over a historic pan down the side of one of the twin towers of the World Trade Center. That this particular archival road will end with '9/11' is reinforced by a complex, yet nevertheless symbiotic sequence involving on-screen text and images that unfolds thus:

On-screen text	Image
At the end of the 20th century	Man (a banker?) looking out from a window at a cityscape at dusk.
	A helicopter disappears behind a skyscraper.
... faced with a complex and chaotic world	Cars on a freeway at night.
	Chain of most likely Russian ballet dancers gliding out left of frame.
... politicians retreated into simple stories of right and wrong:	End of dancers shot.
	Fuzzy video image of President Bill Clinton on a diegetic television set.
	UK Prime Minister Tony Blair driving a car.
... moral fables of good versus evil.	Continuation of Blair driving, glancing briefly into the camera.
	Short, dark purplish image of bodies on a dance floor, eerily shimmying in time to the beat of the electronic music. (Recognisable from earlier.)
	Outtakes of BBC newscaster Huw Edwards in the studio at the end of a broadcast.
	Older film footage of a speckled bird at night.
	A foreign news report (Afghanistan?) interrupted by a fight breaking out between two men, one clutching a tripod.
Politicians in America and Britain gave even more of their power away	Bill Clinton waving as he boards Air Force One.
... to the banks.	Circling nocturnal helicopter shot of Citicorp building.
	Woman's hand gesticulating.
	Upwards travelling shot through windows in a glass lift.
The financial technocrats promised they could manage the new complexities,	Lift shot continues upwards.
	Outtake in South East News studio, anchorman flapping his arms about, joking.
	Intercutting between a woman dancing, looking into camera in a different club and the flapping spotted bird.
	Blair walking through a train carriage.
... but the politicians still wanted to change the world.	Continuation of Blair walking shot.

(*Continued*)

(Continued)

On-screen text	Image
So, they did what President Reagan had done:	Dingy descending subway escalator. Fighters (Afghans?) aboard an open-topped jeep, machine guns in hand.
. . . they ruthlessly simplified the complex struggles around the world	Fighters on jeep. More similar vehicles driving through crowded Arab street. Bombing of city at night (Baghdad?).
. . . into simple stories of good versus evil:	Dark, purplish dance floor footage. A woman's hand (with extravagantly long maroon coloured nails) waving.
Kosovo 1999	Tony Blair waving, being applauded as he walks through Kosovo street.
. . . and intervened to protect the innocent victims.	Blair continues. View through nose of fighter plane, flying towards snow-capped mountains (Afghanistan?).
Osama bin Laden sent a team of jihadists to attack the far enemy.	The plane shot continues towards mountains.
The majority were Saudis. They could get US visas easily.	Montage of passenger planes taxiing and taking off at night.
Because of the special relationship between America and Saudi Arabia.	Plane montage continues.
	Black smoke billowing out of one World Trade Center tower; second tower is hit, accompanied by zoom in as orange cloud bursts from it.
	Cut to black.

There is little that is tricksy about this layered, yet straightforward sequence, despite the more elliptical images (the dancers; the bird). Editing between text and illustrative image is largely synchronised, and if the visual edit pre-empts the text it is by only a few frames. Curtis self-identifies as a journalist and establishing the causal chain of such a sequence remains the defining factor. There is minimal dialectical distance created here; linear storytelling is paramount: bin Laden's targeting of the US and the US and allies' reciprocal attempts to quash the international forces of 'evil'. The images, whether straightforwardly illustrative of the inter-titles (the roll call of characters – Blair, Clinton – is familiar) or more opaque 'wallpaper', such as the dancers and bird, serve to bolster the central argument. The tight cause-effect chain of this tightly synergistic sequence is definitively explained with the final edit to the twin towers.

Curtis also deploys archive *representatively* or *symbolically*. Again, in *Bitter Lake*, after having more simply catalogued the failures of the Soviet campaign in Afghanistan, there is a cut to an unidentified scene of a violently traumatised Russian veteran of the 1980s' Afghan War on a train. In close-up the soldier – his hands in black leather gloves, his face sweaty and grimacing – uses the carriage's overhead bars to do pull-ups. Subtitles translate his words: 'we're going to fry their village!'. He shouts and falls back into his wheelchair, as a brave fellow-passenger asks, 'why don't you shut up?' until the soldier turns on her and remonstrates menacingly: 'We're your boys, you stupid bitch'. A friend hurries to wheel the soldier off, at which point he takes off his sunglasses and continues to shout: 'We've brought back Mujahedin ghosts!', laughing maniacally as he is pulled back further. Such an insert does more than give a potted history of the doomed Soviet engagement in Afghanistan; it represents it symbolically, a connotation aided rather than hampered by the lack of information about where the clip comes from. Potency derives from having been preceded by the simpler, expositional sequence. The soldier's crazed laugh is most likely what a viewer will take away from this segment of *Bitter Lake*, as an abstract, expressionistic commentary on a wider argument.

Elsewhere, one can find examples of Curtis using archive in a more nuanced, contrapuntal manner. Earlier in *Bitter Lake*, for instance, there is a chain of three extended sequences that are only symbolically and subliminally linked, echoing the elusive complexities of Eisenstein's category of overtonal montage. The first is a longer section of the purple-lit middle-aged dance floor cited earlier, which ends on a couple ballroom dancing, the man holding his partner's hand very precisely and delicately, with the two smallest fingers on his left hand outstretched. A sharp edit to a close-up of a bandaged child's hand heralds a very different scene, this time with no music (and no narration or subtitles). These are loosely cut rushes of what appears to be the setting up of a current affairs report. A wider shot reveals the full extent of the small girl's injuries – she has bandages on all four limbs, has lost half of one arm and one eye and her face is pock-marked with smaller shrapnel wounds; she is dressed in a clean spotty dress, while a toy tiara teeters on her head. Next to her sits an anxious-looking father glancing warily into the camera's lens. Instructions come from behind the apparatus, which he seems to obey, and we hear a woman's voice say in English 'give her the flower'. On the girl's wheelchair there is a red geranium, which the father dutifully holds up level with his traumatised daughter's face. A man's voice – the director's from behind the camera – then asks for him to 'put it down'; the father obliges. Then there comes a cut to an extreme close-up of the girl's face – intense seriousness emanating from her one eye; glistening tears oozing from the socket where the other one once was – before a slightly wider pull out captures father and daughter talking, the girl shaking her head twice before a pan across to a close-up on the brilliant red flower masking her remaining hand. Left unencumbered in this way, this sequence of tenderness and exploitation lingers as the angriest, most intense and unresolved moment in *Bitter Lake*, a testament to the power of raw, unadulterated archive.

As an antidote, coming out of this visceral sequence there is a cut to the use of archive as *interlude*, as vehicle for having a breather or taking stock. Again, unadorned with narration or text, there follows an image of a western soldier studying a map, his concentration ruptured by the tinny familiarity of distant gunshot. He looks into the distance and the camera follows his gaze, focusing on some brown smoke and then the blue sky beyond; Arabic music starts up, swiftly followed by a sharp edit to a close image of a brown bird perched on a machine gun lying in the grass. With a wit reminiscent of Vertov or Cavalcanti, a wider image reveals another hand, this time belonging to a different soldier, who outstretches his arm and strokes the soft stomach of this remarkably passive bird. The bird pecks at the soldier's fingers and it comes to stand on them, until bird and soldier are in profile communing with each other. The soldier says something inaudible to whoever is behind the camera and continues to pet the bird; he and we are transfixed as the bird flutters up to sit on his helmet. Although artificially generated (in that it is edited to look as if it is the same soldier who hears the gunshot and then befriends the bird), this completes an associative chain of images that exemplifies a subliminally meaningful deployment of archive and editing. The repetition of the hands draws us into the details of this sequence; the injured girl reminds us of the violence underpinning the battles for Afghanistan, while the soldier and the bird transports us out of that narrative by compelling us to look most intently at the archive fragment's only tangentially related content, noting the awe on the soldier's face matched by the bird's softness and composure.

At the other end of Curtis's archive spectrum is his deployment of appropriated segments as decisive points of *rupture*, in either signification-heavy or signification-light modes. Exemplary of the former technique would be the injection of references to '9/11' throughout *Bitter Lake*, when the subject under discussion is not the terrorist attacks themselves. This example is somewhat obvious, whereas the film's repeated references to *Carry On Up The Khyber* is more nuanced, initially appearing 'light', but over the course of the documentary becoming 'signification-heavy' by virtue of their cumulative effect. Curtis, deploying synergistic archive alongside a didactic voiceover, concludes that proof came in 2009 of the failure of the British and the Americans to bring democracy to Afghanistan, as they failed to stop Hamid Karzai from being re-elected as President, despite allegations of widespread corruption. Cut to *Carry On Up The Khyber* where, following a lingering shot of a pensive-looking Karzai, the dialogue unfolds thus:

SIR SIDNEY ROUGH-DIAMOND (SID JAMES): I still don't trust that fella.
CAPT. KEEN (ROY CASTLE): Things look rather bad sir, what are we going to do?
SIR SIDNEY: Do Captain? We're British – we won't do anything.
MAJOR SHORTHOUSE (JULIAN HOLLOWAY): Until it's too late.
SIR SIDNEY: Precisely. That's the first sensible thing you've said today.
MAJOR SHORTHOUSE: Thank you sir.
SIR SIDNEY: Well gentlemen, as always, we'll carry on as if nothing was going to
     happen.

Without a pause, a hard edit ensues to President George W. Bush in March 2008 outlining, to the Economic Club of New York, measures to 'mitigate disruptions to our financial markets'. Inserting archive as fissure, whether fictional or factual, may, as here, be crudely satirical; however, the act also jolts the audience, using decontextualization and de-sequentialization as the means by which to refocus attention on the deeper argument and break the film's smooth narrative flow. As Catherine Russell observes, 'Decontextualisation is the means by which the archive offers up history as a nonnarrative series of bodies and events' (1999: 258).

Archive as *rupture* also works, in the tradition of Soviet montage, through dialectical cross-editing. The Jane Fonda workout in *Hypernormalisation* is in fact embedded in a sequence focused on the demise of the Soviet Union and eastern European communism in the late 1980s and is, specifically, intercut with the graphic archive – readily available on YouTube – of the trial and execution of Romanian dictator, Nicolae Ceausescu, and his wife Elena on 25 December 1989. The immediate schism lies in the shock of the contrast between the violent sobriety of the events in Romania and the air-headedness of the Fonda work out. Both the death of communism and Fonda's 'feel the burn' ethos were culturally dominant at the time, but what else is insinuated by this stark juxtaposition? On the most banal level, the cross-cutting offers a sort of belated 'be careful what you wish for' warning: to relinquish the idealisms of communism for *this*? In fact, Curtis forgets to extend this Fonda analogy beyond stating blandly (as on-screen text): 'But there was still something you could control . . . Your body . . . A NEW SYSTEM WAS ABOUT TO BE BORN'. With or without the emphatic capitals, this remains a trite and insubstantial, unsubstantiated assertion; the rupture here is more imagistic than anything else and it is not especially profound, unless one extends the comparison between 1980s' Fonda and the death of communism to include the disavowal or suppression of Fonda's own radicalism – the earlier headier days of 'Hanoi Jane'. A dialectical breach of this kind functions neatly as an 'approximation' that leads the spectator to see parallels and hear echoes beyond the text.

Yet ultimately, Adam Curtis's documentaries, for all their structural complexity and implied formal open-endedness, offer temporary stability – a route to *understanding* the 'time of great uncertainty and confusion' in which we live. The trouble is, we live in a perpetual state of 'great uncertainty and confusion', to which archive materials – indexical reminders of events that have occurred and so resonate with some 'certainty' – provide only temporary relief. Adam Curtis's films inhabit a perpetual dualist state, driven by the tension between the act of cutting a path through the chaotic jungle of the 'great uncertainty and confusion' and, as exemplified by the eclecticism, violence and freneticism of much of the archive, of confirmation that the chaos cannot be held at bay. In this respect, the conclusions to his documentaries are key, leaving us, the viewers, in an ironically satisfied state of disavowal, of enjoying the security of having a handle on our chaotic world, while simultaneously knowing this to be illusory. The pact Curtis strikes with his willing spectators is nicely paradoxical: we relish and are comforted by the ephemeral stability his persuasive arguments offer while simultaneously realising that this stability is illusory, an ambivalent state encapsulated by the end of *Hypernormalisation*.

As specified in its accompanying blog, the aim of *Hypernormalisation* is to 'tell the epic story of how we got to this strange place' of 'Donald Trump, Brexit, the War in Syria, the endless migrant crisis, random bomb attacks' (Curtis, 2016). Symptomatic of this 'strange place' is the eclecticism of the archive recycled to identify it. Eisenstein sometimes concludes lengthier montage sequences (the Odessa Steps sequence in *Battleship Potemkin*, for instance) with, once his argument is well-established, a short collage of more elliptical, abstract images. The effect is to both cement the argument being propounded symbolically and to underline the impossibility of a neat conclusion. Curtis, like Eisenstein, wants to have his cake and eat it too: the compulsion to explicate a complex argument is irresistible, but he is forced into uncomfortable cohabitation with a latent acknowledgement that, convincing analysis or no, the residual messiness of history remains. While the putative aim behind Curtis's documentaries has been consistently to offer a means of controlling such chaos through reassuringly complicated argument, the films rarely conclude with comparably comforting moments of closure. Instead, *Hypernormalisation* plunges us straight back into the 'strange place' whence we started. Reasoned argument – centring on Abu Musab al-Suri and the new small-scale terrorism, the Paris attacks of 13 November 2015 and the insurgence of the reactionary, racist and fearful populist forces exemplified by Brexit, gives way to one final, rousing archival fireworks display. After Stephen Colbert on *The Late Show* has confessed to having been 'genuinely freaked out by this whole Brexit thing. . . . It's just not supposed to happen', there is a cut to Sissy Spacek in Brian de Palma's *Carrie* (1976) being showered in blood during her high school prom, followed by a post-Brexit interview with a visibly distressed British woman talking about 'the stirrings of fascism in Europe'.

Hypernormalisation's frenzied last hurrah follows immediately on from this and splices together pithy shards of archive from earlier: 1960s performance art, Bill Clinton, Blair, Cameron, *Carrie*, Syrian explosions, Putin, Obama, Hillary Clinton, a capsizing immigrant boat, a campaigning Trump, a US citizen flaunting his 'Fuck Islam' t-shirt, a fashion show, all set to Barbara Mandrell's rendition of the Loretta Lynn country classic 'Standing Room Only', about a soul being turned away on Judgement Day as the 'world went up in smoke'. Although *Hypernormalisation*'s last image is of a teenage girl (again familiar from earlier), bored of dancing with her friends and turning off her selfie camera, any sense of closure this delivers is, after the unsettling montage, totally fraudulent. The heady formal turmoil of the montage sequence signals that, even as the film draws to its logical conclusion, things have already moved on and this is no longer 'the end'. The pervasive intention behind Curtis's documentaries has consistently been to proffer an analysis of the state of the world *now*, to open up the debate before setting out to tie up all strands of the argument to reach a superficially simple, but disingenuous, conclusion.

Curtis, like US assemblage artist Bruce Conner, unleashes in his films an 'avalanche of imagery' (Russell, 1999: 251). Although Curtis does not see himself as an artist (even eschewing the nomenclature 'director'), Conner, like de Antonio and Eisenstein, is a crucial antecedent. From the late 1950s (*A Movie* came out in 1958) to the early 1980s, Conner assembled films out of fragments of stock footage which he bought in bulk, splicing together trivia with significant events as he does in *Report* when he juxtaposes a television ad for a refrigerator with Jackie Kennedy getting into an ambulance car carrying her assassinated husband to Dallas's Love Field airport. Curtis, like Conner, reminds us that all images – be they ads, popular fiction films or raw news reportage – comprise and contribute to the narrative of and play a role in our 'complicated' world. And so, Baron's proposal not to view 'the terms "found" and "archival"' in binary opposition but rather to regard '"foundness" as a constituent element of all archival documents' (2014: 17) ultimately works well for Curtis, who nevertheless does not quite acknowledge, as Steedman readily does, that the 'tiny flotsam that has ended up in the record office' (aka the BBC Archives) is but an insignificant, arbitrarily selected tributary of 'the great, brown, slow-moving strandless river of Everything' (2001: 18). Curtis is not yet able to relinquish his desire to understand 'everything' through witty re-appropriation and understanding of flotsam. His documentaries offer subjective, polemical and selective narratives; for all the centrality to them of *archive* – that is the products of other people's engagement with the original events – they do not easily permit one to stand back from it or to formulate a counter argument. Images come at you so fast and Curtis's voiceover is so insistent (and erudite and convincing) that an understanding of 'Everything' is, albeit temporarily, promised. That is, until the documentaries' explosive, inconclusive finales. Although the post-'9/11' documentaries all embark upon similar journeys to tame and understand the 'great uncertainty and confusion' around us, each also invariably acknowledges that things have already changed, and events moved on. Each Adam Curtis's film, therefore, is illustrative of the destabilizing realization that we live in a perpetual state of 'approximation'. Archive may be the window onto the past, found footage might offer indexical ballast, but the images' meaning is never that fixed or secure. Montage is the very articulation of the fact that archive is constantly undergoing reassessment and realignment, that the meaning of each individual sequence is in a constant state of flux and shifts according to what it is juxtaposed with, is reinter-preted through knowledge of later events that were not known at the time or had not occurred last time it was appropriated. Curtis theoretically offers stability in the form of logical intellectual argument but, ironically, built into each of his later documentaries is the idea that similar, even identical, archive will, at another time, help formulate an entirely different story or narrative and reach a different conclu-sion about the reasons for our 'great uncertainty and confusion'.

Archive footage embodies 'approximation' because it is mutable. In the hands of a different filmmaker, or made at a different time, each of the films discussed above would have, in turn, been different. In archive one finds the shapes of randomness as well as intentional, constructed meaning. Each time we visit *the archive*, we are confronted with this duality. Above, I describe visiting the Pathé archive; just now I have instead visited the BBC Archive Homepage.[17] The arbitrary resonance of archive is there on the (inevitably ephemeral) landing page, on which one could click: 'Hop-pickers return to Kent, 1972' (a short film about East-enders returning to the fields where they used to work); 'Musical Pioneers'; 'Men with long hair, 1967' (subheading: 'I think it's disgusting, disgraceful and effeminate'); 'Experimen-tal Mobile Phone, 1976'. There were other boxes, but these were the ones I visited. Sometimes there is a logic to the films featured on the secondary page below any one of these (alongside Michael Rodd's *Tomorrow's World* item about a hefty port-able phone there are, predictably enough, other items about mobile telephones); the selection around the hop-pickers film is wider, and includes a news item from 1960 on Petticoat Lane market (the link here is presumably working East-enders). Depending on the order in which I click on these windows, I will navigate the archive differently, make different connections, have different thoughts – and almost certainly will have forgotten how it was I got to where I end up and will, even more certainly, not be able to retrace my steps.

Each visit to *the archive* will be different, just as each piece of archival footage will, depending on context and time, yield different meaning(s). And within that frame there resides the flexible unstable archive documents themselves. The different archival selections made by Rithy Panh and Emile de Antonio (discussed at the outset of this chapter) are revealing about how and what archive can mean. Whereas Panh's historical footage carries solid and transparent meaning with it, the inferences of de Antonio's rickshaw-travelling colonialists (though not quite Steedman's 'flotsam' in the way Curtis's Jane Fonda 1980s work out is) are significantly more flexible and susceptible to context. Something the flotsam demonstrates is a fundamental truism of archive, namely that most history happens *without* being recorded or made into *archive*; the instabilities of unarchived memories then predominate over an unpredictable past. As with other illustrations of 'approximation' (and notwithstanding archive's conventionally indexical link to past events) fiction has emerged as part of *the archive* of film and media, a generic disjunction to match the temporal disjunction between past and present inherent within every archival fragment. Alongside and underpinning both of these is the added awareness that the 'present' of the triangular relationship between factual event, representation and consumption is perpetually shifting; its instability is the factor that ultimately defines archive's 'approximate' status.

Notes

1 Cf. Jay Leyda, *Films Beget Films – Compilation Films from Propaganda to Drama*, London: Hill and Wang, 1971; Alan Rosenthal and Emile de Antonio, 'Emile de Antonio: An Interview', *Film Quarterly*, 32:1, Autumn 1978, 4–17; Jaimie Baron, *The Archive Effect: Found Footage and the Audiovisual Experience of History*, London: Routledge, 2014.
2 www.britishpathe.com/search/start/1890/end/2011. Accessed 9 February 2017.
3 Gallery notes from Tate Modern Rauschenberg exhibition, 1 December 2016–2 April 2017.
4 That it was ruled over by a series of 'kings, known as shahs', as the female voiceover states, until Mohammad Reza Shah Pahlavi was overthrown by the returning cleric Ayatollah Khomeini, who became leader in December 1979 and established the Islamic Republic.
5 The adoption of the storyboard cartoon style of animation presages the film's storyline, in which a fake science fiction film screenplay becomes a weapon in the CIA's successful plot to free the hostages.
6 Rumours abounded at the time and since that tip-offs on Red Brigade hide-outs and potential locations of the apartment in which Moro was being held were either ignored by the authorities or followed up too late.
7 O'Leary comments how this was the first time (in Italy, presumably) that there had been 'blanket, round-the-clock news reporting' of an event (2011: 31), to which the omnipresent television broadcasts attest.
8 Whose dramatization and narrativization of contemporary history is discussed in Chapter 3.
9 Cf. Chapter 4, 'The Transition to a Narrative Cinema, 1904–1907', in Richard Abel (ed.) *The Ciné Goes to Town: French Cinema, 1896–1914*, expanded and revised ed., Berkeley and Los Angeles: University of California Press, 1994.

10 Available at the John F. Kennedy Presidential Library and Museum. www.jfklibrary.org/asset-viewer/archives/THWPP/059/THWPP-059-011. Accessed 1 September 2019.

11 'Item III-A: A Copy of Theodore White's 19 December 1963 Interview Notes', *Kennedy Library*. www.jfklibrary.org/Asset-Viewer/Archives/THWPP-059-013.aspx. Accessed 1 September 2019.

12 Cf. *In the Line of Fire* (Wolfgang Petersen, 1993). The protagonist of *JFK* is Louisiana District Attorney, Jim Garrison.

13 Cf. Samuel Johnson idea that a characteristic of metaphysical poetry was that 'heterogeneous ideas are yoked by violence together', *The Lives of the Poets, Vol. 1*, London: J.F Dove, 1826, 18.

14 Cf. Weiner and de Antonio, 1971.

15 *It Felt Like a Kiss* was a collaboration with theatre company Punchdrunk and Damon Albarn.

16 One such parody is 'The Loving Trap', a short look at Curtis's career and his fantasy that '200,000 *Guardian* Readers Will Change the World'. www.youtube.com/watch?v=x1bX3F7uTrg. Accessed 2 September 2019.

17 www.bbc.co.uk/archive/. Accessed 19 September 2019.

2

'9/11' AS 'NOT 9/11'

United 93 and Man on Wire

Gerhard Richter's 2005 painting, *September*, gives a loose, abstracted representation of the twin towers on 11 September 2001 just as the second plane has struck. It offers an elliptical response to the terrorist attacks, blurred and fuzzy in a way that his series of 15 paintings depicting the deaths of Red Army Faction members (18 October 1977) had not been.

The grey of the traumatised towers melts into the plume of dirty grey smoke threatening to engulf them; lines of paint knifed into the canvas dissect it as the planes have just done the blue skies behind. Richter was uncomfortable with the notion of rendering the attacks literally, producing instead an image 'at the very edge of being recognizable, at that liminal point where the information it contains could be read any number of ways', as New York art critic, Robert Storr, observed (2010: 48). For Storr, *September* opens 'meaningful gaps between us and the onsite images we know so well' (that is, the video and photographic archive images of the moment United Airlines Flight 175 slammed into the South Tower) and presents 'a figment rather than a record of history' that questions 'the photographic fiction' of being able to straightforwardly capture 'the decisive moment' of, for example, the point of death (Storr, 2010: 50–51).[1] The truth of '9/11' cannot simply be 'distilled' into any one image taken that day, and 'Richter's blur' – having created a spectral image whose indexicality is literally buried under layers of paint – 'makes that flux and indeterminacy explicit' (Storr, 2010: 51). Richter's image is only an approximation of the explosion of the second plane into the World Trade Center and, as such, represents the paradox of a representation: how to create distance between itself and memory, while conveying its visceral intensity.

Others are discussed, but the two films that are the focus of this chapter are Paul Greengrass's *United 93* and James Marsh's *Man on Wire*. Both, from very different perspectives, offer 'approximations' of '9/11' and embody the paradox of Richter's *September* as they seek to create intensity through distance, and stand apart critically from the dominant narratives that built up around '9/11'. Simultaneity between images and events ostensibly negates the formation of a counter-narrative, and yet *United 93*, which recounts '9/11' from its epicentre, from the unimaginable perspective of its immediate victims, evades being subsumed into the dominant narrative by virtue of having come into being before that narrative was formed. In this way it dramatizes the new unfathomable abstraction of the pre-'9/11' narrative which Don DeLillo describes at the outset of *Falling Man* when he talks of the site where the twin towers had once stood as 'not a street anymore, but a world, a time and space of falling ash and near night' (2007: 1). By enacting a distant pre-moment that occurred decades before the attacks (Philip Petit's 1974 high wire walks between the freshly constructed twin towers), James Marsh in *Man on Wire* instead evokes '9/11' subliminally. This is more clearly a 'not-9/11' film, as the events of 11 September 2001 are never cited directly, though they maintain a constant and spectral presence that creates distanciation, a critical alienation between its temporal layers. Both are 'approximations' of and to the ways in which '9/11' has been narrativised, and so are framed here, alongside Richter, as 'not-9/11' narratives.

Recalling André Bazin's excitable championing of the photographic image over the painting (that while the painting offers only '*a mere approximation. . . .* The photographic image is the object itself' [1967: 14; my italics]), it has become the case that, increasingly, proximity elicits quite different responses as we come to expect virtually instantaneous verification – via television and social media – of 'decisive moments' such as '9/11'. And yet, 'EVERYTHING IS NOT ABOUT 9/11!' (Turpin, 2012), as one exasperated contributor wailed in an online debate about the minimalist poster to *Mad Men*'s Season 5 (a solitary silhouetted figure of a falling man accompanied by only a date) which for many was perceived to be a direct allusion to '9/11'. This discussion examines some of the implications of cinematic narratives that complicate, contextualise and work around the official '9/11' narrative that started to form immediately. *September* adds, according to Storr, a 'third term' to the 'familiar binary tensions in Richter's art between the photograph and the painted picture' (2010: 9); likewise, these 'not-9/11' texts create a 'third term', a new and unique space in which the proximate photographic image is both remembered and erased by its approximate, more nebulous or refracted incarnation.

Defined by its instantaneous mediarisation, '9/11' joined the ranks of what Douglas Kellner terms 'megaspectacles', events that 'become defining events of their era' and which 'dramatize its controversies and struggles . . . while taking over media culture' (2005: 25). '9/11', like 'megaspectacles' before and since, ceased very swiftly to be a series of individual constituent parts as it became transformed, even as the events were still unfolding, into a *narrative*. This narrativisation occurred rapidly, as perceived gaps were filled and 'something closer to the cinematic assemblage of images was offered' (King, G., 2005: 51). By the day after, such sequences were already able to include the narrative's very beginning in the form of Jules Naudet's accidental video capture of the moment American Airlines Flight 11 crashed into the North Tower. 'By editing the fragmentary shots into a continuous sequence', Bolter suggests, 'the networks were helping to provide an interpretation of the events and thus to cover over the sense of dislocation that their audience felt', thereby providing them with supposedly 'total coverage' (2005: 11). However, the networks' coverage was not 'total', as features 'deemed too brutal' (10), such as the images and sounds of bodies falling from the twin towers, were soon excised from the larger collective narrative of '9/11', which conceptualised the terrorist acts as a 'heinous and unprovoked attack on a virtuous and blameless nation' (McSweeney, 2014: 10). Like all 'decisive moments', '9/11' came to be viewed not as a 'third term' at all, but rather 'in binary terms – good versus evil, us versus them' (Westwell, 2011: 816).

Such instant narrativization left Susan Sontag 'appalled' and 'sad' on the day, as

> America had never seemed farther from an acknowledgement of reality. . . . Where is the acknowledgement that this was not a 'cowardly' attack on 'civilisation' or 'liberty' or 'humanity' or 'the free world' but an attack on the world's self-proclaimed superpower, undertaken as a consequence of specific American alliances and actions.
>
> *(2007: 105)*

The macro-narrative of '9/11' started to be formed on the evening of 11 September 2001 as President Bush addressed the nation from the Oval Office and framed the tragedies as attacks on 'our way of life, our very freedom',[2] and continued – through the commencement of military action in Afghanistan (October 2001), through the 29 January 2002 State of the Union address in which he identifies Iraq, Iran and North Korea as 'an axis of evil, arming to threaten the peace of the world' – to the moment on 20 March 2003 when the US-led invasion of Iraq commenced with a 'shock and awe' campaign of aerial bombardment of Baghdad. The aftershocks (or postscripts) were the capture and execution of Saddam Hussein and the eventual hunt for and murder of Osama bin Laden.

Francis Fukuyama asked, in the summer of 1989, as communism unravelled, if the world was witnessing 'the end of history'? 'What we may be witnessing', he continued, is 'the end of history as such', which he characterised as the demise of 'Western liberal democracy as the final form of human government' (Fukuyama, 1989). In this respect, '9/11' was firstly the end of one and secondly the commencement of another battle between conflicting ideologies, as represented, in cinema and media studies terms, by the many books, collections and journal editions (many of which I site below) 'about' films 'about' '9/11'. The majority of books 'about' cinema and '9/11' discuss films, from *World Trade Center* (2006) with its digitally recreated dust cloud, to *Zero Dark Thirty*, that outwardly conform to the official '9/11' narrative, from terrorism to war, to torture. The references are explicit in a film such as the 2011 adaptation of Jonathan Safran Foer's novel, *Extremely Loud and Incredibly Close*, about a boy whose father dies in the World Trade Center, though more tenuous in films set in the wars in Iraq and Afghanistan, such as Clint Eastwood's *American Sniper* (2014) or Kathryn Bigelow's *The Hurt Locker* (2008). Nevertheless, the context is clear.

The 'not-9/11' narrative – of films such as *United 93, Man on Wire*, the portmanteau film *11'09"01, September 11* or Matt Reeves's found footage monster film, *Cloverfield* – admits the instabilities of history and accepts that there are multiple, frequently conflicting, ways in which it can be viewed. '9/11' becomes a fragmentary, shifting 'approximation', which puts the primary events in and out of focus, as articulated explicitly in Michael Moore's *Fahrenheit 9/11* (2004), in which Moore claims that the Bush administration exploited the events of '9/11' for its own benefit 'in order to embark on an imperialist war in the Middle East' (Westwell, 2014: 64), the roots of which, Moore argued, pre-dated the terrorist attacks of 2001. A pre-requisite of the 'not-9/11' narrative is not necessarily the absence of the events of '9/11', though this is the case in a film such as *Cloverfield*, shot in ultra 'queasy-cam' and featuring a surprise catastrophic attack on New York City by a monster and smaller creatures. Alternatively, Spike Lee's *25th Hour* (2002), which had been shot in the summer of 2001 but was subsequently reworked after '9/11', refers explicitly to the iconography of '9/11' but not in a way that straightforwardly reinforces the notion that the attacks (as the monster attacks do in *Cloverfield*) came 'out of the blue' and 'changed everything' (Westwell, 2014: 33–38). Echoes of '9/11' extend to the spate of films about contemporary and historical terrorism, such as *The Hamburg Cell* (2004), *Buongiorno, notte, The Baader-Meinhof Complex* (2008) or even *Shadow Dancer* (2012), that were released in its aftermath. The two principal examples discussed below offer quite distinct 'not-9/11' models, one from the eye of the storm (*United 93*), the other from a position of detachment and accidental encounter (*Man on Wire*. Both face outwards from the closed '9/11' narrative'.

It is true that 'EVERYTHING IS NOT ABOUT 9/11!' . . . but 'Nearly everyone in the whole world understands immediately what is meant by the phrase "September 11th"' (Croft, 2006: 15). A few years ago, I was giving a research seminar at the University of Nottingham when, *a propos* of *Mad Men*, I said pretty much precisely this. An unexpectedly hostile member of staff retorted that, if I had asked her incoming first years what they understood by '9/11', none of them would have heard of it. I found this hard to believe and wondered if her antagonism stemmed from a residual resentment at the US hegemony contained in the branding of '9/11'. The political, ideological and cultural reach of '9/11' is such that, when asked, only weeks after the attacks, if he agreed that '*Le 11 septembre*' had already become 'one of the most important historical events we will witness in our lifetime', Jacques Derrida responded:

> We will have to return later to this question of language. As well as to this act of naming; a date and nothing more. When you say 'September 11' you are already citing, are you not? You are inviting me to speak here by recalling, as if in quotation marks, a date or a dating that has taken over our public space and our private lives for five weeks now.
>
> *(Borradori, 2003: 85)*

'9/11', 'September 11', '11 September' was placed almost immediately, as Derrida notes, in quotation marks; it became a globally recognised shorthand. But as Derrida also intimates, the date is only a date – *we* have given it resonance, *we* permitted it to 'take over our public space'. Whatever the appellation and however brief, Derrida continues, repetition is crucial to its effect because, fundamentally, repetition has taken the place of understanding, 'for repetition always protects by neutralizing, deadening, distancing a traumatism' (Borradori, 2003: 87). 'This act of language', Derrida argues, helps us to forget 'to think the thing in question', for all we can say – and all the enunciation '9/11' can say – is 'something terrible took place on September 11, and in the end we don't know what' (87). The identification of a series of collective events as the singular '9/11' also became the mechanism by which the unknown (and frightening) became the known (and familiar). '9/11' was a way of containing an imaginative threat.

In the immediate aftermath of the *tragedies*, their collective identity was formulated as an extra-ordinary *singularity*, as when (New Yorker) Don DeLillo, writing in *Harper's Magazine* in December 2001, wrote of 'this catastrophic *event* that changes the way we think and act' (DeLillo, 2001: 33, my italics). A recurrent corollary of this singularity became the conceptualisation of '9/11' as 'unreal', 'too real' or 'unaccountable' within conventional frames of reference (38). Narrative simplicity became a way of fixing the narrative of '9/11' in the imagination and history, of not permitting it to change or be changed by global contextualisation or understood within a complex series of historical events as Sontag had argued. The first 'not' in this debate, therefore, is that, despite the frequency with which '9/11' is discussed as a singular event, there was not just *one* attack but four coordinated attacks, as al-Qaeda terrorists seized control of four passenger jets bound on journeys from north eastern airports for California. Two were crashed into the World Trade Center, another struck the Pentagon and a fourth, the hijacked United Airlines Flight 93, was intended for Washington DC but came down near Shanksville, Pennsylvania. In total, around 3,000 people were killed in the attacks and another 6,000 injured. The characterisation of '9/11' as a single public event is over-simplifying and indicative of its collective impact on global politics, culture and the media but not of what it felt like to inhabit. In accepting the events' plurality, the 'not-9/11' text seeks the alternative, potentially global, point of view in order to break down simplifying binary oppositions.

Conceptualising 'not-9/11' is also about remembering media- and genre-specificity and understanding that it was not only mainstream narrative film, but also television, that was responsible for the representation of '9/11'. In *Postmodernism: Or the Cultural Logic of Late Capitalism* Fredric Jameson contended that, while

> memory seems to play no role in television, commercial or otherwise . . . nothing here haunts the mind or leaves its afterimages in the manner of the great moments of film (which do not necessarily happen, of course in the 'great' films).
>
> *(1991: 70–71)*

Jameson's polemical (and snobbish) dichotomy from 20 years before was to play out interestingly in the aftermath of the attacks. While television (news especially) was central to remembering both what '9/11' was and shaping how it came to be memorialised, academic discussions of the events in 'afterimages' have been dispro-portionately biased towards fictional *films*, as Hollywood film swiftly became, in terms of screen cultures, the go-to way to examine '9/11' narratively and cultur-ally. *Man on Wire*, for instance, features in discussions about '9/11' and film far less frequently than Oliver Stone's infinitely inferior *World Trade Center*, but the latter is both bigger budget and studio-backed, and tackles the events of '9/11' explic-itly. Indirect allegories of 'not-9/11' surfaced more readily (though not exclusively) among other sorts of screen media: documentary; low-budget film; television. So, maybe it is possible to argue that while the '9/11' trauma was acted out on televi-sion, it was allegorised by Hollywood.

The visual parallels between the attacks on the twin towers of the World Trade Center and Hollywood disaster movies, many reasoned, rendered those real events 'cinematic', so they both *echoed* and subsequently *influenced* big budget disaster mov-ies. As Hollywood director Robert Altman remarks in '9/11''s immediate aftermath:

> The movies set the pattern, and these people copied the movies. Nobody would have thought to commit an atrocity like that unless they'd seen it in a movie. . . . I just believe we created this atmosphere and taught them how to do it.
>
> *(Hoberman, 2001)*

The parallels between the spectacle of the planes hitting the World Trade Center's two towers and Hollywood disaster movies have been noted many, many times; what is still interesting about Altman's comment is the *guilt* that Hollywood in par-ticular felt over having 'taught them how to do it'. In an article that considers film studies after '9/11', B. Ruby Rich says of Gillo Pontecorvo's *The Battle of Algiers* (1966) that it virtually resembles 'a recruiting film for Al-Qaeda' (Rich, B., 2004: 111); but what Altman is inferring from the '9/11' attacks is that it had been the grand narratives of mainstream cinema, more than the overt politics of films such as *Algiers*, that had influenced the terrorists. The impact of the events of '9/11' on film and media was, of course, profound. Lynn Spigel argues, for example, that the day's events changed attitudes to the 'de rigueur violence of mass media – both news and fiction – (that) no longer seemed business as usual' (2004: 235), while McSweeney articulates that Hollywood especially 'had a distinctly problematic relationship with the traumatic events of 11 September 2001. . . 9/11 was paradoxically both erased from the cinema screens and returned to in film after film' (4).

Slavoj Žižek focuses on the visual parallels between the attacks and 'catastrophe movies' when he asks in *Welcome to the Desert of the Real*:

> For the vast majority of the public, the WTC explosions were events of the TV screen, and when we watched the oft-repeated shot of frightened peo-ple running towards the camera ahead of the giant cloud of dust from the

collapsing tower, was not the framing of the shot itself reminiscent of spectacular shots in catastrophe movies, a special effect which outdid all others, since – as Jeremy Bentham knew – reality is the best appearance of itself?

(2002: 11)

Just as Žižek here sees the real 'giant cloud of dust' of '9/11' as recalling past movies, so every CGI (computer generated imagery) wall of dust, since 2001, almost inevitably recalls that horrifically authentic precursor (McSweeney cites *Cloverfield*'s DVD extras, for example, in which crew members spoke of intentionally using a 'wall of dust' as a way of evoking '9/11' [151]). The symbolic relationship between '9/11' and Hollywood disaster narratives were doubly uncanny, for the real events of 11 September 2001 both echoed the narratives and iconography of earlier movies (the construction of the WTC towers seen in *The French Connection* or flaming skyscrapers from *The Towering Inferno* to *Independence Day*) and helped reinforce this hegemonic narrative. Cameron Crowe's decision not to excise the twin towers from *Vanilla Sky*, or Steven Spielberg's to computer-generate them for the final scene of *Munich*, were noted and loaded.

In her 2004 article 'Teaching 9/11 and why I'm not doing it anymore', Louise Spence notes, that, while after the terrorist attacks she 'noticed a similarity between images of Hiroshima after the dropping of the atomic bomb and the wreckage of the World Trade Center', in popular discourse the tragedy came more readily compared not with 'the devastation of a civilian population but with the attacks on our military ships at Pearl Harbor' (2006: 100). Unlike its counterpart, the '9/11' narrative film, Spence implies, narrowed down historical and ideological spectra, and, discussing Michael Bay's *Pearl Harbor*, released the summer of 2001, Cynthia Weber cautions 2001 viewers against 'allowing their desire for their perceived moral clarity of the past to overwrite their concerns about the moral uncertainty of the present' by equating the two attacks (2006: 11). '9/11' was hastily conceived of as what Hayden White might have termed a 'holocaustal' event, one of a group of traumatic events that 'function in the consciousness of certain social groups exactly as infantile traumas', which cannot either 'be simply forgotten and put out of mind' or 'adequately remembered' (White, 1996: 6). The recourse to familiar narrative forms and older 'holocaustal' events speaks to the ambivalence White identifies: of both facing up to and turning away from '9/11' by seeking refuge in a simpler historical past.

Susan Faludi, at the outset of *The Terror Dream: Fear and Fantasy in Post-9/11 America*, raises the issue of conceptualising '9/11' as a 'holocaustal' event that 'changed everything', but which culture found difficult to 'remember':

'Everything has changed' was our insta-bite mantra, recited in lieu of insight . . . Our media chattered on about 'the death of irony' and 'the death of postmodernism', without ever getting close to the birth of comprehension.

(Faludi, 2007: 2)

'Comprehension', Faludi maintains, came very late, leaving the nation 'still sleep-walking' five years after the events. 'Virtually no film television drama, play, or novel on "9/11" had begun to plumb what the trauma meant for our national psyche', she continues, because 'slavishly literal reenactments of the physical attack . . . or unrep-resentative tales of triumphal rescue at ground zero seemed all the national imagina-tion could handle' (2). Faludi is here fingering two films in particular: Greengrass's *United 93* and Stone's *World Trade Center*; her criticism of the latter seems justified, but when it comes to *United 93*, she misses the point and the effectiveness (as I will discuss) of Greengrass's brand of 'slavish re-enactment'. There were some immedi-ate responses to the attacks but, as Faludi implies, they simplified the narrative: sequences that featured the World Trade Center, were excised and serial episodes re-drafted so as not to offend or hastily written.

The West Wing, in its third season (the start of which was postponed for a week as a response to the attacks) put out just such a special, 'Isaac and Ishmael', (scripted by *West Wing* creator, Aaron Sorkin), which aired on 3 October 2001 in advance of the intended opening episode. The terrorist attacks on New York, Washington and Pennsylvania are not mentioned directly, although we infer the context from *extra*ordinary factors such as the cast coming out of character to address viewers directly and announce that profits from the episode will go to charities estab-lished to help families of emergency services personnel and victims of '9/11'. In serial terms, 'Isaac and Ishmael' is an aberration: a televisual *event* that exists outside the series' (and television's) linear narrative. As Hayden White suggested about the assimilation of 'holocaustal' events, the episode signals the primacy of '9/11' while choosing (within the diegetic frame) not to remember it directly.

'Isaac and Ishmael' is awkwardly didactic. It presents a contrived lesson in US/ Islamic relations whose plot revolves around a terrorist alert at the White House, as a worker in Chief of Staff Leo McGarry's office is briefly suspected of being part of an Arab terrorist network. Entrapped White House staff members offer (literally) an *impromptu* history lesson to a group of teenagers on a school trip to The White House. The attacks of 11 September 2001 are not the episode's ostensible subject, yet they cast a bleak shadow over this trundle through political history as the chil-dren ask naïve but universally pertinent questions such as, 'So, why is everybody trying to kill us?'. The episode both conforms to the swiftly forming official '9/11' narrative that cast the US as victim and counters some of the accompanying hate-mongering; Josh reminds the schoolchildren, for example, not to assume that all Arabs hate the US while First Lady Abigail Bartlet tells the eponymous Old Testa-ment story of Abraham's sons 'Isaac and Ishmael', one the ancestor of the Jews, the other the founder of the Arabs. This episode of *The West Wing* simplifies issues and its message is both forced and false (the children are reassured, for instance, that ter-rorism has a '100% failure rate'). The episode's self-conscious balance is concluded by Josh as he assures the schoolchildren that pluralism is the key to destroying 'them', the amorphous enemy that is not 'us': 'keep accepting more than one idea' he tells them, 'it makes them absolutely crazy'. This atypically wooden episode with, at its heart, a condensed parable of 'them' vs. 'us', neatly demonstrates the extent to which, in the immediate aftermath of '9/11', basic and simplistic narrative construction were adopted as the means of containing the perceived imaginative as well as ideological threats posed by the attacks. The series' subtler and more nuanced response to topical global politics only came much later, in the form of Season 3's final episode 'Posse Comitatus', in which the series' own 'war on terror' plotline concludes with President Bartlet ordering the assassination of terrorist leader Abdul Shareef.[3]

It was arguably too early for Sorkin to construct a narrative out of the terror attacks, for '9/11' had not yet, over the latter months of 2001, become 'history'. Sontag was heavily criticised for her contribution to the *New Yorker*'s 'Talk of the Town: Tuesday, and After' in which, on 24 September 2001, the magazine invited selected staff writers and contributors to 'reflect on the tragedy and its consequences' (2001). Sontag, a New Yorker, effectively produced a challenging response to *The West Wing*'s tongue-tied liberalism as she critiqued the 'disconnect between last Tuesday's monstrous dose of reality and the self-righteous drivel and outright deceptions being peddled by public figures and TV commentators' (Sontag, 2001). Sontag railed against the infantilization of the public, as no acknowledgement was forthcoming that the attacks were 'a consequence of specific American alliances and actions' such as the 'ongoing American bombing of Iraq' (2001). The public, she surmised, was not 'being asked to bear much of the burden of reality'; its grief was being managed and politics was being 'replaced by psychotherapy'. For one vital episode of *The West Wing* 'grief management' came in the form of a therapeutically elementary 'everything is OK' narrative that effectively replaced what Sontag identified as 'historical (and self-) awareness' (2001).

The boldness of Sontag's call to her fellow citizens possesses the clear-sightedness of hindsight (as when she warns: 'Let's by all means grieve together. But let's not be stupid together' [2001]) because even so close to the events she *is* looking back and refusing to see '9/11' exclusively as the start of a narrative not embedded in history. Writing three years after Sontag, Judith Butler, in *Precarious Life*, revisits this issue of how '9/11', as an affective and affecting experience, obscured historical and global awareness. Butler is interested firstly in how the story of '9/11' was being told, and from whose perspective. 'We have to shore up the first-person point of view', she contends, 'and preclude from the telling accounts that might involve the decentering of the narrative "I" within the international political domain' (2004: 6–7). The narrative arc of '9/11', Butler suggests, centres on the personalised experience – one that had lost the 'ability to narrate ourselves not from the first person alone' (8). Underlying the personal, selective and limited ways in which Americans narrativised '9/11' was, she detects fear, for a fear of 'understanding a point of view belies a deeper fear that we shall be taken up by it, find it contagious, become infected in a morally perilous way by the thinking of the presumed enemy' (8). Many books and films bear this out as a way of telling the story of '9/11', concomitantly limiting its intellectual, ideological and symbolic connotations. The priority given to first person testimony is exemplified by the Library of Congress's 'September 11, 2001

Documentary Project' in which are captured 'the reactions, eyewitness accounts, and diverse opinions of Americans and others in the months that followed the terrorist attacks'. The collection – comprising audio files (of interviews and other things), poems, pictures, banners, photographs and other artefacts – sets out to

> capture the voices of a diverse ethnic, socioeconomic, and political cross-section of America during trying times and serves as a historical and cultural resource for future generations.[4]

That is, to speak for and to the current trauma and to the more formed histories of the future.

Conversely, the narratives that emerged from inside Butler's framework of fear were also in denial about '9/11''s relationship to history, as the first-person narration runs the danger of de-historicising the traumatic effects of the attacks. One fundamental way in which the events of 11 September 2001 were narrativised, Butler outlines, was to exist outside history:

> There is no relevant prehistory to the events of September 11, since to begin to tell the story in a different way, to ask how things came to this, is already to complicate the question of agency which, no doubt, leads to the fear of moral equivocation. In order to condemn these acts as inexcusable, absolutely wrong, in order to sustain the affective structure in which we are, on the one hand, victimized and, on the other, engaged in a righteous cause of rooting out terror, we have to begin the story with the experience of violence we suffered.
>
> *(2004: 6)*

Butler here characterises with consummate clarity the dilemmas facing filmmakers and others who want to examine '9/11' and its repercussions, but not in a manner proscribed by the official '9/11' narrative. To choose not to abide by the 'them and us' binary of that narrative is, as Butler states, to face the 'fear of moral equivocation', potentially to be deemed unpatriotic, to knowingly construct subversive or radical alternative accounts. The fear of which Butler speaks is, fundamentally, the fear of the Other: not just Islamic fundamentalism, but anything that challenges US ideological and cultural hegemony, hence the dominance, where the telling of the story of '9/11' is concerned, of the conventional 'well-made' film, which elides and suppresses differences of ideology and dialectical interpretation, a dominance perpetuated by critics continuing to be overwhelmingly drawn to the direct Hollywood treatments of '9/11'. The 'not-9/11' story Butler ushers us towards is less commonly told.

'Not-9/11' films do not ignore the events' 'relevant prehistory', nor do they begin with 'the experience of violence we suffered'; they do not exclusively tell the story from the first person US-perspective but rather open it up to other viewpoints – the universality of experience as well as the feared and loathed Islamist

'Other' with whom, for example, Paul Greengrass defiantly opens *United 93*. For Butler, as for Sontag, the United States, through its reluctance to engage with other perspectives, 'was missing an opportunity to redefine itself as part of a global community' (Butler, 2004: xi). So, Butler asks: 'Can we find another meaning, and another possibility, for the decentering of the first-person narrative within the global framework? (7). Although she does not mean that 'the story that begins with September 11 should not be told' (7), Butler makes a case for not simplifying it to '9/11', the singular, reductively de-historicised and iconic moment, but rather to see it as part of a historical continuum, as a chain of events with global reach and implications. '9/11' need not inevitably be a break with history, the definitive start or end of a narrative journey. Whereas the convention of the '9/11' text is for the narrative to either actually or intellectually *end* with the attacks, the 'not–9/11' film presupposes that, for all its significance as a moment of traumatic rupture, '9/11' did not bring narrative to a halt or define everything that came after. 'Not–9/11' films do not deny the 'holocaustal' nature of attacks but instead take as their starting premise the idea that the same events, while points of fracture and destabilisation, did not bring finality and closure and extended the opportunity to explore the events' multiple ambiguities. Central to 'approximation' is the idea of the inherent instabilities of history and memory, and also the *articulation* of this, in films and pro- grammes, as fragmentariness and dislocation.

'Not–9/11' texts are founded on the dialectical tension generated by being about events that rapidly became allegorically as well as historically dominant, even when not directly recalled. There is also a temporal claim that could be made here, not exclusively to do with the terrorist acts of September 2001: that we at the start of the 21st century were already becoming far more accepting of media culture that blurred the boundaries between fact and fiction, reality and construc- tion, even before events occurred that re-defined reality and defied representation. Having, for example, sent out a call for contributions to a special issue of *Studies in Documentary Film* about '9/11', Christian Christiansen explains how he received critical emails from scholars and filmmakers, including one that queried another endeavour that placed 'the United States (yet again) at the centre of our under- standing of popular culture and media in general' and consequently ignored

> the myriad other social, economic and technological factors that have impacted the development and evolution of documentary film in recent years (such as the democratic possibilities provided by low-cost, high-quality digital cameras).
>
> *(Christiansen, 2009: 197)*

The notion that '9/11' 'changed everything' is maybe just another assumption; that inversely, the events of 11 September 2001 coincided with the era of 'constructed reality', 'approximation' and the new democratisation of media rather than trigger- ing it. In keeping with this, '9/11' thereby appears as both ascendant and incidental across such media examples as Ken Loach's section of *11'09"01, September 11, United 93, Mad Men* or *Man on Wire*, as discussed below.

As Ken Loach explores in *11'09"01, September 11*, there have been other, overshadowed, '9/11's, notably the Chilean coup of 11 September 1973 and the overthrow by US-backed military forces under General Augusto Pinochet of the democratically elected government of President Salvador Allende. As Noam Chomsky forcefully reminds us in *9–11: Was There An Alternative?*, there were historical antecedents to '9/11'. The 2001 attacks, Chomsky contends, could 'have been a lot worse' had they, for example,

> gone as far as bombing the White House, killing the president, imposing a brutal military dictatorship that killed thousands and tortured tens of thousands while establishing an international terror center that helped impose similar torture-and-terror states elsewhere and carried out an international assassination campaign; and as an extra fillip, brought in a team of economists – call them 'the Kandahar boys' – who quickly drove the economy into one of the worst depressions in its history.
>
> *(2011: 22–23)*

Chomsky views the terrorist acts holistically and historically, going beyond framing them as horrific personal tragedies, and the 'lot worse' did happen in Chile after, during the 'first 9/11' of 1973, when 'the US succeeded in its intensive efforts to overthrow the democratic government of Salvador Allende' (23).

The portmanteau movie *11'09"01, September 11* (in which 11 directors each creates a segment lasting eleven minutes, nine seconds and one frame around the events of that day) makes explicit use of the events of 11 September 2001 as the motivation for reflecting on past and other histories. The reaffirmation, even re-categorisation, of '9/11' as a global, not exclusively US-centred narrative emerges clearly from such a universal and collective endeavour, albeit one which, through depicting, in each mini title sequence, New York City as a pulsing heart linked by a line to various countries across an atlas, acknowledges the city as its epicentre. As the film's producer, Alain Brigand, attests: 'September 11 was an American tragedy, but also a universal catastrophe . . . an American drama, but also a drama that affected humanity' (quoted in Dixon, 2004: 5–7), an ideological backdrop that immediately confirms the existence of the multiple perspectives found in *11'09"01* and the events' status as global experiences on a historical continuum. *11'09"01* also succeeds in de-Westernising '9/11': Samira Makhmalbaf's mini film features an Iranian schoolteacher standing under an incinerator tower to help her pupils understand and empathise with those trapped under the World Trade Center rubble; Egyptian director Youssef Chahine's contribution self-reflexively centres on Chahine himself playing a director shooting a sequence in New York City on 11 September 2001; Amos Gitaï's Israeli segment focuses on a tenacious journalist who, thwarted in her attempts to film the chaos after an explosion on 11 September 2001 in Tel Aviv, resorts instead to itemising previous global events that share this same date. The US point of view is represented by the penultimate segment directed by Sean Penn. The most celebrated of the interlocking tales proved to be Loach's – the sixth film in the sequence – which won the 2002 Fipresci Critics' Prize for Best Short Film at the Venice Film Festival. Loach formally question '9/11''s uniqueness by bringing the 2001 events into dialectical dialogue with the forgotten 9/11 of 1973.

Loach's contribution opens with Pablo, a Chilean, sitting at the table of a modern, local authority London flat writing and narrating a letter to the 'mothers, fathers and loved ones of those who died on September 11th in New York'. 'I am a Chilean', he writes, so 'we might have something in common'. Immediately, 2001's '9/11' is displaced as the image switches from this present-day drama to grainy, hand-held, monochrome archival footage of the violence that ensued on the day of Chile's military coup on the same date in 1973. In this way opens a classic Loachian drama in which fiction is deployed as an instructive tool, a means of both teaching the 21st century audience about Chile's 9/11 and de-centring – or at the very least complicating – US hegemony. In Loach's mini-film the US relinquishes symbolic ownership of '9/11', it is also compelled to give up its exclusive claim to the personal affect and experience of the date's violence. Although Loach refrains from making explicit reference to this, Pablo is played by Chilean singer, Vladimir Vega, who had fled to Britain in the late 1970s after years in jail following the Pinochet coup, and who remained in England until his death in 2013.[5] The implication of the US in the Chilean coup is underlined as Loach's episode doubles as a letter of condolence and a stark history lesson, crafted as an eloquent but uncompromising reminder that it had been Richard Nixon's US administration that had refused to let Chile, as Pablo (citing Nixon's Secretary of State, Henry Kissinger) says, 'go communist'. Chile and the US, Loach argues, were conjoined from the moment Nixon declared his intention to make the Chilean economy 'scream'. This historical battle between the conflicting ideologies of Allende's Chile and the US resonates uncomfortably, recalling Sontag's courageous acknowledgement, only days after 2001's '9/11', that the al-Qaeda attacks (symbols of a later ideological conflict) were in part 'a consequence of specific American alliances and actions' (2001).

Located within a portmanteau film that, by its very nature, widens the commonly narrow frame of reference for '9/11', Loach's part mobilises overtly the notion, by cross-referencing New York City and Santiago, that historical hindsight informs our understanding of current atrocity. Pablo asks, the film having shown Chile's popular defence of Allende in the face of US aggression, 'In municipal elections we actually increased our support, so what did the US do?' A hard edit follows, to 2001 colour footage of a steely-faced President George W. Bush speaking to Congress about how 'on September 11th enemies of freedom committed an act of war against our country, and night fell on a different world, a world where freedom itself is under attack'. In this archetypal moment of intellectual montage, Loach cuts not, as might be anticipated, to the familiar footage of planes crashing into the twin towers, but instead to black and white archive of another aircraft (one of the Chilean air force's Hawker Hunters) dissecting the skies of Santiago on 11 September 1973, interlaced with the frequently recycled juddering images of their bombardment of La Moneda, the official seat of the President of the Chilean Republic. Pablo's (now ironic) repetition of Bush's words presages a description of what transpired that 1973 morning, his calm voice ultimately giving way to archive of President Allende's, equally calm delivery of his iconic final address to the people of Chile. The scratchy recording provides an emotive epitaph to one '9/11' and a complex reminder, to use Sontag's words, of 'the disconnect' between the other '9/11' and 'how it might be understood' (2001):

> They have the power. They can enslave us. But social progress cannot be halted, not by crimes and not by force. History is ours. It is made by the people. Long live Chile! Long live the people! Long live the workers!

That both '9/11's occurred on a Tuesday is another poignant parallel, and in yet another example of the instabilities of history and the value of hindsight, the controversy over whether or not Allende committed suicide or was shot by Pinochet's soldiers (as propounded by, for instance, Fidel Castro as well as by Loach whose protagonist repeats 'he was murdered; he *was* murdered') has since been settled by the 2011 exhumation and autopsy which confirmed that Allende shot himself with two shots from an automatic assault rifle.[6] Loach's focused film concludes with Pablo/Vega at his table once more writing his letter to New Yorkers and vowing to remember them as he hopes they, in return, 'will remember us'. He signs off, emits a sigh and the screen cuts to black. 'The first 9/11', as Chomsky writes, 'did not change the world. It was "nothing of great consequence", as Henry Kissinger assured his boss a few days later' (2011: 24).

Reflecting, in 2004, on the teaching of film studies after '9/11', B. Ruby Rich remembers how her 'first impulse, faced with writing and teaching the events of '9/11' in a cinematic context' was to go back to a previous traumatic event and to seek out Theodor Adorno's dictum 'To write poetry after Auschwitz is barbaric' (Rich, B., 2004: 109).[7] Rich also found, in 2004, that '9/11' 'left me less interested in Baudrillard than I would ever have imagined' (113). Representation no longer started from the principle, as Baudrillard had argued in the 1980s, 'that the sign and the real are equivalent' (170); rather, for Rich, '9/11' reinforced the schism between representation and reality, although, as Brian Urquart argues about Gerhard Richter's canvas, *September*, events of '9/11' were still performative and 'designed to be witnessed' (quoted in Storr, 2010: 6). Baudrillard's intellectual excitement in *The Spirit of Terrorism* at finding himself in possession of 'the absolute event, the "mother" of all events' (2002: 4) that affirms his notion of the simulacra makes for seriously uncomfortable reading:

> The fact that we have dreamt of this event, that everyone without exception has dreamt of it – because no one can avoid dreaming of the destruction of any power that has become hegemonic to this degree – is unacceptable to the Western moral conscience. . . . At a pinch, we can say that they *did* it, but

we *wished for* it. If this is not taken into account, the event loses any symbolic dimension. It becomes a pure accident, a purely arbitrary act.

(Baudrillard 2002: 5)

Baudrillard's attachment is to symbolism, not reality. Having concluded that 'in a very real sense, the events of 9/11. . . have rendered inadequate the theoretical approaches and analytic habits on which film studies as a discipline has relied for the past several decades' (Rich, B., 2004: 109), Rich chooses a different route when she identifies some of the films she chose to teach, from the 'totemic film' *The Manchurian Candidate* (John Frankenheimer, 1962) with its 'eerie' premonitions of the Kennedy assassination, to (as mentioned earlier) *The Battle of Algiers* and Lizzie Borden's *Born in Flames* (1983) in which 'a tiny revolutionary cell of lesbian feminists blows up the top of the World Trade Center to destroy its lie-disseminating television transmitter after the government has assassinated the group's leader' (112). One way in which we might start to comprehend '9/11', Rich implies, is via 'not-9/11' texts – that is, films that unwittingly or indirectly help to make sense of the events of 2001, as well as those later examples overshadowed by them. 'Not-9/11' films and other screen texts are both inhabited by and go beyond the specifics of '9/11'; they are not afraid to 'tell the story in a different way' or accept that no event, however history-changing, exists in a historical vacuum. Instead, events haunt and are haunted by each other and our perceptions of reality alter when those events become juxtaposed with others – both fictional and actual.

Haunting is a crucial element of how the events of '9/11' have been assimilated into collective memories and culture, and a sense of hauntedness, as opposed to direct address, permeates 'not-9/11' texts. As Žižek argues, a 'real' that is so 'traumatic' or 'excessive' in character compels us 'to experience it as a nightmarish apparition' as opposed to 'the thing itself' (2002: 19). '9/11', like previous traumas, will hang over culture by virtue of its atrociousness, to assimilate Susan Sontag's command to 'let the atrocious images haunt us' (Sontag 2003: 102). To permit ourselves, our imagination, to be haunted is to admit loss; as Butler, in response to Sontag's powerful imperative reminds us:

> there are conditions in which we can refuse to be haunted, or where haunting cannot reach us. If we are not haunted, there is no loss, there has been no life that was lost.

(2010: 97)

Butler is here specifically referring – as was Sontag – to the still photographic image, which, Sontag had suggested, is both aesthetic and objective; it 'gives mixed signals. Stop this, it urges. But it also exclaims, What a spectacle!' (2003: 68). In addition, Butler is arguing for a multi-layered and complex understanding of the 'haunting' photographic image: that the arrested 'presentness' of a photograph both perpetually re-evokes the loss it captured while at the same time preserves its subject's 'presentness'; that it is specifically tied to the subject it depicts while nevertheless being able to outlive, transcend and go beyond it. Concluding that the inherent 'pathos' of the 'haunting' photographic image 'is at once affective and interpretative' (98), Butler opens up the possibility that it is thereby capable of being specific as an agent of grieving at the same time as being able to function as a more uncanny abstraction. The photograph is not the event, although the event is persistently recalled by contemplation of it.

One photograph that locked the story of '9/11' in our minds (cf. Sontag 2003: 77), was Richard Drew's 'The Falling Man', taken at 9:41 A.M. on 11 September 2001 and showing a male figure either falling or jumping from the North Tower. The 'falling man' is facing straight down, in seemingly perfect parallel and synchrony with the vertical axes of the exterior of the World Trade Center. One of a series of photographs, others of which showed the same figure tumbling and flailing through the air, this 'perfect' image was, inevitably, the one selected by newspapers as a talismanic image for the day's tragedy, although newspapers soon withdrew it on account of it being too upsetting. One reason for the image becoming instantly compelling must have been, simply, that it was beautiful, synchronous, *too* perfect: the sublime mingled with raw tragedy. Iconic photographs, Rob Kroes posits, 'do the work of memory for us' (2011: 2). As an image of a catastrophe the photograph makes its viewer uneasy; it appears so choreographed, the figure so calm and serene, so poised; its tremendous stillness and grace make it even harder to look at than, for example, the skeletal remains of buildings that were photographed and filmed endlessly after the towers' collapse. The photograph's perfection always sat in violent and disquieting contradistinction to what it represented literally, specifically. Drew's falling man stood for the approximately 200 people who jumped from the burning towers – the 'disappeared' of 9/11/2001, whose actions were immediately excised from the day's news bulletins; as Meek comments, 'the exclusion of images of falling bodies from media coverage of 9/11 resulted in a failure by the American public to confront this horrific aspect of the events' (Meek, 2010: 181). In the 2006 documentary, *9/11: The Falling Man*, director Henry Singer attempts to determine the falling man's identity (which he does so erroneously) as well as discuss the photograph's cultural importance, echoing Meek when he asserts in his voiceover: 'No one wanted to confront the existence of the jumpers . . . America had recoiled from the falling man'. The 'fearful symmetry' of Drew's iconic image has been evoked several times in books such as *Extremely Loud and Incredibly Close* and DeLillo's *Falling Man*.

Another fictional falling man arguably haunted by Drew's photograph, is the silhouetted figure who tumbles past skyscrapers and stylised advertising hoardings in the title sequence of the television drama series *Mad Men*. These animated titles start with the male figure on the periphery of a stylish retro office. After a close-up of the figure's lower legs walking (accompanied by the credit for Jon Hamm, who plays Don Draper, hence the assumption that the series' troubled protagonist is also *Mad Men*'s 'falling man'), the monochrome man puts down his suitcase, as sketched artwork for late 1950s/early 1960s ad campaigns start to slide down the blank office wall. The office melts away and there is another edit to the black male figure as he starts his tumble down the vertiginous sides of anonymised high-rise blocks adorned with stylised, faded images of vintage advertisements. The man continues to plummet, hurtling towards and past us. However, instead of hitting the ground (which is allegedly how, in an early incarnation, the sequence was to conclude) the titles end with this suave but desperately out of control figure metamorphosing just in time into a calm seated man, one hand hanging nonchalantly over the edge of a sofa arm, white cigarette between his fingers, panic suppressed and tragedy averted.

The suited tumbling figure at the start of *Mad Men* will always inevitably be, to some, an elliptical 'not-9/11' (in)version of Drew's almost monochromic 'falling man'. Stripped of all information, narrative and words bar the start date 'March 25', the poster announcing the imminent arrival of Season 5 (as mentioned at the outset of this chapter) courted controversy 'for looking like [the] tragic 9/11 photograph' (Zutter, 2012). Another respondent on the same online page saw alternative contexts: both 'the pain of 9/11', but also 'Black Monday or Tuesday . . . the October 1929 days when the stock market took a massive dive' (Turpin, 2012). One of the original title sequence's creators, Mark Gardner, admits that some 'saw references to 9/11 and all that, and in the beginning, AMC[8] were totally against the idea'. They 'got away with it', Gardner concluded, because of the title's ambiguous status: part dream; part reality. (Art of the Title, 2007).

'They got away with it' because the 'decisive moment' of '9/11' was often assumed to permeate everything even loosely related to it, to be the start or the conclusion to a narrative arc, the primal trauma of the collective twenty-first century US imagination. Events that preceded it were conceived to have been merely a dress rehearsal.[9] *Mad Men*'s title sequence is not about '9/11', but then neither is it not-not about it, an ambivalence it shares with a very different 'not-9/11' text, Paul Greengrass's *United 93*. On the surface it might seem perverse to categorise Greengrass's frantic, traumatising, shot-in-almost real time, shaky cam film about the final hour of the fourth hijacked plane, United Airlines Flight 93 (from Newark, New Jersey) as 'not-9/11', and yet (unlike the more overtly patriotic television films about the same event),[10] it explicitly returns to and inhabits that limbo time of the dress rehearsal, the pre-state just prior to the '9/11' narrative starting to take shape, while at the same time remaining mindful (through its months of research, the close links forged with the victims' families, the provision of detailed dossiers for the actors about the characters they were playing) to honour the consequent official narrative (Greengrass, 2006: 94). Greengrass included in the cast non-actors enacting their own or similar roles from the day including, most notably, Ben Sliney, who reprises his role as the Air Traffic Command Center's national operations manager and who, on his first day in the job, 'gave the unprecedented order, after the Pentagon was hit, to ground all the nation's air traffic' (Prince, 2009: 108).[11] The film's extreme authenticity extends to the use of locations and sets such as the decommissioned Boeing 757 reassembled for principal filming at Pinewood Studios, whose cabins, to increase authenticity during filming, remained segregated, with the four terrorists being kept apart from the 40 other passengers and crew.

Although, by the time he made *United 93*, the events were in the past and the '9/11' narrative formed, Greengrass's dramatic evocation of Flight United 93 is a complex act of disavowal that enacts events as if that narrative was still unfolding. In choosing to re-enact Flight 93, on which 'a group of citizen soldiers ... rose up, like their forefathers to defy tyranny' (*Newsweek* quoted in Faludi, 2007: 59), Greengrass also chose to 'think the unthinkable' (Bradshaw, 2011), which was to recreate '9/11' from inside the public archive. The story of the fourth plane occupies a liminal space and time and, as Greengrass observes, its crew and passengers became 'the first people to inhabit the post-9/11 world' (Greengrass, 2006: 89). 'For the rest of us', he adds:

> whether we were in civilian air traffic control, Presidential bunkers, or just ordinary folks like us watching on TV, we knew something terrible was happening, but we didn't really know what. . . . But for those people on the airplane they knew exactly what it was.
>
> *(89)*

United 93 evokes the preconsciousness of a 'third term': a suspended moment before the living, unfolding reality of 11 September 2001 became the symbolic entity '9/11'. Greengrass's re-enactment of the fourth plane's flight offers us the means to forget the '9/11' narrative just as we are compelled to relive it and, like Gerhard Richter's, 'September', suspends but does not ultimately embody '9/11', for this would be to foreclose that narrative.

The film largely maintains its disavowal of the symbolic narrative of '9/11', but only once the anomalously and resonantly conventional opening sequence has been completed. The murmur of Muslim prayer ('what has come to be known as the "sound of terror"', as Burgoyne identifies [2010: 196]), can be heard over a gliding, nocturnal aerial shot looking directly down at a busy New York City street. Surreal and dreamy in its smoothness, this image then gives way to one that is forward-facing, as if from the point of view of a cockpit, as the aircraft skims and skirts around the peaks of skyscrapers twinkling in the subdued dawn skies. This introductory sequence would be blandly familiar if it were not for its elliptical referencing to the events and iconography of '9/11' and its emblematic sideways glance at the Hollywood movie tropes that echo and find themselves echoed in those attacks. The perspective of this first sequence is ambiguous; at first, it feels as if it adopts the anonymous perspective of the generic disaster film, but the ensuing edit to the hijackers in their cramped hotel rooms preparing themselves for their imminent acts of terror instead posits that this is their internalised fantasy of the crimes they are about to commit, that the terrorists, as Altman had suggested, had 'copied the movies' that 'taught them how to do it' (Hoberman, 2001). The events' prehistory is discretely distilled into and informs this fictive moment.

The crucial juncture at which hindsight and official '9/11' narrative both intrude and are formally acknowledged comes a little less than mid-way through the film when

Greengrass inserts an iconic piece of archive footage of the second plane hitting the South Tower of the World Trade Center. Full-screen television news archive of both New York City terrorist strikes is used in *United 93*. The first (when news filters through to the air traffic control rooms that CNN is reporting the attack) is more conventional in that the visuals cut from characters watching a diegetic screen to the image becoming full-screen. Instead, the second piece of news archive is integrated into action as a substitute for reality, not television. Knowing and having just seen that a plane has struck the World Trade Center, Newark air traffic controllers (among them controllers who had been on duty on the day) are informed that there is a second aircraft 'rapidly descending' towards the city. They switch from observing its trajectory on their digital monitors to looking directly out from the tower's window towards Lower Manhattan (as they had done when news filtered through of the first attack). One of them spies and points to a plane as it hurtles, as if in a movie, through the bleached skies. There ensues a hard edit to a hugely magnified, pixelated piece of television archive showing that second plane strike.

Familiar, terrifying, ugly, incontrovertibly indexical, this archival fragment functions, as it had done on television screens across the globe, as a point of coalescence as well as trauma for different audiences and communities, as all operators across the film's various air traffic control suites (US Federal Aviation Administration FAA]; North Eastern Defense Sector [NEADS]) react in unison to this collective moment with gasps of disbelief and horror. This, Martin Amis had written in *The Second Plane*, was 'the defining moment', the moment when the '9/11' began to be understood and formed:

> Until then, America thought she was witnessing nothing more serious than the worst aviation disaster in history; now she had a sense of the fantastic vehemence ranged against her.

> *(Amis, 2008: 3)*

FIGURE 2.1 CNN footage of the second plane, used in *United 93* (Paul Greengrass, 2006)

The archive fragment is only a few seconds long, but its inclusion as live action as opposed to archive breaks with convention and holds a dual focus: as representative of the reality of '9/11' and as a reminder that the remainder of *United 93* is a fictionalisation.

To recall Jameson's contentious view that it remains film, not television, that holds and consolidates our memories of 'big news events' (Holdsworth, 2010: 130), it is at a juncture such as this that we witness the clash between the two 'memory media'. Here, cinema memorialises the iconic televisual images that became central to the memory of what '9/11' felt like to watch on television. Television, Jameson posits, equips us with information, but cinema shapes information into narrative; the use of enlarged, imperfect televisual archival images here serves as an indication that the transformation from 'information' to 'narrative' is still incomplete; the 'not-9/11' narrative is still feeling the aftershocks of the disruption of 'the everydayness of television itself' (Spigel, 2004: 237), which '9/11' brought about.

Greengrass's fragment of imperfect, expanded, full-frame archive remains a point of schism, a definitive and defiantly nonfictional (neither simulation nor re-enactment) moment that throws into sharp relief the realistic 'look-alike-ness' of the rest of *United 93*, which conforms to the *verité* style with which Greengrass's name has become synonymous and which he has adopted throughout his career for both drama documentaries, from *Bloody Sunday* (2001) to *22 July* (2018) as well as for pure fictions, such as *The Bourne Supremacy* and *The Bourne Ultimatum* (2004, 2007). The conventional assumption is that this style 'makes the film readily readable as authentic' and to look like 'a documentary more than a fiction film' (Westwell, 2014: 83), although that it is also intricately and methodically crafted betrays its fictional status; as Prince details, for instance, Greengrass used 'multiple cameras, with staggered start and reload times', which permitted him to lengthen takes and film 'in real time for extended intervals' (Prince, 2009: 108).

The agitated, wobbly-cam style approximates the inherent fragmentariness of the day's events; it inverts expectation by making the familiar public-facing, archive- and news-focused narrative uncannily *unfamiliar*, while paradoxically constructing, with its documentary-simulating look (Director of Photography, Barry Ackroyd, was first a documentary cinematographer), its editing of verbatim testimonies and its use of non-actors, a film that proclaims its very *realistic fictiveness*. Greengrass's loose, surveillance style is now so ubiquitous that its documentary roots – and inferences – have largely been superseded and replaced with an alternative ultra-reality. Greengrass constructs a 'third term' reality, the bastard offspring of both documentary and action movies, and hopes that, 'when you think of my films . . . you think of an extreme sort of real unfolding', with events 'unfolding as if just captured (Eisenberg, 2010). The director has talked of his influences being 1960s' observational documentary and (once again) Pontecorvo's *The Battle of Algiers*, when an immediate and urgent visual style (made possible by newly available lightweight cameras and sound recorders) came to signal cinema's evidentiary potential, and an alluringly idealistic belief that the new equipment 'would allow for reality to be documented in an unmediated fashion' (Winston, 2008: 149). The observational filming of Robert Drew or Richard Leacock made it possible, the filmmakers contended, to blend into reality and catch it unawares. Leacock, for example, believed that John Kennedy 'hadn't the foggiest notion I was shooting' (Shivas, 1963: 37) during the filming of *Primary* (1960), so absorbed was he in what he was doing. However naïve this sounds, the furtive, eavesdropping photographic mode became cinematic shorthand for the belief that crises transcended the filming process and could be captured without the presence of the crew interfering with or altering the course of events, a belief Greengrass's agitated camera mimics.

David Bordwell accuses Greengrass of superficiality and vacuity, claiming that his handheld style is deployed to mask '*three mistakes: bad acting, bad set design, and bad directing*' (Bordwell, 2007); furthermore, he adds that it is 'pretty incoherent and nowhere near as engaging as most critics claim' (2007). This, however, is to downplay Greengrass's reflective, knowing invocation of observational documentary's ability to 'approximate quite closely the flexibility of the human senses' (Peter Graham quoted in Winston, 2008: 150). Greengrass's conscious appropriation and refinement of observational documentary techniques exposes the inherent paradox of the responsive observational camera (namely, that its supposed *objectivity* is rooted in its ability to simulate the *subjective* gaze of the human eye) while embodying postmodernist doubts over whether or not the photographic and cinematic image can ever authentically capture reality. *United 93*'s 'observational camera' is quite different to Leacock's; for one thing (as intimated by Prince) it generates multiple, frequently conflicting, points of view rather than authenticating just the one. Greengrass's mimicry of the direct cinema style thereby merely *affects* the idea that the camera is reacting to a crisis.

Notions of authenticity, science journalist John Whitfield surmises, 'depend as much on emotional and psychological plausibility as they do physical accuracy' (Whitfield, 2006: 922). The 'conventions of realism' change, British neuroscientist, Chris Frith, adds; whereas 'People once believed newsreels only if they were in black and white', now, 'the mark of authenticity . . . is wobbly handheld footage' (923). Greengrass is not therefore merely replicating reality in a superficial and unthoughtful way as Faludi accuses him of doing, but is instead mobilising the tools his audiences most readily associate, culturally and technologically speaking, with the effective representation of reality which, in turn, enables them to re-inhabit the lost, pre-narrative reality of Flight 93. Illustrative of this is the scene in which news reaches all control rooms that American Airlines Flight 11 has hit the North Tower of the World Trade Center, at which point Barry Ackroyd's *faux*-documentary camera becomes increasingly agitated. Cutting back from the darker Defense Sector control room to the FAA, the first image is an extreme, shaky close-up of Sliney and colleagues, mimicking the bemused perspective of a concerned, invisible interloper into this moment of crisis. Rushed whip pans and lurching focus pulls try frantically to find level and sharpness as the huddle of men discuss having 'lost American 11'. The confusion of shots, the mixture of blurred, over the shoulder close-ups and wider framings – especially the hesitantly wavering close shots of Ben Sliney's face – conveys Sliney's mental computation of what he is hearing.

The studied imitation of the observational documentary camera outwardly suppresses while paradoxically confirming that this is a fiction film; the wobbly-cam style has now become ubiquitous when it comes to conveying fictional emergency: an instrument of tense disavowal.

The dialectical friction created by having suppressed knowledge in order to more emotively and effectively engage with such a complex simulation of an incomplete and traumatic narrative reaches its climax during the final sequence, as Flight United 93 hurtles towards its tragic end. An empathetic perspective has gradually been established aboard United 93 and for the final few minutes the camera adopts an unaligned, quasi-subjective point of view stance from the position of an imaginary representative passenger cowering in their seat, a nightmarish phantom perspective that charts terrorists and passengers racing up the aisle as the latter try to ram their way into the cockpit. For the final couple of minutes, rapid parallel editing alternates between cabin and cockpit as passengers attempt to take back control of the plane. An unruly juddering camera struggles to keep the sweating, grimacing face of principal hijacker Ziad Jarrah's face in frame as he, in turn, battles to pilot the aircraft. The anonymously subjective, anxious camera, whether in the cabin or the cockpit, is no longer tied to any, even putative, fixed vantage point, and as Robert Burgoyne observes, 'becomes increasingly jagged' as the film goes on, 'with the speed and intensity of movement, the fragmentary split-second images, and the whip pans . . . creating a tachycardic rhythm that pummels the audience' (2010: 199). With echoes of Sam Peckinpah's *The Wild Bunch* (1969), one tension-building irony throughout this fragmented sequence is that, despite the rapidity of the parallel editing and the freneticism of the photography, actions (such as Jarrah repeatedly failing to secure his seatbelt) are repeatedly interrupted, their conclusions delayed, in a seemingly perverse reaffirmation of the film's generic status as a fictional action movie. A series of short, wild, almost abstract close-ups are intercut – hands wrestling, alarmed faces, the swaying cockpit, the canted cabin – ever more frenetically, a bewildering diversity of perspectives that culminate, inevitably, in one longer image looking out from the cockpit window as United 93 spirals towards the ground before cutting to black.

United 93's status as fictional action movie sits in contradistinction to its actively close rendition of the true story – of having Ben Sliney rather than Nicolas Cage (who starred in *World Trade Center*) play himself. However, although Sliney on 11 September 2001 and Sliney in *United 93* enact the same events and impart comparable information, they are not equivalents, but rather protagonists in alternative narratives: the '9/11' narrative and its 'not-9/11' counterfoil. The later re-enactment is not only a simulation of an unwitnessed, unrecorded though authentic 'act', it is a performance that exposes the tensions and fissures in how that original '9/11' story has subsequently been scrutinized or rendered as narrative. While it might seem perverse to argue that a visceral, forensic film is not 'about' '9/11', it is important to understand, as with Bigelow's portrayal of the Algiers Motel in *Detroit*, in what ways *United 93* fails to affirm or conform to the official version of events. That narrative is *public*, generated from the outside, mediarised and mediated; conversely, *United 93* re-enters the eye of the storm and knowingly denies itself (and its viewers) perspectival acuity. Paul Greengrass, when asked by journalist Gavin Smith if *United 93* is a re-enactment, responds: 'it's a catharsis, it's a reliving, it's a reconstruction. It's a hypothesis' (Smith, 2006: 26). The kind of active simulation Greengrass creates does not quite forfeit the 'indexical bond to the original event' that, according to Bill Nichols, taints re-enactment (Nichols, 2008: 74); *United 93* is, therefore, more a reliving than a haunting. In the case of Ben Sliney, he is not so much Nichols' absent 'specter' that *haunts* the text as a shadow *reliving* it. Re-enactment – resonant as it is with detachment and intellectual understanding – would presuppose an engagement with how history has framed and narrativized '9/11', whereas simulation of the kind seen in *United 93* does not.

United 93's status as a 'not-9/11' film is tied to its prioritisation of proximity and simulation of action over the construction of a framing narrative that attempts to make sense of or contextualise the events' overwhelming, emotional presentness. As Judith Butler had argued, the question of whether or not the US, in the aftermath of '9/11', was ever able to narrate itself 'not from the first person alone' (2004: 8) was fundamental. To prove able to narrate the '9/11' story from 'say, the position of the third, or to receive an account delivered in the second, can actually work to expand our understanding of the forms that global power has taken' (8). *United 93* enacts a collision of these multiple points of view, a metonym for which becomes the paradoxically unaffiliated point of view of the handheld camera; whether it is hovering over Sliney's shoulder or cowering from the terrorists in an unoccupied passenger seat, the camera's perspective is both subjective (in 'the first person') and anonymised, universal (in the second or third). The obdurate myopia of simulation, which re-enters both the site specificity of where events happened (the Newark control tower, the air traffic control centres, Flight 93) and the state of agitated presence which that repositioning engenders, represses or, at the very least, disavows, the desire to conceptualise or *make sense of* '9/11'.

Elizabeth Cowie's contention, in relation to Hollywood melodrama, that 'the opposition real/not real is wholly inappropriate to a consideration of fantasy' (1992: 149) proved, as mentioned in the Introduction, an unlikely but liberating springboard for thinking about 'approximation'. Hypothetical re-enactment, as found in *United 93*, is a fragmented, kaleidoscopic fantasy based on real historical events. The phantasmatic potency of hypothetical re-enactment is especially pronounced, for *hypothesis* bundles together what *really happened* with the fantasy of what *could have happened*. As confirmed by comparisons with the retrieved black box, Greengrass has not constructed a conventionally hypothetical drama-documentary, such as the rash of post-millennium 'hypothetical docudrama(s)' on UK television such as *Smallpox 2002* (2002), *The Day Britain Stopped* (2003) and *Death of a President* (2006) which, in their inclusion of *faux* documentary interviews and archive, owed much to Peter Watkins' *The War Game* (1965) (Stewart and Butt, 2011: 75). Instead, *United 93*'s cabin sequences, through their use of fictional tropes and constructs, embody and honour the personal tragedies of '9/11'.

As Žižek pinpoints, 'the September 11 attacks were the stuff of popular fantasies long before they actually took place' (2002: 17), so we collectively (referencing Lacan) 'traversed the phantasy' not in order to abandon our 'involvement with fanciful caprices', as Richard Boothby explains, but rather 'to be more profoundly claimed by the phantasy than ever' (quoted in Žižek, 2002: 18). Žižek then extends Boothby's analysis when he says: 'a fantasy is simultaneously pacifying, disarming (providing an imaginary scenario which enables us to endure the abyss of the Other's desire) *and* shattering, disturbing, inassimilable into our reality' (2002: 18). One might consequently argue that Greengrass's shard of archive (of the second plane) breaks the illusion of the faux-reality of the near-real-time re-enactment of United Flight 93's last journey and is the definitive moment of *United 93*, as it is the juncture when we 'traverse the fantasy' and, as Boothby suggests, admit the 'limit of everyday reality' (18). While it is common to caution against mistaking fiction for reality, Žižek concludes:

> the lesson of psychoanalysis here is the opposite one: *we should not mistake reality for fiction* – we should be able to discern, in what we experience as fiction, the hard kernel of the Real which we are able to sustain only if we fictionalise it.
>
> *(19)*

That fiction can be experienced as reality even as it signals its epistemological difference to it, lies at the heart of *United 93* as an 'approximation'. Its hypothesis is not that the events of '9/11' are repeatable, but rather that they are not, although this does not prohibit them from being assimilated into our memories as well as fantasies of the past.

The disruptive grey area of fantasy described by Žižek is the one inhabited by James Marsh's documentary *Man on Wire*, at once elegiac and prophetic – certainly unique in its absenting of '9/11' while being *all about* the World Trade Center, in the form of Philip Petit's successful tightrope walk between the not quite completed towers in 1974. As it remains resolutely focused on Petit's escapade on 30 May 1974, so inversely *Man on Wire* is superficially *not about* '9/11', but rather conjures up the equally tenaciously unspoken *fantasy* of '9/11', through centring its narrative on the twin towers. Made in 2008, *Man on Wire*'s relationship to '9/11' is complex and nuanced; critics of the documentary have accused its director of using the story's '9/11' backdrop for commercial gain; Ruth Mackay, for instance, reflects on Marsh's disingenuousness in his 'attempt to cover up the fact that he must have been acutely aware that 9/11 would at least inform, if not guarantee, the success of *Man on Wire*' (Mackay, 2011: 9). This seems grossly unfair, for *Man on Wire*, very effectively, retains a dual focus, being both about Petit's walk while not forgetting or circumventing the later destruction of the World Trade Center. The film's liminal references to '9/11', though knotty and subtle, are not repressive acts of denial; Marsh acknowledges that *Man on Wire* 'has a poignancy for that reason, but not one that needs to be overstated' (Marsh quoted in Mackay, 2011: 9). Likewise, the film's producer, Simon Chinn, says on the DVD commentary:

> I don't think it crossed any of our minds ever that 9/11 would be part of this film, even to the extent that there's the one photo coming up . . . with a

plane in the background. . . . We talked about how to use this . . . this always gets a delayed reaction, people sort of respond to it with a 3 second delay and there's nervous laughter.

The photograph being alluded to here (and discussed briefly in the Introduction) comes 1.18.38 into *Man on Wire* and is a low angle black and white shot of Petit walking between the towers, the blob that is his body and the perpendicular lines of his wire and his balancing pole just about perceptible against the white of the sky. What prompts the 'nervous laughter' and causes the documentary's producers to discuss how to use the image is that, in the top right of the picture, there also happens to be a large passenger jet. As Marsh affirms, that this moment is 'not even paused or remarked upon. . . [is] . . . absolutely right. 9/11's there the whole time, the last thing we should do is mention it'.

There is little need to mention it because a modern audience would most likely feel the *frisson* of this moment acutely. That such a *frisson* is accidental makes it all the more potent as well as poignant as a catalyst to remembering; it would simply be unnecessary to exploit the photograph's residual symbolic complexity. Instead, the innocence of that extraordinary, as yet resonance-free, image from 1974 liberates it from, rather than imprisons it within, history. All representations of factual moments are, as I argue throughout this book, fluid and approximate; we can never with any confidence say, 'there is no more to be said about this'.[12] For Mackay, this accidental image of a passenger jet between the World Trade Center towers is fixed, determined by '9/11'; but just as Petit's high wire feats were audacious, so too, because it resists such rigid compartmentalisation, is Marsh's cinematic interpretation of them. Other planes are featured in *Man on Wire*: the comically oversized animated planes that cruise over a map of the world and represent the global travels of Petit's group from Paris to Sydney, or to New York City, for instance. And then there is the archive footage of a plane coming in to land over Sydney in June 1973, just after Petit has, during his interview, confessed to having thought: 'If I die, what a beautiful death, to die in the exercise of your passion'. Once the aircraft has glided over Sydney's Opera House and Harbour Bridge, there is a cut to it touching down on the runway, before another edit to more archive of Petit's successful walk between the towers of the bridge, against a beautifully cloudless, limpid azure sky. The image of Petit silhouetted against the faultless blue of the Australian skies equally well summons up the clear skies over New York City on 11 September 2001, although the sequence's temporal innocence lures viewers into a superficially uncontaminated world, momentarily unpunctured by the trauma of the disruptive monumental event that complicates its beauty. Petit treads a fine line, and so does Marsh, between responding tactfully and appropriately to the tragedies of September 2001 and downplaying them. Arguably, the most uncomfortable moment of this Sydney sequence is actually the cut from Petit speculating about dying 'a beautiful death' and the passenger plane: as if the terrorists that hijacked the four planes in 2001 might have, as they hurtled to their deaths, found a comparable beauty in their extremist actions.

Man on Wire neither affirms nor denies that all the planes or uncontaminated skies are subliminal references to '9/11'; nor, by the same token, does it admonish us for thinking that they are. As we lose ourselves in Petit's breath-taking story, we ultimately do not know whether or not to believe in its ghostly allusions to '9/11'. During her interview, Petit's then girlfriend, Annie, instinctively looks up as she recalls the moment in 1974 when she saw Petit on his wire between the towers. Not only was this a 'defining moment' for all of Petit's group of collaborators and friends as Chinn states, but it also proved a moment when, as Marsh continues on the DVD commentary:

> the imagery of the film starts to bang against the later imagery of the destruction of the buildings and there were quite a few iconic and terrible shots of people looking up in horror as the buildings were being destroyed, and here they're looking up with awe and joy and wonder.

The awe and wonder reignited and re-enacted in *Man on Wire* opens up the possibility for us to temporarily repress our knowledge of later events; Petit's majestic, quasi-ethereal suspension in mid-air could make an apt metaphor for our suspension of disbelief. For Mackay – as, undoubtedly, for many others – *Man on Wire*'s ambiguity and playful, intellectual elasticity is disingenuous; 'clearly', she posits, the film 'could not stand free from its audience's awareness of 11 September, and the film's creators would surely have known this' (11). However, the absence of any 'mention, discussion or imagery of the towers being destroyed', does not consequentially mean that Marsh is trying, with *Man on Wire*, to 'push away the horrific association of 2001' (Mackay, 2011: 9–10); references do not have to be literal in order to be *there*.

Like Barthes's distinction in *The Pleasure of the Text* between a text's *plaisir*, which is 'linked to a comfortable practice of reading' and its *jouissance*, the 'Text of bliss: the text that imposes a state of loss' (1975: 14), the stratified ambiguities of Marsh's account of Philippe Petit's walk between the unfinished twin towers is simultaneously *about* and *not about* '9/11'. The pleasure of watching *Man on Wire* stems from its 'comfortable practice' of giving us the chance to recognise and dwell upon the familiar, if painful, events of 2001, even as its 'bliss' transcends this literalness – imposing a 'state of loss', as Barthes intimates, by, as he goes on to say, unsettling 'the reader's historical, cultural, psychological assumptions' (14). Such loss is felt keenly, for instance, at archival footage of the World Trade Center under construction. Early in *Man on Wire*, archive shows the WTC foundations being laid and the grid-like metal frames being slotted into place: similar jagged, shard-like frames to those that lay at 'Ground Zero' after the towers had collapsed in 2001. As Marsh comments on the DVD over these library images: 'some of the iconic elements created by the disaster now feature in the construction of the building'. These sequences, in their relative mundaneness, are rendered poignant – though not defined – by their *approximation* to later realities. *Man on Wire*, for all its attention on Petit's exploits, is careful not to violate that approximate bond; the DVD commentary track informs us, for instance, that the filmmakers had a 'long and protracted debate' about Petit's concerns that the windows of 7 World Trade Center (where the re-enactments were filmed) might have been wider than the familiar ones of the destroyed North and South Towers. Authenticity, albeit approximate, remained crucial. To return to Barthes, absence in *Man on Wire* (what is left unsaid) is dynamic; the void at its heart is active if silent recognition, not denial, and the root of approximation is the notion that fantasy and desire can be channelled into textual gaps and fuelled by their ambiguities. Events become imaginatively accessible by not being fixed.

One way of understanding this fertile ambiguity is via Freud's notion of the uncanny, and *Man on Wire*'s uncanniness has, of course, been remarked on many times, as when Hamilton Carroll introduces the documentary as 'cut through with uncanny resonances' (2011: 83). The film's uncanny echoes do not, though, begin and end with the World Trade Center, as intimated by the use in the background of one of the reconstructions a television set replaying news footage from 6 August 1974 of President Richard Nixon making the infamous televised address in which he vows 'I'm not a crook, I've earned everything I've got'. To us now, *Man on Wire* might be a film overburdened with uncanny echoes of September 11, 2001; in 1974 Petit's walk shared the moment with the culmination of the Watergate scandal, as two days after this press conference Nixon resigned rather than face impeachment. There are not simply two layers to *Man on Wire*, as symbolised by the film's ellipses and ambiguities. The uncanny is an indistinct and uncertain sensation, not a clear state; it is not built merely on the binary opposition between the *heimlich* and the *unheimlich*, for although, as Freud writes, 'we are tempted to conclude that what is "uncanny" is frightening precisely because it is *not* known and familiar', it is not the case that 'everything that is new and unfamiliar is frightening' (1992: 341). Just as Freud finds the equation 'uncanny' = 'unfamiliar' reductive, so it is reductive to only find in *Man on Wire* echoes of 11 September 2001. Marsh's film inverts the temporality of Freud's uncanny, as the events that reverberate uncannily with the primary narrative of Petit's 1974 walk happened decades *later*; what is 'familiar' or *heimlich* in *Man on Wire* is the tragedy of '9/11', so the reversal is twofold: firstly temporal and secondly that the 'familiar' ('9/11') is also the frightening, while the unfamiliar or *unheimlich* (Petit's walk) is sublime and joyous.

Re-enactments are always uncanny, and documentaries are always re-enactments of sorts. As Paula Rabinowitz wrote pre-'9/11':

> Walter Benjamin, chronicler of modernity, called for a history that could redeem the past by catapulting it into the present. . . . Documentary is usually a reconstruction – a re-enactment of another time or place for a different audience, a graphing of history in and through the cinematic image and taped sound into the present.
>
> *(1994: 16)*

Conversely, what *Man on Wire* offers is a graphing of more recent events onto history, so although it contains conventional re-enactment sequences (such as the reconstructions of the 'coup' as Petit refers to the World Trade Center walk), it is not otherwise the conventional documentary reconstruction Rabinowitz identifies. Neither does *Man on Wire* conform to Nichols' reading of re-enactment, in which re-enactments are seen to 'occupy a strange status in which it is crucial that they be recognized as a representation of a prior event while also signaling that they are not a representation of a contemporaneous event' (2008: 73). According to this model, re-enactments abide by a chronological temporal logic. Here too, *Man on Wire* inverts Nichols' anticipated chronology by positioning '9/11' as the phantasm haunting the enacted, but much earlier, events of Petit's high-wire exploits and staging re-enactments of *prior events* that evoke tragedies *yet to occur*. Just as Barthes resists the need to define a text's '*brio*' beyond its '*will to bliss*' (1975: 13; italics in original), so *Man on Wire* ignores basic causality and the logic of standard documentary time.

Butler had intimated that 'there is no relevant pre-history to the events of September 11, since to begin to tell the story in a different way . . . leads to the fear of moral equivocation' (2004: 6). Amid its playing around with time, causality and expectation, the boldness of *Man on Wire* is that it dares to 'tell the story a different way' by beginning with the towers' construction not destruction. Its narrative arc begins and ends before 2001, starting with Petit's fixation on the twin towers before they were even built and concluding with his eight successful walks between them in the summer of 1974, for which he was first charged with trespassing and disorderly conduct and subsequently given a permanent WTC pass. The notion of permanence, as Marsh acknowledges, 'has a huge connotation now', but that some people remarked, as Simon Chinn notes at the end of the same DVD commentary, how they 'left the cinema with a different memory of those buildings' suggests that permanence and impermanence can coexist, just as *Man on Wire* can both be *about the coup* and *not about '9/11'*.

These two states exist alongside each other throughout the film, exemplified by a section such as the one that includes the 4 April 1974 WTC dedication ceremony. Immediately prior to footage of the ceremony, there is a lengthy black and white reconstruction sequence of Petit, Jean-Louis and others hiding out in the South Tower to prepare for the coup. 'To ease the torment' (of hiding from the security guard), Petit recalls in voiceover, 'I returned to my memories . . . years of dreaming, months of organizing. I dive back into the past for a long while', words spoken over a montage of grainy, faded film archive footage of the towers captured from below, above, alongside. After the ceremony archive, comes a strange interlude in which Petit describes standing on the roof of a little house over a re-enactment of himself when young on a unicycle; Petit's memory of then shouting, 'I'm coming to America!' coincides with an animated oversize plane flying over an atlas from France to New York, before further archive of commuters pouring up the World Trade Center subway station escalators to the accompaniment of Michael Nyman's musical score. Over a shot of the completed towers, Petit talks about his dream being 'destroyed instantly' because it was 'impossible, impossible'. Yet, after a sequence of still photographs showing him at the World Trade Center planning the coup and again repeating 'It's impossible', Petit this time goes on: 'OK, let's start working'. On this occasion the Nyman music becomes more upbeat and determined, and Jean-Louis recalls getting a postcard from Petit of the twin towers with a wire drawn between them and thinking: 'Of course! That's why these towers are there, I mean for Philippe'.

The towers existed for Philippe and their destruction was embedded in their symbolic narrative; in the collective imagination they have become, perversely, familiar as the embodiments of loss and lack, a tragic assumption countered by Jean-Louis's alternative Petit-centred conclusion that they existed 'for Philippe'. *Man on Wire* is shot through with moments when these two narratives collide, most notably when Petit steps out onto the wire between the towers – according to Jean-Louis, the worst wire they had ever laid. A 16mm camera had been loaded with the intention of filming Philippe's 'coup', but after carrying the heavy cable up so many flights of stairs, Jean-Louis was too exhausted to lift the camera; what exist are a series of still photographs, one of which (a point of view image of Philippe on the edge of the South Tower looking down) is animated to make it look like moving footage. This brief moment unfolds thus:

Petit, in interview, explains how he 'had to make a decision of shifting my weight from one foot anchored to the building. . . .'

Cut to the moving photograph from the South Tower roof, with a view of the ground hundreds of feet below, sidling forwards and upwards as Petit continues (in voiceover) . . .

'. . . to the foot anchored on the wire'.

Cut back to Petit being interviewed admitting how at the time he had thought: 'This is probably – I don't know – probably the end of my life to step on that wire, and on the other hand, something that I could not resist . . . death is very close'.

Man on Wire's distinct temporal planes shiver like vibrating musical strings that create untranscribable reverberations as opposed to distinct notes. The tonic through this brief, animated point of view photograph is Petit's walk, his imminent triumph, while the sub-dominants are the allusions to height, desperation, falling and death contained within the lurching movement. 'I start walking as a wire walker studying his cable', the older Petit says, 'Now I'm going to perform'. Just as the sensation of shifting one's weight to look into the urban abyss below the South Tower memorialises the dead and dying on '9/11', Petit's instinctual transition to the present tense here as he relives the glorious moment of stepping out reclaims the narrative as his.

Presentness offers a further means of displacing the monolithic relationship between 1974 and 2001, as interviewees, archive footage and re-enactments converge on the singular sublime moment of the walk. The notion of being transported back to that day is felt most powerfully in the interviews during the final twenty minutes of the film, several of which are characterised by physicality and tearfulness. Jean-Louis, the most emotional of Petit's troupe, cries first as he recalls seeing that Philippe was 'secure' on the wire then later, as he finds it impossible to conclude the thought 'you can't take away what happened', intimating that the crowning moment of their collaboration also led to the end of their friendship. Similarly, Annie's eyes swell with tears as she remembers the beautiful moment of Petit kneeling down on the wire and saluting – a gesture Annie mimics. Finally, Jim's eyes look a little watery as he refers to the walk as 'beyond anything you could have imagined'. And yet, however keen it is to evoke the sublime, *Man on Wire* does not over-romanticise the 'coup'; just as you might have been forgiven for thinking it is fine to momentarily forget '9/11', *Man on Wire* punctures its own sublime by harking back to it. During Annie's awed, transcendental descent into the memories of Philippe's magnificent walk, there comes a harsh interjection of later reality with a crisp black and white photograph of Annie amidst a crowd of gawping bystanders staring heavenwards at the twin towers. The image is canted, off balance, in direct contrast to Petit; such subliminal allusions to '9/11' jolt us with more force than more obvious references might have done. Likewise, the image of the plane flying between the towers is inserted during Jim's last interview – as he labels what Philippe has achieved 'mind-boggling'. After the brief, jarring sign of future tragedies, Jim explains how it 'took my mind into a place where I wasn't that concerned about him . . . it was magical'.

The sublime perfection of the eight high wire crossings over New York City is summed up in the end not by one of Petit's accomplices but by one of his arresting officers, who in his press interview on the day talked of how 'I personally figured I was watching something that somebody else would never see again . . . it was once in a lifetime'. *But*, this spiritual transportation notwithstanding, *Man on Wire* does not focus on the sublime perfection of Petit's walk *at the expense of* remembering '9/11'. Beauty is only part of truth; to distil the World Trade Center down to '9/11' is to forget its past, its lofty magnificence and its historically untethered symbolic value. To underline this point, *Man on Wire* closes with the comedy of the aftermath of the walk (Petit being arrested, taken away for a psychological evaluation and having sex with a stranger) and then laughing at having been asked repeatedly why he had done it. 'There is no why', he says, as *Man on Wire*, totally unexpectedly, starts to resemble Marleen Gorris's 1985 feminist masterpiece, *A Question of Silence*. Asked by a bank of bemused male judges why they had killed a male shop manager whom none of them knew, Gorris's three female protagonists and all the other women sitting in the public gallery, start to laugh uncontrollably, until the defendants are escorted from the courtroom. Marsh explains that he and his producers never asked Petit 'why?' because: 'if you can't see the virtue of something beautiful and dreamlike and wonderful, I can't help you really'.

In an essay published in the wake of '9/11' in 2004, Juan Suárez explains how he screened *Manhatta* (1921), a short silent, non-narrative documentary portrait of

Manhattan by painter, Charles Sheeler, and photographer, Paul Strand, to his students. 'I could not help but notice', Suárez writes,

> how elegiac it had become under the pressure of recent events. What had always seemed a rather 'full' text, a self-assured homage to New York and its modern cityscape, had suddenly become mournful, inhabited by loss – by the open wound of the bombed World Trade Center.
>
> *(2004: 103)*

The 'dreamlike' beauty of *Man on Wire* is that it has not reduced the memory of the twin towers to the act of mourning their loss; it is still a celebration of a feat not defined by the events of 2001 as Suárez finds *Manhatta*'s cityscape to be. But Suárez raises a fundamental issue for *Man on Wire* as a 'not-9/11' film, namely that mourning or perceiving the shadow of '9/11' in the film is a function of spectatorship; it is the viewer who makes the links, hears the echoes between 1974 and 2001, mourns the loss of the towers even as they marvel at their construction. It is in these ways that *Man on Wire* becomes an 'approximation' of '9/11': an event distant from but informed by it. Historical detachment is likewise the defining characteristic of Loach's contribution to *11'09"01, September 11* and what makes it an 'approximation', as he argues against the marginalisation of the 'other' '9/11': the Chilean coup of 1973. Conversely, temporal distancing does not mark *United 93*; instead here, the convergence of Greengrass's extreme shaky-cam style and his subject matter create a different gap – between the speedily constructed, dominant public narrative of '9/11' and the alternate perspective the film represents. Firstly, *United 93* offers the 'unimaginable' point of view of the victims on the planes (the swiftness with which sight and sound of the World Trade Center 'jumpers' and close-up images of the planes were excised suggests how controversial such images were at the time); secondly, the film enters the tragedy's core and thereby inhabits the brief period before the '9/11' narrative started to assume its official, public structure.

One of the starting points for this study was a consideration of the chicken and egg of '9/11' and the representation of reality. Did instant conversion of the terrorist attacks into media images and narrative, for instance, change the ways in which we thought reality could be represented, or were those changes (towards 'constructed reality', towards mash-ups that incorporate both fact and fiction) already afoot? Douglas Kellner, for one, argues that 'Real-life events' had taken over from 'television spectacle' before '9/11', specifically during the 'intense battle for the White House in the dead-heat election' between George W. Bush and Al Gore (Kellner, 2005: 29) as the new millennium ushered in a radical reassessment of the generic boundaries 'factual' and 'fictional'. With these shifts the contemporary notion of 'approximation' started to be formed, of finding it as valid, as vital to *approximate* reality as it had been to 'represent' it. The '9/11' attacks were so excessive, so movie-like, so 'ready-made for CNN' (Rodney, 2005: 38), so likely to have been conceived to be looked at, that a natural response was to view them as performances – not the binary opposite of fiction, but as images that shared much with fictions of disaster and spectacle. Representations of '9/11' both defined and were defined by the era of 'approximation'.

Notes

1 Storr compares *September* to Robert Capa's 'Loyalist Militiaman at the Moment of Death, Cerro Muriano, September 5, 1936' and Edward T. Adams's 'General Nguyen Ngoc Loan Executing a Viet Cong Prisoner in Saigon' (1968).
2 Cf. www.nbcnews.com/now/video/from-the-archives-george-w-bush-s-oval-office-speech-on-9-11-68719685777. Accessed 18 September 2019.
3 For a fuller discussion of this episode and *The West Wing* more generally see Gregory Frame, *The American President in Film and Television: Myth, Politics and Representation*, Oxford: Peter Lang, 2014.
4 Cf. www.loc.gov/collections/september-11th-2001-documentary-project/about-this-collection/. Accessed 3 September 2019.
5 Vega also starred in Loach's *Ladybird, Ladybird*, 1994.
6 Of course, it could still be argued that Allende was pushed to suicide and so 'murdered'.
7 Cf. Theodor W. Adorno, 'Cultural Criticism and Society', in *Prisms*, Cambridge, MA: MIT Press, 1981, 34.
8 The production company behind *Mad Men*.
9 In the early months of 2002, the fashion designer Kenneth Cole ran a series of advertisements entitled 'On September 12'. Across each ran the tagline: 'Today is not a Dress Rehearsal' as each ad placed models and clothes in ostensibly but skewed domestic settings (for example, a model in a little black dress eating whilst sprawled over a weathered wooden table) in what many considered to be a campaign that was 'one of the most sophisticated produced in the first months after 9/11' (Sturken, 2007: 36).
10 Such as *Let's Roll: The Story of Flight 93* (2002), *Last Hours of Flight 11* (2004), *Flight 93: The Flight That Fought Back* (2005), *Flight 93* (2006).
11 Others who play themselves in the film are: Boston air traffic controller Thomas Roberts, military specialist Colin Scoggins and Major James Fox of NEADS. Other non-actors include commercial airline pilot J.J. Johnson, who had flown extensively with United Airlines and plays United 93's Captain Jason M. Dahl; experienced pilot Gary Commock who plays First Officer LeRoy Homer; Trish Gates, who plays flight attendant Sandra Bradshaw and had both acting and steward experience prior to filming and was, when cast, 'still working in the field' (Greengrass, 2006: 96).
12 For further discussion of this image, cf. my contribution to the British Academy podcast series 'From Our Fellows'. https://soundcloud.com/britishacademy/from-our-fellows-01-november-2016. Accessed 22 August 2017.

3

MAD MEN AND THE INCIDENTAL EVENTS OF THE 1960S

In Steven Spielberg's *Lincoln* (2012), the Speaker of the House gives as his justification for deciding to cast a vote on the 13th Amendment: 'This isn't usual, Mr Pendleton, this is history'. In this moment of reflexivity, as Spielberg highlights the importance of history, he also signals his film's place within it. By drawing attention to the event being re-enacted, *Lincoln* itself lays claim to being a historical act. Though it as much steeped in familiar history as *Lincoln*, in *Mad Men* something different and subtler occurs, namely the 'incidentalisation' of history, the components of which are relatively specific, in that fiction pursues a parallel track to the factual events it references, with history as its counterpoint, as chords might be to the dominant tune, but stories and characters do not interact with that history directly. In Matthew Weiner's series which ran from 2007 to 2015 and charted the story and multiple reincarnations from 1960 to 1970 of fictional Madison Avenue ad agency, Sterling Cooper, history (that is, almost exclusively US history) is clearly and self-consciously signalled, at the same time as it is narratively marginalised. The claims to 'approximation' are relatively telegraphed, as the series relates dialectically to the history it depicts. Unlike copious other historical dramas, however, the series does not construct a transparent Lukácsian microcosmic metafiction through which 'history' can be better understood, a distinctiveness which makes it doubly intriguing. Internal crises in *Mad Men* tangentially and unconsciously mirror external ones (more than once, for example, an external crisis precipitates an internal crisis in Don Draper, *Mad Men*'s protagonist), but the series' narrative is not redirected or defined by its interaction with the timeline of typically familiar events it rubs shoulders with.

Unlike a film such as Pablo Larraín's *No* (2013), which blends archival footage and fictionalised characters to recount, from the point of view of a young (and fictional) ad man, the story of the advertising campaign that helped oust Chilean dictator Augusto Pinochet in 1988, *Mad Men* does not contrive an excuse to inveigle itself into history (or very, very rarely). Like Hitler driving past in his car in Robert Harris's *Munich* (2017), 'big history' in *Mad Men* happens elsewhere – on television, in newspapers, away from the diegetic action. Fictionalisation, in however small a way, interacts with history in dramas such as *No* or, more overtly, a biopic such as Roger Donaldson's *Thirteen Days* (2000), in which Kenneth O'Donnell's central-ity to the Cuban Missile Crisis negotiations is beefed up for dramatic effect (and played by its 'star', Kevin Costner). Going one step further, in *The X-Files* episode 'Musings of a Cigarette-Smoking Man' (Season 4:7, 1996) two shadowy FBI agents, having intervened in many of the events that figure in *Mad Men* (the assassinations of John Kennedy, Martin Luther King and Robert Kennedy) muse: 'how often did we make or change history?' In this instance, drama sheds doubt on received history, on how it has been formed and on how individuals have impacted upon it. The interaction becomes more proactively ideological in an example such as Jonathan Coe's 'Brexit novel', *Middle England* (2018), which situates fictional char-acters within contemporary politics in order to offer an interpretation of them – specifically, the 2016 Referendum and the UK electorate's decision to leave the EU. In one chapter, two characters are watching Boris Johnson (leader of the 'Leave' campaign and later Prime Minister) draw an analogy between the European Union and Nazi Germany:

> Both, he argued, had the design of creating a German-dominated European superstate. Benjamin (Trotter), whose interest in politics had grown expo-nentially in the last few weeks, was aghast. Was this what political debate had become in this country, now?
>
> *(Coe, 2018: 292)*

Coe is not making this up – 'BoJo' did make such an analogy, which seemed at the time desperate as well as desperately offensive; what he does make up is the meta-commentary on the remarks and what it might have said about the level of 'political debate' in the UK in 2016. This is not just a comment on a factual event, it is an aside made with hindsight, which is something notably lacking in fictions that 'incidentalise' history.

Mad Men is engaged in a particular *pas de deux* of entanglement and disengage-ment. It touches and shimmies past history (in the way any of us might stand next to a celebrity and note them but say nothing); history is 'incidental', but not *irrelevant*. Events are there, and there to be noted; and yet, the encounter between narrative and events remains casual, often uneventful, at other times indirectly impactful. Even when 'history' does not impinge on the narrative, its shadowy pres-ence inflects it and, however ephemerally, pricks its surface. *Mad Men* is especially drawn to the 'incidentalisation' of significant and familiar factual events – events that even its contemporary audience would most likely recognise as 'history': the Cuban Missile Crisis; the assassinations of President Kennedy and Martin Luther King; the first moon landing. Likewise, fleeting mentions of the 'Arab Spring' in the 2016 BBC Television adaptation of John Le Carré's 1993 novel, *The Night Manager*, or the references to immigration into Sicily and Southern Italy in the film *A Bigger Splash* (Luca Guadagnino, 2016), or the just audible car radio news item about Vietnam in Quentin Tarantino's counterfactual film, *Once Upon a Time . . . in Hollywood* are almost throwaway – but not quite – interjections, there for someone, presumably the viewer, to pick up on. Such *sprezzatura* is exemplified by an earlier film such as Ettore Scola's *Una Giornata Particolare* (*A Special Day*, 1977) in which Hitler's historic encounter with Benito Mussolini in Rome is the narrative trigger but is never seen, as the action becomes absorbed instead in the nascent relationship between housewife Sophia Loren and her neighbour, Marcello Mastroianni. The incidental event is not simply background noise but an interruption, a reminder of the facts that lurk behind fiction which, in the Tarantino, is heavily ironic, as the whole movie tells a parallel counter-historical narrative to the real story (which, though referenced, does not happen) of the murders of Hollywood actress Sharon Tate and friends.

Mad Men has been regularly scrutinised and praised for its 'truthiness' (Varon, 2013: 257) and, as Dana Polan is moved to observe, 'is somehow taken to be, and admired as, a *document*, or even a *documentary* of upper-middle-class suburban life in the late 1950s and into the 1960s', as 'viewers assume it offers a picture of the way things were in those times' (Polan, 2013: 39–40). 'Documents' in the form of authentic historical artefacts (cumbersome television sets, Eames chairs and teak desks, grey flannel suits) and archival material (newspapers, radio and television news broadcasts) are regularly integrated into the series, but self-evidently *Mad Men* is not a documentary. However, Polan's hyperbole touches on the extent to which viewers put their faith in the series' historical fidelity and 'lovingly tended mimicry' (Goodlad et al., 2013: 3). The series inhabits a design-oriented space that lovingly recreates, via interior décor and costume, an 'authentic' 1960s' milieu, so its viewers would have sought and found a comparable 'authenticity' in its referencing of background factual events: the series' authenticity when it comes to its use of television and media in the dissemination of news is impressively, even fetishistically, accurate. The insertion of real events into this pristine pastiche leads to a re-evaluation of authenticity on various levels and exemplifies the manner in which 'approximation' works towards the imaginative reconfiguration of history through inter-layering and cross-referencing across the supposed factual/fictional 'divide'. *Mad Men* remains both authentic and contemporary, able to capture both a documentary sense of 'being there' in the 1960s and something about the collective (US) unconscious, at the same time as contributing instrumentally, alongside series such as *The Wire* and *The Sopranos*, to the evolution of television drama in the millennial era. *Mad Men* prompts the viewer to look both at and through its 'tender mimicry' of the times it depicts, by not ignoring when it was made – a multi-directional focus that finds an echo in the character of protagonist, Don Draper, whose dissembling and mental instability function throughout as metaphors for the turbulence of the 1960s. With its pervasive interaction with key moments in history alongside its emphasis on 'how history is experienced', *Mad Men*, Goodlad et al. argue, 'altered the vision of the 1960s and of pastness itself' (Goodlad, 2013: 2). The discussion below will look first more broadly at *Mad Men*'s inclusion and configuration of 'incidental' events before paying particular attention to the episode 'The Grown Ups' in Season 3, which charts the assassination of President Kennedy.

The *Mad Men* 'vision' of the 1960s is built on the series' successful integration of a fastidiously detailed and richly evocative *mise-en-scène* (into which broad category fit Janie Bryant's precisely selected and meticulously designed vintage costumes) and its historical accuracy and specificity. 'History' is here made material, tangible and *lived*, as *Mad Men* argues against the received wisdom that 'proper' history is written down, because 'print is deep, images are shallow' (Schama, 2004: 24). Despite the prompting of a more nebulous or emotive nostalgia for some of the series' surface trivia, such as Betty's more outré fashion choices (her predilection for stiff anaglypta-like fabrics, for instance), the office's retro lamps or cigarettes, *Mad Men* takes the representation of history seriously. Just as Schama celebrated the fact that the arrival of television's popularisation of history in the early 2000s meant that 'In place of a profession, we now, at last, have the real possibility of a community' (28), *Mad Men* constructed a comparable history 'community' whose central symbol became characters congregating around television sets watching the highlight moments of 1960s history unfold. The series' engagement with historical detailing is deemed to be, by Ono, '*sublime*' (Ono, 2013: 302; my italics), a magnificent obsession with drawing together décor, fashion, technology and historical events.

One feature of *Mad Men*'s engagement with real history is its attachment not to the forgotten marginalia of history, but rather to a '*Life* magazine timeline of political turmoil and change' (Stanley, 2010), 'a past of knowable events about which one might read in the *New York Times*' (Goodlad, 2013: 2), starting with the Kennedy vs. Nixon presidential race of 1960. Its reassuring mainstreamness is developed across and complemented by the extensive 'paratextual' material made available as DVD and website 'extras',[1] or within the drama itself as dramatic irony. When invitations are sent out to Margaret Sterling's wedding on 23 November 1963, for instance, audiences probably realized that the nuptial celebrations will be overshadowed by a momentous event that will have occurred the day before. The series maintains a persistent tension between textbook history and narrative progress. In *Mad Men* narrative and history are symbiotically and symbolically linked. Archival records of event are temporally transported out of 'history' to be recycled and repeated as markers of events that are yet to be concluded. Archive is essential in this respect as it carries with it an eternal, irrepressible *presentness*, a sense that this is taking place *now*. The event, as Mary Ann Doane argues, 'is a pure indication, deprived of meaning' (1990: 140), whose readability is generated via context and contingency; *Mad Men* returns its incidental events to their primal, pre-historical state, moves them from their 'context and contingency' to the still emerging (hi)story of *Mad Men*. The big crises of 1960s' US history are interpolated into the series as indexical evidence of a historical narrative as yet unshaped: film or video archive, radio bulletins, newspapers, unformed until situated or explained.

To take one of *Mad Men*'s early examples: the Cuban Missile Crisis ('Meditations in an Emergency', Season 2:13). A standard fictionalised retelling of those 13 days in October 1962 culminates in relief and joy at Kennedy's brinkmanship winning the day and saving the world from a third World War after Khrushchev orders the cessation of a Soviet nuclear build up on Cuba. In *Thirteen Days*, for instance, after the White House has received Krushchev's final missive, Kennedy (Bruce Greenwood) enters a room full of staff to be greeted with applause and praise, while the film overall closes soon after on audio from Kennedy's post-crisis television address calling not just for 'peace in our time, but peace in all time'. Conversely, *Mad Men*'s Cuban Missile Crisis episode is aptly named 'Meditations *in* an Emergency', not *on* an emergency, as the external emergency precipitates internal crises and contemplative introspection, but does not define the episode, whose narrative contains many threads and, as in other 'big crisis' episodes, storylines that are *especially* momentous and so distract from the 'crisis' at hand. Archive footage of the escalation of military tension between the US and USSR punctuate the drama, and a fuzzy replaying of Kennedy's national address detailing the fact that 'unmistakable evidence has established the fact that a series of offensive missile sites is now in preparation on that imprisoned island' plays on Don's diegetic television set. And yet, the external crisis does not cause the dramatic narrative to 'stand still'; rather it becomes indirectly symptomatic of internal crises for which it acts as a catalyst and focus point. The episode opens, for instance, with Betty Draper, Don's first wife, visiting her gynaecologist and being told she is expecting their third child. As she and Don are at the time living separately (Don is watching television in a hotel room), this is not, as she tells a friend later, a good time. Betty's marital crisis continues as she leaves the two children with Don and goes to a bar in which the words 'Cuban Missile Crisis' issue audibly from its television set. Conventional yet spectacular in a stiff, golden, embroidered dress and jacket, Betty has sex on the sofa in the bar's powder room with a stranger who had just bought her a drink, leaving the bar with lipstick and recently coiffured hair intact. Running in parallel with Betty's marital crisis is the announcement that Sterling Cooper has been taken over by London-based company, Puttnam, Powell and Lowe. And, finally, there is the conversation, late at night in the office, between Pete Campbell (who works in the accounts department at Sterling Cooper) and Peggy Olson (one of its copy chiefs) in which Peggy reveals to Pete information viewers have known since the last season but of which he has remained ignorant, namely that Peggy was pregnant, had a baby and 'gave it away'. The two domestic crises converge with the brutal edit from a devastated Pete to Don going home (in direct response to the as yet unresolved political crisis), to be greeted by his children, Sally and Bobby, calling 'Daddy! You're home!' before discovering that Betty is pregnant. As the episode closes with a slow pull out from this tense, quiet and unresolved scene and fades to black, the cathartic relief generated by a declaration that the Cuban Missile Crisis is formally over (the scenes in Times Square as relieved New Yorkers look up at celebratory neon headlines) is denied. World War Three was averted, but the Cold War continued, just as the cracks in the Draper marriage are only temporarily papered over.

Over its seven seasons, *Mad Men* constructs a dynamic dialectic between its linear and familiar *Life/New York Times* historical trajectory and its tonally nuanced, multi-planed dramatization of that history. Its narratively complicated re-enactments of that history also enact the notion that, though comprising those events, time is not constrained by them. The collision with its fictional events renders the (within the conventions of drama) unfinished external crisis 'readable'; one result of the 'incidentalisation' of the Cuban Missile Crisis is that it impinges and reflects on *Mad Men*'s fictional crises. The series offers a particular, though not necessarily subversive, way of recounting history (its events timeline, for example, is not only mainstream but parochial, and, despite the series' global reach, rarely looked beyond the forming of a modern American identity and consciousness) exemplified by the combative diachrony between the potentially disruptive external event and the seamless narrative 'flow' through each episode, across every series and from season to season. The ultimate and ironic paradox of the moments when external crises intrude on the drama is that it is at such junctures that *Mad Men* feels most retrospective, contemporary and of its own millennial time: the time of retrospection and knowing where things end up, the time of its title sequence of the silhouetted 'falling man', a reminder of its 21st century, post-'9/11' origins.[2] *Mad Men* was not just about a past time, it was so much *of* its time, a television event in its own right; consequently, one obstacle to immersive engagement with *Mad Men*'s ostensibly flawless depiction of history is its persistent presentness: that it was, for its seven seasons, such a noughties television event. It is against this temporal duality – as both a contemporary televisual event and an 'authentic' evocation of the past – that the historical events of the 1960s unfold; informed by the knowledge that ultimately they will remain incidental, subsumed into the flow of historical and narrative momentum, they mimic the fantasy that an event even momentarily makes time 'stand still'.

The series' notable complementary supply of 'paratextual' materials is just one feature that marks it out as millennial, as Jackie Kennedy's 1962 tour of the White House was uploaded in its entirety onto the series' website, as was Martin Luther King's 'I Have a Dream' speech from the steps of the Lincoln Memorial, 28 August 1963. Even if the series itself only incorporates edited highlights and iconic snatches of US 1960s' history, such secondary materials attest to the barely veiled earnestness of *Mad Men*'s claim to historical accuracy. Such subsidiary constituent historical contributions function in contrapuntal or symbiotic dialogue with the drama, as regular features on *Mad Men*'s official website included: the series blog, 'exclusive' interviews, clips and audiences quizzes; an 'explore' section attached to each season, which includes more detailed discussions of features such as costumes and fashions; a '1960s Handbook' strand of the blog in which the series' incidental historical events are discussed in greater depth via factual blog items; live links to other webpages and relevant newspaper articles. During its run there was also considerable internet trade in *Mad Men* footnotes, such as Natasha Vargas-Cooper's 'footnotes of *Mad Men*' blogs, on her own (now defunct) site *Mad Men Unbuttoned: A Romp Through 1960s America*,[3] which used the series as a launch pad for wider discussions and citations of parallel cultural and political events.

The extra-diegetic materials are straightforward indicators of *Mad Men*'s desire to be taken seriously for taking its history seriously. Just as characteristic is its *sprezzatura* (its nonchalant ability to do something well without showing the effort it took) illustrated by those moments when historical events, both lasting and ephemeral, are casually dropped in and out of the narrative, as when the death of Marilyn Monroe is discussed briefly in the lift (Season 2:9) as characters arrive for work or when the toxic smog that hung over New York City for the period of Thanksgiving is mentioned (Season 5:9). Big events are generally at least remarked on, such as Don and his blind date Bettany's exchange about 'the boys killed in Mississippi' – referring to the case of Andrew Goodman and two other civil rights activists killed on 21 June 1964 by members of the Ku Klux Klan ('Public Relations', Season 4:1).[4] There are also various insouciant references to culture, most prominently the careful selection of popular music.[5] Casual allusions to Don Draper's unlikely consumption of eclectic and up-to-minute reading matter are especially entertaining examples of *sprezzatura*. In the opening episode of Season 2, for example, Don is shown reading Frank O'Hara's poetry collection, *Meditations in an Emergency* (which supplied the title for the season's Cuban Missile Crisis episode), and in the penultimate ever episode he is glimpsed, while holed up in a motel waiting for a replacement car, being diverted by Mario Puzo's *The Godfather*, Michael Crighton's *The Andromeda Strain* and James Michener's *Hawaii* – as well as by a beautiful poolside woman reading *The Woman of Rome* by Alberto Moravia.

A different sort of *sprezzatura* is used for the death of Robert Kennedy, Democratic presidential candidate, on 6 June 1968. Coming relatively soon after the assassination of Martin Luther King Jr on 4 April (an event around which an entire episode, 'The Flood' [Season 6:5], is structured), the decade's second Kennedy death is not narratively dominant. Instead, its referencing provides an interesting insight into *Mad Men*'s linkage of events to character. Pete is with his mother, who suffers from dementia. She comes in, dressed in a silk night turban, to wake him and alert him to the news that 'they shot that poor Kennedy boy'. The following exchange ensues:

PETE: That was years ago mother.
MOTHER: I just saw it on the television.
PETE: It's 6 A.M. [sighs.]
MOTHER: You'll be late for school.
PETE: Please just let me sleep.
MOTHER: I don't understand what's going on. They're shooting everybody. [She walks out.]

As archival footage is played across other scenes in the episode, characters watch the news horrified; Pete, however, remains oblivious – a minor but entertaining intra-textual reference to how he had also been one of the last people to hear the news of John Kennedy's assassination in Season 3. Only occasionally does *Mad Men* treat factual events heavy-handedly, one example being the inclusion of the death of civil rights activist, Medger Evers, assassinated 12 June 1963. Evers' death comes up when Don and Betty Draper have been asked to go and see their daughter

Sally's teacher to discuss Sally's recent and uncharacteristically bad behaviour. In the process of trying to determine the cause for this, Betty reveals that her father had died two weeks before, at which point the teacher (Suzanne) appears relieved, sensing she has now alighted upon the reason for why (nine-year-old) Sally was 'asking all those questions about Medger Evers' murder' (Season 3:5, 'The Fog'). As compensation, perhaps, for this clumsiness, and in inverse proportion to the narrative time given to Evers' assassination, the Season 3 'extras' DVD includes a two-part documentary about him.

Sprezzatura also characterises the series' referencing of sexual politics, which, though not signalled overtly, is subtly omnipresent throughout, in characters such as Betty. It often feels as if Weiner et al. want to see how far they can push the parallels between Betty Draper Francis's unspecific discontent and Betty Friedan's identification of 'the problem that has no name' without citing *The Feminine Mystique* directly. Betty Draper Francis – Bryn Mawr-educated and, by the end of the series enrolled in a psychology degree at Fairfield University, Connecticut – is the masquerading, high-functioning embodiment of Friedan's depressed housewife who wants more than her husband, her children and her home. By the end of Season 7, in the knowledge that she has terminal lung cancer, Betty ignores her second husband Henry Francis's wishes to undergo chemotherapy, informing him she is tired of others telling her what to do. *Mad Men*'s 'extreme-authenticity' is uneven; in terms of history, timeline events are prioritised over chronic issues such as feminism, gay rights, student unrest. The decision not to bring 1960s politics of identity and consciousness-raising is, though, symptomatic of wanting to remain faithful to the deeply unenlightened realities of Madison Avenue's own identity politics. *Mad Men*'s overarching fictional structure is focused and unified, yet its sampling of history is, though not random and tokenistic, then kaleidoscopic. Its history of the 1960s is a vibrant but selective bricolage of transformative events and incidental cultural or factual detail, some minutely observed, some merely glanced. Although sometimes the series' fictional characters do inhabit real situations (for example Henry Francis going to support the real [but not seen] Mayor Lindsay who visited Harlem on the night Martin Luther King was assassinated),[6] there is no faked archive, no matting of actors' faces into real actuality footage, no Oliver Stone-esque mash-up and remarkably few anachronisms.[7]

History is not randomly treated in *Mad Men*, although, as intimated above, it is not the case that the biggest events make the biggest narrative interventions (again mirroring how 'history' is maybe consumed). Whereas a whole episode revolves around an archival moment as relatively trivial as 'A Tour of the White House by Mrs John F. Kennedy',[8] the Vietnam War, despite having dominated news bulletins on an almost nightly basis throughout the second half of the decade covered by *Mad Men*, impinges on the series only sporadically and tangentially through such details as Joan Holloway's husband Greg enlisting as a military doctor and brief snatches of dialogue. It seems remarkable that Vietnam, in so relatively short a time, might have fallen from US collective consciousness but, writing significantly earlier than *Mad Men* in 1984, Fredric Jameson speculates that 'Vietnam vanishes from American consciousness as completely after the American withdrawal as did Algeria from French consciousness after the Evian accords of 1963' (Jameson, 1984: 183). Betty twice in Season 7 (Episodes 5 and 10) spouts the 'wrong' views on the war, the latter instance being twinned exchanges (in 'The Forecast') with a young former neighbour, Glen, who has just enlisted. Glen comes to the grand (Republican) Francis residence to say his goodbyes to Betty's daughter, Sally, as he is 'shipping out next week'. The first exchange goes as follows:

SALLY: Are you fucking stupid? . . . You hate the war. What about Kent State? You were crying. You were going to join the movement.
GLEN: What about a bunch of negroes dying while we sit at home getting stoned? It's immoral.
SALLY: You're going to die. For what?
BETTY: Don't listen to Jane Fonda here. It's a very brave thing to do.

This tense exchange functions on both a general level (the generational divide, the clashing idealisms and ideologies of youth) and on a more profound if elliptical one by joining up the dots of Vietnam, Kent State, young African Americans dying, the counterculture and 'Hanoi Jane'. The reference to the 4 May 1970 Kent State shootings of students protesting against the bombing of neutral Cambodia by members of the Ohio National Guard indicates how, even when it makes little of it, *Mad Men* uses some of the intricate detail of consequential history. Such a fleeting aside about such 'big' events has a dual purpose: by feeding the complex fantasy that the series' fictional characters are living through real history and inhabiting an off-screen space of unseen nightly news bulletins and newspapers, it reinforces the significance of those events.

Sally flounces off and this scene concludes, though Glen returns soon after to the Francis home to find Betty alone. This time the simmering erotic *frisson* between them is made explicit as Glen goes to kiss Betty just after she has reassured him that 'from what I read in the magazines, they [troops in Vietnam] have all the comforts of home'. He is rebuffed and admits to having joined up because he had messed up at school and saw it as a way of regaining his father's approval. Betty's facile suggestion that Vietnam soldiers are surrounded by their creature comforts is tricky to read and has been taken to be straightforwardly indicative of the privileged perspective of the upper-middle-class 1960s housewife who believed all that her magazines told her. And yet, there is also a meta-dialogue going on here with the audience that disrupts the un-ironic interpretation of the exchange. This meta-commentary works as an alienation device or disengagement tactic; it reminds viewers of how Vietnam concluded, of the hindsight they bring to the scene – much in the same way as Joan's suggestion in 'Meditations in an Emergency' that she might run through with colleagues 'the protocol for civil defence' elicits from Don the cynical response: 'trust me, I don't think there'll be a point to taking the stairs or diving under a desk'. Most informed citizens believed that in Vietnam US troops had 'all the comforts of home' as much as they would have believed the 1950s public information film

'Duck and Cover' to which Don is alluding here. There is an argument that the series' sumptuous aestheticism 'is itself an obstacle to pleasure' (Goodlad, 2013: 9); in a comparable way, its elaborate weaving of history into narrative is an obstacle to pleasurable immersion, forever interrupting the narrative flow and compelling viewers to recall the extra-diegetic space of fact and history that continues to exist outside of the fantasy of its fictionalisation. *Mad Men* is so often referred to as being 'nostalgic', but nostalgic for what? For sexism, racism, homophobia and the Cold War? If anything, it is nostalgic for profoundly mixed pleasures, of entering the foreign country of a past where casual adultery and recreational alcoholism were taken for granted.[9] 'The show's embrace of the past', as Kent Ono suggests, 'is not merely a loving but also an uncomfortable one' (Ono, 2013: 300), as its equivocal evocation of the 1960s probably, and paradoxically, became part of its allure: that it reconstituted mid-century stylishness while simultaneously permitting its audience to stand aloof from it, secure – even smug – in the knowledge that 'Now We Know Better', whether about 'male chauvinism, homophobia, anti-Semitism, workplace harassment, housewives' depression' (Greif, 2008).

Dramatic characters cannot live through every news story as if aware of its infinite potential to become a transformative event; not only would that be exhausting for the audience, but the strictures and conventions of dramatic irony that dictate historical drama are such that characters must live in presentness and ignorance, not fully comprehending how 'appalling' aspects of their lives are, negotiating both seismic and trivial events without the perspective that might facilitate the differentiation between them. *Mad Men*'s characters are tantalisingly imprisoned in their ever shifting 'now', forcibly denied any awareness of their present's implications for the future. Betty, therefore, lacks self-reflectivity, whether about sexism, Vietnam or the dangers of smoking. At the same time, for a cognisant millennial audience, watching *Mad Men* is a headily dialectical experience built on the disavowal and repression of, on the one hand, knowledge and, on the other, the triumph of hindsight. The series inhabits the *mise-en-scène* of fantasy history, a world of fastidious historical accuracy haunted by the feint shadow of a post-millennial present. When, therefore, in 'Nixon vs. Kennedy' (Season 1:12), company founder, Bert Cooper, tells Don that the Nixon camp had not asked for a recount of the extremely close 1960 presidential race because 'you don't want to win like that', many viewers might well have felt a subliminal brush with the equally contested election of 2000, when a recount in the state of Florida confirmed George W. Bush as president against Democrat Al Gore (like Nixon, the incumbent Vice President) by the narrow margin of 537 votes or 0.009% of the vote.

One dominant 1960s story that *Mad Men*'s characters live through is the civil rights movement, which surfaces sporadically but not uncontroversially, for the series' treatment of race (more than its treatment of gender politics) has been much critiqued. Blackness is conspicuously peripheral to *Mad Men*; while some have accused the series of tokenism in its depiction of race, others have argued that the 'invisibility of racialized "others" is a key political strategy of the show' (Beail, 2015: 236) in keeping with the series' stubborn allegiance to authenticity. Yet, in an era of 'colour-blind' casting, this jars. Throughout, *Mad Men* remains tentative in its treatment of racial difference and the issue of civil rights, like Vietnam, is largely kept in the background until, that is, Martin Luther King Jr's assassination in 'The Flood' (Season 6:5), first transmitted 28 April 2013, soon after President Obama had started his second term in office. In this episode Weiner and colleagues effectively counter the criticism (published in 2013, so most likely formulated before Season 6 aired) that the series 'decontextualises the experience of black characters by banishing the civil rights struggle to the South' (Lang, 2013: 76–77). *Mad Men*'s perspective on race is, Ono argues, one of '*demographic realism*' for 'the show documents the actions of characters through the lens of white society, from the vantage point resonant with contemporary logics of whiteness' (301), which include the 'national hunger for racial optimism' that followed Obama's election (Thomas Pettigrew in Ono, 2013: 301). *Mad Men* overlapped significantly with the Obama presidency of 2009–2017, and the discourse on race is one of the areas where indubitably 'Now We Know Better'. Racial optimism, if not the 'postracialism' which Ono also finds in *Mad Men*, is concentrated in 'The Flood'.

As the event of King's death is again embedded in a complex web of pre-existent narrative threads, a source of tension becomes how its historical effect is collapsed into or becomes synonymous with the impact it has on the lead characters' world of white privilege. The individual stories introduced at the outset are: Peggy's viewing of an apartment on the Upper East Side; Don and Megan Draper's neighbours, the Rosens, setting out for a conference in Washington DC; Don and Megan heading for an advertising industry awards ceremony, compered by Paul Newman; Michael Ginsberg (copywriter at Sterling Cooper) arriving home to discover that his father has arranged a date for him with Beverley, the daughter of a Jewish family friend. It is not insignificant that King's assassination is about to take place against a backdrop of casual inattention to the differences amongst white immigrant groups. In 'The Flood', the news of King's murder first impacts as an interruption to the award ceremony, just as Newman has started his speech in which he offers outspoken support in the forthcoming presidential race for Eugene McCarthy. The brief impersonation of Paul Newman (albeit from a distance, as those seated at the Sterling Cooper table 'need binoculars' to see him) is, for *Mad Men*, a unique and uniquely awkward moment of re-enactment, soon cut short by a muffled voice from the crowd asking the actor: 'Do you know, Mr Newman, sir, that Martin Luther King is dead, sir? What have you got to say'? The decision to 'take ten minutes to talk out this terrible event' before resuming 'festivities' sticks very close to events as they transpired: Newman was shocked, people rushed to make phone calls and yet the evening's scheduled programme resumed ten minutes later, albeit in a more sombre mood.[10] (The ceremony's resumption is not dramatized, though it is mentioned later.)

Further details of the assassination emerge from a radio bulletin, which interrupts Ginsberg's date. As the report plays (at a higher volume probably than it would have done in reality, so as to render it audible) there is a jump cut from Ginsberg looking shocked to a high angle wide shot of the diner: the others eating there are exclusively white, but as the news of the attack by 'an unknown assailant' in Memphis breaks, black staff members emerge, mute and stunned, from the kitchen. Exemplifying the awkward narrativization of King's assassination from a white perspective, the kitchen workers remain mute and the black experience instead becomes the collective, universal experience as it is Ginsberg who voices the diners' disbelief at the news when he exclaims, 'they *had* to do it'. Ginsberg's stress here is odd, the 'they' presumably being his fellow white Americans, unless it is that, as a Jew, he is somehow distancing himself from 'them'. Otherwise, this is yet another instance of the white saviour eliciting sympathy and understanding for the racial 'other'.

Civil unrest following King's assassination is not, in 'The Flood', confined to the South and arrives in New York City as Abe, Peggy's photo-reporter boyfriend, leaves the awards ceremony to go and photograph the looting and tension in Harlem. Later, Don drives home with his kids through the same streets and worries for the Rosens' safety in Washington. The tone of these scenes depicting the effect of King's death on *Mad Men*'s white community is complicated; Abe is evidently excited at the prospect of going to Harlem still 'in a tuxedo', while Henry Francis admits to Betty when he returns home that accompanying Mayor Lindsay 'was exhilarating'. Don's brief drive through Harlem is interesting in a different way in that, alongside the Newman impersonation earlier in the episode, the sequence provides another rare moment of awkwardness. Represented through a close-up of the car reddened by the flames outside, Don and the kids look out towards the streets, but the car glides along in the strangely dreamy manner of a stationary car in front of a moving backdrop on an old Hollywood studio stage. It might be too much to suggest that the episode's instances of technical maladroitness (this driving and the re-enactment of Newman) are pieces of meta-meta-commentary on 1960s' racism, but the thought did cross my mind as they are anomalous; whether conscious or not, *Mad Men* is always more successful at conveying the impact of historical events on its characters when those events are observed *mediated* and from a distance. The awkwardness continues through standard meta-commentary the following day as Dawn, Don's black secretary and at this point the only African-American employee, looks bemused when Joan hugs her and offers her condolences, Peggy's estate agent has the canny idea (which backfires) to go in with an offer on the apartment of 'five thousand under . . . and let the TV news do the rest', and Don's son Bobby tells a black cinema worker, as he is about to watch *Planet of the Apes* for a second time: 'everyone likes to go to the movies when they're sad'.

The narrative integration of external crises is conventionally, as here, reflexive and visible; differences are not elided. The interesting consistency of some characters' responses to such crises serves to emphatically reassert the dominance of narrative over events and so likewise underscore the distinction between fact and fiction. Roger Sterling's response to transformative events, for example, is to become uncharacteristically contemplative, whereas in Don Draper they prompt episodes of existential anxiety, in the case of 'The Flood', taking the form of an extended rumination on fatherhood. The evening after King's death, his second wife, Megan, has just chastised Don for not 'being there' for Sally when his daughter needs him.

Don confesses, 'I only ever wanted to be the man who loves children, but from the moment they're born, that baby comes out and you act proud and excited, hand out cigars, but you don't feel anything'. As he continues, now in close-up (and having winced at remembering his 'difficult childhood'), he tells Megan: 'You want to love them, but you don't'. For Don Draper fatherhood (like the series' representation of race) is performative; he re-enacts the enactment of genuine fatherliness, an apt incarnation of the arch, self-consciously choreographed ways in which real events are treated in *Mad Men*, as if the wider series, like Don's contemplating on of fatherhood, recognises the events' authentic impactfulness and endeavours to re-evoke it, while at the same time knowing it will perennially remain one step removed from it. This is frequently the poignancy that accompanies the watching of *Mad Men*, that its rendition of history is perfect, but detached. Like being Don Draper, maintaining its pristine 'truthiness' is such a strain.

Symbiosis between Don and 'big history' permeates the series. In her discussion of race in the episode 'The Crash' (Season 6:8), Linda Beail observes that the 'dishevelled black woman' who breaks into Don and Megan's apartment when the kids are there alone not only serves as a device 'to reference white middle-class fears of black crime and violence in 1968' but also as 'one of the many doppelgangers for Don Draper. A grifter, claiming a false identity, using deceit and charm to gain access to people or wealth in order to survive' (Beail, 2015b: 249–250). Beail quotes Ta-Nehisi Coates when he remarks that 'Don Draper is, in the parlance of old black folks, passing' (250); he, as Hollis the lift operator says of Marilyn Monroe, 'hide(s) in plain sight'. Of course, as viewers have known since Season 1, 'Don Draper' is not Don Draper at all, but Dick Whitman, having assumed the dead Draper's identity in Korea. Don is therefore perpetually inauthentic, a performative fantasy figure playing at being an advertising 'creative', a duality that goes some way towards explaining why each real historical crisis precipitates in him a (fictive) personal collapse: Don's grasp of reality is tenuous and his trauma stems from the real historical trauma of the Korean War. The 'falling man' of the title sequence may be an elliptical homage to those who jumped from the World Trade Center towers on '9/11', but he is also Don on the verge of crashing out before just managing to hold himself together.

The extent of Don's masquerade emerges at the end of the first season in 'Nixon vs. Kennedy'. In response to the mini crisis of a news bulletin declaring that John Kennedy is narrowing Nixon's early lead (Sterling Cooper had worked on Nixon's campaign), Pete Campbell once more goes through a box, which, unbeknownst to Don, had been sent to him but which Pete had intercepted. The box contains some possessions belonging to Dick Whitman, the real Don Draper, and had been delivered by Dick's half-brother, Adam. The next day, Nixon's defeat confirmed, Pete goes into Don's office brandishing the box that he has kept at home – a crude blackmailing tool for getting Don to reconsider him for the role of Head of Accounts Services. The minute Pete is out of his office, Don rips open the box. Over an urgent zoom into his back, the sound of a jeep rises, heralding the start of the first of two flashbacks to Korea and revelation of his suppressed identity. In this war scene, Dick Whitman arrives at a lonely posting and meets his Commanding Officer and the man whose persona he later steals: Don Draper. Later in the episode, as the prelude this time to a second extended and more intense flashback, Pete, not content with the news that he is, after all, to be Head of Accounts, feels compelled to tell Bert Cooper everything he knows: that 'Donald Draper is not who he says he is . . . he is a deserter at the very least and who knows what else'. A pause ensues as Bert, eccentrically shoeless, shuffles quietly around from his desk towards Pete. 'Mr Campbell, who cares?' he repeats thrice, 'This country was built and run by men with worse stories'. In the second flashback, Dick Whitman (digging a trench) and the real Draper come under heavy bombardment but think they have survived until Dick drops his lighter on the ground, triggers an explosion and Don dies.

Comparisons have been made between Don's repressed memories and those of Tom Rath (Gregory Peck) the eponymous *Man in the Gray Flannel Suit* in Nunnally Johnson's 1956 screen adaptation of Sloan Wilson's emblematic 1955 bestseller. Like Dick Whitman/Don Draper, Rath is traumatised by his wartime experiences of the Italian campaign of 1944–1945. Rath is also harbouring a secret: that he fell in love with an Italian woman who later bore his child. Following the explosion at the end of the second flashback, Dick Whitman swaps identity tags with the dead Don Draper and with that act kills off his old self. An edit from the flashback to the new 'Don Draper' on his regular commuter train home again recalls Tom Rath, whose flashbacks occur during his commute out of New York City. Don (in another gesture towards Gregory Peck) puts on his trilby and with it puts the lid on his unwelcome memories of the old era of Rath, Nixon and Eisenhower. As Polan observes, *Mad Men*'s Don Draper 'is shown to be on the wrong side of history', having had his 'conversion of identity' long before the transition to the 1960s and the new Kennedy era (Polan, 2013: 43). In 'Nixon vs. Kennedy', Don Draper arrives home in time to see a snippet of Nixon's concession speech and with that enters the 1960s.

As the suited man of the title sequence, Don's masquerade is superficially successful as he has seemingly reinvented himself and loosened the chains of history. Each historical crisis to impinge on *Mad Men*, however, in turn precipitates in Don a personal crisis that instead suggests that he finds it impossible to shake off the past and reinvent himself. In 'The New Girl' (Season 2:5) there is a flashback to when Don paid Peggy a hospital visit after she has given birth to the baby she gave up for adoption. Don's advice to Peggy is to do what he has done, to 'Get out of here and move forward. This never happened. It will shock you how much it never happened'. He, though, cannot heed his own advice and 'cares' more than Bert Cooper about his fraudulent identity, and certainly more than he wishes to let on. One of the key themes of *Mad Men* is 'the contradiction between appearance and reality' (Beail, 2015a: 5) and Don is the series' talismanic reminder that the present cannot shake off the past, as each critical historical moment in turn prompts an internalised emergency, as he repeatedly re-enacts the impossibility of leaving history behind, an anxious tension that extends to his attachment to his grey flannel suit into the 1960s.

To return to the notion that *Mad Men* constructs and operates across a dialectic between a linear historical trajectory and its dramatisation: if Don Draper personifies the desire to *forget* or redraft official history, the media (and specifically the primary archival material) through which that history is relayed, is the series' symbol of *remembrance* – the verification of that past and the embodiment of history's intransigence. In her discussion of *Mad Men's* fashions, Mabel Rosenheck draws on Pierre Nora's distinction between *history* and *memory*, 'history' being the official timeline or the 'authoritative accounts of what happened', and 'memory' how individuals lived through and recalled that timeline (2013: 162). The simple divide between 'history' and 'memory' is one that *Mad Men* problematizes, endlessly revisiting the liminal boundary between drama and fiction on the one hand and archive and fact on the other, not in order to reaffirm their smooth symbiosis but rather to draw out their perpetually live and agitated binary interaction. Don, the wilful amnesiac, represents the desire to suppress 'memory' and to sever ties with his own 'history' in order to rewrite it. But, just as Hamlet hopes that 'foul deeds will rise, though all the world o'erwhelm them to men's eyes' (Act 1.2), Don's conscience and unconscious are repeatedly caught out by the 'big' events along *Mad Men's* historical chronology. From Kennedy's narrow victory in 1960, to his death in 1963, to the assassination of Martin Luther King Jr and the 1969 Apollo moon landing (in the immediate aftermath of which Bert Cooper dies, thereby depriving Don of his protector), Draper is destabilised by history, a destabilisation which frequently takes the form of the resurfacing of unwanted memories and emotions. Don forever treads the series' fault-line between the immovability of the past, the recognition that *things happened* and historical re-enactment, with all the potential for revision and excision that brings. *Mad Men's* re-enactment of history, as outlined previously, is frequently praised for its 'authenticity' and 'accuracy', but its *too* perfect, *too* pristine *mise-en-scène* masks residual tensions. Not only are there very few anachronisms in *Mad Men*, but there is very little that is *old*. Most homes, most offices are made up of collections of old and new pieces of furniture, as only technology really has to 'move with the times', but here the past is suppressed. The present in *Mad Men* is authentically, but, like Don, only superficially, perfect. Bad news, the crises and momentous events of history, disrupt the drama's poise and literally puncture its flawless surface, for archival television images from the 1960s might possess some vestiges of nostalgia and they can certainly be dramatic, but they are rarely pretty.

Diegetic television sets in *Mad Men* – bulky, veneered boxes with thick curved screens yielding grainy, imperfect images – evoke the past through 'materiality' (De Groot, 2016: 89). As de Groot explains (before going on to discuss smoking in *Mad Men*), material objects in historical work 'seem to provide a way of moving between the past and the present' although ultimately they serve merely 'to demonstrate the unknowability of the past and its strange presence in the present' (89). Objects and bodied 'artfully draw attention to the ethical and ontological gap between then and now', de Groot argues, while carrying the burden of the knowledge that such closure is 'impossible' (89). De Groot's conceptualisation of the object or person who aids the transition between past and present finds its ultimate expression in

Mad Men in the series' deployment of television sets, which are generally obtrusive and visually dominant, representative of an era when 'more than half of American homes installed a television set and the basic mechanisms of the network oligopoly were set in motion' (Spigel, 1988: 11). Spigel pursues the idea that, as it entered the home, television led to 'the theatricalization and spectacularization of domestic space' (12), that it eradicated the distance between domestic and outside domains and, quoting from a general readership book from 1950, provided 'a form of "going places" without even the expenditure of movement' (15). And yet, in *Mad Men's* 1960s, televisions feel more Sirkian: they prompt (as does the delivery of Carey's television set in Douglas Sirk's *All That Heaven Allows* [1955]) tense introspection, they transfix, curtail movement and bring characters (especially Don) reluctantly back into the domestic or work space and remind them of the dullness or fraught-ness of the here and now. Television also brings reminders of the dangers as well as the freedoms of the world beyond the confines of the domestic space. They do, as Spigel suggests of the 1950s, bring 'to the home a vision of the world which the human eye itself could never see', though the 'perfection of human vision through technology' (Spigel, 1988: 35) also brings with it access to a world that appeared threatening and uncertain. Just before being summoned by Betty to pick up the kids, Don is at home watching the rioting in Washington DC the night Martin Luther King died; news images are graphically beamed into his apartment via dra-matic colour images of the capital engulfed in flames, their orange literally bleeding into and threatening Don's dark and tidy interior. Spigel writes of how the post-war television set 'would seem to hold an ideal place here because it was a "window on the world" which could never look back' (Spigel, 1988: 34). In fact, the actual and implied figures on *Mad Men's* television screens (in the form of news anchors, reporters, presidents, or voices narrating upsetting actuality footage) often break the fourth wall, compelling their viewers to take notice of the dangers, trauma and chaos portrayed in the archival images. Television in *Mad Men* brings with it crisis not escapism, hence Don's often pointed interaction with it.

Mad Men's implicit contention is that live, breaking television news coverage offers access, albeit mediated, to the events it conveys. When, as Abe leaves the advertising awards ceremony to see first-hand the eruption of Harlem, he is head-ing up town to experience the news *un*mediated. The repeated use of the live bulle-tin mimics the act of watching undigested, as yet unassimilated, events unfold; with television's indexical link to the truth, comes chaos and instability: what will hap-pen next and how will lives be changed by this? In this way, the series mimics the experience of the collective experience of the 'average' US citizen (whether as part of an actual or a virtual group) learning about events for the first time. With the col-lective act of watching the decade's big formative news stories, 'real' history became personal, became part of life and sometimes fictional drama become part of 'real' history, as when Henry Francis crosses over from his fictional marriage to Betty to accompanying the real Mayor Lindsay on his visit to Harlem. Although *Mad Men* is probably not what most critics would think of as 'historiophoty', Hayden White's term to describe 'the representation of history and our thought about it in visual images and filmic discourse' (White, 1988: 1193), it does nevertheless provide – with the diegetic television at its core – a historiographical inquiry in images. *Mad Men* is careful not to simply confuse the boundaries between truth and fiction and the diegetic role of television is frequently central to this.

One crucial factor is the sets' physicality, that they are always diegetically present, their archival images never becoming full-screen, a framing that would elide the differences between their retro contours and the programme's 21st-century retrospective dramatisation. The physical presence of these television sets is, in part, a performative 'textual gesture' that announces *Mad Men*'s status *as* television,[11] just as, simultaneously, one effect of the diegetic television sets' conspicuousness is to draw even more attention to the historicity of the crises they relay. The diegetic televisual image is generally incorporated in one of three ways: almost full-screen with its casing still discernible; slightly smaller within the frame, with more set and surroundings captured as well; shot straight on, central or to the side of frame but taking up roughly half of the screen's surface area. The last is generally used for when characters are actively engaged in watching television. There are also examples of televisions being on as background, when the *mise-en-scène* is generally more cluttered, with characters, furniture (and dialogue) obscuring its image and sound, although this is not usually the way in which breaking news is relayed (an exception being the ignored first bulletin to announce the attempt on John Kennedy's life, discussed in the second half of this chapter). Television in *Mad Men* is the bridge to the verifiable past, watching it an act of authentication, as history becomes insinuated into the drama's collective consciousness.

In *Camera Lucida* Roland Barthes asks:

> Is history not simply that time when we were not born? I could read my non-existence in the clothes my mother had worn before I can remember her. There is a kind of stupefaction in seeing a familiar being dressed *differently*.
>
> *(Barthes, 1981: 71)*

This process of looking at history and 'seeing the familiar being dressed differently' is complicated significantly in *Mad Men* as real and 'familiar' television archive (within living memory for some viewers) is firstly shown on and through television, then 'dressed *differently*' as it is watched by characters impersonating those who had watched the bulletins at the time before they became archive. The televised archive in *Mad Men* goes through three degrees of separation: firstly, the real mediarised 'national events' provide 'experiences of shared grief that can help knit generations together' (Frew and White, 2013: 2), then, transposed to the fictional domain of *Mad Men*, fictional characters mimic the reactions of the citizens of history who lived through those original crises, before, finally, millennial audiences vicariously experience the imaginative creation of those same 'flashbulb memories' enacted by *Mad Men*'s fictional characters as they '[weave] together . . . personal history with traumatic, public events' (Godbey, 2012: 228). *Mad Men*'s past *is* a foreign country where they do things differently, and in spite of – or maybe *because* of – its assiduous, defiant authenticity, this multi-layered, multi-mediarised imaging brings home the 'wroughtness' (De Groot, 2016: 91) and constructedness of its historical representation. *Mad Men* possesses a ubiquitous reflexivity. It is neither the equivalent of a documentary, nor is it *The Crown* (Netflix, 2017) or *Chernobyl* (HBO, 2019); it is not *about* history, a dramatization *of* historical events, but a fictional series *situated alongside* and *enlivening* history, which would otherwise remain remote.

In a chapter concerning his past television history productions such as *The World at War*, Jeremy Isaacs cites executive producer David Elstein's comment that, while historians 'present the evidence they have accumulated, weigh it, and reach conclusions based on it', television history 'is simply unable to handle material in that way, because the audience cannot be expected to keep several conflicting pieces of evidence in mind' (Isaacs, 2004: 42). *Mad Men*, being drama and not 'television history', is able to keep these multiple, conflicting strands 'in mind'; its 'history' is an amalgam of several perspectives across different genres and different eras, as history is filleted to produce complex, often dialectical and seldom neatly resolved arguments. Vivian Sobchack argues that

> Forrest Gump — the character, not the film — denies the hermeneutic necessity (perhaps even the hermeneutic possibility) of understanding the significance of that 'larger' temporal spread we live and narrativize socially (rather than individually) as 'History' or 'histories'.
>
> *(Sobchack, 1996: 2)*

The characters in *Mad Men* (being more than cyphers or palimpsests) are given greater historical awareness than this, though their history's full hermeneutic possibility is constructed around them.

Mad Men both inhabits and sets itself apart from history; its 'greatness' (to borrow from Georg Lukács's praising of Walter Scott and the 19th century historical novel) lies in its 'capacity to give living human embodiment to historical-social types', to render in 'typically human terms', to make 'tangible' 'great historical trends' and to put that *embodiment*, that bold bodily *occupation* of history 'at the centre of the representation of reality' (Lukács, 1981: 34–35). The focus, as Lukács saw it, of the historical novel remained the 'objective *outer* world'; the 'inner life of man . . . his feelings and thoughts' only made 'manifest' when in 'visible interaction with objective, outer reality'; it is only via a committed integration of the personal into the universal, the internal into the external experience, that 'great epic and drama' can give 'a *total picture* of objective reality' (103). In his discussion (and demolition) of 'the modernist event', Hayden White soon outlines how more recent works of 'historical metafiction' such as Truman Capote's *In Cold Blood* (1965), Norman Mailer's *The Executioner's Song* (1979) or Oliver Stone's *JFK* 'differ crucially from those of their generic prototype — the nineteenth-century historical novel' (White, 1996: 18). For White the contractual obligation of the historical novel to its reader was, despite the 'interference' between 'imaginary events' and the 'concreteness of reality', to 'distinguish between real and imaginary events, between "fact" and "fiction", and therefore between "life" and "literature"' (18). Conversely, the 'new genres' usher in 'the dissolution of the event as a basic unit of temporal occurrence' and thereby threaten 'the distinction between realistic and merely imaginary discourse' (18). The result, 'as Gertrude Himmelfarb tells us, is "History as you like it"', the treatment of 'an historical *event* as if there were no limits to what could legitimately be said about it' (19). The blurring of fact and fiction which White finds so disagreeable in *JFK* brings 'under question the very principle of objectivity as the basis for which one might discriminate between truth on the one side and myth, ideology, illusion, and lie on the other' (19) and 'undermines the very notion of "fact" informing traditional realism' (18).

Within the parameters of White's argument, *Mad Men* is more closely aligned to the historical novel than to *JFK*, and yet, however 'big' the events and crises referenced and lived by its characters, history ultimately remains incidental to its dramatic narrative as storylines continue on through and past even the most 'holocaustal' events,[12] ultimately remaining unaltered by them as opposed to integrated with them. As with the audible but fleeting radio bulletin about the Cuban Missile Crisis in *A Single Man* (Tom Ford, 2009), or Margaret Thatcher's attendance at a party at the house of Gerald Fedden in Alan Hollinghurst's novel *The Line of Beauty* (2004), the 'incidentalisation' of history in *Mad Men* does not bring with it 'the dissolution' of the event or the elision of the differences between 'fact' and 'fiction'. *Mad Men*'s fictional characters come up against and get engrossed in factual events; the difference, however, between Scott's *Waverley* novels and *Mad Men* is that, while the latter's characters are touched by and watch history unfold, they do not inhabit or make interventions into it. The sense of an ongoing developmental narrative that overrides history is very strong; equally powerful is the sense that history has happened and is not there to be changed or messed about with. *Mad Men*'s treatment of archival materials is precise, even rigid – it is significant, for example, that news footage is not projected full screen but is instead transmitted on diegetic television sets whose frames literally mark out the boundary between 'fact' and 'fiction'. On the rare occasions when characters do inhabit history or, vice versa, when real people are fictionalised, as Paul Newman is in 'The Flood', the clumsiness of such episodes rather telegraphs their very out-of-place-ness. Facts almost always happen elsewhere: on television, on the radio, recounted in the newspapers; so, when Abe and Henry vacate the fictional diegetic space, we do not pursue them into some smudgily 'metafictional' re-enactment.

In Dealey Plaza, Every Day is 22 November 1963: 'The Grown Ups', repetition and the death of JFK

The death of John F. Kennedy in Dallas on 22 November 1963 is *Mad Men*'s most notable footnote, evoked in 'The Grown Ups' (Season 3:12). An inherently and quintessentially diachronic event whose cultural meaning and significance has altered over time, the assassination was, for the US at least, the defining moment of the 1960s whose repercussions resonated globally, politically and culturally. Its 'incidentalisation' within the context of *Mad Men*, therefore, is ironic, and offers the most profound test of the series' narrative strategy with regards to historical events. 'The Grown Ups' is *Mad Men*'s ultimate duet between history and narrativization and its quintessential lesson in 'approximation'. In response, the following analysis, in a demonstration of the mechanics of 'approximation', pursues a deliberately discursive pattern in which the discussion oscillates between narrative (how the episode enacts 'incidentalisation') and the metaphorical depository of subsequently acquired information about the assassination (the history, the conspiracies, the Zapruder footage, cultural responses to it, re-enactments and commemorations of it). The latter forms the heady amalgam of history, fact, fantasy, symbolism and emotions that characterises both the commemoration of one of the defining episodes in twentieth-century history and, more broadly, 'approximation'. The dynamic dialectic between the event and its 'incidentalisation' is, in its decontextualization, and yet quintessentially enacts 'approximation' as it is taking shape and as it is experienced by viewers. 'Approximation', as here, comprises largely of details that exist subliminally; not often, though, do they remain quite so literally subliminal as in 'The Grown Ups'.

As Fredric Jameson argues in 'Periodizing the 1960s', it seemed clear (in 1984, when Jameson was writing) that, notwithstanding the realisation that the reality of the Kennedy regime might be quite different, for many

> the assassination of President Kennedy played a significant role in delegitimizing the state itself and in discrediting the parliamentary process, seeming to mark the decisive end of the well-known passing of the torch to a younger generation of leadership, as well as the dramatic defeat of some new spirit of public or civic idealism.
>
> *(1984: 182–183)*

The shooting of the 35th President of the United States is generally perceived to have been not only a tragic event, but a transformative one that marked the transition from one era, one state of consciousness both within the US and more widely, to another; it is commonly framed as a terminus – a point of departure, arrival or severance. Documentaries and books about the events of 22 November 1963 in Dallas, Texas, go by titles such as *The Day the Dream Died*, *The End of Camelot*, *Reclaiming History* and *Farewell America*;[13] whereas JFK himself continues to have the sort of symbolic resonance that prompts Oliver Stone's Richard Nixon, as he looks up at a portrait of him, to muse: 'People look at you and they see who they want to be. They look at me and they see what they are'. 'Even Kennedy's critics', Christopher Lasch wrote on the 20th anniversary of his assassination, 'have to admit that things haven't been the same since he died', for his murder 'still haunts the American soul. . . . No other postwar president has inspired so many people with such hope, whether or not it was justified' (Lasch, 1983: 32). Kennedy is defined by his death, and the assassination is perceived to have altered the course of history – whether, as Jameson argues, by enabling us to mask Kennedy's failures as president, or by permitting speculation that things would have been better had he lived.

Alongside documentaries such as *Virtual JFK: Vietnam if Kennedy had Lived* (Masutani, 2008), which maintains that, had he lived, Kennedy would not have let the Vietnam War escalate as his successor Lyndon Baines Johnson did, many time travel novels have revisited the assassination and speculated on what might have been had the assassination been averted. In one of the more recent of these, Stephen King's 2011 novel, *11.22.63*, something bizarre occurs that tangentially informs this ambivalent nostalgia. In an already very long and detailed novel in which Jake Epping is tasked by his dying friend, Al, to go back in time and stop Lee Oswald from assassinating President Kennedy in order to (as Al writes in his deathbed note) ensure that 'everything changes' (King, S., 2011: 241), the build-up to the momentous day, revolving as it does around Jake's love affair with fellow teacher, Sadie, is so interminably long that it starts to feel as if Jake, in dragging his feet, is after all reluctant to change the course of history. Pleasure in *11.22.63* derives from being able to fantasise that the past could be changed, while living through all its immovable imperfections. In tune with this ambivalence, saving JFK from Oswald's bullets makes the world a worse not a better place in which, 'The great civil rights reforms of the sixties never happened. Kennedy was no LBJ', 'the North Vietnamese armies overran Saigon', Martin Luther King was still assassinated 'a month after the fall of Saigon' and 'George Wallace was elected president' (815). Looking further into the future, in 2005 Maine became part of Canada (810), the globe is subject to persistent earth tremors, 'four of the Japanese islands are gone' (811) and a nuclear reactor 'blew up in Vermont' (812). Stephen King's view of history is rigidly causal; history cannot be altered and repeatedly fights back against attempts to change it.

'The Grown Ups' characterizes the tension between fantasy and history as a dialectic between innocence and experience. As with the series' other incidental events, Kennedy's death, self-evidently, does not for long halt *Mad Men*'s narrative course, although in its powerful suppression of the event's afterlife and metaphoric potency, the episode does nevertheless precipitate the series' most forceful act of historical disavowal. The amount of historical knowledge and accompanying baggage accumulated between 22 November 1963 and November 2009, when 'The Grown Ups' was transmitted, is considerable, and yet it is also liberating that *Mad Men* could remain disingenuously innocent of this. Innocence is a powerful condition. William Blake's *Songs of Innocence* might lack the imaginative force of the accompanying *Songs of Experience*, and yet the two books, the two states are symbiotically linked; on their own would each offer only incomplete views of life and reality. Innocence, the pre-Fall state, is not complete 'goodness', it also carries with it connotations of ignorance, lack of awareness and of not having reached fulfilment, fruition or maturity. Of what, in 'The Grown Ups', are the *Mad Men* characters 'innocent'? Crucially, they are ignorant of the aftermath of the assassination – the official Warren Commission report, the conspiracy theories, subsequent assassinations; they also do not know how Kennedy's presidency came to be viewed; they also, importantly, are unaware of the images of the assassination to emerge soon after, in particular the 26.6 seconds of 8mm home movie footage shot by Dallas dressmaker, Abraham Zapruder, an iconic piece of film that has since cast a long, indelible *cultural* as well as political shadow on the events it captured.

As befits the characters' collective state of 'innocent' unawareness, the assassination narrative is told with slavish authenticity and evolves across the day as characters cluster around television sets to learn the news as if for the first time. 'The Grown Ups', in many respects, forms part of a long tradition of repetitions of the assassination of November 1963, of which there are a multitude, although many of these still find it impossible not to buckle under the strain of knowing what happened next. The mini-series *The Kennedys* (2011), for instance, fantasises that, just moments before his brains are blown out, the President and First Lady reach a point of ecstatic rapprochement, as he pledges to do everything 'to be the man you deserve' while she declares herself to have 'never been so happy in all my life'. *Mad Men* eschews all such schlocky, tragedy-fuelled speculation as it inhabits the assassination from the inside. One corollary of *Mad Men*'s lack of leaden dramatic irony is that it implicitly indulges a very particular form of nostalgia for the assassination as an event which is pleasurable to relive because it remains, as yet, unresolved (and quite possibly unresolvable). I have written before of how familiarity with how the assassination story ends ironically liberates us when watching repeated footage of it, permitting us to fleetingly indulge in alternative endings and suppress the finale we know is coming. The impulse to do this has always felt strongest when reviewing the frames in the Zapruder film immediately prior to the bullet impacting Kennedy's head. The pause between second and third gunshots seems implausibly, temptingly long: Kennedy slumps towards his wife and almost slips out of view. Mad Men offers a twist to the fantasy that maybe this time he will survive.[14] Through its meticulous reliving of how the news broke and its concomitant suppression of all subsequent knowledge of the assassination, 'The Grown Ups' awakens two fantasies: the 'what if?', 'if only' variety that it might turn out differently and the cathartic one of working up to the moment as if for the first time.

In its faithful rendition of 22 November 1963, 'The Grown Ups' invites an extreme form of collective amnesia, especially considering that the Kennedy assassination was one of the most extensively *imaged* as well as *imagined* pre-digital events in history, from the live local news television broadcasts on the day, to the home movies and photographs snapped in Dealey Plaza. To repress knowledge acquired and collated since 22 November 1963 is impossibly perverse – volatile proof that no event is hermetically sealed or immune from re-configuration or re-invention. 'The Grown Ups' wilfully denies its inherent iconic-ness and status as a rebus puzzle by repressing all awareness of the event's afterlife. Unlike Pablo Larraín's *Jackie* (discussed in Chapter 1), into which hindsight is subtly etched, 'The Grown Ups' compels its viewers, if not its characters, to feel the tension between innocence and experience, between conscious recognition and disavowed cognition of this uniquely mysterious and catastrophically violent event that has been repeated multitudinous times.

What Caroline Levine refers to as 'the shock of the banal' (2013: 134) is instrumental in establishing the episode's anticipatory tension and dramatic irony. 'The Grown Ups' opens with a paean to inconsequentiality as Pete Campbell huddles in his overcoat on a sofa as the Sterling Cooper office finds itself without heating. Pete is summoned by Lane Pryce, the company's British finance officer, attired in a

FIGURE 3.1 The first CBS bulletin, 22 November 1963 in 'The Grown Ups' *Mad Men*

pale grey three-piece suit, plaid scarf and black leather gloves while sipping from a blue and white cup and saucer like some parody English gent, to be told that Kenny Cosgrove has been preferred to him as the new Head of Accounts Services. After a snappy montage of brief scenes, the heating gets sorted and Duck Phillips (the former Head of Accounts) invites Peggy to spend her lunchbreak with him in his hotel room. In the background is the episode's first television set – muted, showing the soap opera *As the World Turns*. Campbell, who had briefly gone home, goes to relay his disappointing news to Harry Crane, whose television remains permanently on by virtue of him being in charge of television advertising. Considering Harry's role, his studied, unwavering *lack* of attention to what is unfolding on his television set resonates with ironic bathos. In blocking reminiscent of Vincente Minnelli, this dextrously modulated build up to the first news flash about the assassination positions Harry in profile to left of frame behind his desk, Pete in profile to the right, either side of the now semi-audible, prominently stationed television. Dovetailing neatly with the relative 'banality' of Pete's extended moan, the first 12:40 (Central Standard Time) news flash about the attempt on the president's life interrupts the soap opera, as 'CBS Bulletin' comes up, unnoticed, on the television screen. During a heavy sigh from Pete between two lines of dialogue, it is just possible to make out Walter Cronkite's iconic words 'from Dallas, Texas, three shots', before Pete resumes 'there's no future for me here'. In the subsequent pause, the words 'Kennedy's motorcade, downtown Dallas' are audible, before the television briefly slips from view.

The multi-layered texturing of this exchange – with its dual points of focus, one 'banal' yet foregrounded, the other peripheral, though far more momentous – extends into full dramatic irony with the subsequent edit to Don barging into Lane's office brandishing a memo to ask, 'Is this official?' The possibility that this is the moment that news from Dallas reaches Sterling Cooper is soon quashed, however, as Lane confirms that he cannot replace Art Director Salvatore Romano (the subject of the memo). Don offers to walk Lane 'through a delivery schedule' before a cut to Duck in his hotel room watching, we realise from the swift reverse shot, Cronkite's first CBS in-vision bulletin confirming that 'there has been an attempt, as perhaps you know now, on the life of President Kennedy'. Direct interweaving between narrative action and historical events is soon curtailed, though, as Duck, who has been waiting for Peggy to arrive, pulls the television's plug out of the wall and goes to let her in. As the action reverts to Sterling Cooper, Don storms out of Lane's office as his phone rings; Lane's exclamation of 'What?' is maybe the news finally trickling down, although, if it is, the sharp edit back to Harry's office denies the audience the equivocal pleasure of witnessing a character's anagnorisis. The two-shot of Harry and Pete is a little tighter than it had been and the television is still on; this time the image is less ambiguous: behind the curve-stemmed desk lamp Cronkite sits at his desk wearing his heavy-framed glasses, reading papers on his desk. We are willing Harry or Pete to finally pay attention to the omnipresent television, but it is only when others, spear-headed by Don's secretary, Allison, finally tumble into Harry's office to collectively watch the news that the two of them register what is happening and the external news finally penetrates the Sterling Cooper bubble, to the full cathartic relief of *Mad Men* spectators. In an extreme act of *sprezzatura* (for how many millennial viewers would notice the shift from one channel to another?) Allison manually switches channels from CBS's coverage to NBC's as she asks: 'Is he dead?', a question, as there is then a cut to Don walking into the secretarial pool and an eerie choir of abandoned, ringing telephones, that is left hanging.

FIGURE 3.2   Allison, Pete, Harry and others watching NBC coverage of Kennedy's assassination in 'The Grown Ups', *Mad Men*

As Don enquires, 'what the hell is going on?', the frenzied chorus of unanswered phones suddenly falls silent. The sequence concludes with a cut to further NBC coverage on a different diegetic television set (this time the Drapers') as Frank McGee interrupts the live studio coverage to deliver the flash from the Associated Press (intercut with Betty watching anxiously and Carla, the family's African-American maid, arriving home with the Draper children) that two priests confirm President Kennedy has died.

The shared televisual moments cut across various locations, mirroring the relatively swift spread of the momentous news of Kennedy's death. The three and a half minutes of screen time from the first CBS bulletin appearing on Harry's television to Betty's tearful 'they say he died' leaves only Peggy, out of the main characters, oblivious to what is going on. This gap in knowledge is significant, for it prizes open the space for 'approximation': as we watch Peggy continuing to be ignorant of the news all her colleagues by this stage in the episode are cognizant of, we not only enjoy the dramatic irony but also inhabit that innocence and reignite the fantasy of the assassination having un-happened. An incredible and oft-cited fact about the assassination was that 68 percent of US residents had heard the news within an hour of the initial broadcast and 92 percent within two. By six o'clock that evening only 0.2 percent of the population had *not* yet heard the news, testament to both the 'overwhelming authority of television during the four days following the assassination' and its 'capacity to unify a national audience' (Simon, 1996: 136, 152) – but also to the medium's shortcomings, as the day Kennedy died also demonstrated how the US networks had been 'ill-prepared and ill-equipped to deal with a breaking story of such enormity' (Knight, 2007: 17). Television cameras were not positioned in Dealey Plaza, where the assassination occurred, although they had been located at the airport, earlier along the parade route and at the Trade Mart, where Kennedy was due to deliver a speech. 'Never again', Simon argues, 'would television be caught without the apparatus to supply important images' (1996: 152), and later that day, convergence between news and image was re-established, with live transmission of Mrs Kennedy, still wearing her blood-stained suit, accompanied her husband's corpse from Andrews Air Force Base to Washington DC, and of Lyndon Johnson being sworn in as President. The reactive liveness of television is captured by *Mad Men* as characters congregate around the same (relative paucity of) grainy, wobbly television images over the 'four-day telethon' (Knight, 2007: 22). As Jane Feuer argues, 'Television *is* live in a way film can never be' and it looks 'more "real" to us than does film' (Feuer, 1983: 13).

The bathetic contrast between Betty and Carla crying and smoking in unison on the sofa and the next image of Peggy in bed asking Duck (also lighting up) if he gave her a hickey 'because I get questions from my mother', could hardly be more extreme. Duck them claims to have been 'distracted' by a report he had been watching before she arrived and re-plugs the television.

Marita Sturken, like Feuer, remarks on television's centrality to the solidification of collective memory when she comments: 'When an image coincides with traumatic events of historical rupture, it plays a central role in the construction

FIGURE 3.3 Walter Cronkite on CBS announcing the death of President Kennedy, in 'The Grown Ups', *Mad Men*

of national meaning' (Sturken, 1997: 26). As testament to this, the diegetic set in Duck's hotel room fires up again in symbolic synchronicity with Walter Cronkite putting on his heavy black spectacles, touching his upper lip with his thumb and shifting the tenor of his voice slightly from conversational ad-libbing to announce-ment mode in order to read the most familiar, most frequently recycled soundbite of television's coverage of that day: 'From Dallas, Texas the flash, apparently official: President Kennedy died at 1 P.M. Central Standard Time'. It is at this moment, in the decorous hiatus between Duck and Peggy's responses to the news, that the alignment of hitherto misaligned points of view finally occurs – an alignment, moreover, marked by the replaying of the day's most iconic, most often repeated news broadcast.

In 'Kindergarten', under the subheading 'Rhetoric of the Too Late', Franco Moretti analyses why it is that certain scenes in novels 'move' us to tears. 'Point of view is grounded in a symbolic hierarchy' and 'Tears are always the product of *powerlessness*' (Moretti, 1983: 161) he writes, coming at a time in a novel when one character, hitherto in the dark over something, finally acquires the knowledge oth-ers and the reader have already acquired, only to realise that such knowledge comes 'too late'. The tears therefore emanate from 'two mutually opposed facts: that it is clear how the present state of things should be changed – and that change is *impos-sible*' (162). The orchestration of the first phase of the assassination's narrativization in *Mad Men* culminates in Cronkite's near-tears, Peggy's disbelief and, in the next scene, Margaret Sterling's profusion of tears as she selfishly (but understandably) cries 'it's ruined' as she, clad in the wedding dress she will wear the next day, sits crumpled on the floor in front of her television. The framing of Cronkite's historic announcement on Duck's hotel room set is as full-screen as the replay of actuality footage gets in *Mad Men*: taking up three-quarters of the screen, with only the curved inner frame and the control buttons down the right side completely visible. The reverse framing of Margaret is complementary and completes Moretti's binary; as a low-level camera glides behind her television, looking back out at its diegetic viewer, it returns their gaze and in so doing cements Moretti's idea of poignant, too-late convergence. From this juncture, when the last of *Mad Men*'s central characters discovers what is going on, fictionalised reaction and the day's most familiar, iconic archive are increasingly matched with shock and tears, for instance as the Drapers watch eye-witness Charles Brehm's tears as he recounts seeing Kennedy smiling back at him just as the first bullet struck.

Mad Men's group of characters live the day of Kennedy's assassination as lived, imbued with the 'rhetoric of the too late' and confirming, as they all watch the same coverage, Patricia Mellencamp's observation that it was the looped coverage of the assassination that realised 'television's potential for collective identification – television's democratic dream' (Mellencamp, 1990: 254).[15] Alongside its collectivity, television's 'temporal dimension', suggests Mary Ann Doane, is 'that of an insistent "present-ness" – a "*This-is-going-on*" rather than a "*That-has-been*", a celebration of the instantaneous' (Doane, 1990: 222). As we, the millennial viewer, watch the characters inhabit their 'present-ness' we become ever more acutely sensible to our 'too-late-ness', which interrupts the way in which the catastrophe unfolds. Catastrophes, Doane argues, are inherently televisual – on the 'cusp of the dramatic and the referential' (228), still lacking a shape or an end that would permit them to be analysed or explained. As occurs with each catastrophe (see the discussion in Chapter 2 of '9/11'), a narrative starts to take shape even as the crisis unfolds. The compulsion to establish a continuous sequence of events that gives them structure and cogency is universal, as coherence masquerades as understanding. So, like the tears of Cronkite, the televisualisation of a catastrophe becomes a point of coalescence: between ignorance and knowledge; between continuity and discontinuity; between technology and emotion. Conversely, for the *Mad Men* viewer, the process is one of watching the characters in their state of '*This-is-going-on*' from a perspective (whatever one's grasp on the Kennedy assassination) of '*That-has-been*'; Barbet Schroeder's episode is a masterful example of keeping our double-vision in abeyance and at maintaining a meaningful differentiation between what was known and seen at the time and what has become known or been seen since. There is little discernible hindsight in *Mad Men*, although, over the course of the series, Pete Campbell does offer, as each crisis unfolds, a slightly broader perspective on events than others. It is Pete, for instance, who voices, while watching, on the morning of 23 November, the then Mayor of Berlin, Willi Brandt, offering his condolences, the widely espoused view that, with Kennedy's election, 'it felt for a second as if everything was about to change'. He also, the day after, as he and his wife Trudy watch NBC's slow-motion re-run of Jack Ruby's shooting of Lee Oswald on live television, remonstrates that 'they just stood there. No security, the most wanted man in America' – which is as close as 'The Grown Ups' gets to acknowledging the assassination's afterlife.

A notable aside to the relationship between the twin temporal tracks of innocence and experience, but one pertinent to us as viewers, is how accessible all television archive of that day (or that of any other notable news event) has become.
As the World Turns, the first CBS bulletin and, of course, Walter Cronkite's iconic
announcement, are all readily available on the internet, ensuring that a modern
viewer could closely mimic and piece together the viewing experience of their
1963 counterparts (although the existence of 'David von Pein's JFK Channel' renders this exercise redundant).[16] The dialogue between our privileged instant access
to, among a well-stocked bank of other things, the same archival material watched
in *Mad Men*, produces a dually uncanny effect as we watch characters watching television and maintaining their ignorance of the assassination's afterlife while we have
ready recourse to, should we wish to access it, all of this information and more. The
reason for the Kennedy archive being so extensive is, of course, that his assassination
remains unsolved, meaning that the assassination's '*that-has-been*' afterlife is dominated
by conspiracy theories that proliferated throughout the 1960s and 1970s, largely (but
not exclusively) as a result of the public unavailability, until 1975, of the conspiracy
theorists' ur-text: the Zapruder film. The insistent '*this-is-going-on*' present-ness of
'The Grown Ups' is fuelled by a total, defiant suppression of the most dramatic, most
gruesome 'ocular proof' of Kennedy's death; of all the elements to bring 'approximation' to bear on 'The Grown Ups', the marginalisation of Zapruder is the most
significant – and it could have been easy to include reference to it had the episode's
action been extended beyond the morning of Kennedy's funeral to encompass CBS
journalist Dan Rather's evocative and controversial 'word picture' account after having seen the iconic home movie footage later on 25 November 1963.[17] Although
conspiracy theories are no longer as compelling as they might once have been (as
Chris Petit admits in his essay film, *Content*, he is 'not that interested in who killed
him, more in the permutations, like a gambler'), Zapruder's footage is still mes-
merizingly horrific and still the quintessential artefact many of us will call to mind
when the assassination is mentioned. Though many falsely remember having seen
the Zapruder as part of the television coverage (Patricia Mellencamp remarks how
'Zapruder's amateur/tourist movie footage was endlessly rerun on television and
scrutinized for clues . . . the horror of Kennedy's assassination was in what we saw'
[1990: 253]), one thing television audiences definitely did *not* 'see' until its first public broadcast in 1975 was Zapruder's 'amateur/tourist movie footage', so absence of
any mention of it in *Mad Men* mirrors the disavowal of the 1960s.

The life cycle of the Zapruder film is roughly as follows. On 22 November 1963
local businessman Abraham Zapruder captured on his Bell and Howell 8mm camera from his vantage point just in front of the Grassy Knoll in Dealey Plaza the
death of President Kennedy. Unlike many of the other photographs and home
movies taken at the scene, the film was not at the time made public. On the morning of November 23 CBS lost the bidding war for it to *Life Magazine*, who made
three copies, one for themselves, one for Zapruder and one for the FBI. Bootlegged
duplicate copies of the film circulated and were certainly readily available after

lawyer Jim Garrison subpoenaed the home movie film in 1969 (Garrison, played by Kevin Costner, is the protagonist of Oliver Stone's *JFK*). Then, in 1973, technician Robert Groden created an enhanced version, the copy which was shown on Geraldo Rivera's *Goodnight America* on 6 March 1975, the film's first networked broadcast. Eventually, copies became readily available and now on the internet there are multiple versions. In 2000, $16 million was eventually paid to the Zapruder family for copyright to transfer to Dallas's Sixth Floor Museum.

The Zapruder film's 'absent presence' through the 1960s was a 'kind of 18.3 fps phantasm' that 'lurk[ed] behind' contemporary renditions and accounts of the assassination (Beck, 2005: 186). Despite being 'our nation's first official snuff film' which, as Steve Seid posits, 'in a mere handful of frames, encapsulated the loss of the real' (2004: 32), the viewing experience of 22 November 1963 lacked the *direct* 'horror' of witnessing the second plane crash into the World Trade Center on 11 September 2001. Zapruder's film and conspiracy theories are symbiotically linked; although the official Warren Commission Report into the assassination concluded that Lee Harvey Oswald acted alone, Zapruder's graphic visual evidence is commonly invoked to prove otherwise, namely that JFK was the victim of a conspiracy. On visiting Dealey Plaza when making, *Content*, Chris Petit (born in 1949) feels drawn to reconsidering one of the 'two defining moments' of his childhood (the other having been the Holocaust). Over a series of travelling shots from the uncanny viewpoint of a car driving very slowly along Elm Street, past the picket fence and finally going under the Stemmons Freeway Bridge as did the presidential motorcade, Petit's voiceover ruminates on conspiracy theories and their value. Having established that 'the conspiracy theory becomes a perfect complement to the state of religious lapse, becomes the substitute for lost beliefs' whose 'appeal', despite repeated 'epiphany and revelation', is that it will never reach closure, Petit puts forward his own theory. 'Given that conspiracy is so often fiction', he begins, 'I offer my entirely satisfactory version' which is: fearing 'the church would be rocked to its foundations' if details of sexual scandals involving Kennedy, the second most powerful Roman Catholic in the world after the Pope, were to emerge, the Vatican 'did the necessary, using its Mafia contacts, and Jack became a martyr, reputation intact'. The fictionalism of a conspiracy theory does not stem necessarily from its implausibility, but from its unprovability; so Petit's is just as fictional and plausible as is Santiago Alvarez's theory, put forward in his agitational collage film *LBJ* (1968), that it was LBJ, Kennedy's Vice President and successor, who was behind the murders of John Kennedy, his brother Bobby and Martin Luther King.

The truth remains that, however graphic and tragic the Zapruder footage is, and however confident Christopher Lasch was in 1983 that it 'proved that Oswald's rifle could not have fired so many shots in rapid succession' (1983: 35), it 'proves' nothing beyond the fact of death. In Don DeLillo's *Libra*, retired intelligence analyst, Nicholas Branch, is commissioned by the CIA to write a secret history of the assassination and the 'Six point nine seconds of heat and light' (DeLillo, 1988: 15). 'Let's call a meeting', Branch fantasises, 'to analyse the blur' and 'build theories that gleam like jade idols', that 'follow the bullet trajectories backwards to the lives that occupy the shadows' (15). For DeLillo, as for Petit, each conspiratorial narrativization of the assassination is ultimately, in spite of its grounding in the authenticity of the Zapruder film, an ephemeral fantasy. Endlessly scrutinised, enhanced, blown up, slowed down, each pixel has been used at some point to prove something – or nothing. Considering how laden and pregnant with information it is, the Zapruder film makes for an unlikely palimpsest, used to argue for and against a plethora of theories, yet unable to definitively 'prove' any of them, because to be there for the moment of death is to miss the act of killing, a 'catch-22' that engenders a sort of paralysis around it, a need to obsessively repeat and re-run the 26.6 seconds in the futile hope that just once it might unmask 'what really happened'. 'If you are at all sensitive', Geraldo Rivera had warned his viewers before running the Zapruder film on *Goodnight America*, 'if you're at all queasy, then don't watch the film'; but as John Beck remarks about the close scrutiny of its frames: 'The closer one gets, the more one sees. Or, more accurately perhaps, the more one sees, the less one knows' (Beck, 2005: 185).

One could not, in the 1960s, get close to the Zapruder film, it was excised from collective grief and memory, and excision has persistently haunted narrativizations of the Kennedy assassination. *Mad Men* can be viewed as one extended act of excision and disavowal, fuelled by all the previous acts that preceded it, while the most notable excision of all is the omission from various versions of the Zapruder film of frame 313 – the frame in which Kennedy's head is blown apart. Reputedly, after suffering a nightmare in which he was haunted by a headline in Times Square that read 'See the President's Head Explode!', Zapruder persuaded *Life Magazine* to omit the offending frame from the 29 November 1963 commemorative edition, which it only later reproduced (and later still in bright Eastman Color). The viewing of Zapruder's frame 313 – whether in paused isolation or as part of a moving continuum – is an intensely visceral experience; its excision thereby makes it possible to suppress awareness of many things: pain, violence, macabre fascination, conspiracy. Ultimately, death itself is, if not denied, then veiled or complicated through the omission from assassination narratives of its incontrovertible 'ocular proof'. To cut out the assassination's 'money shot' is an act of radical suturing that sanitises the narrativization of Kennedy's life history as well as death. Official early biographies of JFK (by insiders such as Ken O'Donnell, Arthur Schlesinger, Theodore White and Theodore Sorensen) skirted over the assassination,[18] and Jackie Kennedy sanctioned only an anodyne, diluted version of the 'Camelot' years in her published interview with White for *Life Magazine* on 6 December 1963 (whereas White's notes, published after Jackie Kennedy Onassis's death and the source for Pablo Larraín's *Jackie* are far more graphic).[19]

In commemorations of JFK the excision of frame 313 and the gruesomeness of death is telling. The official Warren Commission version of the assassination most likely performed the original and ultimate excision, flowing into the revisionist versions of the JFK story proffered Boston's John F. Kennedy Presidential Library and Museum where (at least when I visited in 2012) the events of 22 November 1963 are marked only by five small monitors along a dark, empty corridor each running a snippet of archive, including the first CBS bulletin and Cronkite's choked announcement that the President was dead, the aftermath of the shooting in Dallas and the funeral. Having received the official endorsement of the Kennedy family, Boston's museum tells the authorised story, jumping from life to legacy. A very different museum experience is granted by the Sixth Floor Museum in Dallas, a site-specific, assassination-focused museum situated on the floor of the Texas School Book Depository on the corner of Elm and Houston Streets from where Oswald allegedly shot the three bullets that killed Kennedy. The Sixth Floor Museum's attitude towards the assassination is surprisingly contradictory; its discourse is, as Vågnes Øyvind observes, 'troubled by the pressure to visualise' (2011: 128), while it has also 'ultimately contributed to transforming the site into something like an assassination theme park' (129), making the presence of key excisions from the assassination narrative all the more unexpected. Owners of the Zapruder film, the museum runs the footage continuously on a loop, but each replay stops just short of the 'head shot' of frame 313, before fading out and starting again. A museum dedicated to the commemoration of a death that it does not visualise is heavily ironic. Dramas have likewise acted ambivalently towards Kennedy's blood. Whereas, despite the relative authenticity of its assassination re-enactment, David Greene's counter-factual *The Trial of Lee Harvey Oswald* (1977) minimises the bloodiness, the 1980s mini-series, *Kennedy*, becomes unexpectedly sacrilegious as its hoses Jackie (Blair Brown) and her replica pink Chez Ninon suit in Kennedy's blood, much more in keeping it has to be said with Lady Bird Johnson's remark that 'one of the most poignant sights' of the day was 'that immaculate woman, exquisitely dressed, and caked in blood' (quoted in Lubin, 2003: 196).

The assassination's 'incidentalisation' in *Mad Men* is another quasi-excision. Before it is fully comprehended quite how *un*-incidental the assassination was to become, the *Mad Men* episode proceeds to make it both incidental to the narrative and yet more symbolically entwined with it. Paradoxically, as confusion escalates, the more direct its impact on the characters and their lives becomes. When, for example, characters congregate in the hotel kitchen during Margaret Sterling's wedding dinner to follow the news of Lee Oswald following his arrest, the sequence's *mise-en-scène* goes beyond the immediate reference point of the JFK assassination as it encompasses an oblique premonition of a future catastrophe, namely the assassination in 1968, in the kitchen of the Ambassador Hotel, Los Angeles, of Robert Kennedy, President Kennedy's brother. The pairing of the tenuous allusion to Robert Kennedy's assassination and the audibility of Oswald's iconic soundbite as he proclaims himself to be 'just a patsy', neatly exemplifies the tussle between history and drama that runs throughout *Mad Men*, their conflicting narratives and their divergent imperatives, many of which viewers will pick up. The symbolic complexity of Margaret's wedding scene is apt because it soon becomes clear that this is the episode's crossroads moment, the moment when the balance tips towards the fictional narrative and away from history. Betty Draper, for example realises conclusively at the subdued wedding dinner that she has fallen out of love with Don and is falling in love with Henry Francis, her future second husband. Before leaving the nuptial celebrations, Betty visits the washroom. When she emerges, both Don and Henry are in the hallway and both look over at her; both meet her distant gaze and presume she is looking at them. As she walks towards them, she goes to her husband, but this has been her moment of choice and we sense that she will eventually take the road 'less traveled' and choose Henry.

Back in his hotel room after his daughter's 'disastrous' wedding, Roger Sterling calls colleague and confidante Joan Holloway at home, and what ensues is a conversation highly relevant to how the drama enforces the incidentalisation of history:

ROGER: Hey, she (Margaret) pulled through, I pulled through, we all pulled through. I can't believe how quiet it is out there.

JOAN: Not everywhere. Greg just called. He's working the night shift at ER. People are still getting sick, car accidents are happening, babies are being born.

ROGER: I'm glad he's not home. I had to talk to you. [Silence]. Nobody else is saying the right thing about this.

JOAN: My god, you're really upset.

ROGER: What's that about?

JOAN: Because there's nothing funny about this.

What is Roger 'really upset' about? That life still goes on, even in the face of tragedy? Whatever the reason for this cryptic exchange, it offers a neat illustration of what Beck touches on, namely that the assassination seemed clearer and could more easily be *felt* before much was known about it. Just after Roger and Joan have said their goodbyes, there is a cut to live television coverage (the morning of 24 November) of Jack Ruby's murder of Lee Harvey Oswald in the basement of Dallas police station. Betty's decision to leave Don for Henry is eventually enacted in synchrony with and, in many ways, becomes inherently symptomatic of, this second public murder. She is watching television while Don is in the kitchen; the image switches to NBC's live coverage as Ruby fires at Oswald at point-blank range; hearing her cry of 'Oh my God!' (dovetailed with the reporter's commentary, 'He's been shot. He's been shot. Lee Oswald has been shot') Don rushes in; 'What's going on?' Betty asks rhetorically, but as Don goes to comfort her, she shrugs him off brusquely and tells him to 'please, let me alone'. Their daughter, Sally, then comes in and asks, 'what happened?', which has just become appreciably harder to answer. Again, television is important. One small aside to their marital disintegration is that Don and Betty prefer different television channels: she watches NBC (which had 'acted on its hunch and cut away from its coverage of the funeral preparations' to cover Oswald at the police station [Knight, 2007: 20]) while he favours CBS.

The following day (November 25, the date of Kennedy's state funeral) roles are reversed as it is Don (asleep on the sofa) who has been glued to the television. Betty comes in to tell him she is 'going out. . . . I need to clear my head'. In fact, she has arranged to meet Henry, which she does – in the bright winter sunlight, leaving Don alone in the introspective interiority of his sitting room oppressed by windows swathed in net curtains. 'Have you thought there are other ways to live?',

Henry asks Betty, assuring her that he can make her happy; then they kiss. Upon her return home Don is (still) watching the funeral preparations in the suffocating suburban gloom. Oswald's death, Ruby's violence, the funereal preliminaries all lend background consequence to her resolution to end their marriage. At the very end of the scene the multiple crises (external as well as internal) are conflated as, with Don leaving the room after Betty has told him 'I don't love you anymore', she, after switching channels, takes his place in front of the television.

Several narrative strands converge and ultimately it takes two globally significant deaths to make sense of the demise of *Mad Men*'s central relationship. In 'Observations on the Long Take', Pier Paolo Pasolini writes about the narrative of death in relation to the assassination and 'the short sixteen-millimeter film of Kennedy's death' (Pasolini, 1980: 3). Though he does not name it, it is Zapruder's film that is, for Pasolini, 'the most typical long take imaginable': subjective and unfinished 'reality as it happens' (3). Reality, Pasolini argues, is captured '*from a single point of view*' and '*always in the present tense*', while the long take is cinema's (or live television's) 'primordial element' (3). Just as basic, unedited 'cinema', for Pasolini, only becomes 'a film' through the splicing together of different points of view (or a '*multiplication of "presents"*' [4]), so the subjective reality of unedited life only acquires narrative structure and meaning through death. However, the simple act of dying itself is not enough: '*Kennedy, dying, expresses himself in his final action*', but 'Like every moment of the language of action, *it requires something more*. It requires systematization' (4) to be understood. As soon as a 'multiplication of presents' is brought together and 'montage intervenes', then 'the present becomes the past' and actions start to acquire meaning. Pasolini concludes by relating these ideas to death, through which comes completeness and knowledge. Until that moment, life, like language, remains 'indecipherable' (6). Alive, we remain 'untranslatable: a chaos of possibilities' (6) so it is only in death, '*which performs a lightning-quick montage of our lives*', that we acquire meaning.

Pasolini was writing in 1967, in the messy limbo of the aftermath of Kennedy's death between the publication in November 1964 of the Warren Commission's 26-volume report on the assassination and later events (such as the assassinations of 1968) which gave it renewed context and meaning. He probably did not imagine that, more than 50 years later, we would still be inhabiting the 'multiplications of presents', obsessively repeating events of unfinished, tantalising blankness with Kennedy's death still unexplained. To subject the events of 22 November 1963 to endless repetition (as occurs in *Mad Men*) is to admit this impasse. In the same year as Pasolini's article was published (and recycling archive footage that was available at the time), Bruce Conner finished his short 13-minute avant-garde found footage film *Report*, which the editors of *October* reference in the issue that contains 'Observations on the Long Take', arguing in a footnote that Conner's film 'in fact illuminates, through its serial structuring of such footage, Pasolini's speculations' (Footnote 2 to Pasolini, 1980: 4) that each 'present', each repetition of the events from a single perspective, postulates 'the relativity of all others, their unreliability, imprecision and ambiguity' (4). In *Report*, a seminal example of 'Kennedy death art' (Tuchman, 1978: 18), repetition and collage-like montage become Conner's motifs for expressing multiple perspectives, but each reiteration in *Report* (especially images that are returned to several times, such as the First Lady smiling broadly from the presidential car, or going to open the ambulance door, or the ecstatic crowd at a bullfight) serves only to annunciate the inability to move beyond the traumatic present. Repetition also, however, brings welcome stasis (part of *Mad Men*'s nostalgia is about not having to yet acknowledge the unresolvedness of an event such as Kennedy's death), as it does in *The Eternal Frame* (1975), a 23-minute film by art collectives Ant Farm and T.R. Uthco structured around a series of site-specific re-enactments of the assassination. Performed and recorded not long after Robert Groden's enhanced copy of the Zapruder film had first been broadcast, *The Eternal Frame* was 'undoubtedly in part as a response to that screening' (Øyvind, 2011: 47). With its repetitions of the moment of death, *The Eternal Frame*, like *Report* and *Mad Men*, does not decipher or bring 'systemisation' to the assassination in the form of narrative understanding, but in terms of its rebirth through media: the reimaging of Kennedy as mythical as well as the emergence of the assassination as spectacle.

In seeking a way to conclude the death–narrative, Pasolini does imagine the film that would be capable of taking us past repetition and '*Rendering the present past*': 'the hypothetical projection one after the other of the various films at FBI headquarters' (Pasolini, 1980: 5). The National Archives, Maryland, house a series of FBI video files, riveting in their repetitiveness and raw fragmentedness, one of which – a short montage film, dating from 1978, which collates together into a sequential narrative the extant archive of Kennedy's journey from Love Field Airport to Parkland Hospital[20] – (in theory at least) equates to Pasolini's 'hypothetical projection' and could (in theory at least) move beyond the nightmarish, stuttering present and 'complete' the act of the Kennedy assassination. Many subjective viewpoints are represented in this crude montage of the available files, from both sides of the presidential limousine, from the road, from the crowd, in black and white and colour and including Groden's enhanced Zapruder footage. However, far from taking us beyond repetition, to watch this compilation is to enter a state of purgatorial unfinishedness; the pieces of footage from that day might present a 'self-authenticating evidentiary basis' as author Josiah 'Tink' Thompson suggests to Errol Morris in his short documentary 'November 22, 1963',[21] but one that has not been definitively 'read', leaving a narrative that remains – for all the 1,000s of classified files released in 2007 – incomplete.

Conversely, *Mad Men* needs to transcend the paralysis of repetition and move its narrative on, but not before a last, audacious, wry reference to the assassination proper. After his terminal argument with Betty the day before, Don leaves for the office on the morning of Monday, 25 November 1963, the date of the state funeral and a day of mourning, Sterling Cooper is officially closed, but when Don arrives, he finds Peggy at her desk working on the artwork for a campaign. Don picks up the storyboard and looks at one final, uncanny repetition, for the images Peggy is working on depict four figures seated in an open-topped limousine. Don says nothing. 'We'll be okay', Peggy assures him, 'doesn't shoot till after Thanksgiving', before she goes to watch some of Kennedy's funeral. Don does not join her – one of only 7 percent of the television-equipped population not to do so. The brief closing shot of the packed episode is of Don in his office, pouring himself a drink, before a final cut to black and the first line of Skeeter Davis's country hit, 'The End of the World': 'Why does the sun go on shining?' With an oblique nod to the way in which the Kennedy assassination has been conceptualized as a terminal end point, this fictional ending reminds us that *Mad Men* occupies an alternative temporal plane and that this, of course, is not the 'end of the world', for not only will the 'sun go on shining', but Peggy will have overhauled the storyboard for the campaign before Thanksgiving. The Kennedy assassination is both imaginatively invasive and incidental; while it remains open and unconcluded, the episode's ending is markedly closed and conclusive, informed and haunted by the broad plethora of disparate elements and references that have illustrated, scrutinised and defined the assassination since it occurred: the documents, the 'long takes', the documentaries, the dramas, the conspiracy theories, the art.

'Approximation' is made by the awareness and knowledge of its viewers. The unrelenting dramatic irony of 'The Grown Ups', its dogged attachment to its state of innocence, to the era of not knowing any of the subsequent myths and theories about Kennedy's death sit in weighty contradistinction to everything we can bring to the episode's viewing. Ours is a double vision as knowledge and disavowal jostle for position. Nearly everything that is known of Kennedy's assassination is missing from 'The Grown Ups', and yet it is not: the archives and depositories of future knowledge and paraphernalia are the episode's spectral presences lurking in its wings. Though absent visually from *Mad Men*, Dealey Plaza, the Texas School Book Depository, the Grassy Knoll, the Stemmons Freeway Bridge haunt its innocent repetitions. As an onlooker to the re-enactments in *The Eternal Frame* observes of Dealey Plaza, 'it's so small' – certainly smaller than it becomes in the imagination. And the picket fence – for any lone-gunman-disbelieving conspiracy theorist, the most likely position from which a sniper could have fired the fatal bullet at Kennedy's head – is very close to the road. Dealey Plaza is spooky and uncanny: small and ordinary; symbolic and resonant. Standing at the site is to evoke both the reality of the event and to inhabit one more re-enactment. I spent three full days in Dallas; in truth, I spent three full days hanging around Dealey Plaza. Looking on as, in the traffic light changes, tourists posed for photographs – smiling, waving, thumbs up – while standing on the X that marks the spot on Elm Street where the limousine was when the president received his fatal wound, I was inhabiting my own long take and multiplication of presents. Moving from vantage point to vantage point, I experienced most of the meaningful points of view of the tight, iconic space; all different but all also hopelessly blurred, except for the position behind the white picket fence from where it felt that even I would have been able to inflict harm on a motorcade crawling by.

The site prompts reverence, but also provokes irreverence: for the video to accompany her 2010 song 'Window Seat', Dallas resident Erykah Badu mimics being shot in Dealey Plaza and falls to the ground on the asphalt near the X; and

Vågnes Øyvind describes a limo tour ('widely regarded as inappropriate' [2011: 179] and no longer available) that for $25 offered tourists a ride from Love Field airport to Parkland Hospital in a Lincoln convertible, following the route of the presidential motorcade, replete with an audio track of cheering crowds and gunfire. Tourists are drawn to 'sites, attractions and events that are linked in one way or another with death, suffering, violence or disaster' (Sharpley and Stone, 2009: 4), and dark tourism – or the desire to visit 'a socially acceptable environment that provides them with an opportunity to construct their own contemplation of mortality' (Frew and White, 2013: 3) – has clear parallels in historical drama. If dark tourism is related to fantasy – that going to the site is morbid but also potentially a catalyst to the development of imaginative scenarios that do not necessarily need that physical proximity to the original event – then those dark places can likewise be revisited via the generation of fictional and hypothetical narratives. In this way, drama functions as another location where our personal memories and fantasies interconnect with historical events.

The display in the corner of the Sixth Floor Museum (boxes in situ, the lower window ajar) replicating Lee Harvey Oswald's vantage point looking down on Dealey Plaza, is somewhere in between. Tourists are not allowed to enter the space, though they can gaze out from an adjacent window at the familiar scene below. As with the absent frame 313 from the Zapruder projection, decorum sits shoulder to shoulder with morbidity. The second chapter of DeLillo's *Libra* opens with Branch, in his fifteenth year of labour, contemplating his room of 'documents, the room of theories and dreams' (14) about the assassination. These all blur in Dealey Plaza; they do not, in some postmodern mélange, become one, but they all lead, circuitously or directly, back to the primal scene. But there is so much crowding in, so many disparate, eclectic, contrary 'documents, theories and dreams' that that primal scene no longer simply defines the countless re-enactments it has spawned but is also defined by them. Dealey Plaza exemplifies a *reverse* uncanny, or a return to a real event that has become familiar in the imaginary, or as a re-enactment or fantasy. In such cases as the Kennedy assassination, a fictional 'original' base layer of knowledge has become how we have gained access to or got to know a 'familiar' factual event; the full 'reverse uncanny' effect is most strongly felt when visiting the site of a momentous historical occurrence that has become more familiar through subsequent, often repeated, re-enactments. Dealey Plaza is so familiar through dramas, photographs, documentaries and video games that visiting it feels like being on a film set.

Symbolic order has been reversed as the Kennedy assassination is now informed by its secondary texts and Dealey Plaza has become a performative site. The JFK limousine tours might have ceased, but tourists can still experience the 'Trolley Fun Tour' charting the route Lee Harvey Oswald took after he left the Texas School Book Depository. The car stops at each important landmark – Oswald's dwellings, the site of Officer Tippett's murder, the cinema where he hid just prior to his arrest – and passengers are invited to get off and snap away. As our tour guide told me and my fellow travellers: 'Here in Dealey Plaza, every day is 22 November 1963'.

'Back then was a time of innocence', he reminds us, as the trolley car slowed to 5 mph, the speed at which the motorcade was travelling up until the moment when the three shots rang out. There is a strain as well as a liberation involved in watching a fictionalised account of the Kennedy assassination without explicit and immediate recourse to any of the archival material that depicts it. The *incidentalisation* of the assassination within 'The Grown Ups' becomes part of a wider 'approximation' as we recall past versions of it that inform but do not directly destabilise our viewing.

Very occasionally, characters in *Mad Men* do more than brush past or observe history, but such engagement is not dramatized, instead, it happens off-screen. The series' alienation from 'history' is an integral part of how it uses 'approximation' and of how it enacts history's lack of closure or finality. Vivian Sobchack remarks of *Forrest Gump* (Robert Zemeckis, 1994) that it 'tells us with great sincerity not to worry: one can be *in* history, can *make* history, without paying attention and without understanding' (1996: 2). *Mad Men*'s choice was far from empty or uncomprehending; the series shadowed history, it slid in and out of it; it did not fictionalise it but rather observed it from within fiction, a decision that is altogether bolder, if more elusive. External crises mirror and even precipitate internal narrative crises, but there is no conscious or reflexive connection, none of the overt distinction between the historical consciousness of the series and the historical ignorance of its characters that Sobchack discerns in *Forrest Gump*. *Mad Men*'s characters are not merely naïve, passive or disinterested in events around them, as exemplified by the centrality accorded television news. If, as Robert Rosenstone argues when discussing the historical film, documentary's asset is 'that it gives us direct access to history' (20), then the 'indexical relationship to actual people, landscapes, and objects' can provide an even more 'unmediated experience of the past' (2012: 20) when it comes in the form of news coverage. The television set and the communal moments it supplies are, in terms of how *Mad Men* 'incidentalises' history, resonantly significant. The series' characters believe in the image's indexicality, in its ability to offer an 'unmediated experience' of current events. Conversely, the *Mad Men* audience can observe the dialectical permutations of these accidental encounters, as 'incidentalisation' builds a dialectical relationship between narrative and viewer whereby it is the latter who brings to the series' integration of the landmark events of the 1960s the knowledge, opinions and hindsight the characters so stubbornly lack. Their perspective may be constricted and their hands tied by the conventions of dramatic irony and history – but ours are not, and in this endlessly replayed dislocation resides the series' most notable evocation of 'approximation'.

Notes

1 I have applied the term 'paratext' as used by Allison Perlman in 'The Strange Career of *Mad Men*: Race, Paratexts and Civil Rights Memory', in Gary R. Edgerton (ed.) *Mad Men: Dream Come True TV*, London: I.B. Tauris, 2011.
2 Discussed in Chapter 2.
3 http://madmenunbuttoned.com/. Accessed 30 June 2014. The book *Mad Men Unbuttoned: A Romp Through 1960s America*, New York: Harper Collins, 2010 is still available.
4 This case was dramatized in the film *Mississippi Burning* (Alan Parker, 1988).

5   The choice of music for the end credits is usually interesting and significant – see for example the choice to run the end credits to the Martin Luther King episode not to the then current (to 4 April 1968) No.1, Otis Redding's '(Sittin' on) The Dock of the Bay', but to its far less familiar predecessor, Paul Mauriat's 'easy listening' arrangement of Andre Popp's 'Love is Blue'. Redding's posthumously released iconic single would have been significantly more conspicuous and would have imposed itself on the episode's troubled conclusion of Don smoking a cigarette silhouetted against the evening Manhattan skyline, police sirens still wailing in the distance.

6   Henry works for John Lindsay, a liberal Republican mayor of New York City from 1966 to 1973. Civil unrest erupted in over 100 US cities in the wake of King's assassination. Lindsay, who had been at the theatre, immediately went to Harlem, a visit that is credited with preventing more serious violence occurring on Manhattan.

7   Goodlad et al., writing in all likelihood somewhere between the transmissions of Seasons 4 and 5, only identify relatively inconsequential 'occasional inaccuracies', such as Bryn Mawr not having sororities when Betty Draper would have been a pupil, an IBM typewriter arriving in the Sterling Cooper office a year ahead of schedule and, most interestingly, a reference to Marshall McLuhan's 'the medium is the message' three years ahead of publication (Goodlad, 2013: 2).

8   Hugely popular with audiences, Jackie's tour of her newly refurbished home first aired on 14 February 1962 and then four days later across all three main networks: CBS, NBC and ABC.

9   As Katie Roiphe said of her mother Anne's autobiography about the *Mad Men* era: 'I can't help but think the modern reader of my mother's impending memoir will be a little appalled by the casual adultery, the recreational alcoholism, but also just a little bit intrigued; it's like reading about a foreign country, or Margaret Mead's Samoans' (Roiphe, 2010).

10 Cf. https://adage.com/article/special-report-mad-men/mad-men-recap-ad-biz-reacted-mlk-s-death/241169. Accessed 30 July 2019.

11 See Charlotte Brunsdon, '"It's a Film": Medium Specificity as Textual Gesture in *Red Road* and *The Unloved*', *The Journal of British Cinema and Television*, 9:3, Autumn 2012, 457–479.

12 White's term for events that function as traumas that 'remain ambiguous' and cannot easily be consigned to 'the past' (White, 1996: 20).

13 Titles such as: *The Day the Dream Died* (*Dispatches*, Channel 4, 1988); Bill O'Reilly and Martin Dugard, *Killing Kennedy: The End of Camelot*, London: Palgrave Macmillan, 2012; Vincent Bugliosi, *Reclaiming History: The Assassination of President John F. Kennedy*, New York: W.W. Norton, 2007; James Hepburn, *Farewell America: The Plot to Kill JFK*, Roseville, CA: Penmarin Books, 2002.

14 Cf. Stella Bruzzi, *New Documentary*, 2006.

15 This is viewed very much from a US perspective; a comparable 'collective identification' occurred in the UK, for example, as on 2 June 1953 over 20 million British viewers watched Queen Elizabeth II's coronation live on the BBC.

16 Cf. www.youtube.com/channel/UCF_mQgKpqDBPDWF-pHRTMgg. Accessed 17 September 2019.

17 Dan Rather's account of the Zapruder film on the whole coincides with the film. However, his description of the president's head going 'forward with considerable violence' as opposed to back and to the left as is visible in Zapruder, has caused significant controversy.

18 Cf. Knight, 2007: 23.

19 Cf. www.jfklibrary.org/asset-viewer/archives/THWPP/059/THWPP-059-011. Accessed 17 September 2019.

20 'The Assassination of President Kennedy: What Do We Know Now That We Didn't Know Then?' 21.2.78 c/o Syndicate Services. Reference 233JFK.F555 PART1.

21 Cf. www.youtube.com/watch?v=5ICxqP-t1Ms. Accessed 11 August 2019.

4

DOCUMENTARY AND THE LAW

True crime and observation

'Approximation' is, for every legal case and every trial, a residual state of being, as each is a series of competing perspectives on the same story and evidence. The law's relationship to 'truth' is inherently unstable as it transpires that 'truth' and 'evidence' are not invariably synonymous, nor that 'justice' necessarily follows on from the truthfulness of a case's evidence (if indeed that can ever be determined). Trials, the formal examination of this evidence, are, as Charles Musser surmises, 'only incidentally about establishing the truth, for they are "truly" about determining guilt or innocence using the evidence that has been admitted within the court rules' (1995–1996: 964). Just as 'approximation' is a process of negotiation and reassessment, so the law documentary is not merely 'about' the law or a particular case, but is also about how to represent and visualise and negotiate the fragilities of 'truth'. As countless advocates and scholars have noted, a legal case is won by whichever litigant crafts the most convincing version of 'the truth' from the available evidence; there are no consistent and simple guarantors of 'truth', the law and documentaries about the law suggest, which is potentially epistemologically as well as legally problematic. Likewise, there is no guarantee that a dispute will ever be definitively closed – in fact, most evidence points to the contrary. An interest in justice motivates documentaries about the law, although the elusiveness of 'justice' and the vulnerabilities of 'truth' remain their establishing premise.

This chapter examines two very different illustrations of this that make for a compelling juxtaposition: the observational law documentary and the true crime documentary, one discursively interested in the symbolic entity of 'the law' and how people (defendants and lawyers) interact with it, the other forensically focused on the frequently horrific nitty-gritty of individual cases. Though both are examples of the law documentary, these two groups occupy opposite ends of that spectrum. The true crime documentary is a phenomenon, which has become an industry; punch 'true crime' into the *Netflix* search page and rows of such series, documentaries and dramas appear. The observational documentaries are, by contrast, niche. And yet, despite the multitude of differences (of budget, style, length, for instance), their concerns are surprisingly similar. The observational studies of courts in Raymond Depardon's *The 10th District Court: Moments of Trials*, Marc Isaacs's *Outside the Court* and Carey Young's *Palais de Justice* emphasise the fragmentariness, mutability and elusiveness of the law and of legal procedure, its repetitiveness and its lack of finality. True crime documentaries are underpinned by comparable concerns and realisations, although their explicit attention remains trained on the specifics of evidence, testimony and argument in individual cases.

Also worth noting is that these two groups of law documentaries exist within a much broader tradition of law and film that extends from feature films to verbatim plays, some of which went on to be filmed.[1] Until recently, academic discussions of the law and film or media have focused largely on mainstream fiction films, to the conspicuous marginalisation of documentary. The first of many law and film studies textbooks, Greenfield et al.'s (2010) *Film and the Law*, devotes a mere handful of pages (out of 300+) specifically to documentary, while, much later (in 2013), Asimow and Mader in *Law and Popular Culture*, though putatively interested in 'the importance of films based on actual events', proceed instead to single out fiction films that 'put flesh and blood on historic events' as opposed to documentaries (2013: 250). The reasons for this are the formal affinities between the law and narrative film as explained by Carol Clover who, from her perspective as a film scholar, contends that 'trials are already movie-like to begin with, and movies are already trial-like to begin with' (2000a: 99). Clover identifies – with its opening statements, examination and cross-examination and then closing statements – the trial's tripartite (and quintessentially Aristotelian) structure which, she concludes 'matches the architecture of the standard screenplay' (Clover, 2000a: 103). 'With the closing arguments', she continues, 'the text reverts to syntactic narrative with a vengeance as each side tries to gather all the evidence into a master bundle' (108).[2] 'Many trials fall short of full closure' (2000a: 108), she observes, the reality that ultimately proves to be the jumping off point for law documentaries.

However, as demonstrated throughout this book, documentary and fiction are not polarities so much as opportunities to offer alternative perspectives. Some true crime documentaries, ironically, have had alternate (and arguably less successful) lives as fiction films: before *The Jinx: The Life and Deaths of Robert Durst* (2015), for instance, Andrew Jarecki had made *All Good Things* (2010), a fictional account of Robert Durst's life, while the drama–documentary series, *The People vs. O.J. Simpson, American Crime Story* (2016), aired a few months before Ezra Edelman's documentary epic *O.J.: Made in America* (2016) premiered at Sundance. Then there are Joe Berlinger's two virtually contemporaneous Ted Bundy projects, *Extremely Wicked, Shockingly Evil and Vile* (2019) starring Zac Efron as Bundy and the documentary series *Conversations with a Killer*. And *The Keepers* is in many respects the companion piece to the feature film *Spotlight* (Tom McCarthy, 2015), from two years earlier and dramatised the true story of how the *Boston Globe* exposed the cover up of child abuse within the local Catholic diocese. That these legal tales move with relative ease between documentary and fiction demonstrates their inherent acceptance of permutation, nuance and ambiguity. As an addendum, it is also striking how frequently luck, chance and fluke are factors in the documentaries, complementing their fascination with the incompleteness and the chaotic unpredictability of 'real life'. Jarecki ended up making *The Jinx* as a result of Robert Durst (as documented in the series) making contact with him after having seen *All Good Things*, while *Murder on Sunday Morning* was nearly not made because de Lestrade and his producer Denis Poncet 'had been planning an entirely different documentary project when they happened upon Butler's case' (Fuhs, 2014: 786).

Across both documentary and feature films and across selected non-fictional case studies, the fractures and collisions that characterise 'approximation' more broadly are in evidence: the vulnerabilities of individuals pitted against the immovability of the institution of law; the turbulent and unpredictable interaction between narrative, truth and evidence; the unexpected disparities between justice and truth. Neither the observational nor the true crime documentary is simply concerned with rendering justice, but in rendering justice through images; they ask to be considered as part of visual as well as legal culture for, as legal scholar Richard Sherwin determines, 'Visual meaning-making is different from the way we make meanings in words alone. . . . We respond to images quickly, holistically, and affectively' (2011: 2). Part of the task here is to engage with the visual complexities of these films and series, to not just consider how they, from the perspective of the law, negotiate the impenetrability of 'the truth' or the instability of evidence, but how they 'make meanings' in images.

'Approximation', as far as the law is concerned, is not about believing the real to be irretrievable, but rather that it cannot be easily solved. Several ages and writers have pronounced the loss of the real, and it is arguably no coincidence that the burgeoning interest in true crimes, especially those that are older, unsolved or ambiguous, should occur against the backdrop of 'post-truth' agendas and the perceived elusiveness of the real. Over the past few decades, as academic interest in the intersection between the law and film has grown,[3] a scholar sporadically declares, as Jessica Silbey did in 2007, that a new crop of trial- or law-based films and documentaries 'suggests more than a trend; it suggests an inherent affinity between law and film' (Silbey, 2007: 131–132). There is also an enduring affinity, I would continue to argue, between the law (with its multiple, frequently colliding perspectives, its alternative narratives or tendency to reopen and reinterpret evidence, fact and history) and 'approximation'.

The true crime documentary

More than three years after *The Jinx* first aired, news broke that director, Andrew Jarecki, had significantly edited Robert Durst's crucial audio confession with which he concluded the series, a confession which had, at the time of the episode's release, led (more or less directly) to Durst's arrest for murder. Ethically, Jarecki was already on slightly shaky ground with this 'confession' as Durst had mumbled it while speaking to himself, unaware that his microphone was still on, but the evidence seemed convincing. By having tampered with the evidence, however, Jarecki potentially jeopardised any future case against the eccentric real estate multi-millionaire. Whereas, in the final moments of *The Jinx*, Durst is heard to utter the semi-audible but pretty incontrovertible confession, 'What the hell did I do? Killed them all, of course', it later transpired that Jarecki had inverted the order of the two sentences. A fuller transcript of the accidental recording is as follows:

> [Unintelligible] I don't know what you expected to get. I don't know what's in the house. Oh, I want this. Killed them all, of course. [Unintelligible] I want to do something new. There's nothing new about that. He was right. I was wrong. The burping. I'm having difficulty with the question. What the hell did I do?
>
> *(quoted in Bagli, 2019)*

The filmmakers defend their edits 'as being entirely representative of what Mr Durst said', whilst others, such as documentarian Mark J. Harris, deem the editing to have been 'problematic'. As a result of these revelations, Durst's defence team is 'seeking to have all the evidence compiled by the filmmakers thrown out' (Bagli, 2019). Either way, if Jarecki's furtive editing exemplifies nothing else, it illustrates the extreme volatility of both documentary and legal 'truth'. The law enters the shifting sand of 'approximation'. *The Jinx* was a popular series, also the trigger to the post-2015 explosion in true crime documentary series on Netflix and other platforms and channels; it remains hugely enthralling, but its compelling finale is now compromised. Jarecki et al. might well maintain that their edits did not distort what Durst said; we might well believe them; but even if 'true', this has become a far more chaotic and unstable truth.

The allure of both the certainties and the instabilities of the law are exemplified by the true crime documentary, a subgenre that is vast and growing. The true crime documentary canon is so extensive that picking out representative examples is near impossible, and any selection is bound to seem, in no time at all, out of date. There is, for instance, no mention below of *Don't F**k with Cats: Hunting an Internet Killer* (Mark Lewis, 2019) or *Killer Inside: The Mind of Aaron Hernandez* (Geno McDermott, 2020), the main illustrative examples being: the series *The Staircase* (Jean-Xavier de Lestrade, 2004), *The Jinx, The Keepers* (Ryan White, 2017) and *Conversations with a Killer: The Ted Bundy Tapes* (Joe Berlinger, 2019); the one-off documentaries *Murder in Mansfield* (Barbara Koppel, 2017) and *Out of Thin Air* (Dylan Howitt, 2017) and the podcast *Serial* (2014). There were notable documentaries dating to before *The Staircase* (which followed the trial and conviction of North Carolina author and Vietnam veteran, Michael Peterson, for the murder of his wife, Kathleen), such as Joe Berlinger and Bruce Sinofsky's *Paradise Lost: The Child Murders at Robin Hood Hills* (1996), as well as de Lestrade's own Academy Award-winning *Murder on a Sunday Morning* (2001), but de Lestrade's series is still the most significant earlier text which Sarah Koenig, for one, stressed had influenced her equally influential podcast, *Serial*, the first true crime podcast sensation which was, in turn, followed by later examples such as *Black Hands: A Family Mass Murder* (Martin van Beynan, 2017) and *S-Town* (Brian Reed, 2017).[4]

The most notable formal feature that *The Staircase* brought to the genre was, unlike other precursors such as *Paradise Lost*, a longitudinal episodic structure. *The Staircase* ran for eight original 50-minute episodes and subsequent updates, and was repackaged in 2018 by Netflix into a complete series. Like other long-running true crime series, it was detailed and *forensic*, it mimicked and enacted legal procedure, and led to not just further true crime series, but also a long list of one-off true crime documentaries such as Brett Morgen's animated *Chicago 10* (2007), Werner Herzog's *Into the Abyss: A Tale of Death, A Tale of Life* (2011), Nick Broomfield's *Tales of the Grim Sleeper* (2011), Ken Burns's *The Central Park Five* (2012) and Amy Berg's *West of Memphis* (2012). The films and series share many tropes and motifs (and indeed invite consideration *as* a genre), and the ensuing analysis will discuss discursively the most significant and characteristic of these, starting by considering how, typically, true crime documentaries begin, to how they structure and shape narrative, to how they deploy the generic suitability of the serial form, to how they layer time, to how they work through the binary opposition of people and evidence, to how they use re-enactment and finally to how they end. Behind the creation and repetition of generic conventions, there resides a deeper, more abstract interest in the true crime documentary with the ceaselessly approximate nature of the law, the elusiveness of truth and the impossibility of closure. True crime documentaries seldom follow neat and tidy trajectories and rather more frequently *start* and *stop*; beginnings are frequently as abrupt as their finales are inconclusive. Series in particular are episodic and their narratives fragmented; whether retrospective or contemporary, they are meandering, accepting of inconsistency, constitutively fluid and almost certainly neither neatly nor chronologically structured. In some cases, such as *The Staircase, The Jinx* and *Making a Murderer*, the filming process was entered into speculatively, the filmmakers not knowing what direction their cases would take and consequently where the series' *narratives* might end up. Some true crime documentaries also embark on one path but change tack during the course of production, as occurs in *The Keepers* and *S-Town*, though all imply in some form the embarkation on a journey.

The most common true crime opener is, from *Paradise Lost* to *Killer Inside: The Mind of Aaron Hernandez*, gritty archive footage (a sensationalist news report; a crime scene video) that hurls the viewer into the thick of it. Viewers are thereby made party to a case being blown open or an investigation being initiated. After an opening statement that 'The following events took place in Jacksonville, Florida', there ensues in *Murder on Sunday Morning*, for instance, a rapidly edited sequence of gruesome video images of the crime scene accompanied by the sounds of a gunshot and flashbulbs firing, followed by a cut to black. Public defender, Pat McGuinness, who will feature prominently in the documentary, tells how 'everything important took place in two hours on a Sunday morning': the two hours of screen time, this statement attests, will scrutinise these and their aftermath exhaustively. This is a quintessential true crime documentary beginning. In its immediacy, its capture of raw, unadulterated fact and its brash, heady disregard for aestheticism (there is something more important to think about than what this looks like, it seems to declare), the archival fragment lays claim to the truth, to the crime 'as it happened'. But these are false assurances, and such an opening also, crucially, invites the viewer to reopen a case, to scrutinise the authentically unadulterated footage afresh, and follow the film or series as it unpicks, challenges or complicates the disingenuous simplicity of the archival opening.

Another classic way of launching a true crime documentary is to start speculatively, to tiptoe into a case, feel a way into it, as if conscious from the outset of this latent, inevitable lack of surety. Whereas the one-off documentary most likely feels the need to establish its premise early and quickly, the longer serial can afford to be more relaxed and reflective, *The Keepers, Serial* and *Conversations with a Killer* offer classic illustrations of the ruminative beginning. Starting in the casual, conversational manner which will soon become a defining characteristic of her style, Sarah Koenig in *Serial* sets out her case for looking again at Adnan Syed's conviction for the 1999 murder of his ex-girlfriend, Hae Min Lee. Koenig explains that

> For the last year, I've spent every working day trying to figure out where a high school kid was for an hour after school one day in 1999. Or, if you want to get technical about it, and, apparently, I do, where a high school kid was for 21 minutes after school one day in 1999.

Although she is not 'a detective or an investigator... [or] even a crime reporter', Koenig, through the podcast, fixates on one 17-year-old's alibi. This conversational start speaks to many things, notably the intimate camaraderie she intends to establish with her listeners, and the obsessive, pedantic precision they should expect from her painstaking reinvestigation. The ruminative beginning has comparable underlying intentions to the archival opening, as both make explicit their attention to evidence and detail. *The Keepers'* introductory sequence highlights a slightly different trait of the true crimes opening, namely the oftentimes amateur investigation (as here, in *Making A Murderer, Serial* or *The Jinx*) as *quest*.

Wrapped in crepuscular dinginess, *The Keepers* opens with an exterior shot of a suburban home; a cut to an equally dark interior shows a man walking up towards his attic. The camera follows. The disorganisation of the attic finds an echo in the rough and ready following-the-subject hand-held camerawork. Panning across the gloomy disorder as the figure almost trips up as he seeks out and starts to rummage in boxes of papers, journalist Tom Nugent's voice starts up: 'I've spent the last 30 years as a freelance writer. . . . It's been a life of wandering around and finding a good story'. The boxes are full of his journalist's notes. He finds and pulls out a tabloid paper which he holds aloft for his interviewer behind the camera: 'Who

Killed Sister Cathy?' Tom introduces the story of Cathy Cesnik, whose murder in Baltimore in 1967 remains unsolved. The case was reopened in 1994, when the first (as yet undetailed) 'stories started to emerge' of, as Tom again puts it, 'an on-the-record public story', under which lurked 'the world beneath that was actually being lived'. Part of the appeal of *The Keepers* is its residual inelegance and unkemptness; while we probably think at the outset, for example, that Tom will be the one to lead the investigation into Cesnik's murder, it soon emerges that it is instead two of Cesnik's former pupils, Gemma Hoskins and Abbie Schaub, who have reopened and will lead the reinvestigation. Such beginnings telegraph the fact that the series' narrative paths will not be linear or direct, that not all questions will be satisfactorily answered, that ultimately (as in *The Keepers*) audience and investigator convictions about what actually occurred might not finally be matched by either the films' or the legal conclusions.

Just as the good detective novel is at its most engrossing in the middle of a messy investigation and becomes progressively less interesting as a solution looms, so ultimately the ambiguity and lack of certainty promised by true crime documentary beginnings entice rather than deter audiences, even when the conclusion is known and seemingly clear cut. Even a case as well-known and conclusive as that of Ted Bundy, the serial killer and necrophile who killed 36 young women in the 1970s and was executed in 1989, can come laced with anticipatory uncertainty, as Joe Berlinger's *Conversations with a Killer: The Ted Bundy Tapes* draws us in with journalist Stephen Michaud's opening voiceover: 'I had no idea what I was doing. I had no idea who I was dealing with'. Michaud's admission segues into an especially visceral example of the true crime documentary's fragmented opening, a quintessentially 21st-century documentary 'mash-up' that mirrors what we may assume to be (despite his protestations that he is 'just a normal individual') Bundy's fractured personality. This busy montage splices together reporters' descriptions ('diabolical genius, deceptive, manipulative'), news footage of a handcuffed, smiling Bundy personifying the 'handsome devil' of the episode's subtitle, a kaleidoscope of other voices from Bundy's childhood confirming that he was 'very nice' and assumed to be on track to becoming 'a lawyer or a politician', and Bundy's mother Louise's voice commenting that he was 'the best son in the world'. The editing becomes increasingly staccato and each shot or sound bite shorter, as the sequence starts to evoke the brutality of Bundy's crimes. A sequence of the smiling, innocent faces of Bundy's 36 victims is roughly intercut with shots of (their) skeletal remains, fractured skulls and bloody clothes, while an agitated cacophony of soundbites reduce Bundy's crimes to their savage, extreme essence: 'bludgeoned, raped'; 'mutilation, necrophilia'; '36 sex killings'; 'sexually mutilated by mouth, by teeth'; 'bite marks'. The disjointedness of this opening in which virtually no single shot represents a unified action and almost no statement is complete, symbolically disputes Bundy's self-assessment and sets up, with elegant economy, a series that will enact not only the serial killer's staggering violence but the disconcerting realisation that truth is endlessly refracted and rarely distilled. Information is overloaded and overlaid, spewed out.

Such a refraction of truth often also features in the genre's increasingly compositionally homogenous title sequences; interesting because they promote a sense of generic certainty that masks the inherent uncertainties of the individual cases. Distinctive common features such as a tense, ominous score featuring a clearly defined instrument or instruments (the preponderance of the lonely violin likely stems from Jocelyn Pook's delicately melancholic strings-dominated score for *The Staircase*) is one such motif that both embodies narrativised uncertainty and cements a sense of generic affiliation. Alongside this, *The Staircase* established the predilection for the kaleidoscopic assemblage of archival and other images whose sense becomes clearer as a series moves forward. Each episode of *The Keepers* repeats its splintered, montage title sequence in which are brought together a series of archival and reenacted images that become familiar over the course of the series: St Keough's School, nuns and others going to church, portrait shots from a girls' high school yearbook and a final one of a smiling Sister Cathy. The generic significance of the title sequence montage lies in the way that its repetition mirrors the progress of the investigation from ignorance to knowledge, but it also appears that such generic 'packaging' may have developed consciously as the genre has become increasingly popular. *Making a Murderer*, for instance, is an intrinsically craggy, rough-edged, observational series, but one given an anomalously slick title sequence, again comprising a montage of talismanic series images cross-fading into each other and set to an overwrought, violin- and snare-drum-led score that rises to a screechy conclusion. These titles consciously or not merge *The Staircase*'s score with the double-exposures that kicked off *The Jinx* (the void left by which *Making a Murderer* was seen by many media journalists to have filled)[5] and throw in for good measure the double-exposed drawl of the titles for the cold case drama series, *True Detective*. These echoes are unlikely to be coincidental, as the title sequences for *Making a Murderer* and *True Detective* were made by sister companies and shared an executive producer,[6] and such synchronies construct a collective identity across otherwise distinct series. In sum, the shared features of these beginnings, especially the puzzle-like, pixelated qualities of their visual imagery, signal a common understanding that the truth is messy and its pursuit often tortuous and inconclusive.

The true crime narratives that ensue follow the leads set out in their introductions and are propelled by a shared compulsion to solve a crime (whether or not this turns out to be possible). Legal cases are narratives and narrative, therefore, becomes integral to the true crime documentary as it works towards solving or recounting a crime. Law scholar Peter Brooks, who starts his 1996 co-edited collection, *Narrative and Rhetoric in the Law*, with the assertion that the collection will be 'different' from previous studies of the law by virtue of its focus on the law as 'stories' and 'as narratives and rhetoric' (Brooks and Gerwitz, 1996: 2), later commends narrative for its 'unique ability to embody the concrete experience of individuals and communities, to make their voices heard, to contest the very assumptions of legal judgement' (16). The then recent acquittal of O.J. Simpson for the murder of his wife Nicole Brown and her partner Ron Goldman serves 'to remind us', Brooks contends, 'that the law is in a very important sense all about competing stories' (16). Extending Brooks's idea of narrative's omnipresence in the law, celebrity criminal defence lawyer Alan Dershowitz (who formed part of O.J. Simpson's legal 'dream team' and whose other clients included Mike Tyson, Patty Hearst and Claus von Bulow) starts his contribution to the same book by recalling Chekhov's purported advice to the aspiring young dramatist: 'if you hang a gun on the wall in the first act, you had better use it by the third' (1996: 99).[7] However, as Dershowitz goes on to comment:

> life does not imitate art . . . Events are often simply meaningless, irrelevant to what comes next; events can be out of sequence, random, purely accidental, without purpose.
>
> *(100)*

True crime documentary narratives are notably anti-Chekhovian (as characterized by Dershowitz), their stories circuitous, filled with incidental, jumbled events that lack discernible logic and structure, and so often thwart the lawyer's professional predilection for imposing form on randomness. Dershowitz warns of the 'profoundly important implications for our legal system' when we 'impose order' on life's 'chaos' (1996: 100), for 'when we import the narrative form of storytelling into our legal system', he contends, 'we confuse *fiction* with fact and endanger the *truth-finding function of the adjudicative process*' (101; my italics).

The question of narrative as a means of making sense of facts and evidence is fundamental to the law; but problematic for *documentary* is the fact that Dershowitz conflates narrative with *fiction*. The questions for documentary, as demonstrated by the beginnings of true crime examples are different. Finding parallels between the seamless linearity of the trial and the equally coherent unities of the mainstream fiction film is infinitely possible and richly rewarding; as I discovered when researching my doctorate, the classical narrative film and the adversarial trial share a common structure that observe the unities of Aristotelian drama. Neither, as implied earlier, merely starts or stops, but rather begins and finishes; both adhere to the appeal of closure and determinism, and both embody purposefulness. The classic trial and the classic fiction film both obscure and marginalise the shambles, irregularities and unresolved tensions of life as lived. But to infer from this that (inherently chaotic) life is *narrativeless* or that to impose narrative onto it is to fictionalise it, is misguided for, as Hayden White argues, 'to raise the question of the nature of narrative, is to invite reflection on the very nature of culture and, possibly, even on the nature of humanity itself' (White, 1980: 5). Narrative is as intrinsic to 21st-century true crime documentaries as it was to Stanley Kramer's courtroom drama, *Judgement At Nuremberg* (1961); they all, for example, set out to make sense of and navigate a path through the muddle of life, the fallibility of memory and procedure, the lack of determinism or certainty of outcome and the centrality of luck and chance.

Mainstream fictional legal dramas frequently use the process of law to iron out life's chaos or memory's frailties, using these processes *en route* to surety and closure;[8]

but, as Jennifer Mnookin observes in her discussion of *Paradise Lost*, the affinities between trials and documentaries are slightly different. Both, Mnookin argues,

> are 'productions' – elaborate staged dramas whose relation to the real is very far from indexical. . . . And yet, both documentaries and the trial have a generic similarity: they both overtly aspire to produce the truth.
>
> *(Mnookin, 2005: 157)*

The 'production' of this 'truth' has its roots in narrative production or story construction, for as Brooks, surmises: 'No doubt any courtroom advocate knows the importance of narrative presentation instinctively' (Brooks, P., 1996: 16–17). Or, as Judge Alex Kozinski writes in the Preface to *Reel Justice*, 'the moviemaker's art is not all that different from the lawyer's. . . . Both must capture, in a very short space, a slice of human existence and make the audience see a story from their particular perspective' (Kozinski, 2006: xv). Documentary filmmakers and advocates alike aim for 'truth' but ultimately present their judgement, which is rendered most affective or dramatic by virtue of being narratively as well as evidentially compelling. True crime documentaries appreciate the inbuilt fragility of legal systems, they frequently emphasise the complexities of evidence gathering and evidence contamination, and they possess a deep understanding of the fragilities of human memory, from the alternative eye-witness accounts juxtaposed in Errol Morris's *The Thin Blue Line*, to an interviewee in *Out of Thin Air* noting how 'memory is such a fickle thing'. An acceptance of doubt is fundamental to the very nature of the law; as David Rudolf, Michael Peterson's Defence Attorney, clarifies in *The Staircase*: a criminal verdict determines either 'guilt' or not; even on acquittal, a trial judge or jury is only ever asked to decide that a defendant is 'not guilty', not that they are conclusively innocent.

The episodic structure of the true crime serial raises alternative implications for narrative. As previously intimated, doubt, luck, fickleness, fluke, forgetting, misremembering, lying, evidence contamination, believing in the wrong guy . . . the list of things that get in the way of lawyers or filmmakers, journalists and podcasters from getting at 'what really happened' in any given case is lengthy. True crime serials are, by their formal nature, episodic and eclectic, mixing archive, interview, narration and frequently some form of re-enactment. They display an attachment to forensic detail, at times to a fetishistic degree. Episodes frequently end on cliff hangers, while new evidence surfaces unexpectedly. Exemplary of how the true crime series' meandering structure can be both satisfying and inconclusive is the final, twelfth, episode of the podcast *Serial*, 'Finale: What We Know'. Sarah Koenig, a year after she first contacted him, is on the phone to Adnan Syed; the latter asks, in disbelief, 'you don't really have no ending?', to which Koenig sighs, then rallies and confirms she will have an ending, before describing how, over the course of making *Serial*, she found herself repeatedly 'upended' by new revelations that led her to discard previous convictions. She professes astonishment at 'how the back and forth hasn't let up, after all this time'. Right up until this, her last day of writing, Koenig confesses, 'I'm learning new information all the time'. 'What's hard about this story', she admits to one witness, is 'there's something that's not computing here'. As is so often the case, the piece of conclusive evidence that could either prove Syed's guilt or innocence definitively has remained elusive. *Serial*'s longitudinal structure complements and emphasises this inconclusiveness. It is intriguing that, after so many hours dedicated to listening to *Serial* or watching *Making a Murderer* (which is not only longitudinal in form but was also filmed over many years) listeners and viewers are not exasperated by such ambivalence. Increasingly, despite the attractions of the narrative trial film's symmetry and closure, the true crime documentary's defiance of determinism and finality is perceived to not only more accurately approximate the messiness of life but become more appealing as entertainment.

An essential component of the true crime documentary's value as *entertainment* is the way in which it integrates viewers into the investigation and commonly treats them as quasi-jurors. To waver alongside Sarah Koenig is to be an investigator, a juror, someone implicated in attempting to solve a crime, though legal scholar Paul Gewirtz cautions against the conflation between jurors and members of the public (characterised as 'voyeurs'). Writing from the perspective of the post-O.J. Simpson mid-90s, Gewirtz argues: 'Law is all about human life, yet struggles to keep life at bay' (1995–1996: 863); the 'rules of procedure, jurisdiction and evidence' that 'define law's autonomous character' are in place to keep out 'the mob' whose faces are 'pressed hard against the courthouse windows' (863). For Gewirtz there is 'considerable ambivalence about the general public's relationship to the trial' because the public is both 'an indispensable audience and participant' (when, for example, lawyers and defendants address the gathered public and press from the courthouse steps at the end of a trial), but also 'a deeply distrusted one, always in danger of becoming a mob of "public opinion" that can assault and undermine legal processes' (883). 'Surely there is a problem', Gewirtz surmises, with the 'jurification' of the viewer, for 'the general public are not jurors' who have been selected from a cross-section of society to minimise bias – or at least to bring to bear on a trial 'a collection of representative biases' (887); the viewer-jury is only an 'intermittent audience' that 'hears only part of the story' (887) – and in the case of the documentary, potentially only the parts of the story that the filmmakers want them to hear. Most problematically, 'the public feels itself entitled to pass judgement' (887), rendering the trial 'a mass political event, not a legal process' (888).

While there are series such as Channel 4's *The Trial: A Murder in the Family* (2017) that construct a more explicit parallel between viewers and on-screen jurors,[9] true crime documentaries do so implicitly, although to many series and cases there is an afterlife during which 'the court of public opinion' can continue to garner evidence and protest a defendant's innocence or *vice versa*. The 'jurification' (Mnookin's term) and mobilisation of the lay-audience of viewers and listeners is just one mechanism for ensuring that a case is never conclusively *closed*. Recent cases such as the convictions of Adnan Syed (*Serial*) or Steven Avery and Brendan Dassey (*Making a Murderer*) have spawned action groups and campaigns established to fight perceived miscarriages of justice. Ricciardi and Demos re-examined the Avery and Dassey convictions, and the information they present in Season 1 'led viewers to respond with near-universal outrage about the verdicts' (Schulz, 2016). Explicit public involvement in the Avery/Dassey case escalated to the level of a petition (of some 130,000 signatures) for their pardon, which was sent to then President Obama. In the wake of *Serial*, Syed family friend and lawyer, Rabia Chaudry, and others established the Adnan Syed Trust to crowdfund Syed's legal defence; Chaudry later extended her advocacy for Syed by executive producing the four-part series, *The Case Against Adnan Syed*, released (by HBO) on 10 March 2019, the day after the Maryland Court of Appeals quashed an appeal for a new trial. Many documentaries have been clearly advocational and have led to further legal proceedings. *Out of Thin Air*, for instance, reopened the unsolved 1974 murders of Gudmundur Einarsson and Geirfinnur Einarsson; what happened to the murder victims 'remains a mystery', on-screen text at the end of Dylan Howitt's film states, 'Their bodies have never been found' – but crucially (in a manner that obliquely vindicates Gewirtz's distrust of public 'voyeurs') the Icelandic Supreme Court agreed to reopen the original murder convictions, the original verdict having been deemed (like the one in *Murder on a Sunday Morning*) prejudiced by the surrounding 'trial by media'.

And yet there remain significant and interesting parallels between jurors and audiences, between trials and series; as Carol Clover surmises, 'we' (speaking of the US) 'are a nation of jurors' and that the marriage between entertainment and the law 'makes jurors of us all' (2000b: 258). Our collective 'jurification' is collateral of the longitudinal form itself, measured by the commitment those long-running series expect from their audiences. The series' loose, directional but largely non-didactic structures and their forensic attention to detail recall the actual trial's rumination on similar elements such as archive images, interviews and testimony. The series permit longueurs, ponderings, silences and the like, while archive is frequently not edited down into concise, punchy 'sound-bites' but extended, as it might be in a courtroom. Tangential rambles, conversations and speculative reflections with little ostensible narrative 'value' are allowed, a tendency counterbalanced by pacey interjections of significant revelations often at the start of an episode that remind audience-jurors that 'truth' is seldom arrived at via a straightforward linear route. About one such reveal – the discovery at the start of the final episode of *The Staircase* that the alleged murder weapon (a blow-poke) has come back free of Peterson's DNA – David Rudolf remarks directly to camera and his audience-jurors: 'it's one of those moments that trial lawyers enjoy – trial lawyers and filmmakers'. *The Keepers* holds in reserve some unexpected details such as the revelation of 'Brother Bob', introduced mid-way through the series as a means perhaps of punctuating and focusing its otherwise winding – though compelling – narrative. Alongside the viewers' 'jurification', these documentaries also imitate (and permit the same audience-juror to indulge in) the research process; any researcher will be familiar with the experience of entering a library in order to find out one thing, only to unearth something potentially just as interesting but entirely tangential. The research trail motif surfaces many times, most directly in the podcasts, as in Rabia

Chaudry's revelation of a boot full of documents relating to the Adnan Syed case mentioned in *Serial* – and subsequently re-enacted again for the benefit of the cameras in Amy Berg's later HBO series. Though Koenig and her team's fixation on minutiae tips over into the obsessive (which Koenig intermittently acknowledges), it is not ultimately the case that *Serial*'s immersing tactics detract from the bigger picture of whether or not Syed was wrongly convicted of Hae Min Lee's murder.

Underpinning the circumlocutory longitudinal structure is often a complex relationship to time, as (in both series and individual films) the documentaries' multiple temporal layers collide, interact and prompt re-evaluations of historical outcomes or received facts. A crucial dimension of these documentaries' retrospection (and one that underscores their 'approximate' status) is often the desire to reopen or reinvestigate a case, to re-consider verdicts from the past. Some, such as Berlinger's *Cold Blooded: The Clutter Family Murders* (2017) and *Conversations with a Killer*, explicitly emphasise their retrospective and historical dimension, while many others probe less directly the relationship between history and the present, often in the form of a personal confrontation, which is the essence of Barbara Kopple's *Murder in Mansfield*. In this instance, the titular case is the murder of Collier Landry's (then Boyle's) mother, Noreen, for which Collier's father, John Boyle, was, in 1990, found guilty. After its conventional archival opening (in which a disarmingly articulate and composed 12-year-old Collier testifies at the 1990 trial against his father), *Murder in Mansfield* cuts to 26 years later, as Collier returns to his hometown in an attempt to 'heal' himself. Collier's therapeutic journey takes him to his childhood home where the murder took place, his high school, his foster parents' house and finally to the prison where he confronts the father he has not seen for many years. Collier's mission is to get John (Jack) Boyle to 'finally come clean' and admit his guilt, which Jack will not do. Instead, Jack calmly offers his counter-account of what happened the night Noreen died: that they fought, and that she hit her head on a table as she fell; that it was manslaughter, not murder. Intuitively and sentimentally we are not, by this late stage in the film, predisposed to believe Jack; we know Jack buried Noreen under the patio and have witnessed Collier break down in tears when seeing for the first time the graphic police photographs of his mother's corpse. And we have travelled the film flanking Collier, have observed him opening up to his therapist and have been fed his side of the story. Jack repeatedly tells Collier in the documentary's painful denouement, 'I'm very sorry', but he does not confess. Temporal distance does not, in this case, bring affirmation or closure to the case.

All documentaries, to a greater or lesser degree, are constructed around a juxtaposition of past and present, between events that have already occurred and the presentness of the filmmaking process itself. An interesting disavowal of this established relationship occurs in *The Staircase* as the distinct temporal plains of past and present are elided. *The Staircase* recreates presentness and a sense of events unfurling as they are being filmed, despite the fact that it was broadcast a year after the actual trial (one of the longest in North Carolina history) had, on 10 October 2003, concluded. The outcome of Michael Peterson's original trial, therefore, was known before transmission, even if the story – whether implicitly or explicitly – is not narrated with hindsight. One reason for this is that the 8 episodes of the original 2004 series resulted from director, de Lestrade, on the back of the success of his earlier real-case documentary *Murder on Sunday Morning*, being invited to follow and film the murder case as it progressed to trial, so, after filming commenced in January 2002, a mere six weeks after Kathleen Peterson's death, he was filming events as they happened. De Lestrade was originally granted access to both legal sides, though the prosecution team, led by Durham Country District Attorney, James Hardin, proved less welcoming. On the back of renewed interest in *The Staircase* after the re-release of all episodes, from 2004–2018, on Netflix, David Rudolf (Peterson's lead defence attorney) undertook a global lecture tour. In one talk he explains how the filming came about and the deal he struck with de Lestrade. It was Peterson who had been 'enamoured of the idea of having this Academy Award-winning French film crew filming' as he was 'convinced he would not get a fair trial in Durham'. Rudolf was more circumspect so, though he 'wasn't controlling what was being filmed', he did set down certain conditions: all material shot prior to the trial had to be 'covered by the attorney-client privilege'; concerned that the DA might subpoena them, dailies had to be sent back to France; no footage would be shown publicly until all trials and appeals had been exhausted; Rudolf would be permitted to see the finished films prior to release. Rudolf also stipulated that nothing was to be filmed twice, so all footage is 'real-time video' and, as the crew was based in Paris and so 'weren't there 24/7', he would alert them in advance of something critical coming up, which they might want to capture.[10] These filming conditions no doubt contribute to the series' lack of retrospection.

Most documentary filmmakers, as Rudolf acknowledges, would not normally agree to these conditions, though the relationship between filmmakers and their subjects (on the defence side) was close, and de Lestrade was able to film events outside the courtroom as well as proceedings within it, notably inside Peterson's family home after court business had concluded. One potential effect of this proximity and insider knowledge is that audience and filmmakers alike would incline towards favouring Peterson, a perennial issue for many such documentaries (see the charges of bias levelled at the directors of *Making a Murderer*, for instance) and one confirmed by *Staircase* producer, Denis Poncet, when he says that de Lestrade told him 'this is a great story, but I could only do it if I believed he was innocent'.[11] Later, in 2013 (after Peterson's eventual release from prison), the director further commented that 'It has been immensely frustrating that the truth of this story has remained so obscure for so long. I never believed the prosecution's murder story. The evidence contradicted it'.[12]

This camaraderie as well as the film's constructed presentness is exemplified by the series' first extended sequence (after the conventional prelude of archival television news footage establishes the premise for the case, namely, Kathleen's death the night before) in which Michael Peterson walks through his home and towards the garden, pursued by a handheld camera.

FIGURE 4.1   Michael Peterson 'walks through' Kathleen Peterson's final actions in *The Staircase* (Jean-Xavier de Lestrade, 2004)

In the matter-of-fact tones that characterise his delivery throughout, he recounts in detail his version of events the night Kathleen died: how they drank two bottles of wine, watched a rental movie and went to sit outside by the pool. This length of shot, observational camera style and level of detail are all common features of the true crime documentary's relaxed treatment of time; the implications for *The Staircase* are also significant, for Peterson, in his domestic domain, is manifestly at ease, as he ushers the camera out onto the deck, and towards the pool, where he sits on a sun lounger, pats one of the family dogs, and recounts Kathleen's final moments as she left him to go to bed. Peterson then (unconsciously one presumes) merges past and present as he starts to enact and retell Kathleen's last moments as well as his own observation of them (as in the image above). Though Peterson's slippage is less common, to-camera testimony in the present tense, as here, is a staple feature of true crime documentaries, summoning into the 'now' a charged historical moment that, even as it recedes further into the past. *The Staircase* offers a particularly clear example of the true crime documentary's adoption of the continuous historical present, a dual time zone that enables retrospection at the same time as it opens up the potential for the unearthing of new truths or the overturning of verdicts. Its compulsiveness as a viewing experience (and one emulated by subsequent true crime documentaries) stems from this uncanny temporal duality, that it is simultaneously both a re-enactment of past events and an enactment of them as if they have not yet occurred. The two basic strata – the historical and the present – lie in contradistinction to each other, they mutually inform each other and change in relation to each other. However, there are a multiplicity of presents at play in a series such as this: the shooting/filming present; the broadcast present(s); the viewing present(s). These shift in perpetuity and never completely come to rest, and so, inevitably, neither does the legal case.

Within the framework of these moveable temporal dynamics and complex narrative structures, the essential components of the true crime documentary are the paired or competing stories of people and evidence. For all the uncertainties and fluctuations described, truth is not relative, it happened – but ascertaining *how* or *why* it happened in the way that it did is far from simple. People and evidence are, within the frame of the law, the two crucial means of accessing that truth, although they are also the surest means of complicating, obfuscating or masking it. Before the delayed title sequence of the final episode of *The Jinx*, there is a fascinating example of the hindrances as well as insights that comes when 'people' are brought together with 'evidence'. On camera Robert Durst is asked to comment on an envelope (a copy of which has been placed before him) addressed to 'BEVERLEY HILLS POLICE' (written in capitals, 'Beverly' misspelt); still on camera he speculates, in the third person, what the sender (who, it is to be inferred, was Durst himself) must have done, namely to 'take a big risk' by writing a note which 'only the killer (of Susan Berman) could have written'. Inside the envelope was a note (the perusal of which is re-enacted) on which is written Berman's address and 'CADAVER'. Copies of the two letters – one sent to the police, the other to Berman – are then, on camera (and in an unedited shot), handed by Jarecki to Jeanine Pirro, Former District Attorney, Westchester County, New York. Pirro is prompted to look at 'the rest of that letter' and quickly exclaims, 'Oh, Jesus. Beverl(e)y', at which point the (very, arguably too, swift) personal response and the evidence coincide as Jarecki's complementary visuals offer split screen images of the envelopes, both halves zooming in on the two versions of 'BEVERLEY HILLS'. As the quietly anxious soundtrack continues over the edit, the same photocopies are then handed (again on camera) to Chip Lewis, Attorney for Robert Durst. Lewis is not so quick to speak and Jarecki fills the short silence by remarking 'I couldn't help but recognise a similarity between the two, and I wanted to know what you thought of it?', a comment that straddles a jump cut from a mid- to a close-up shot of Lewis, who appears to be nodding in agreement. The edit is important in terms of what we now know of Jarecki's tidying up of the final taped confession as it here obscures how long Lewis takes to respond, which he then does, but in a significantly more circumspect manner to Pirro, admitting he sees similarities but also differences. Cut back to Pirro, who has no such doubts as she scrutinises the letter 'B's and pronounces them 'exactly the same. Son of a bitch'. With the strident title sequence starting directly afterwards, it is as if this mini sequence has reached its conclusion and found, through bringing people and evidence together, Durst to be guilty – in a short space of time and with no handwriting expert, as yet, consulted. The synchrony between personal opinion and evidence is a frequently compelling (if not necessarily watertight) documentary moment. (At the very end of 2019, Durst's lawyers admitted that their client had written the 'cadaver' note, but not that he had killed Berman.)

The importance of the personal angle to both the law and the true crime documentary is manifested in multifarious ways. The criminal trial's 'money shot', for instance, is the reaction shot after a verdict, the moment when courtroom television cameras rest on a defendant's face as they await a jury's decision: Michael Peterson's despondency, followed by his children's tears; Robert Durst's relief (or was that surprise?); Ted Bundy's inscrutability. The 'personal angle' spills over into content, from the (surprisingly rare) featuring of defendants and witnesses from 'ordinary' backgrounds (as in *Making a Murderer, The Keepers, Serial*) as opposed to extra-ordinary or comfortable and/or celebrity ones (Peterson, Bundy, Durst), to the 'social justice component',[13] as Joe Berlinger conceives of it, that ensues. Filmmakers give a voice to the Avery family, the abuse victims of St Keough High School and the Muslim community of Baltimore so as to ensure that they are no longer, in the words of Jean Wehner in *The Keepers*, 'invisible'. The personal angle makes a profound contribution on the part of the documentary to the pseudo-process of law, as when Gemma and Abbie in *The Keepers* stand up, like David against the Goliath that is the Roman Catholic Church, for all the 'ordinary' women who have reported being abused by the priests at St Keough.

In turn, the 'personal angle' also spills over into the relationship with the 'jurified' audience and others beyond the immediate parameters of the investigation. In Episode 3 of *The Keepers*, some 40–50 women are reported to have responded to an appeal for information that Abbie and Gemma placed in the local paper; such direct appeals to the public in turn corroborate the series' allegations by going beyond the text and cementing the bond between victims, investigators, the wider public and the viewing audience. Direct, personal appeals to the public are by now generically familiar forms of active spectatorship which constitute an extra-legal form of 'instrumental advocacy' (Mnookin, 2005: 154). As Mnookin observes of *Paradise Lost*, that a film can stir spectators 'from quiescence to advocacy' illustrates how the 'law's moving image can, on occasion, be a truly *moving* image . . . designed to effect a change in legal outcome' (2005: 154). There is a personal, bodily and emotive connection between individual on-screen and off-screen perspectives which can transcend and colour responses to evidence and clinical legal inquiry which documentaries exploit. For Sherwin, 'Visual meanings are written in the body, so to speak' (2011: 2); the personal is also the bodily and instinctual. Evidence alone is not what makes a case or cause compelling; what is needed by way of augmentation, true crime documentaries suggest, is the bodily presence – of personal advocates, interjecting filmmakers and viewers. In *Discipline and Punish*, Michel Foucault refers to instances when 'accounts of crimes and infamous lives were published' in advance of trials in order 'to force the hand of a court that was suspected of being too tolerant' (1977: 66). The true crime documentary engages its wider public by making the film or podcast a 'spectacle' for change whose primary mechanism is the personal dimension that brings evidence to life as well as to light.

'In the last twenty-five years words like *proof*, or even *truth*', writes historian Carlo Ginzburg, 'have acquired in the social sciences an unfashionable ring, evoking positivist implications' (1991: 294, italics in original). Ginzburg calls for the rejection of the 'element in positivism' that leads to 'the tendency to simplify the relationship between evidence and reality' (294), before returning to the tricky congregation of argument, personal intervention and evidence when considering the status and permutations of the document, which can, in his estimation, be many things: 'a fake', 'authentic, but unreliable' or even 'authentic and reliable' (294).

Ginzburg treads a line between those (the 'positivists') for whom evidence is not merely 'a historical document' but 'a transparent medium . . . an open window that gives us direct access to reality' (294), and those (the modern sceptics) for whom, conversely, evidence becomes a 'wall' which 'precludes any access to reality' (294). Ginzburg concludes that 'there are no neutral documents' (Donaldson, 1991: 313). Evidence, like Ginzburg's document, might appear superficially to be the binary opposite of personal intervention, but firstly it requires individual scrutiny to be understood and, secondly, it is seldom neutral. The point in *The Staircase* when things are looking especially bad for Michael Peterson comes in the third episode, 'A Striking Coincidence', which opens with his attorney, David Rudolf, watching ABC news report on the death, 17 years previously, of a female family friend and biological mother to Peterson's daughters, Margaret and Martha. Elizabeth Ratcliff's body, like Kathleen's, had (in 1985) been found at the bottom of a staircase. In court, the prosecution has emphasised the striking similarities to Kathleen Peterson's death, and Rudolf indirectly once again acknowledges his wider jury as he looks into the camera and remarks: 'Well, you guys got a much better film now' and ruminates sardonically on the 'stairway killer' who 'strikes like every 17 years'. Rudolf's combative response nevertheless admits that, to the 'jurified' lay-viewer, the 'striking coincidence' probably seemed like pretty damning evidence. And yet, evidence still needs people (lawyers, witnesses, spectators) to construct convincing arguments around it, just as the document requires the historian to interpret it.

The Staircase, like many subsequent true crime documentaries, raised particularly interesting questions about what legal scholar Jessica Silbey terms 'evidence verité', namely the 'film footage of arrests, criminal confessions, and crime scenes' routinely admitted in US courts of laws as 'the best evidence of what happened', especially of past events 'about which there is a dispute' (2009–2010: 1257). Such evidence can be especially powerful – and problematic – when presented to the largely untrained eyes of a television audience (if not Gewirtz's 'mob', then the court of common sense), such as my colleague who pointed to the gruesome images of the death of Elizabeth Ratcliff as *the* piece of incriminating evidence against Michael Peterson. Silbey contends that such 'evidence' 'is rarely analysed for its ambiguity, its bias or its incompleteness' or subjected to 'critical reflection' (1257–1258); in the court of law, as it does in culture, the photograph 'becomes iconic . . . more than mere evidence of some fact' (1260–1261), and as a result is deemed to be above analysis. To an obsessive, fetishistic, voyeuristic degree, detailed analysis of evidence is the epicentre of the true crime documentary: just as it gradually becomes apparent to viewers that the case against Father Maskell and others in *The Keepers* is weakened by the lack of 'evidence verité', so police crime scene videos in a number of documentaries are replayed repeatedly for their evidentiary as well as dramatic effect. Detailed scrutiny of evidence regularly interrupts and informs the fluency and cogency of the law narrative, as exemplified by Sarah Koenig and colleagues' exhaustive analysis of phone records or, as occurs in Episode 3 of *Serial*, 'Leakin Park', a single crime scene photo.

The analysis of 'evidence verité' without visuals is surprisingly compelling (although much 'evidence verité' could be consulted on the series' website if desired). In the middle of the episode – in which 'Mr S', who discovered Hae Min Lee's body in Leakin Park, is interviewed by police – Koenig describes poring over, at the State's Attorney's Office, the Baltimore Police Department's box of crime scene photographs with *Baltimore Sun* crime reporter, Justin George. Koenig remarks how she 'didn't understand how camouflaged the body was until I saw photos of the crime scene, the way Mr S found it before they removed the body'. As they look at the one photo, we hear Koenig and George exclaim in synchrony their disbelief at Mr S making out the body as he described: 'how did he notice [the body]? . . . it's pretty well covered . . . yeah, there's barely anything showing. Wait, are we supposed to be looking at something there? . . . Is that her? Is that all he saw? . . . I expected it to be more visible than it is'. In their stumbling, detailed scrutiny Koenig and George demonstrate that 'evidence verité' is rarely incontrovertible. As Silbey advocated: 'We should not be looking at the *photograph* for its meaning but at *the story in which the photograph is situated*' (italics in original, 1293–1294), before setting out to 'temper the illusion of objectivity and of "the whole truth" that *evidence verité* is perceived to project' (1298) by proposing a set of 'practical changes' that could be effected in the courtroom to minimise the 'illusion'. Considering our residual belief in photographic evidence, these 'changes' seem strikingly progressive and include the recommendation to judges that, 'When faced with the choice between a personal viewing of a crime scene . . . and a viewing of a photo or video of the same' they 'might consider opting for the personal viewing to avoid the mediation of the camera and the exaggerated effect of *evidence verité*' (1297).

Silbey's is, for documentary as well as for the law, a radical proposal, as 'evidence verité' at least putatively remains, for the documentary as well as the law, its trump card. 'Memory', as Errol Morris states, 'is an elastic affair. We remember selectively, just as we *perceive* selectively' (Morris, 2008); conversely, 'evidence verité', with its raw and direct indexical link to reality, is presumed to be less fallible, less tainted by the subjectivity and bias of 'the personal viewing'. And yet, as intimated already, personal engagement with evidence is the beating heart of the true crime documentary, drawing together its two primary mechanisms for accessing the truth. The dialogue between the two is a crucial narrative component repeatedly performed in the form, for instance, of the amateur investigator or filmmaker (be this Koenig, Jarecki, Gemma and Abbie of *The Keepers*, my colleague) scrutinising a document. However, it is this favoured interaction between evidence and people that most clearly enacts the impossibility of knowing conclusively that the right decision has been reached, that justice has been done; just as it is the trial lawyer's job to construct the most plausible narrative from the evidence and testimony provided, so the true crime documentary filmmakers take it upon themselves to use the tools at *their* disposal to construct their (often contradictory and open-ended) version of the story.

One of these tools is the re-enactment, the clearest expression of the law documentary as 'approximation'. In his discussion of Natalie Davis's *The Return of Martin Guerre*, Ginzburg ponders what the historian does when faced instead with *absence*. The absence of transcripts compels Davis to work from the judge's commentary on Guerre's trial and she is 'careful', in Ginzburg's words, to distinguish 'truth from possibilities' by adopting 'the conditional mood' with terms such as 'perhaps' or 'may have been' (Ginzburg 1991: 301). Re-enactment is, I suggest, the filmic or televisual equivalent of the conditional mood, the tool wielded in the true crime documentary to signal doubt or ambiguity as opposed to surety. Discussed in more detail in Chapter 6, it is often re-enactment that is used to give the films and series a speculative voice (transmuted, in podcasts such as *Serial* and *Black Hands*, into the voicing of speculative hypothetical scenarios). Re-enactment's primary role in the true crime documentary is to fill the gaps in the available archive and/or human memory, to bridge the divide, perhaps, between evidence and personal opinion or testimony.

The most prevalent form of true crime re-enactment is the blurred reconstruction that accompanies an interviewee's personal account of past events. In such cases, re-enactments serve a dual function: they convey the subjectivity and potential frailty of human memory, while also compensating for the lack of archival material. Their haziness does not necessarily connote unreliability; often it indicates the need to maintain a respectful distance from criminal and violent events. In *Cold Blooded*, for example, Berlinger reconstructs the Clutter family murders and their aftermath via soft and slowed images, leaving to the audience's collective imagination the full brutality of the attacks, while Ryan White in *The Keepers* uses indistinct re-enactment repeatedly as a tacit means of reinforcing the accusations of sexual abuse that ultimately, however, remain uncorroborated. Re-enactment is deployed in these instances to fill archival gaps, but feels less tentative than Natalie Davis's circumspect 'conditional mood'. At the outset of Episode 3 of *The Keepers*, as Jean lights a candle, lies down and closes her eyes as a means of enacting what she does to prompt the recall of repressed memories, she affirms in voiceover: 'This is not just a story. This really happened'. A close-up of Jean's horizontal profile fades to black before the image fades up again to a black and white re-enactment. Through tangled undergrowth and branches two figures can be made out – a blonde girl and a man – as Jean's voice continues: 'He took me to her body'. A point of view walking shot along a woodland path is then replaced by Jean in interview repeating: 'I know that I saw her. I know that I saw her'. The 'her' is Sister Cathy Cesnik's corpse, memories of which Jean had repressed since her schooldays; the 'he' is Father Maskell. In such an instance re-enactment functions as Ryan White's far from conditional affirmation of Jean's story. *The Keepers* builds up a re-enactment roster to counter the church's denials and to accompany the memories of abuse at the hands of Maskell and colleagues. These repeated emblematic re-enactments, though superficially elliptical serve to draw together the collective memories of the priests' victims – from the slow motion image of a girl walking into Maskell's office to her hand turning the door knob or the door clicking back shut, the sequence represents the experiences of all the victims.

In *Out of Thin Air* re-enactment is similarly deployed not to highlight the vagueries and instabilities of human recall but as advocacy, to reinforce a particular point of view. The film is noticeably re-enactment-heavy: reconstructions are used literally to illustrate on one level the perspectives of individual interviewees (accused, experts, journalists, etc.) and yet, on another, to bring these together into an all-encompassing distrust of the confessions extracted by the Icelandic police from Erla Bolladóttir and Sævar Ciesielski, two of the six suspects in the Einarsson and Einarsson case. Sævar was detained in solitary confinement for 615 days and interrogated 180 times for a total of 340 hours, leading forensic psychologist, Gisli Gudjonsson, and others to conclude that the confessions were 'in all likelihood fabricated'. That *Out of Thin Air* makes such liberal use of intense and hyper-aestheticised re-enactments performs this unreliability and strengthens Gudjonsson's conclusion that five out of the six detainees suffered from 'memory distrust syndrome'.

The Jinx (also overloaded, its critics maintained, with glossy, highly wrought re-enactments) ties reconstruction to human memory but uses it in a more Errol Morris-like fashion as the means to query the existence of any ultimate and undisputed truths. Though re-enactment is sometimes eschewed in favour of interviews in such investigative documentaries, it becomes especially powerful when linked, as it is in *The Jinx*, to direct and positive intervention into a criminal investigation. Whereas *Out of Thin Air* does not ultimately come up with a new solution to the double murder, *The Jinx* stumbles across fresh evidence (the 'BEVERLEY' envelopes and the audio confession) that does assist the case against Durst, who was arrested on 14 March 2015 for the murder in 2000 of his old friend Susan Berman.[14] In its use of re-enactment alongside old fashioned investigation, *The Jinx*'s most obvious antecedent is Morris's *The Thin Blue Line*, which likewise caused a murder case to be reopened on the presentation of a surprise confession. *The Jinx*'s re-enactments play reflective roles as opposed to an interventionist role; they do not posit alternative theories about Durst's crimes, but rather point to the value of speculation and rumination that ultimately makes way for the series' evidence-heavy and re-enactment-light final episode. Re-enactments also, quite simply, like the fast-cut montages of the opening sequences, heighten the dramatic tension of the true crime story, and in this respect Jarecki sets out his stall at the start of *The Jinx*'s first episode, 'A Body in the Bay', which opens with a broody night-time reconstruction of detectives attending a crime scene following a report that in September 2001 'a young kid' had discovered a body in the Bay of Galveston, Texas. A very Morris-esque police car, blue and red lights flashing in the gloom, creeps along a road; almost impossible to see in the darkness, a pair of legs get out of the car; in an eerie blue light and with the car lights still flashing, the figure of a policeman walks towards the water, as the voiceover details what he expects to find: 'a torso – no head, no arms, no legs, just the torso'. The re-enactment is replaced by 'walking through' enactment – of Jarecki being taken by the policeman to the bay in daylight as he describes having to put his arm down the torso's throat in order to pull it out of the water – and brutally graphic crime scene photographs of the dismembered body of Durst's friend, Morris Black. The early, swift juxtaposition of these three elements cements re-enactment's status, in Jarecki's estimation, as an investigative as well as a creative tool.[15]

Re-enactment is the element of *The Jinx* and the true crime documentary more generally to have received most criticism; Richard Brody of *The New Yorker*, for example, argues that 'What's lost in re-enactment isn't the logical verifiability of truth but the tonal notion of authenticity . . . the actual thing is a relic, a physical connection to the event' (Brody, 2015). Significantly, Brody considers re-enactments to be 'as-ifs' (2015) that undermine 'authenticity', and he is especially critical of the repeated – as he sees it gratuitous – simulation of Berman's body falling in slow motion. A comparably aestheticised re-enactment dramatizes the death of Durst's mother in Episode 2. Over home movie footage of him playing in the swimming pool with his mother as a child, Durst says his memories of his time with her are 'happy, happy, happy'. There is then a cut from his grinning boyhood face to a dark, slow pan up a woman's body, her light nightgown, then hair fluttering in the breeze. As the camera reaches her head, Jarecki's voice is superimposed asking Durst what his first memory is of 'that night your mother died'. The contrast between question and the enigmatic elegance of the re-enactment is stark and brutal, and symbolically marks this as the point that changed Robert Durst. Durst continues to narrate the re-enactment, which switches to the point of view from over the shoulders of the actors playing him and his father looking out of a leaded window at his mother on the roof.

As he recalls hearing the maid shouting 'she's off the roof', the re-enactment has moved much closer again, as Bernice Durst's body tumbles slowly, surreally, almost balletically towards the ground. 'It was a long, long fall', Durst remarks, his glacial drawl mirroring the length of her fall. At the time (corroborated by a newspaper clipping), Bernice's death was reported as an accident, a conclusion

FIGURE 4.2   Robert Durst's mother's unbloody suicide in *The Jinx* (Andrew Jarecki, 2015)

supported by the subsequent re-enactment shot of her artfully posed and conspicuously unbloody body on the ground. Durst casts doubt on this version when he tells Jarecki: 'It happened, I was there, I saw it – whatever I saw'. *The Jinx*'s smudged re-enactments do not posit concrete alternatives to evidence or truth, rather their indistinctness creates the space for doubts and re-evaluation.

So, what do re-enactments add and what roles do they play in the true crime documentary? They are not evidence, although it is possible for them to build a convincing narrative about the events they depict. Errol Morris, in his *New York Times* blog, argues that re-enactments 'burrow underneath the surface of reality in an attempt to uncover some hidden truth' (Morris, 2008). They are not just about looking again; they are concerned with discovery, unravelling and re-examining. *The Jinx* is not a drama, but through its hyper-stylised re-enactments it does raise key questions about how fictionalisation tempers what Dershowitz termed 'life's chaos'. While Jarecki's grandly stylised re-enactments add little by way of fresh evidence, they do enable the otherwise comically unbelievable catalogue of bizarre events that make up Robert Durst's life to be dramatized.[16] At one stage, Durst flees from the police disguised as a mute woman named Dorothy Ciner and rents an apartment in Galveston where he subsequently murders and dismembers Morris Black. In the full-blown, in-focus dramatization for Jarecki's feature film, *All Good Things*, the absurdity of this image is distracting, whereas Jarecki's blurred re-enactment, being less outlandish, maintains its dual status as both proxy evidence and narrative fiction.

Re-enactment brings together multiple, often conflicting points of view, different temporal layers, reality and fantasy. It permits perspectives to be countered or strengthened and, most fundamentally, offers up the space for judgements or verdicts to be questioned and reopened. The re-enactment is the articulation of an absence of knowledge of evidence and can only offer *a* view, not *the* view of truth, but it also stems from personal interpretation and brings an emotional and psychological proximity that many other elements in both law and documentary lack. The re-enactment rarely brings certainty (at the conclusion of *Out of Thin Air*, for example, we are told that the 1974 Icelandic double murder has been reopened, but what 'really happened' to the victims 'remains a mystery. Their bodies have never been found'), but it prises open cases and facts to enable re-scrutiny.

Shoshana Felman comments how 'A trial is presumed to be a search for truth, but technically, it is a search for a decision, and thus, in essence, it seeks not simply truth but a finality: a force of resolution' (2002: 54–55). It remains acceptable, almost mandatory, for true crime documentaries *not* to 'conclude' or reach 'finality', *not* to 'end' or to resolve themselves in a determinist, definitive way, but rather to stop on a note of ambivalence or uncertainty, which the re-enactment embodies. Truth, like life (to echo Dershowitz) is messy, cases are often legally closed but unresolved. When he started filming *The Staircase* Jean-Xavier de Lestrade 'was convinced that in the end I will know about him (Peterson), but after two years and a half, I cannot say for sure',[17] though he remained convinced that 'that the trial was not fair to him'.[18] The inconclusive conclusion can take many forms: *The Jinx*'s mousetrap finale brings only problematic certainty, while Sarah Koenig's subdued lack of surety at the conclusion to *Serial* is ironically just as satisfying. Whatever their tone, conclusions rarely signal finality, as exemplified by the true crime series' afterlives: the perennially updated websites, or more importantly the retrials and subsequent acquittals that have come about as direct or indirect results of the series themselves. Jarecki might superimpose a sense of formal closure on *The Jinx* when, following Durst's shocking testimony, the lights for the final interview are shut down one by one, but this denouement is really only the beginning: following his initial arrest in 2015, Durst's trial was due to begin early in 2020 (but was delayed following the revelation that Jarecki had doctored the final confession). In March 2019, just after Maryland's Court of Appeals denied Adnan Syed a new trial, Koenig posts a blog on the *Serial* website in which she finally (for now) states very clearly where she stands on this judgement at least: 'Now I'm going to say it: I disagree with the Court of Appeals decision. . . . He should get a new trial'. When responding to questions about whether or not she will undertake more episodes as the story unfolds, Koenig is equally adamant: 'I don't have anything to add to the deluge of reporting that's already aswirl. Like millions of people, I've become a spectator'.[19] Koenig's characterisation of herself as 'a spectator' is salutary and moving: for all her instrumentalism in helping the Syed case gain national and international prominence, the case soon breaks free and (re)becomes an entity in its own right.

All true crime endings should be seen from the perspective of independence and openness. Even in a definitively closed case such as that of Ted Bundy, the ending of *Conversations with a Killer* comprises a set of disparate perspectives on Bundy (proffered by various of the series' previous interviewees) interposed with elegant, expansive aerial landscape shots. The juxtaposition of Stephen Michaud likening Bundy to a 'taint you can't get rid of' and a staggeringly beautiful pastoral sunset – golden flames centre frame, encircled by grey clouds and mountains – functions as a simile for Bundy's unknowability (that we might understand what he did but not what drove him) and the case's complexity. The final (for now) episode of *The Staircase* ('Flawed Justice', 2018) shows Peterson rejecting the opportunity of a retrial and instead taking the Alford manslaughter plea, which leaves him, in the words of the presiding judge, 'free to go' as 'he has served his time'. Outside the courthouse Peterson comments ruefully to the assembled media: 'This deal is not a good one for me. . . . There is no closure. This is not an end'. *The Keepers*' frustrating circular narrative ends, in a superficial sense, where it begins: with the diocese's denial of abuse and Sister Cathy's murder as yet unsolved, but Jean – who is drilling a memorial plaque into a tree at Cathy's death site – warns: 'Before you know it, the pressure of that voice [of the abuse victims] creeping through the cracks, is going to shatter it!'. The subsequent cut to black, like Jarecki's symbolic extinguishing of the lights, is a powerful and decisive *formal* gesture, but sadly a toothless one. The final sequence of Kopple's *Murder in Mansfield* shows Collier with his therapist, who is keen for him to 'let go', which Collier does – although not in the way he has led us to think he wants. Instead, he describes the relief of having 'lost that man' (his father), although his quest for some more definite 'closure' (an infinitely loaded term in which emotional, psychological and narrative needs are conflated) is referenced more than once through the course of the film. Is his father Jack a sociopath, intransigent or cynical (he has sought to enlist Collier's support more than once to help him gain parole)? Or is he just plain innocent? Does Collier press him so hard to confess because he believes he committed first-degree murder or because 'All I've ever wanted is a father who loved me'? Viewers of *A Murder in Mansfield* might prefer the catharsis that comes with emotional certainty and narrative resolution, yet irresolution remains a way of life, and there is often a painful and insoluble schism that opens up between what a documentary posits as the truth in a case and the verdict or conclusion arrived at. 'Closure' too eagerly sought makes of the law a crude and blunt instrument. The nuanced, complicated consolidation found in these true crime documentaries between the chaotic randomness of life and complex, incomplete narratives is doubtless less consoling than the emotional predictability of the traditional fictional linear form, but it befits an era attuned to the realisation that any event or verdict is vulnerable to being changed, to being overturned or viewed entirely differently as fresh insights, new evidence, further witnesses come to light. These are living 'approximations' that will never reach Felman's 'force of resolution'.

Unresolved observations of justice: the 10th district court, outside the court, palais de justice

Only relatively recently has law on screen become dominated by the true crime documentary; the final portion of this chapter will look briefly at an alternative: the observational law documentary. From the outset, *The 10th District Court: Moments of Trials*, *Outside the Court* and *Palais de Justice* share a sense of the law as a force for *irresolution*. In 1995, John Fiske and Kevin Glynne argued that 'symptoms of postmodernity' such as the loss of truth's 'finality and objectivity' (505) had already destabilised television and were threatening to do the same to the law; they ask, 'in an age of multiple and shifting realities, how can lawyers represent *the* reality of an event to a jury?' (506). The films of Raymond Depardon, Marc Isaacs and Carey Young extend the doubt running through true crime documentaries that *the* reality is ever attainable. No less attuned to its entertainment potential, these films reflect more upon the law's ritualised performativity (its conventions and rhythms) and provide more abstract ruminations on the institutions of the law and the relative opacity of different legal systems (those of France, the UK and Belgium). The legal outcomes of cases are marginalised in favour of attention being placed on the individuals who partake in and are affected by the law, as these documentaries are above all artistic as opposed to investigative responses. In his inaugural lecture at UCL (University College London, 15 March 2018), Anthony Julius posited that 'law and literature are alien in their respective modalities'. 'Law oppresses art' and 'literature is suspicious of the law' he continued; and yet, without both, a society would be incomplete. Although formally fragmentary, poetic and narratively inconclusive, these films also embody the artistic, and as such express the idea that it is the two sides of the law – its internalised structures and its social-facing aspect – that render it complete.

The shifting sands of the law, truth and justice inform Depardon's *The 10th District Court*, a portmanteau of 'moments', as its subtitle indicates, from cases that, in early 2003, came before Madame Justice Michèle Bernard-Requin, presiding judge in a busy Parisian district court. Bernard-Requin's bench is adorned with daunting piles of case documents as she and the lawyers plough through cases one after another and pass verdicts at the end of each session, sometimes late into the night. Depardon was permitted to show only segments of individual cases, as opposed to entire trials, and had to change the names and personal details of the 25 people (out of 169 filmed) featured in the documentary. The incompleteness of the narrative is signalled from the outset. The start of *The 10th District Court* (on 15 May, 11.30 A.M.) is announced via courtroom 'white noise' of footsteps on stairs, fidgeting and the shifting of chairs, immediately after which, with a mid-action low angle mid-shot of a male defendant, poised in the witness box waiting to be addressed by the judge, the film proper begins. The documentary likewise ends (4.26 P.M., 19 June 2003) mid-action and on a parallel low angle and out of focus shot of the courtroom's wood panelling and the top of one of its doors as the judge's off-screen voice summons the 'next case'. The film's focus is the fragmented, unstructured workings of a local court and the people in it; less interesting to Depardon are the criminal cases and legalities *per se*.

Depardon's scrutiny of minutiae is enthralling; segments from individual cases are spliced together kaleidoscopically, neither explained nor completed, and filmed via a fixed, outwardly inexpressive, tripod-mounted camera that does not respond as figures walk into or drop out of shot. Cinematographers Depardon, Justine Bourgade and Fabienne Octobre use a limited, repetitive range of framing options: front on or low angle mid-shots, low angle or eye level close-ups. The fleeting glimpses into personal traumas and chaotic lives are, paradoxically, enabled not diluted by Depardon's inscrutable visual style, for fragmentation or stylistic minimalism do not prove impediments to emotional involvement in the cases, exemplified by the charged example of Karim Toulbia (not his real name) and his former partner, Laura Lekouby (also a pseudonym), who has brought charges of harassment against him. There is considerable and powerful tension between the cool manner in which the sequence is filmed and its visceral content. We have become accustomed by this point in *10th District Court* to the presiding judge's wit and eloquence (Michèle Bernard-Requin is the true star of this documentary) but rarely to that of those defendants (intoxicated, mumbling, confused, angry) who come before her. Lekouby, with her calm fluency, is the exception. She recounts seven years of abuse, how Toulbia 'still beats me in my dreams, beats me every day' and speculates that, if he is given a light sentence today, he will 'be patient, and try again to ruin my life'. There is a cut away to the seated Toulbia, looking over at his accuser as she continues: 'I won't give up. He's afraid of the law; that's why I'm here'. Toulbia, who remains as inscrutable as Depardon's camera, is ultimately found guilty and given a 16-month suspended sentence. He is also served with an injunction preventing him from entering the 11th Arrondissement, where Laura Lekouby lives.

In a sequence such as this, the profound potential as well as the arbitrariness of the observational trial documentary emerges. On the one hand, reality has its own potency that does not need to be 'constructed' or scripted; on the other, the 'moments of trials' brought before this Parisian court are merely random stations along a continuum – on other days Depardon would have found himself equally engrossed in entirely different stories and lives. It is accidental and lucky that Depardon is there to witness this striking 'performative moment'. *The 10th District Court* is situated at the other end of the law documentary spectrum to the true crime documentaries, underscoring (via its tonal detachment or lack of strong formal linearity) the acceptance that the act of filming is incidental to the court's business, testing to the limit Mnookin's assertion 'That observers affect what they watch is practically axiomatic' (2005: 154) as it emphasises its own residual lack of influence over events. True crime coverage (as when a camera anticipates a defendant's reaction to the verdict) largely represses or elides this realisation. Depardon's camera is not hidden, but that nobody looks into its lens resonates with something equally axiomatic, namely that courts of law will go about their business and justice be meted out regardless of a camera's presence.

Marc Isaacs' *Outside the Court* is similarly focused on the individual stories (as opposed to testimonies) of the defendants Isaacs accosts outside Highbury Magistrate's Court across two seasons, 'Summer' and 'Winter'. Like Depardon, Isaacs's focus is the process of law and its effect on individuals' lives, expressed via a similar compendium of incomplete, splintered testimonies, this time told to the camera outside not inside the court. Isaacs only seeks out one side of the story; his viewers never have it definitively confirmed whether or not the truth of the performances in front of the camera corresponds to the unobserved actions or truths that unfold once the interviewees have disappeared through the courthouse's revolving door. The film features no lawyers, only defendants (and on two occasions family members). Remaining 'outside the court' becomes a potent metaphor for the exclusivity of the law, its impenetrability, but also for its intransigent strength; 'outside the court' is a space that is both real and metaphoric, a 'thirdspace' as Laura Rascaroli (after Soja) terms the space in Isaacs's *Lift*, 'which is simultaneously real and imagined . . . a space of extraordinary openness, a place of critical exchange . . . enabling the contestation and renegotiation of socio-geographical boundaries and cultural identifies' (Rascaroli, 2013: 5).

The law hangs over *Outside the Court* as a ghostly presence, the film's immovable object represented literally in its first frame by a close-up of the crest mounted above the dreary mid-century doorway to the Magistrate's Court. Justice's traditional blindness is here transmuted into anonymous muteness. In terms of their relationship to the legal *system*, the defendants are powerless, only able to respond to the fines and sentences meted out; but as with Depardon's defendants, this relative passivity does not, within the film, equate to subjective power. Also, obviously, 'outside', Marc Isaacs (interviewing whilst operating one of the two cameras) establishes a symbolic camaraderie with his subjects as another 'outsider'. 'Outside' is a figurative space beyond the jurisdiction and confines of the courthouse arena; it is also the documentary's literal domain. The local colour of the Highbury streets forms the film's backdrop – the string of dust carts, the assured urban fox, the unremitting traffic – bathed poignantly in beautiful sunlight (warmly golden in summer, coldly blue in winter) that lends the otherwise drab urbanism an awkward beauty. Brief interludes punctuate the drama of the interviews, drinking in the metropolitan environs and capturing its arresting complexity. Though focused on the defendants' backstories and not their appearances in court, Isaacs, like Depardon, remains non-judgemental. He is a patient interlocutor who says little, but rather poses broad and brief questions in order to engage his interviewees and get them to open up, a tactic that, in turn, invites his viewers to observe, to spend time scrutinising the facial details and expressions his camera has alighted on. His strategy brings to the surface a series of individual tales of hardship and misfortune, and elicits surprising details, such as the revelation by the father awaiting the release of his son that, for 12 years, he was a professional soccer player in Madeira. 'What was that like?' Isaacs asks; 'good life', the father replies, 'but everything is finish. Now it's a different life'. Then there is the alcoholic Frenchman, Michel, who later on (so after we feel we have got to know him) recounts his abuse as a child: 'always running away to avoid a beating. Always cold and hungry. . . . I have never been normal. I never will'. Isaacs gives his subjects time and attention, he elevates them from being the string of anonymous cases they most likely become the other side of the revolving door; as Michel remarks, it 'makes me feel good to speak in front of the camera'. This is their moment in the sun.

Isaacs's shoulder-mounted camera gets stuck in; it is immediate and there: in the moment, the moment of encounter between director and social actors, further captured by the second contextualising camera. Interviews framed from a variety of angles gesture to the idea that there is always more than one way of seeing or looking, more than one truth. Isaacs forges a visual style that is rougher, more energetic and overtly responsive than Depardon's; one that creates solidarity with his subjects and their own roughness and edginess. He often elicits unexpected information, as with Michel or, most wrenching of all, the woman before the court on charges of Actual Bodily Harm, committed on the day her mother died. When Isaacs asks if she has been to visit the grave, the woman answers 'no, because she's buried with my son. I don't like going up there'. From behind the camera Isaacs's shock at this appalling, unanticipated revelation of her infant son's cot death is palpable, but he does not retreat; instead, his camera becomes a means of access rather than a barrier. Unlike his putative Direct Cinema antecedents, Isaacs's method, as Rascaroli notes, is to draw attention to 'the director's presence in situ . . . his camera is not invisible' (2013: 5). His presence is felt, for instance, in the exchange with the alcoholic father, Mark, estranged from his son and about to receive a custodial sentence. In the second dialogue with him, Mark is heavily inebriated and desperate; he holds his head in his hands and then walks off. Isaacs's camera lingers on him sitting on a bench, before an edit to a closer shot as Mark takes a gulp from his can; the switch to the more supportive image presages Mark saying to himself, to Isaacs and to us: 'I'll take an overdose. It don't bother me'. Isaacs's voice from behind the camera pleads with him 'don't do that', but to little avail. Mark takes some pills, vows to 'fuck 'em all' and lies down. Mark's hopelessness is starkly juxtaposed with another luminous sun; he gets up and, as he lurches towards the doors of the courthouse, imploring Isaacs's camera to 'help every addict in the country'. Crafting a quite different tone to Depardon's more strictly observational tripod-mounted images, the camera in *Outside the Court* becomes a tool of active engagement.

The 'outside' space Isaacs inhabits is not just a convenient backdrop; it is fundamentally a discursive space for rumination as well as dialogue. We the viewers cannot but see the law in its social context. The law is shut off and insular in Isaacs's film, contrasted directly and symbolically with the sublimity of the summer's golden light and the eclecticism of the social world that continues on its way 'outside the court'. The revolving doors become the crucial metaphor for this. Through the course of the documentary we become intensely aware of their status as a liminal barrier between the openness of outside and the closedness of inside, between a space of non-judgemental dialogue and exchange to the internal courtroom arena of judgement and sentence.

Doors as barriers also feature throughout Carey Young's video artwork, *Palais de Justice*, which transports its spectators to the interior of the colossal Brussels central court, a large, crumbling edifice that houses some 7000 working lawyers (the majority of whom are women), although, as Linda Mulcahy observes, 'Like Josef K we always stand on the outside looking in' (Gaakeer et al., 2018: 291). Young, became fascinated by the Palais as 'monumental labyrinth', its imposing omnipotence but also its 'signs of decay' that converted it 'somehow in[to] a zone of neutrality, beyond anyone's full control' (Carey Young in Gaakeer et al., 2018: 306). The Palais de Justice feels anachronistically grand: in the UK we have courts not 'palaces of justice, which, as barrister Barbara Rich points out, lends the institution of the law a 'sense of grandeur'.[20] Anomalous though it might seem, the Palais' grandiloquence becomes a discernibly subversive if not anarchic space, with greater affinities to the disorderly urbanism of Isaacs's street than first appears likely. Young's work conceptualises the law's power through filming only lawyers, not defendants, and by focusing deliberately on female lawyers, a tactic that presents 'a legal space decisively occupied by women' (Joan Kee in Gaakeer et al., 2018: 288) and places the female judges and lawyers 'in dialectical relationship to the building's innate patriarchal symbolism' (Carey Young in Gaakeer et al., 2018: 306). (Although the similar gender balance of *The 10th District Court* is probably simply random, it makes for an interesting comparison.) Young filmed illicitly in the Brussels courthouse over the course of two years, producing, from hours of High Definition video rushes, a film of 18 minutes (itself a form of advocacy, as Philippe Sands remarks).[21] Not only is the Palais de Justice enormous, but it is, Young observes, filled with iconography that 'feels very patriarchal'.[22] Counterpointing this, the masculine point of view is marginalised; as Gary Watt comments, when there is a 'rare close-up study of a male advocate' he is 'lingering outside a courtroom door and peering, like us, through the port-hole window' (Gaakeer et al., 2018: 302), an image that asks: 'Would a legal system run by women be a better thing?'[23]

It is interesting if not contrary that one way in which Young confronts the complex gender dynamics is through the adoption of an explicitly voyeuristic gaze trained on female workers. The film's voyeurism is overtly expressed through Young's intense fascination with the porthole windows that provide her only access to the courtrooms. Viewers, as they are also in *Outside the Court*, are made reflectively aware of the camera and the art as well as the act of looking. Watt says of one shot in *Palais de Justice* that it 'compel[s] us to look at the circular glass window, and not merely through it. The result is alienating. We feel the edifice of the building, of law, looking back at us' (Gaakeer et al., 2018: 301). The doors that house the portholes are, for Young (as they were in a different way for Isaacs), metaphors for the law, thresholds onto a legal system that both protect its workings and bar us, the observing outsiders, from it. Doors can welcome, but in *Palais de Justice* they universally keep the viewer out: they prevent sound from carrying, thereby enacting legal proceedings as mute moments of theatre, and they intensify the importance and impact of the visual. The porthole windows provide restricted views, cropped yet luminous points of access onto a spectacle that we are never intended to fully comprehend. Their very shape echoes the shape of the eye, spectacles and the camera lens and their *alter ego* is the camera, which here functions as a go-between, as a means of accessing the elusive subject of law. The advocates and judges spied in *Palais de Justice* might, as Philippe Sands suggests, have 'placed themselves in a special, exclusory space that says we are above you, we won't connect with you',[24] but the still intransigence of Young's tripod-mounted camera (another similarity with Depardon's film) is equally redolent with a sense of control having been snatched back. The static camera most clearly recalls the similarly fixed and objective CCTV lens, an insinuation that especially comes to the fore when coupled with the ongoing soundtrack of indistinct voices and footsteps echoing across marble. The soundtrack, as Young specifies, did not use only the diegetic sounds, but mixed the building's sounds 'to create a distinctive "sonic environment", an abstraction of the Palais' unique auditory personality' (Gaakeer et al., 2018: 308).

The gaze in *Palais de Justice* manages to evoke both the oppressive orchestration of the panopticon and the loose informality of eavesdropping, of just stumbling across an image worth looking at, which intensifies in the final third of the film as the scopophilic gaze is increasingly prominent. With her 'paparazzi-style lenses' (Gaakeer et al., 2018: 309), which compel us to home in on the physical femininity of the women lawyers, in particular their hair, necks and hands, Young's stated intention is to 'convey a sense of tenderness and tactility – or the desire to touch' (Gaakeer et al., 2018: 309). Periodically, the ostensible casualness of the camera's gaze is scrutinised and undermined when women judges appear to make eye contact. In fact, they were simply staring into space, but with this illusion of the fourth wall being broken comes the possibility that power is reverting back to the anonymous, detached institution of law, which in turn draws our attention to the complexities of the act of filming women who do not realise they are being filmed. 'There's a celebratory quality to just looking' and the 'feminist gaze should be pluralistic', Young attests,[25] but there are moments when the focus on the mute female advocates and judges unsettles the viewer and makes them feel uncomfortable with the position of control and domination in which they unwittingly find themselves. At screenings of *Palais de Justice* these are the moments that women find most problematic. For women, just such a conflicted moment comes when there is a lingering shot of the wisps of hair on the back of one lawyer's neck, an image of intricate ambiguity. In one sense such an image is objectifying and reductive, for as we are unable to hear the legal argument she is making, the female lawyer is reduced to the level of fetishised image. Conversely, these shots resonate with their poetic beauty, arrestingly uncomplicated by words, and cement the sense that it is women who are in control – and they *are* in control of the law, for it is in the initially troubling objectification of the female form that one ultimately finds, in *Palais de Justice*, its clearest, and most ironic, embodiment of the pervasive sense of the law's all-consuming omnipotence. The piece's sustained reflexivity (that it refuses to let the viewer forget they are watching a constructed film) mitigates against the concern that it is conforming to rather than rebelling against the law's patriarchy; the act of filming is omniscient and all-controlling. *Palais de Justice* is an involved tug of war between the law and the female filmmaker it tried unsuccessfully to keep out.

'The law' in *Palais de Justice, The 10th District Court* and *Outside the Court* is a quasi-independent entity to 'the crime' or 'the evidence', which are precisely the facets that preoccupy the true crime documentary. In this trio of films, the law, though not necessarily ennobled, is rendered opaque through its muteness, absence, blindness and its sheer scale. When compared to true crime documentaries, these three pieces offer uncanny 'approximations': discursive, fragmented and ambiguous; they express an alternative idea about truth, which extends beyond the frustrations of the true crime documentaries' frequent realisation that, because justice and truth are not necessarily related, resolution and closure remain out of reach. Truth, like justice, is perpetually transient the observational documentaries proclaim; there is no such thing as the complete and indisputable truth, or justice, so why seek it out? In all three, the institution of law is likewise unstable and inconsistent, a series of performative acts. In a documentary, the performance in front of the camera may or may not correspond to the 'truth' that might have unfolded had the cameras not been there; these works by Depardon, Isaacs and Young are similarly not *about* the truth or otherwise of the defendants' stories, the judgements; their focus, rather, is the *process of law*. The films extend a view of justice as a multifaceted idea not necessarily couched within the institution of the law.

Tyrone Kirchengast argues that the modern trial is more than 'the popularly conceived notion of the adversarial trial before judge and jury' and needs instead to be understood as a 'discursive institution of social power that . . . transforms to meet social needs' (2010: viii). Just as the criminal trial, according to Kirchengast, is now open to new, less 'narrowly conceived' discourses, so the true crime documentary as well as the observational law documentary has freed popular representations of the law from the equally 'narrowly conceived' law as portrayed by law and film studies.

The modes of representation and narrative have become richly varied and roving, while the notion that a case can reach simple closure is not merely dismissed but rendered irrelevant, as all the crimes, trials and cases featured are layered, mutable and perpetually open to new, additional information that could transform them. Neither the true crime documentary, with its focus on the specifics of cases, nor the observational law documentary, with its interest in the process of law and the individuals it affects, follow the 'syntactic narrative' Clover detects in the traditional adversarial trial (2000a: 108), and in this they are both accepting of the unpredictabilities that underpin justice and the search for truth. In their formal fracturedness and narrative incompleteness they are all 'approximations', sitting at a tangent to and acknowledging the mutabilities of reality and evidence, in dialectical dialogue with both the abstractions and the specifics of the law (evidence, lawyers, courts).

Notes

1 Cf. Bruzzi (2016a) for a discussion of theatre director Andres Veiel's film adaptation of his own production *The Kick* (2005), a prime exponent of the true crime 'performative documentary', which comes from another, notably German tradition, of documentary or verbatim tribunal-form theatre and whose antecedents include Rolf Hochhuth, Peter Weiss and Heinar Kippardt, as probably does the work of experimental Swiss theatre director, Milo Rau, whose tribunal plays include *The Last Days of the Ceausescus* (2009) and *The Moscow Trials* (2013). The tribunal form has more recently been revived by the Tricycle Theatre, London under Nicolas Kent's Artistic Directorship, with a series of documentary plays about topical miscarriages of justice produced between 1994–2012 (now published as a single anthology). Topics tackled by the Tricycle playwrights included the murder of Stephen Lawrence, the Saville Enquiry into Bloody Sunday, the 2003 inquiry into the death of government arms inspector, David Kelly, in *Justifying War – Scenes from the Hutton Inquiry* (2003) and Richard Norton-Taylor's later play, *Called to Account* (2007) which presented a succession of charges against Tony Blair for crimes of aggression against Iraq. The Tricycle tribunal cycle has proved influential on, for example, British playwright Alecky Blythe (whose 2011 play *London Road* about the Steve Wright murders of 2006 was made into a film in 2015), Nicolas Kent's *All the President's Men? Scenes from the Senate Confirmation Hearings of President Trump's Cabinet*, performed for one night only in London's West End in 2017 or J.T. Rogers' 2017 play *Oslo* centred on the 1993 Oslo Accords). This theatrical heritage, and earlier film documentaries such as Frederick Wiseman's *Law and Order, Juvenile Court* or *State Legislature* and Emile de Antonio's one foray into the verbatim tribunal tradition, *In the King of Prussia* (1983) informed the discussion of the film and television documentaries that follows.

2 Like so many film and law scholars, Clover's examples are taken largely from Hollywood (even branching out into European 'art cinema' and a film such as Marleen Gorris's *A Question of Silence* [1984] would have problematised if not undermined these simplifying assumptions), and the latter part of her article dwells on the 'trialness' (115) of Paul Verhoeven's neo-noir *Basic Instinct* (1992).

3 I was one of those scholars. In the late 1980s I wrote my PhD thesis, *Trial and Error: The Political Use of Trials in Film, Theatre and Television*; I neither published the book of the thesis nor did I even deposit it with either the University of Bristol or British Library. More fool me. Over the latter 1990s, legal scholars and some film academics began to get extremely interested in the law on film, many of them reaching similar conclusions to the ones I had arrived at in my thesis, namely that the law (most explicitly in its Anglo-American adversarial form) is inherently dramatic and that the tribunal form in particular possesses an inbuilt quasi-Aristotelian narrative cohesiveness, which makes it

congenial and convenient fodder for drama and narratives. This affinity between law and narrative cultural forms (film, television or theatre, for instance) has continued to attract scholarly interest, and finally not merely in relation to Hollywood, which has often provided the most accessible if blandest and unchallenging illustrations of this mutuality. Just some of the scholars who have probed the parallels between narrative film and the law are, from the perspective of film studies, Carol Clover and Charles Musser, and from the much more extensive list on the law studies side, Steve Greenfield, Guy Osborn, Peter Robson, Paul Gewirtz, Peter Brooks, Jennifer Mnookin and Jessica Silbey.

4 Journalists also likened *Serial* to *The Staircase*. www.newyorker.com/culture/sarah-larson/serial-really-taught-us; www.telegraph.co.uk/culture/tvandradio/11327934/Could-the-Serial-podcast-trigger-a-retrial.html. Accessed 8 March 2018.

5 In the US, *The Jinx* aired February–March 2015 and *Making a Murderer* started December 2015.

6 *Making a Murderer*'s title sequence is directed by Ahmet Ahmet for Elastic, and *True Detective*'s by Patrick Clair for Antibody, a sister company to Elastic. The share the same Executive Producer, Jennifer Sofio Hall.

7 Though of little consequence here, Dershowitz misrepresents Chekhov, whose plays were seldom so neatly tied up.

8 A rare exception is German émigré Hollywood director, Fritz Lang, who, in films such as *Fury* or *Beyond a Reasonable Doubt*, remains attentive to the role chance plays in arriving at justice. For a further discussion of Lang and justice, cf. Stella Bruzzi, 'Imperfect Justice: Fritz Lang's *Fury (1936)* and Cinema's Use of the Trial Form', *Law and Humanities*, 4:1, 2010, 1–19.

9 Many older antecedents exist, such as London Weekend Television's *The Trial of Lee Harvey Oswald* which, in 1986, staged the trial (using real lawyers and witnesses) of the man accused of killing President John F. Kennedy. After 8 hours of deliberation the 12 Dallas residents of the television jury concurred with the Warren Commission verdict that Oswald was the lone assassin on 22 November 1963.

10 One such talk and Q&A can be found at: 'Westside Bar Association: Inside *The Staircase* – Making Sense of the Madness', 11 October 2018, W Hotel Hollywood, www.youtube.com/watch?v=rrMWi9Be06o. Accessed 29 April 2019.

11 'The Staircase – Inside the Series', *Sundance TV*. www.youtube.com/watch?v=mXLaDPJk1ZU. Accessed 25 August 2016.

12 '*The Staircase*: Director Jean-Xavier de Lestrade on Michael Peterson. Owls and More, *thedailybeast.com*, 4 March 2013. www.thedailybeast.com/articles/2013/03/04/the-staircase-director-jean-xavier-de-lestrade-on-michael-peterson-owls-and-more.html. Accessed 13 October 2019.

13 Berlinger in conversation with Ricky Camilleri for Build Series, 9 February 2019.

14 The police also started to investigate links between Durst and other deaths: that of his first wife Kathleen McCormack Durst in 1982 and the unsolved disappearances of three other women.

15 *The Jinx* was not Jarecki's first involvement with the Durst case, which had been his feature film, *All Good Things*, a fictionalised version of Durst's life starring Ryan Gosling as the Robert Durst-like property heir, David Marks. Durst saw the movie and, as documented in *The Jinx*, called Jarecki's office to offer the director an interview.

16 Other episodes include his conviction for the lesser crime of killing Morris Black in self-defence, despite having cut his corpse up into pieces and dumped them in Galveston Bay, of being apprehended shoplifting when he had $37,000 in the trunk of his car, and of contacting Jarecki and offering him an interview because he had liked the director's thinly veiled fictionalization of his life in *All Good Things*.

17 Interviewed for: 'Inside the Staircase'. www.youtube.com/watch?v=mXLaDPJk1ZU. Accessed 17 April 2019.

18 'Jean-Xavier de Lestrade and Matthieu Belghiti Discuss Truth and *The Staircase*', *London Live*. www.youtube.com/watch?v=Mxpzza702CE. Accessed 17 April 2019.

19 'Adnan Syed's Conviction Reinstated' by Sarah Koenig, *Serial* blog, 15 March 2019. https://serialpodcast.org/posts/2019/03/adnan-syeds-conviction-reinstated.   Accessed 17 April 2019.
20 Q&A after Carey Young in discussion with Philippe Sands after a screening of *Palais de Justice* at the School of Laws, UCL, 4 December 2018.
21 In discussion with Carey Young after a screening of *Palais de Justice* at the School of Laws, UCL, 4 December 2018.
22 Carey Young in discussion with Philippe Sands after a screening of *Palais de Justice* at the School of Laws, UCL, 4 December 2018.
23 Carey Young in discussion with Philippe Sands after a screening of *Palais de Justice* at the School of Laws, UCL, 4 December 2018.
24 Carey Young in discussion with Philippe Sands after a screening of *Palais de Justice* at the School of Laws, UCL, 4 December 2018.
25 Carey Young in discussion with Philippe Sands after a screening of *Palais de Justice* at the School of Laws, UCL, 4 December 2018.

5

POLITICAL MIMICRY

From mimesis to alternate history

The focus of this chapter is the portrayal in drama of former British Prime Minister Tony Blair (primarily in *The Queen* [Stephen Frears], *The Trial of Tony Blair* [Simon Cellan Jones, 2007] and *The Ghost* [aka *The Ghost Writer*, Roman Polanski, 2010]) alongside a discussion of the satirical *A Very English Scandal* (Stephen Frears, 2018). The Blair administration was most likely the most dramatized government in history; 'It was certainly', as Steven Fielding observes, 'the most *quickly* depicted' (2014: 241). In 2012, former British war artist John Keane exhibited a series of paintings in an exhibition entitled 'Scratching The Surface, Joining The Dots'[1] at the centre of which were six canvases depicting Tony Blair testifying on 29 January 2010 to The Chilcot Inquiry: 'Figures at an Inquiry, 1–5' and 'Hands'.[2] Further paintings included 'The Contentious Return of Abdelbaset Al-Megrahi', showing the 'Lockerbie bomber' on his release from prison in 2009 and two paintings entitled 'Sign from God', one of a road sign for Attanf, Iraq and Damascus straddling a lonely desert highway, the other of the same scene, but this time with a blurred, grotesque Tony Blair in the foreground, his distorted red tie resembling blood. The Iraq Inquiry pictures are based on screen grabs Keane took whilst watching Blair answering questions live online. In a 2015 interview with journalist Mark Lawson, the artist commented: 'everything I do now starts life on a computer screen'; images first exist and are worked on digitally before being projected and worked on as paintings. He has 'spanned the pre-digital and the digital age. . . . I still have this sort of pre-digital painterly approach . . . even if I'm working with a screen' (Keane, 2015). Later, he would produce similar sequences of paintings of Vladimir Putin, Rebekah Brooks and Rupert Murdoch for the exhibition 'Speaking Power to Truth'. When questioned specifically about his approach to portraying Blair, Keane commented:

I just couldn't bring myself to address him [Blair] in any sort of literal way. . . .
I spent the whole day watching it [the Chilcot Inquiry]. . . . I was fascinated
and appalled. It was a kind of sanctimonious self-denial. In the face of obvious facts, there was this sense of self-righteousness, which somehow seemed
to trump everything else.

(Brown, 2012)

As Robert Harris does in his *roman à clef* about Blair, *The Ghost*, Keane's emotional
responses to Blair (being both 'fascinated and appalled') become translated into
visceral, figurative and only vaguely literal images.

Keane's paintings, though not strictly sequential, represent a journey into abstraction; the most abstract only truly decipherable by virtue of their titles ('Figure at an
Inquiry') and their contextualisation within the series. 'Figure at an Inquiry no 2'
is the most discernibly both 'not' and 'not-not' Blair; one can make out the distinctive hairline, the blue suit, red tie and hands as he testifies, yet his face is pixelated
out. This and 'no 5', which comprises a series of concentric, television-screen-like
squares that gradually sharpen their focus until at the core there is a totally in-focus
image of Blair's hands in triangular formation with fingers touching and elbows on
desk, are especially successful at conveying the transition from clarity to abstraction.
They are dynamic, suggestive of movement and instability and of the oscillation
between the two – not dissimilar to the dialectical exchanges between fictional and

FIGURE 5.1   'Figure at an Inquiry, no 2' (John Keane, 2010)

factual points of reference in the examples of political mimicry. Insight, these paintings suggest, is generated through the imperfection and instability of the image or performance of reality, not its fixity. As Keane says above, he could not bring himself to address Blair literally (for him, it is the literal that brings with it 'contamination', not *vice versa*) and this second image in the series carries the most palpable force, the greatest anger and outrage, as a series of lines, like cuts, radiate out from the obliterated face. In no 3, only the barest reminders of Blair can be made out under a fog of thick paint and lacerations.

Discussing one image in the Rebekah Brooks sequence, writer Mark Lawson describes how the 'paint gets in the way' (Keane, 2015); observers find themselves mentally trying to peel away the layers to get at 'the truth', although even the most literal images declare this to be permanently out of reach. The blurring, obfuscation or suppression of the literal image is itself a commentary on the subjects' denial of 'the truth': Blair's reluctance to apologise, to acknowledge that he had got it wrong finds its way into the evasive images. Keane refers to the 'small satisfaction' that he 'can muck about with them [Blair, Putin, Murdoch]' as they abused their positions of power, thereby testing the theory that mimesis is knowledge, transgressing the boundaries between knowledge and emotions, and engaging with the deeper, more nuanced knowledge one acquires when one puts the two together. Knowledge is not necessarily in either proportion or in inverse ratio to clarity; Keane's series demonstrate the importance of dialectical exchange as the route to understanding, of the collisions contained within each collage, exemplified by the formative collision between the digital and the painterly. The blurred, kaleidoscopic image more generally enacts the value of being able to see and retain at one time multiple perspectives and ways of seeing; the paintings' style also obliquely recalls the technical imperfections of television news and current affairs broadcasts on which they are based. The last Blair painting, 'Hands', is of the raised, contemplative hands of 'Figure at an Inquiry no 5' magnified. As a coda to the previous five paintings 'Hands' seems to be offering a salutary warning against believing that proximity to an image will bring with it proximity to the truth.

The core of successful political mimicry is not merely impersonation but the productive entanglement of fact and creativity, for it is in that interweaving, as opposed to merger, that critical fantasy resides. The lines and demarcations in Keane's mixed media portraits are, crucially, visible; differences are not elided. Likewise, in the mimicry of political figures, the facts and truths that give substance to those impersonations are maybe masked or tempered, but they are not invisible. As with other drama-based 'approximation', here facts touch their fictional renditions. The reimagining and mimicry of contemporary politics and political figures is immensely popular; one reason might well be that viewers enjoy the game of comparing 'real' people and their impersonation, whether this is from memory or, more likely, from replayed footage (news, archive, photographs, etc.). Peter Morgan (arguably the best known writer of political – and other – mimicry working at the moment) remarked when interviewed after the live screening of his play, *The Audience* (2013), that we had been watching 'an imagined conversation' but that, in the writing of the play, he had been able to 'join the dots' back to research and knowledge about the events either side of these unscripted weekly meetings between the Queen and her Prime Ministers. Emma Freud, his interviewer (for NT Live), suggests to Morgan that perhaps he is pushing for a 'different truth' when writing, to which he responds by pointing out that there is a difference between 'truth' and accuracy' and that, 'many things might be inaccurate, but hopefully not untruthful'. The relationship between 'truth' and 'accuracy' is fundamental to political mimicry, however fictionalised, comedic or satirical the mimicries become (and Morgan's work is at the closer to reality and less politicised end of the spectrum).

This chapter settles for an intentionally narrow definition of 'political mimicry' in that the emphasis is on the *political*, with a concomitant focus, following on from Morgan's comments, on the divergence between the 'real' and its close imitation – and the difference the difference between the two makes. The political 'real' and its shadow are more of less approximate; the intention behind centring the study on the representation of one figure – Tony Blair – is to mark and chart progression along a mimicry continuum, from the extremely close imitation (of *The Queen*) to the more distantly satirical (of *The Ghost*). There is no hard and fast theory to be attached to political mimesis in terms of proximity; it is by no means the case, as Keane's canvases attest, that the closer or more accurate the imitation, the more trenchant or critical it is. Often (but not always) the opposite is true: *The Ghost* is more packed with consummate loathing for Blair than *The Queen*, even though the Blair figure is not even called 'Blair'. The distinction between original and copy is tested in a different manner in *A Very English Scandal*, which remains remarkably faithful to its material while being the most broadly comedic example of mimicry included here. The Jeremy Thorpe scandal is so genuinely replete with bizarrenesses, absurdities and poignancies that you really could not, as they say, make it up. The very whole notion of proximity vs. distance is mocked at the outset of Paolo Sorrentino's *Loro* (2019) which, though manifestly a satirical portrait of Silvio Berlusconi (the central character is called Silvio and Berlusconi was aware of the film as it was being made), opens with a flurry of convoluted and ironic disclaimers that maintain 'this film stems from its authors' independent and free imagination', that the events depicted make no claim 'to represent an objective truth' and that 'No reference to people and/or events except those specifically identified as real is intended or should be inferred'.[3]

The era of Tony Blair's years in office (1997–2007) was marked by a peculiar conjunction of 'extraordinarily important events' (most prominently the Iraq invasion of 2003) and 'politicians – even those on the far Left' starting to 'act like film stars' (Street, 2003: 85). It also became a golden era for political mimicry and satire, and Blair's premiership overlapped significantly with the resurgence of verbatim tribunal plays at the Tricycle Theatre between 1994 and 2012;[4] it also ushered in (in the UK) a time of 'spin' and the mediarisation of politics – the precursors to 'post-truth' politics and news. Political mimicry is a popular, though not often radical, narrative form which, despite not necessarily upholding the outmoded 'great man theory of history' (Carr, 1961: 66), tends to have as its focus individual portraits.

Maurice Gran (co-author with Laurence Marks of series such as *The New States-man*), when asked 'why do dramatists write about politics?', said that he was 'not convinced that the great character, the great man/woman theory of history is all that wrong' (Fielding, 2011b: 351), and the majority of recent works by Peter Morgan, the most prolific political mimicker of the century, centre on politicians – as *opposed to* politics. When questioned about 'the Granita scene' in *The Deal*, for instance, Morgan declared himself to be 'not remotely radical!' (Paget, 2013: 176). Similarly, his other scripts 'about' politicians – such as *Frost/Nixon* (2008), *The Audienc, The Crown* (2016) – are significantly more interested in character and interpersonal relationships.

Attention to personality and character does not automatically bring with it an absence of politics, for, as Linda Hutcheon noted when offering some context to the rise in the 1960s of the non-fiction novel, what was circulating around works such as William Manchester's *The Death of a President* was 'a real distrust of official "facts"' (Hutcheon, 1988: 115). A 'distrust of official "facts"' forms the backdrop for many of the dramatisations of Tony Blair, who, largely as a result of his misjudged and unpopular decision to invade Iraq, inspired a range of copies and satires, ranging from the comic to the more serious, for example Richard Norton-Taylor's verbatim plays, *Justifying War: Scenes from the Hutton Inquiry* (2003) and *Called to Account: The Indictment of Anthony Charles Linton Blair for the Crime of Aggression Against Iraq – A Hearing* (2007). Blair is critiqued across film and television in a variety of genres and modes, and the catalyst more or less explicitly is the disaster of Iraq. From Jon Culshaw's impressionist parody of his speech to the US Congress on 17 July 2003, upon being awarded the Congressional Gold Medal (*Dead Ringers*, BBC2 2003),[5] or Alison Jackson's lookalike spoof film *Tony Blair: Rock Star* (2006) to the Comic Strip's *The Hunt for Tony Blair* (2011), Iraq and Blair's fixation on his legacy figure prominently. There are no overt links to Iraq in *The Thick of It*, but the use of 'spin' and the 'sexing up' of dossiers and documents that formed part of the background to Iraq are implied. Blair became a valued figure of fun; likened or linked to Hitler more than once, in *The Trial of Tony Blair* his legal predicament is compared in passing to Chilean dictator Augusto Pinochet's.

The question of Iraq and Blair's legacy is confronted directly (and comedically) in the counterfactual drama, *The Trial of Tony Blair*. As Blair (Robert Lindsay) leaves office, amidst an otherwise cheering crowd outside Downing Street, he becomes rattled by an anti-war protestor. In the car he turns to his wife, Cherie:

BLAIR: My legacy – do you think my legacy's, you know, secure?
CHERIE: Yes, yes, I do.
BLAIR: Good.
CHERIE: Why?
BLAIR: Well, you know, I just want to make certain, that's all. [Long pause.] It won't be Iraq they'll remember me for will it?
CHERIE: No. [Phoebe Nicholls pats Lindsay emphatically on the knee.] No, I'm sure it won't be.
BLAIR: Good.

The 2003 Iraq War is directly the catalyst for both *The Trial of Tony Blair* and *The Ghost*, two examples of Blair-focused political mimicry discussed below. Two Peter Morgan-scripted/Stephen Frears-directed Blair dramas, *The Deal* and *The Queen*, focus on other political crises (the Labour leadership election following the death of John Smith and the death of Princess Diana in 1997), but Iraq would have been there in the collective unconscious of their respective audiences. The third film in the Morgan 'Blair trilogy', *The Special Relationship* (directed by Richard Loncraine, 2010), which centres on Blair's collaboration with Bill Clinton over the much more positively received military intervention in the war in Kosovo, can and has been interpreted as a sympathetic and extravagant apologia for his subsequent collusion with Clinton's successor, George W. Bush, over the invasion of Iraq.[6] The US/UK invasion of Iraq entered the consciousness of popular drama and is also the motivation for the fictional assassination of George W. Bush during a 2007 visit to Chicago in the counterfactual film, *Death of a President* (Gabriel Range, 2006). A Syrian national is found guilty of the murder, although it later transpires that the assassin was a veteran of the 1991 Persian Gulf War whose son had been killed in the more recent Iraqi conflict (a narrative thread very similar, therefore, to the assassination of the Blair-esque prime minister in *The Ghost*).

Although the frequent issue raised in discussions of mimicry is the snobbery surrounding the notion of 'impersonation', the big question about *political* mimesis is: what can it add? David Morrissey, for one, when detailing how he set about shaping the character of Gordon Brown for *The Deal*, talks of the need to 'be careful' and avoid 'impersonation . . . when you're acting a real person in a *serious* drama' (in Cantrell, 2010: 112–123; my italics), and Tom Cantrell (the editor of the collection for which Morrissey was interviewed) remarks how, 'the cast of *Called to Account* were reticent to use terms such as "mimicry", "impersonation" and "imitation"' to describe their art (Cantrell, 2013: 137) – despite (presumably) realising that, as actors in verbatim theatre, they deployed precisely these skills. Familiarity and proximity are two dominant facets of mimesis: looking like and being recognisable as the person being imitated; hard to execute and yet frequently critically undervalued. The direct performance of actual events, people and words as faithfully as possible grants audiences something approximating direct access to those original realities. This is performative mimicry's uniqueness. But inherent within 'performative mimicry' lies an immovable paradox: that in being 'performed', however proximately, the original people and events are necessarily erased, or more accurately relegated to the wings as their uncanny performative echoes are placed centre stage. A playwright such as Alecky Blythe strives to minimise the distance between the binaries of this paradox by muting the actors' tendencies to 'perform'; she plays the interviewees' actual words directly to her actors on stage through headphones, so they listen to and replicate the audio and repeat exactly what they hear – not just the words but 'every cough, stutter and hesitation'.[7] This way, Blythe explained to me, the actors 'are concentrating so hard they don't have time to *act*'.[8] In this respect, mimicry 'is not a form, it is a technique; it is a means rather than an end' (Hammond, 2012: 'Introduction'). Filmmakers attempt something comparable through not merely performance but the juxtaposition of archive and performance.

The inevitable (but not entirely straightforward) implication of even such a technically sophisticated kind of mimesis as Blythe's is that imitation is no substitute for knowledge; it is not analysis or investigation; it does not *add*, it repeats, an insinuation reinforced by interviews with actors preparing to perform real people in which they stress the need to establish a likeness to their subject or to 'inhabit the character' by refining, adding to and not merely *repeating* their 'visual characteristics and physical mannerisms' (David Morrissey and Roger Allam quoted in Cantrell, 2010: 112, 8). And yet, it is possible for repetition to harbour insight and knowledge. The act of repetition brings a completed, past action into the present; it also, with minimal elaboration or refinement, changes the original and perceptions of it.

The multiple conventions, motifs and tropes of political mimicry are illustrated in a sequence such as the two-and-a-half-minute enactment of the funeral of John Smith in *The Deal*, a dialogue-free sequence accompanied, from start to finish, by Kenna Campbell's reprisal of the Gaelic rendition of the 23rd Psalm, which she performed at the funeral itself. It opens with a montage of eight archival shots showing members of the congregation arriving at Cluny Parish Church, Edinburgh, all of which bear the trademark lines and graininess of live broadcast video: the scars of authenticity that also, alongside Campbell's plaintive strains, make the sequence incredibly moving. The archive has been selected so as not to include the protagonists of the drama, Blair and Gordon Brown (assumed by many at the time to be Smith's natural successor), for one common convention of docudramas about real people is that only the actor/impersonator appears – though another is that the 'real person' often makes a fleeting appearance (sometimes as a photograph and sometimes as Norman Scott does at the end of *A Very English Scandal*, filmed smiling to camera) during a non-diegetic credit sequence.[9] Once established, the funeral sequence is disrupted by two made-to-look-like-archive shots of Michael Sheen as Blair and David Morrissey as Brown arriving, both walking briskly towards the church. (These are not, incidentally, faithful copies of original actuality footage). After archive showing the arrival of Smith's wife and daughters, the action cuts to inside the church, when all the images – of Kenna Campbell (as herself), and of Blair and Brown amidst the congregation – become full-blown and glossy drama-documentary, as smooth pans and a neat focus pull from the back of Blair's head to the back of Brown's two rows in front announce the shift from OB (outside broadcast) (whether genuine or faked) austerity. Outside the church again after Smith's coffin has been conveyed for burial, there are two further paired shots of Blair and Brown in a huddle with their respective advisors, one set is rough faked archive, the other polished close-ups and mid-shots. A sequence such as this draws attention to the pronounced stylistic transitions, suggesting that its inelegance had been contrived for effect. But what effect?

The overall and most blatant effect is to compel us as viewers to notice that this is a sequence that has been *constructed*, that it is not merely a basic re-enactment of a historical scene. The scene's inherent fragmentariness, its explicit aesthetic transitions from archive, to fake archive, to drama-documentary, are all performative acts of judgement, interpretative *choices*, manifest indications of 'approximation'.

A uniform, verbatim dramatisation can still retain complexity, but formally it has narrowed down the interpretative options. Exploring some of the pleasures of reading, Roland Barthes identifies *tmesis* (the separation of parts of a compound word by an intervening word or words) as one source of readerly 'pleasure' (Barthes, 1975: 11), elaborating that 'intermittence', 'tears', 'edges' (10) or 'the *abrasions* I [as reader] impose upon the fine surface' (11–12) are some of the factors that render reading enjoyable. With gaps opened up between the authentically pixelated television news archive, the fake news footage and the lusher celluloid full-blown dramatisations, the textual fissures of the John Smith funeral sequence likewise create depth and complexity. While edited to make a linear sequence, the funeral does not look like one; its dynamic fracturedness performs the idea that history can be opened up to multiple interpretations. Two such (conflicting) perspectives are offered by David Morrissey and Blair's head of communications, Alastair Campbell. For the actor, the funeral was 'the most charged scene [in *The Deal*]'; the actor's inference (probably influenced by Morgan and his own research for the role) was that 'At the moment when Brown should have been at his most galvanised and organising his leadership campaign, he lost his great friend and political mentor and was overtaken by grief' (Cantrell, 2010: 113). This sense of having lost the moment to grief is itself lost in *The Deal*, undermined entirely by the shot-reverse-shots between the politicking rival 'camps' sizing each other up, an exchange that rather echoes Campbell's diary entry for 20 May 1994, the day of the funeral, when he writes that 'Gordon Brown was moving and grooving, really working the room' (2010: 14). While Morrissey feels more compelled to like 'someone I admired' (Cantrell, 2010: 113), the audience is under no such compunction, as the visible textual cracks openly express the residual interpretative tensions.

The 'uncanny', or how something familiar and 'homely' becomes frightening or 'unhomely',[10] is a familiar concept, informing (even if unnamed) a question such as Belén Vidal's about Michael Sheen's portrayal of Tony Blair: 'how should we read a character who exists, first and foremost, through television?' (Vidal, 2014: 145). Likewise, John Corner, in an article that appeared in *The Guardian* the day after '9/11', observes that:

> The piece is doing its descriptive work in a context where most readers will be terribly familiar with the event as a visual phenomenon, through the replays of varied television material the previous day and photographs of the kind that feature on the paper's own front page.
>
> *(Corner, 2007: 10)*

Mimicry, as Michael Sheen suggests when he comments how aware he is of the need to 'meet the audience's demand for familiarity' when playing living people (Cantrell, 2010: 4), is about evoking the familiar, and the Morgan/Sheen 'Blair Trilogy', is not merely concerned with dramatisation but with stimulating 'personal memories, identification, recognition' that surface when a spectator watches a re-enactment of events they 'have lived through' (Reinelt, 2009).[11] Drama meets 'personal memory' repeatedly in the Blair dramas as many viewers will recall the sunny, heady day of New Labour's landslide victory on 1 May 1997, or the shock of Princess Diana's death a few months later. But as Vidal intimates, these memories are themselves heavily mediarised: we most likely did not experience the headiness or the grief of victory and death directly, instead, we watched them unfolding on television. Rather than seeing these as 'uncanny' references, it is perhaps more useful to interpret them as 'reverse uncanny' moments when we are led back to the real person, event or memory by experiencing them most vividly in dramatised form.[12]

Similar confusion reigns between real and fantasy when it comes to the use of the epithet the 'People's Princess' for Princess Diana. In *The Queen*, the term is attributed to Alastair Campbell, in a scene in which the new Prime Minister, dressed in a Newcastle United shirt with 'Blair 10' emblazoned on its back, rehearses down the telephone to his 'spin doctor' what he is going to say about Diana's death before church the following day. However, in both Campbell's diary and Blair's autobiography the implication is that the 'People's Princess' came from Blair.[13] Whatever its derivation, one important facet of the appellation remains that it was a construction that came to stand for and define Princess Diana, masking all her ambiguities and contradictions, and which still evokes the emotive nostalgia of the surreal morning after her untimely death.

After the Blair-Campbell telephone exchange, there is a switch to archive images of BBC news anchor, Martyn Lewis, announcing that 'We're going, I believe to Sedgefield' for the Blairs' arrival at church, conveyed briefly using faked actuality footage before cutting to the first of two busy, fictional press offices (Campbell's) in which assembled staff gather before a bank of four television screens, two showing (Sheen as) Blair in the churchyard delivering to the assembled press his speech about Diana (audible is: *'though her life was often, sadly, touched by tragedy, she touched*

FIGURE 5.2   Made to look like archive shot of the Blairs arriving at church (*The Queen*, Stephen Frears, 2006)

FIGURE 5.3   The bank of television screens in Alastair Campbell's press office

FIGURE 5.4   Full-blown glossy re-enactment of Michael Sheen as Blair delivering 'The People's Princess' speech

the lives of so many others'), the other two relaying footage of Princess Diana alive and members of the public setting down flowers in her memory. There is then a reverse edit back to Blair, not on a diegetic television, but full-screen; the sound edit is seamless as the words continue uninterrupted (*'in Britain, throughout the world, with joy and with comfort'*), although the graininess and thin sound of the previous *faux* archive has now been replaced (as it had been in *The Deal*) with a full drama-tisation using lush celluloid, richer sound and mournful non-diegetic music that will swell as the sequence progresses (a switch that is, later in the sequence, reversed with a return to the *faux* pixelated image). An essential component of the montage here is the sound, so over multiple edits Blair's words remain audible as full-screen segments of him outside the church are juxtaposed with action from both press offices – Campbell's and the Queen's, under Robin Janvrin. Blair's voice reaches the most memorable section of his speech (*'they liked her, they loved her'*) as the image reverts to a tighter framing of Sheen for its iconic climax (*'they regarded her as one of the people. She was [pause] the People's Princess'*) before a final, bathetic return to the royal office's single miserly, old-fashioned television set. The sequence concludes, as it had begun, with a conflict of tonal as well as stylistic registers. Janvrin (Roger Allam), at the end of Blair's speech, quips, 'bit over the top, don't you think?' as he turns around to his staff, only to be confronted by a phalanx of teary, snivelling female colleagues matching the lachrymose Martyn Lewis in the BBC studio, his voice cracking as, in front of an image of the resplendent Diana, he repeats 'she was the People's Princess'. As in *The Deal*, the formal complexity of this sequence brings together a complex of perspectives of the same event and invites a mixture of emotions and responses.

The collage used in *The Queen* adopts a by now familiar format for the political documentary drama; more recently, in Marco Bellocchio's *Il Traditore* (*The Traitor*, 2019), Tommaso Buscetta's arrest and return to Italy is represented by the juxtaposition of full-screen archive, a fictionalised rendition of the archive and the original archive being watched on a diegetic television set. Thinking about some of these shifts in register and style, numerous scholars of documentary and drama-documentary,[14] have made fruitful use of Jean-Louis Comolli's notion of historical fiction's 'body too much': the body of the 'historical character' and 'that of the actor who represents him for us' (1978: 44). In the historical film, Comolli argues, the convention is 'to ensure that the actor's body is forgotten … hidden … beneath the supposedly known and intendedly pre-eminent body of the historical character to be represented' (49). Such a fusion is achieved against the odds (having been prefaced by the coldly sardonic rehearsal of the speech at home in his football shirt and the fragment of faked archive of the Blairs entering the churchyard, both of which emphasised rather than collapsed the difference between 'bodies') in *The Queen*'s rendition of Blair's 'People's Princess' speech. But, testament to the speech's iconic status (that it possesses an identity that transcends its contextualisation) is that such fusion occurs at the moment in Campbell's press office when the speech is broadcast on two of the four television monitors as Sheen-as-Blair, flanked by Diana on the one side and flowers on the other, is literally subsumed by, transported into the historical moment. The actor thus enters history; for the duration of the speech at least, he is no longer simply part of a commentary upon it. Once 'the actor's body is forgotten', the full-screen dramatization commences. Doubly ironic is the fact that Sheen's rendition of the 'People's Princess' is atypically subdued – for both Blair and Sheen – when compared to the news original, a minimalism assisted by Frears's substantially tighter choice of framing. Omitted are the real Blair's expansive hand gestures (out in front of him, usually with fingers intertwined or fingertips touching, sometimes splayed for emphasis), mimicry of which undoubtedly would remind audiences of the fact that Sheen's is the 'body too many'. At this crucial, emotive juncture we do not match Michael Sheen up against the 'real' Blair, but rather we see and (mis)remember him as the 'real' Blair, temporarily forgetting his head ticks, easy smile, choppy hands and odd pauses.

For Comolli, Pierre Renoir, in his embodiment of Louis XVI in *La Marseillaise* (Jean Renoir, 1938), 'brings this body, his own, to the fore: he emphasises its reality and presence. . . . Far from making the spectator forget it, he points it out to him', the result of which is to have a body that 'is seen without being seen' (49). The Peter Morgan/Stephen Frears/Michael Sheen collage sequences foreground an unresolved tension between the single body and the body: the two fused in the full-blown polished drama sections, but remaining distinct elsewhere, as the real 'physicality of documentary expression' (Corner, 2007: 5) persistently punctures the docudrama's veneer. The lines of the video archive scar the film's smooth 'skin', or, to apply, after Derek Paget, Annette Insdorf's inspired notion of the 'danger' in realist drama 'that the aesthetic can become an anaesthetic' (in Paget, 2007: 167), real 'bodies' in the Morgan/Frears films become submerged or anaesthetised within the aesthetics of glossy drama. In the absence of Blair, Sheen *is* Blair and the act of making him look like him, to pursue Insdorf's thought, is also, I would suggest, supposed to make us *like* him (much more easily achievable if Blair is absent).

Talking about playing real people such as English film director, James Whale, Ian McKellen remarked that 'you want to do right by them' (in Cantrell, 2010: 14). Wanting to 'do right' by his characters, wanting us to like them – or at least not to hate them – feels like what propels Peter Morgan. Of *The Deal* Morgan has said that it was not a film especially concerned with New Labour, but was rather 'a film about friendship' (in Paget, 2013: 176). Although this de-politicisation of *The Deal* is disingenuous (for Blair, for all his easy-listening qualities, was a significant politician and not just 'Butch Cassidy' to Brown's 'Sundance Kid'),[15] Morgan uses the anaestheticising aesthetic of historical fiction to make his audience feel for and not just think about his characters. The tears shed by Martyn Lewis and the fictionalised palace press office aides are reminiscent of Steven Lipkin's third purpose of docudrama after 'provoking public memory and shaping national identity', namely: 'the recovery of sentiment as a matter of history, through the foregrounding of the physical and emotional as evidence' (Lipkin, 2011: 91). Morgan links the physical presence of his characters to sentiment; his professed apoliticism (even if every film, as Comolli and Narboni so expertly demonstrated, is political)[16] emerges in these twin attachments, as making his characters *like* their real antecedents (by fusing original and copy into 'one body'), becomes his bid to make us *like* them in the process, a conflation exemplified by twinned acts of *peripeteia* (reversal) by Blair and Queen Elizabeth, later on in *The Queen*.

Before going to London to address the nation about the death of Diana, the Queen visits an adjacent estate to enquire about the death of a stag. She notices that the '14-pointer' was wounded, which the gamekeeper confirms before adding: 'I'm afraid the stalkers had to follow him for miles to finish him off'. The parallels with Diana (Roman goddess of hunting) hounded by the paparazzi are irrepressible.

A more reflective Queen heads off from Balmoral followed by an edit to television archive of the extraordinary bank of flowers encroaching upon the railings of Buckingham Palace, many still encased in cellophane like marine debris brought to shore by an especially violent storm. 'The last time the Queen was among her people outside the palace', a newscaster recalls, 'was the day that war in Europe ended'. Watching this scene on television, after handing Blair a copy of the speech for the Queen's planned televised broadcast, Alastair Campbell emits the last of three snide quips: 'well at least the old bat's finally agreed to visit Diana's coffin'. Blair's patience dissolves and he blasts back:

> You know, when you get it wrong, you really get it wrong. That woman [gesticulating towards the television screens playing the news] has given her whole life in service to her people . . . and now we're all baying for her blood.

After Blair has stormed out, we enter the television archive, as it were, as the image goes to full screen with a cut back to the Queen (Helen Mirren) perusing the line of flowers. She exchanges a few words with a little girl clutching a bunch of chrysanthemums: 'would you like me to place them for you?' she asks; 'no. . . .', replies the girl (the Queen looks dejected) '. . . . these are for you', at which point the Queen's face broadens into a smile. This sequence cements the idea that the audience is to overlook the characters' differences and failings, to *like* them and be moved, as far as the Queen is concerned, to tears. Emotive *volte-faces* for both Prime Minister and monarch accomplished, *The Queen* engineers their mutual rehabilitation, but not before one final reversal. Prime ministerial audiences at Buckingham Palace top and tail Frears's film, and in the one that closes it, Elizabeth II warns her premier: 'you saw those headlines and thought one day that might happen to me [reverse shot of Blair squirming]. And it will, Mr Blair, quite suddenly and without warning'. And, of course, it does – on 19 March 2003, as US/UK-led forces commence the bombardment of Baghdad.

The 2003 Iraq War is the starting point for and explicit target of *The Trial of Tony Blair*, an example of satirical political mimicry written by Alistair Beaton and directed by Simon Cellan Jones. Set in an alternate near future, it possesses an altogether different sensibility to the Morgan/Sheen trilogy. Like Stephen Frears and Russell T. Davies's *A Very English Scandal*, a more recent example of satirical political mimicry, the performances are broader and more comic; the targeting of policy and the establishment altogether more acerbic. Like theatre scholar, Richard Schechner's 1980s' notion of 'restored behavior', the central performances of Robert Lindsay (as Blair) and Hugh Grant (as Jeremy Thorpe in *A Very English Scandal*) use and splice together 'strips of behaviour . . . independent of the causal systems (social, psychological, technological) that brought them into existence' (Schechner, 1985: 35). They emanate from, while not being servile to, the originals they mimic and are able also to maintain their independence as dramatic entities. In relation to performance, Schechner speculates how 'The original "truth" or "source" of the behavior may be lost, ignored or contradicted – even while this truth or source is apparently being honored and observed' (35). Both *The Trial of Tony Blair* and *A Very English Scandal* are faithful to historical detail (Thorpe's dandyish clothes, or Blair's preoccupations with his legacy) while nevertheless feeling empowered elsewhere to depart from authenticity (flying Blair off to The Hague to face war crimes charges, for instance). All forms of 'restored behaviour, surrogation, ghosting, haunting, citation – repetition and/or deferral of meaning' are, to Schechner's mind, indicative of the 'impossibility of defining, no less finding, "originals"' (Schechner, 2014: 25). The 'originals' of either Thorpe or Blair are submerged beneath layers of repetition and ghostly performance, and Lindsay, Grant and their fellow actors appear liberated by the absence (until the closing moments of *A Very English Scandal*) of archive that might have effected a direct comparison with indexical source materials. On the political mimicry continuum (and Schechner determines that the difference between Erving Goffman's notion of the 'presentations of self' and his own of 'restored behavior' or 'me behaving as if I'm someone else' is merely 'a difference of degree, not kind' [1985: 37]) Sheen would be one end, with Lindsay and Grant considerably closer to the other.

Temporal as well as performative distance liberates *A Very English Scandal*, a comedic three-part series about the scandal that engulfed and destroyed, in the late 1970s, the career of Jeremy Thorpe, charismatic leader of the Liberal Party. The trilogy ends (as did Thorpe's political career) with Thorpe being acquitted of charges of conspiracy and incitement to murder of his former lover, Norman Josiffe (known as Scott). Thorpe was free, but he had resigned as Liberal leader and lost his seat in the 1979 General Election. He died in 2014 of Parkinson's Disease, nine months after the death of his second wife, Marion. As British actress Siân Phillips observed when asked about playing real people: 'when they are dead, you are off the hook (to a certain extent)' (in Cantrell, 2010: 7), but temporal detachment notwithstanding, the overriding factor in *A Very English Scandal*'s portrayal of the Thorpe scandal is not merely liberated detachment but an overwhelming realisation that fact is stranger and more hilarious than fiction. The series is comical, parodic and satirical, but it also stays closely tethered to its historical moorings.

The plot to kill Norman Scott involved a chain that ran from Thorpe, his former parliamentary colleague and confidant, Peter Bessell, his best man, David Holmes, a carpet salesman who shared the same name as a prominent actor at the time, John le Mesurier, a fruit machine salesman, George Deakin, to hired gunman and former airline pilot, Andrew Newton, who, in October 1975, succeeded in shooting dead Scott's Great Dane, Rinka, but failed to shoot Scott himself on account of his gun jamming. On Scott's trail, Newton really did mistake Dunstable for Barnstable, while Scott did remain genuinely fixated on needing Thorpe's help in obtaining a replacement National Insurance card. Other incidental details (such as Lord Arran, campaigner for the decriminalisation of homosexuality, giving badgers the run of his home or Scott leaving a suitcase full of incriminating love letters from Thorpe in a suitcase on a Swiss train) are also true. Likewise, Hugh Grant's embodiment of the complex and contradictory Thorpe is equally complex and contradictory. His performance 'may seem like a grotesque caricature. But it isn't'; instead, David Steel (who succeeded Thorpe as Liberal leader) thought it an 'uncanny' and 'genuinely remarkable' likeness (Kettle, 2018). Grant's broad cartoon-like performance is made up of factual details, but also the 'glances, gestures, body language' that sit 'outside the archive' (Martin, 2006: 11).

The truth behind the 'Thorpe affair' was already so colourful as to render archive virtually redundant. The most extended (but hardly extensive) use of archive forms the prelude to the final credits, when there is a sequence of still photographs of the story's principal personalities with bite-size recaps of what happened to them after the trial, a short sequence of Norman Scott outside his current home in Devon and the 'reverse uncanny' to end all 'reverse uncannies': Peter Cook's pointed parody of Sir Joseph Cantley's grossly biased summing up to the jury at the end of the trial. Satirical mimicry in *A Very English Scandal* becomes solid historical commentary. Thorpe and his co-defendants were not on trial for homosexuality, though without homosexuality and, until the passing of the 1967 Sexual Offences Act, its illegality, there would have been no trial. The series essentially and indirectly grants Scott a second trial in which he is not pilloried as he had been by Cantley (who described him as a fraud, a sponger, a whiner and parasite) and gives space and credence to the complexity of Jeremy Thorpe: his attack against a White Paper ('aptly named') advocating tighter immigration legislation; his support for Leo Abse MP's bid to decriminalise homosexuality; his outspokenness on Rhodesia and the supply of arms to Nigeria. Linda Hutcheon proposed a redefinition of parody as 'repetition with critical distance' (Hutcheon, 1988: 26); the juxtaposition of Thorpe's princi-pled intervention into the Commons debate on Nigeria and a meeting with Bessell and Holmes to discuss how they might dispose of Scott's body (Thorpe: 'take him to the pub, get him drunk, shove him in a car, drive him out to Bodmin Moor, . . . shoot the bugger stone dead') exemplifies the intrinsically complex balance of the parodic portrayal. First as reality, then as farce.

In Episode 3, the net starts to close in on Thorpe; a letter in which he refers to Scott as 'bunnies' is published in the press and Marion (Thorpe's second wife) has sent Thorpe's son Rupert (from his first marriage) to stay with friends so they can talk. Dim lighting picks out the high polish of the antique table and two half-eaten plates of cod in parsley sauce. They talk; Thorpe refers to 'unfortunate nights involv-ing alcohol' during which 'I would dabble [in homosexuality] to relieve myself' but denies any involvement in 'that business with the gun and the dog'. Marion (Monica Dolan) pauses, gets up to fetch the water jug and counters:

> For what it's worth. I think people have focused on the word 'bunnies'. But the last thing you wrote in that letter was 'I miss you'. I think that's a wonder-ful thing for a man to say to his friend.

The reverse shot of Grant, so poignantly expressive of a man unable to handle his own partner's emotional perspicaciousness, is a moment of aching melodrama to sit alongside Edith Wharton's description of Newland Archer's realisation in *The Age of Innocence* that his wife May had known all along of his love for the Countess

Olenska. The deep creases on Grant's face, especially the downturned nasal-labial folds, are accentuated by the chiaroscuro light, like profound rivulets of regret and repression. His beady brown eyes fixate on Marion; he might not be able to admit to having loved Norman Scott, but they speak of it. In an incidental, even Sirkian moment, Marion's arm obscures that riven face as she pours the water. By the time the movement is completed, Thorpe has turned away – from confrontation with the truth and the shame. As he half opens his mouth as if to speak, Marion's voice chimes in: 'are you alright?'. Thorpe turns back to face her, still apparently on the verge of uttering a reply, but catatonic. Looks are exchanged and his expression alters, the lines now facing up rather than down with the forced jollity of a comic mask as, with a brief shake of the head, he finally responds: 'very nice dinner. Very nice'. After he rallies briefly at the thought of this 'new start', Marion enquires: 'and what about Norman Scott? Are we finished with him?'. Thorpe looks away evasively: 'absolutely. Absolutely. Damn him, for there's nothing more he can do'. Cut to a sharply dressed Andrew Newton emerging from 'Preston Prison one year later', to be greeted by a journalist willing to pay him £3,000 for his story, and then to another shot of the *Evening News* headline, October 1977: 'I Was Hired to Kill Scott', and then to another of Thorpe returning home in his small, intensely vulnerable, Triumph sports car to a pack of journalists firing cameras. They are not 'finished with him', especially once (a few seconds of screen time later) builders engaged in renovating Bessell's former office discover a briefcase secreted in the ceiling which contains Scott's love letters: 'Jeremy Thorpe, the dirty sod!', one of them says, 'We should take this to the papers'. Second as farce, then as tragedy.

The tragicomic extremes of this sequence, its keen pacing and tonal modulations, exemplify the essential duality of satirical political mimicry – that it is both a performance of and a commentary on the events it depicts; while Grant's intricate performance elicits sympathy for the closeted politician, the abrupt return to the farcical murder plot in which he is embroiled serves as a harsh reminder of Thorpe's callous and criminal ambition. Steven Lipkin argues that 'Docudrama's very acknowledgement of its work as performance argues that we should view its modelling of the past historiographically, as a form of representing history, rather than as a representation of historical fact'; the past on screen, he continues, 'is not meant to be literal . . . but suggestive, symbolic, metaphoric', as he concludes this thought with a question: 'what does its [docudrama's] performance of the past do?' (2011: 15). *A Very English Scandal* does not necessarily 'perform' the 'competing versions of the past' Lipkin then goes on to mention (15), but rather offers, as in the cod in parsley sauce scene, a sensory rendition of extra-factual history, the subliminal history of the factors frequently repressed and shunted aside in favour of *facts*. Jeremy Thorpe was a mercurial character, in the words of journalist Andrew Rawnsley, a 'dandy, exhibitionist, superb showman, shallow thinker, wit and mimic, cunning opportunist, sinister intriguer, idealistic internationalist and a man with a clandestine homosexual life' (Angell, 2019), not abandoned by his party colleagues, according to Hugh Grant, for his sexuality, or even for 'trying to kill someone' but because 'he was very dodgy on money' (Angell, 2019). *A Very English Scandal* renders this complexity in physical, tactile terms on the surface of the film itself, the liminal border between explicit and implicit knowledge. The cod in parsley sauce scene fully embodies, physically and sensually, facts and history.

A Very English Scandal embroils its audiences not only in the intrigues and machinations of Thorpe's criminal actions, but also envelops them in its ornate visual style, often complemented by Murray Gold's score, which manages simultaneously to cherish and mock the narrative's rich absurdities. Take, for example, the sequence in Episode 1 in which Norman Scott (Ben Wishaw), following their bust up, deposits two love letters from Thorpe with the police. Scott slams his suitcase down on the front desk of a police station and announces that he has come to tell them of his 'homosexual relations with Jeremy Thorpe MP'. He hands over 'two of the best' (keeping the remainder as 'my insurance policy'). Gold's jaunty music starts up as Scott shuts his suitcase and a close-up of a typewriter shows the case file being typed up, signed off, put in an envelope and stamped. An edit ensues to another suited officer behind a desk and letters that scroll from the top of the screen announce the case's arrival at Scotland Yard, just before the officer, eyebrows raised, stuffs the forms back in the envelope (an action captured directly from above), the words scurry off left. The man of the Yard writes 'Special Branch' on the envelope and dates it. As the music increases in pace and pitch, 'Special Branch' swoops in from the left, over another surprised and suited man at his desk; he too thumbs through the yellowed papers, the words go off to the left and another high angle shot shows him going through the same ritual of returning the papers to the envelope, naming and stamping them and sending them on to MI5, where they are greeted by yet another besuited, desk-bound operative who, after showing *his* surprise at what he is reading, sheathes them again, but this time places them in the safe next to his desk and turns the lock, an action rounded off by the final note of music, before an edit to Thorpe confiding to Peter Bessell over lunch: 'God knows what he got up to; I thought I was rid of him, and then [pause], out of the blue *that* [pointing at the letter Scott sent to Thorpe's mother detailing his sexual relationship with her son]'. The pacing and repetitions and the 'king asked the queen, the queen asked the diary maid' structure of the sequence presage and predict the return to Thorpe. Frears and Davies's series animates as well as mimics the history it tells; it evokes the events, makes bodily sense of them, as the Thorpe case is re-performed as dynamic history, conveying a sense that it is being re-examined – not just the factual basics of the murder plot, but all the unspoken feelings, desire and tensions that led up to them. The film's presence, the dynamic physicality of its editing, its arch camera style, extravagant performances and jocular musical score, merge into a corporeal concretization of history. This is not living history in the re-enactment sense, but history being re-*lived*, re-inhabited and re-opened. The interaction between past and present is vigorously dialectical.

Frears's series shares some of Paolo Sorrentino's surreal constructedness; certainly, his ironic and dynamic use of moving on-screen script is reminiscent of the introductions to each member of Giulio Andreotti's inner circle as, one by one, they arrive for a meeting at the start of *Il Divo* (2008). As his Chancellor, Pomicino, or businessman Giuseppe Ciarrapico, or Christian Democrat MP, Vittorio Sbardella, emerge from their cars summoned by Andreotti on the eve of his historic seventh term in office, each is identified via text that travels across the screen or emerges from behind buildings or cars, for example. Such reflexive gestures add to Sorrentino's intrusive visual style – the use of slow motion, the extreme low angles – that, in turn, recall Hollywood directors Scorsese and Tarantino and heighten the taint of *braggadocio* criminality that surrounded Andreotti. Although some critics argue that in *Loro* Sorrentino spends too little time exposing Berlusconi's criminality and too much time re-enacting and relishing the surreal sleaziness of his infamous bunga-bunga parties, his satire is, like Frears's, immersive and live, engaged in an energetic game of disavowal with its audience, beginning with the parodic but prudent opening statement cited earlier. In both Sorrentino examples, incisive political criticism (Andreotti's implication in the death of Aldo Moro, for instance) is amplified by the haptic intrusion of surreal moments such as Andreotti's confrontation with a recalcitrant cat or the dopey sheep at the start of *Loro* who, enthralled by the oversized television screen playing reruns of a Mike Bongiorno show, is felled by the villa's fierce air-conditioning. Amidst the films' performative historiography, in which history is being revised at the same time as it is being enacted, Toni Servillo's central performances comprise a series of shorthand gestures and cartoonish prosthetics that belie their insightfulness but likewise subjectify, embody and externalise the films' interior, intellectual consciousness – bringing the past into the present via 'presence'.

In *Il Divo* Andreotti runs through a litany of some of the nicknames (such as: il divino Giulio, the hunchback, the fox, the salamander, the black pope, eternity, Beelzebub) he has acquired through his career. Servillo's portrait of Andreotti, like his Berlusconi, is a type, a distillation of ideas and perspectives; he is not a rounded character of depth and nuance. In *The Historical Novel*, Georg Lukács identifies the significance of typage when he writes of the reduction of characters 'to the typical representation of the most important and most characteristic attitudes of men' which then provide and engage in the central 'collision' of individuals around which the historical novel or drama revolves (Lukács, 1981: 108). Lukács's conception of the collision between broadly drawn, synthesised historical characters representative of wider socio-political forces as the backbone of historical drama offers a useful model for these post-millennial political satires. Typage is an important element of political mimicry; it is a reflexive mechanism that questions, re-evaluates and ultimately rejects straightforward realism as a means of commenting on historical events. Typage creates critical distance, but (as in the case of Grant's portrayal of Thorpe) a reductive portrait is not necessarily a wholly negative one. Tony Blair is often subjected to 'typage': donning his Newcastle United kit in *The Deal;* playing the guitar in both *The Government Inspector* (Peter Kosminski, 2005) and the Comic Strip's *The Hunt for Tony Blair* (Peter Richardson, 2011); brandishing a mug in Molly Dineen's 1997 Labour Party Election Broadcast and copious dramas since. Typage does not please all: Mark Lawson was highly critical of 'the Guitar Scene' in *The Government Inspector*, in which Blair plays blues guitar whilst on the phone to Alastair Campbell during the David Kelly weapons of mass destruction Select

Committee hearings. Though he concedes that 'the dialogue faithfully reflects what they told Hutton [the Hutton Inquiry]' he disapproves:

> It's a nice piece of satire but, in a drama claiming to recreate reality, deliberately weights the scene against Blair. The moment is a variation on fiddling while Rome burns: riffing while Iraq smoulders.
>
> *(Lawson, 2005)*

Of course, typage is used here to 'weight the scene against Blair'; there is no unwritten law of docudrama that states it must maintain neutrality and Kosminski has confirmed that he tries 'to make films that say something, may make people change their minds, affect the prejudices they have developed' (quoted in Paget, 2013: 179). And yet, typage is not always about 'making mischief',[17] but also about making serious political commentary, as in Grant's caricature of Thorpe or Mark Rylance's minimalist portrait of the tragic weapons inspector, David Kelly, the titular *Government Inspector*, whose expression of stoical weariness seems to be permanently etched onto his face.

Labour MP, Hazel Blears, when Secretary of State for Communities and Local Government, claimed in November 2008 that negative depictions of politicians on television, while 'all hugely entertaining and fun . . . reinforces the idea that politics is disreputable and adds to a sense of corrosive cynicism about politics' (Bailey, 2011: 283). When, on the following day, she appeared on BBC Radio 4's *Today Programme* opposite Michael Dobbs, Conservative politician and author of *House of Cards*, Dobbs countered Blears's criticism by arguing that

> if politicians had done a better job – by for example not (allegedly) lying about the existence of weapons of mass destruction in Iraq – they would have been represented more positively.
>
> *(quoted in Fielding, 2011a: 226)*

Blears advocated a British *West Wing*, about which Tony Saint (writer of *Margaret Thatcher: The Long Road to Finchley* [2008]) remarked, though in a different context: 'From my point of view, sitting in this country, watching *The West Wing* . . . I can't understand a programme which is predicated on the idea of political competence. It just doesn't add up, it doesn't make sense' (quoted in Fielding, 2011b: 349). In the latter discussion Alistair Beaton recalls being chastised by another Labour politician, Tessa Jowell, for (in Beaton's words) 'creating public cynicism about politics'; 'this was not long after they [Blair's Labour government] had just launched an illegal war. . . . I thought launching illegal wars was maybe something to do with it. Similarly, lying about weapons of mass destruction' (quoted in Fielding, 2011b: 341). Waging war against Iraq in 2003 on dubious evidence was what turned 'a fundamentally decent man', as Beaton terms Tony Blair (Plunkett, 2007), into the figure put on trial for war crimes in at least three dramas: Norton-Taylor's *Called to Account*, Beaton's *The Trial of Tony Blair* and Robert Harris's *The Ghost*.

With this insertion of the hypothetical scenario – only revealed right at the end, as Robert Lindsay's Blair is flown off to the Hague to face war crimes charges – the hard-hitting satirical intentions behind comedy and typage come to the fore. Set in 2010, *The Trial of Tony Blair* opens with a pre-titles sequence in which Blair is in church to confess his (as yet unidentified) mortal sins, assuring the priest that 'at the time I believed I was doing the right thing'. This nebulous notion of 'doing the right thing' (for the party, the country) is a subtle satirical addition, recalling as it does moments in Blair's autobiography, *A Journey*, or Blair's statement in response to the Chilcot Inquiry Report when he asked 'the British people [to] accept I took this decision because I thought it the right thing to do based on the information I had and the threats I perceived' (Institute for Global Change, 2016). Robert Lindsay's Blair bolts from the church, composes himself and walks out, past the *Evening Standard* headline: 'Ex-PM Faces War Crimes Trial'. Intercut with the opening credits are fragments of doctored news archive of Blair's tenure in office: meeting George W. Bush and Condoleezza Rice, the start of the 'shock and awe' bombing campaign against Baghdad, the 2003 anti-war demonstrations and less politically charged moments such as Lindsay hosting Bob Geldof. *The Trial of Tony Blair* was transmitted three times in 2007, premiering on More4 on 15 January, before being repeated on 5 March and again on 23 June, during Blair's last week in office. Though set in the near future, Beaton and Cellan Jones's film, like much documentary theatre and drama-documentary, is a topical, rapid response to contemporary political issues, most explicitly Blair's actions against Iraq and the sense of gross betrayal they ushered in. Political mimicry treads a fine line between fact and fiction; in such a piece of counterfactual satire, the factual bases for invented actions are referenced relatively directly and revolve almost exclusively around involvement in Iraq.

Iraq and notions of betrayal are brought together near the beginning, just after Blair has delivered his resignation speech and Gordon Brown has won the 2010 election. Cherie questions her husband's sudden eagerness to convert to Catholicism (something Blair *did* do in June 2007, at the point of leaving office) before the Blairs depart from No. 10 for the last time, a sequence set to Katrina and the Waves' catchy 1983 hit single, 'Walking on Sunshine'. Blair and Cherie emerge into the brilliant sunshine to be greeted by ecstatic crowds waving small union jacks; Cherie grins broadly, clings to her husband and lodges her head on his shoulder. All is on schedule until Blair spies a placard that reads: 'BLAIR = 800,000 IRAQI DEAD'. The agitated, rapid-fire shot/reverse-shot sequence that ensues between Blair and the impassive protestor anticipates his later loss of control (one of the few examples in a comedy of Cherie being presented as the sane, stabilising partner in the marriage). This departure sequence faces two ways: it explicitly raises Blair's culpability in Iraq, while also harking back to his triumphant march along Downing Street on 2 May 1997, after being swept to power on a landslide victory – from Cherie resting her head on her husband's shoulder whilst he waves at supporters, to the flag-waving, to the adoption of an even more upbeat track as the Labour campaign anthem: D:Ream's 'Things Can Only Get Better'. Such uncanny satirical references – hypothetical but also uncomfortably close – are revenge for Iraq, but also comprise a lament for Blair's betrayal of his people's optimism and his own earlier principles. In a complementary fashion, Lindsay's nervous, choppy performance suggestive of a man only just staving off encroaching lunacy and collapse, signals far more keenly than Sheen's more temperate mimicry could the terminal loss of the 'frank, even ordinary' man mourned by Robert Harris (Gilbey, 2010) who spoke to Molly Dineen of his childhood dream of playing for Newcastle United. Many supporters on that glorious new dawn of a morning in 1997 no doubt believed that the excited crowds that lined Downing Street had gone there spontaneously, not, as Blair later admits at the very outset of his memoirs (as if feeling the compunction to confess all), that they were party workers 'carefully assembled, carefully managed' (Blair, 2010: 1) by Alastair Campbell. Satirical political mimicry has its source in disillusionment as well as anger.

Disillusionment and anger in *The Trial of Tony Blair* centre on the UK being dragged into the US-led war against Iraq and evolve through the drama in the form of Blair's mounting Macbeth-like nightmares and hallucinations. As the International Criminal Court net tightens, so Blair's tormented fantasies (the rise of his repressed guilt over Iraq) become more frequent and extreme. Returning home having parted company with the intended editor of his memoirs (following his refusal to cut back the Iraq chapters or the number of references to God), Blair turns on the television news: seven British soldiers have been killed in Basra, leading US President Hillary Clinton to conclude that 'the only way forward . . . may be the pathway of peace'. Blair switches off the television, and yet the news continues, segueing smoothly into a further imaginary item reporting the 'mysterious death of former Prime Minister, Tony Blair whose body was found in Connaught Square Gardens earlier this morning'. Layering factual critique over counterfactual drama, Lindsay stares helplessly at the screen as his own body is stretchered into an ambulance after 'it appears that Mr Blair had gone for a walk on his own', another grimly uncanny reference, this time to news reports of David Kelly's alleged suicide (having gone for a walk alone on 17 July 2003).

The last nightmare – an imaginary teleportation from his grand kitchen to a war-ravaged building whose ground is strewn with bodies – prompts the blunt realisation that, despite having 'tried to do the right thing. . . . My legacy's fucked'. His criminal misjudgement over Iraq may have 'fucked' his desired political legacy, but it has secured Blair's legacy to satire, from Peter Kennard and Cat Phillips' photomontages of Blair sidestepping a pool of blood on a London pavement, to the double-layered *Downfall* meme in which Hitler, having revealed his plans to heckle Blair for being a 'bloody war criminal', interrupts his responses to questions live at the 28 May 2012 Leveson Inquiry (Bruno Ganz's head crudely superimposed onto real heckler David Lawley Wakelin's body).[18] *The Trial of Tony Blair* combines an evocation of past optimism with a hypothetical future to call Blair to account for his actions over Iraq. It is a vituperative revenge fantasy in which Blair 'pay[s] for his high crimes and misdemeanours' (Conrad, 2007) and is carted off to a tribunal in the Hague, but not until his memoirs have been rejected by his publisher and a heart problem has landed him in a 'shit-flecked A&E' (Conrad, 2007). In the maelstrom of ignominious farce that sweeps over the end of *The Trial of Tony Blair* lurk vital intersections with real history. Political mimicry in this case remains dependent on the co-presence of recognisable fact and ever more extreme comedic fantasy. For the audience, the interplay between history and fantasy opens up multiple imaginative possibilities for disavowing historical 'fact' and leaving imaginative space for such fantasies to be brought to fruition. In *The Trial of Tony Blair* Beaton is, openly, 'preaching to the converted', but as he continues: 'that's OK, the converted also need a bit of moral support in these hard times' (Fielding, 2011b: 342). Therapeutic support comes in the guise of retelling and working through a traumatic past, rebalanced by the construction of a fantasy future of dystopian retribution, in Blair's case conjoined around his decision to go to war with Iraq.

The 2003 decision to go to war makes for what Derek Thiess, writing about counterfactual historical narratives, terms the 'nexus point': the 'modification of one or several interrelated events after which our recognizable history changes' (2014: 8). One popular historical 'modification' is speculation about how a German victory at the end of World War Two would have altered subsequent events, the subject of numerous 'alternate history' or counterfactual narratives such as Philip K. Dick's *The Man in the High Castle* (1962) or Robert Harris's *Fatherland* (1992). Alternate history stresses the 'role of contingency in history' and in so doing 'is inherently anti-deterministic' (Rosenfeld, 2005: 6); chance, it suggests, is just as important to the shaping of history as determinism: what if Lord Halifax had assumed the British premiership in 1940 and appeasers had agreed peace with Germany? What if John Smith had recovered from his fatal heart attack? What if Al Gore had been declared winner in the 2000 US presidential race? What if Hillary Clinton and not Donald Trump had succeeded Barack Obama as so many counterfactual dramas had assumed? Both fantasies and nightmares could ensue from any number of these hypothetical scenarios,[19] which are as motivated by a desire to analyse and understand the past and how we reached the present as they are by interest in playing around with the future. In such a context, mimicry is of a real and recognisable political situation integrated into a hypothetical plot, as the familiarity of the history to which the drama is the 'alternate' becomes an essential factor in affirming a belief in the 'open-endedness of historical change' (Rosenfeld, 2005: 6).

The night of 26 May 2019 I happened to switch from catching up with the second episode of Russell T. Davies's alternate history drama series, *Years and Years* (BBC, 2019), to coverage of the UK European Parliament election results. The former concluded with the victory in a 2020 by-election of Vivienne Rook, a celebrity candidate who has come from nowhere, the latter, with Nigel Farage's Brexit Party (a party which had not existed a mere six months earlier) winning 31.7% of the vote. To compound this 'reverse uncanny' moment the terrifying 'Four Star Party' leader of *Years and Years* is eerily reminiscent of Sarah Lancashire's businesswoman turned messianic politician, Angela Howard, in *MotherFatherSon* (BBC, 2019), which had aired only a few weeks previously. To put all three together is to create a blurry, not as counterfactual as one might like, alternate history. In Stephen King's time travel novel *11.22.63*, which tries to make history *alternate*, as it were, by intervening in the assassination of President Kennedy, the concept of history *resisting* and *fighting* change recurs, as it does through the various catastrophes in *Years and Years*. The *mimicries* of history perennially both mask and accentuate this resistance. *Years and Years* is more unsettling than *The Man in the High Castle* or *Fatherland* because those counterfactual histories are strictly hypothetical: their history has ended, and we know the Nazis did not win World War Two, so speculating about what might have been if they had is 'just entertainment', whereas *Years and Years* (like *1984* [Orwell, 1949] at the time it was written) is about an uncomfortable present and an even more dystopian future, comprising a jumble of semi-recognisable, ongoing realities which, in turn, may or may not be directly related.

Martin Bunzl offers a simple but important distinction between 'good and bad' counterfactual histories; the 'bad' have no strong grounding in evidence and reasoning (the mainstays of historical methodology), whereas 'good' examples do (2004: 845). *Years and Years* achieves its unhomely effectiveness through remaining disquietingly plausible and closely approximate to recent political events. Implicit references abound. Viv Rook's 'four stars party', for instance, recalls Italy's 'cinque stelle' party which, from June 2018, formed part of the right-wing coalition government with the 'Northern League' under the premiership of Giuseppe Conte, a leader, like Silvio Berlusconi in 1994, with no prior governmental or administrative experience; the collapse of a fictional American investment bank (as occurs in the opening episode) is a composite of three recognisable moments of the 2008 banking crisis namely, the collapse of Lehman Brothers on 15 September 2008, the failure and subsequent nationalisation of British bank Northern Rock that same year and the UK government's ruling, in the wake of the latter crisis, that all personal savings up to £85,000 would be secured and underwritten (legislation to which *Years and Years* makes explicit reference). *Years and Years* is a 'nightmarish' as opposed to 'fantastical' alternate history because its recognisable moments (the echoes of the 2019 trade war between China and the US that leads President Trump to launch a nuclear missile against China at the end of Episode 1) are disconcertingly recent, none more so than the editing into a fictional bulletin news of Doris Day's actual death the day before actual transmission on 13 May.

Alternate histories inevitably blur distinctions between fact and fiction; the temporal compression of the Doris Day moment suspends that differentiation altogether and simultaneously collapses the temporal distance between real present and fictional future. In terms of political mimesis explicitly, temporal as well as performative distance is usually key: indicators such as archive, history or collective memory abound in the Peter Morgan trilogy to affirm that Michael Sheen is re-enacting events and gestures that have already happened; likewise the references to real events and the use of genuine or pseudo-archive in *A Very English Scandal* and *The Trial of Tony Blair*. The link to a recognisable past in alternate histories such as Roman Polanski's adaptation of *The Ghost* or *Years and Years* is more elliptical, and on the level of performance, actors do not ventriloquise individual politicians of the past. Emma Thompson (as Rook) is a composite character who obliquely references a host of male antecedents (Macron, Salvini, Berlusconi, Trump) and bears a physical resemblance to Christine Lagarde, head of the International Monetary Fund. Yet her persona is not shackled to any of these realities.

The Ghost's approximation of real politics is more or less explicit, although Pierce Brosnan (in the adaptation of Harris's novel) maintains the 'gossamer thin' (Freedland, 2007) fiction that Adam Lang is not to be confused with Tony Blair by making no attempt at all to imitate any of the latter's idiosyncratic ticks and mannerisms. A certain semiotic confusion surrounds The Ghost: it reads like, looks like and is a thriller though, by the same token, its fictive veil conspicuously fails to obscure references to real politicians or political events. The relationship between these factors, in particular the disingenuous opacity of those indirect references versus the superficial clarity of the fictional narrative, reconfigures consequent relations between image and truth. If, as Dai Vaughan argues, 'to make a documentary is therefore to persuade the viewer that what appears to be is' (Vaughan, 1999: 59), then what is The Ghost doing, lacking as it does that documentary ingredient 'objective reportage' (Reinelt, 2009: 14) while at the same time retaining close proximity to the reality it critiques? Though it would be overly schematic to propose an inverse ratio between physical likeness and temporal distance, or between a lack of archival authenticity and the capacity to make an effective intervention into contemporary politics, such contrapuntal calibrations define The Ghost's complex relationship to the true histories it 'ghosts'. As one journalist who interviewed Harris at the time of the original novel's publication neatly summarises: 'Fiction allows a great freedom' but it is 'a rather tricky dance' as Harris is both 'asking readers to separate act from character' and to comprehend that 'act is inseparable from character' (Edemariam, 2007). The Ghost's political mimicry is more of a political 'haunting', as reality is the thriller's destabilising spectral presence.

When interviewed at the time of the film's release, Harris was very clear about his motivation for having written The Ghost. Having been a generous donor to Labour and supporter of Blair, after the invasion of Iraq and in response to Blair's alliance with George W. Bush, he became spectacularly and vociferously disillusioned. The Ghost is his bitter roman à clef. 'I liked him' (Blair), Harris remembered in 2010 (interviewed for the release of The Ghost), 'He seemed a member of the human race. . . . He'd drop his kids off at school in the mornings. He liked a drink. He was in every respect a regular guy' (Palmer, 2010), the same 'regular guy' who asked staff to call him 'Tony' and who chatted amiably in a 1997 Party Election Broadcast against a mise-en-scène of mesmeric mundaneness: the back seat of a car, the Blairs' functional and messy Islington kitchen, a football pitch. The PEB's director, Molly Dineen, is an award-winning documentary filmmaker whose short film offers a master class in the effectiveness of observational documentary, and just as exemplary an exercise in the political potency of performativity; Blair's mastery (like John Kennedy's in the early 1960s) of the observational camera and the ordinary location (the male politician in his kitchen soon became a stock feature emulated by others, including Ed Miliband and David Cameron) give the short film a performative accent: that although this is the 'real' Blair, there is no convenient distinction to be drawn between private and public personae (as emphasised in previous PEBs), rather they are both imitations.[20]

Robert Harris repeatedly expresses his shock at the transformation in Blair over the years in office, recounting, for instance, how 'When I looked at him during Chilcot, I thought: "My god, where has that man gone? He has been replaced by this globetrotting, taut-faced, worked-out, neo-con, almost robotic creature that lives behind a security screen"' (Gilbey, 2010). Timings and especially synergies become hugely important to an appreciation and understanding of Harris's projections of his profound personal disaffection onto Blair's mediarised image. Firstly, the book *The Ghost* came out in June 2007, three months after Blair left office, thus becoming an instant and direct comment upon his tenure; its narrative premise is the (ghost)-writing of Adam Lang's memoirs, and, with model 'reverse-uncanny' elegance, it was announced in October 2007 that Blair had signed a deal with Random House (also Lang's publisher) worth £5million to produce his (real) memoirs. *A Journey* was eventually published on 1 September 2010, a few months after the release of Roman Polanski's cinema adaptation (in April) and after the (disastrous for the Labour Party) General Election. *The Ghost* would have been in cinemas during the campaign – another 'reverse-uncanny' for some; it also came out midway through the Chilcot Inquiry (which ran from January 2010 to January 2011), thereby bringing back into the present the historical events and memories both novel and film mimic, as Harris's allusion to Blair's live testimony to the Inquiry attests. Lang's fictional criminality echoes Chilcot as, at the start of *The Ghost*, news breaks that, when Prime Minister, he had secretly approved the capture and extradition of UK citizens to Guantanamo Bay to be interrogated and tortured. The dovetailing of fact and fabrication enriches *The Ghost*'s multi-layered 'approximation' as temporal distances between original events, the Chilcot Inquiry and their fictionalisation are compressed.

Harris's prowess, replicated by Polanski, is to make his references to real figures and events loose enough to work and be enjoyed as fiction, yet sufficiently close to muster a *frisson* of wicked, not quite libellous recognition. The author was keen for the film to come out before Blair's memoir, and self-evidently Blair was never, in light of *The Ghost*, going to employ a ghost writer. His memoirs are neither taut nor elegantly written, but they do describe the life in office of a serious politician; the former Prime Minister did, in advance of their publication, 'let it be known that Robert Harris was a "cheeky fuck" for portraying him as a lightweight in his novel' (Watt, 2010). 'Cheeky fuck' are also, coincidentally or not, the words Lang uses in the film about his former colleague turned whistle-blower, Richard Rycart, after he has watched him on the television expressing his 'shock and sadness' at the news that his 'old friend' Lang is under investigation for war crimes.

Polanski's adaptation of Harris's novel successfully renders the book's eeriness and captures the edgy nastiness of the original portrayal of Blair/Lang in wealthy, miserable isolation, holed up in his publisher/friend Rhinehart's brutalist mansion (on the German island of Sylt instead of Martha's Vineyard) to write his memoirs while mute Vietnamese servants prepare insipid sandwiches and health drinks in the immaculate gloom of its concrete kitchen. Though not subterranean, this is effectively a bunker, in which a small coterie of glamourous, under-employed female staff (led by Amelia Bly [Kim Cattrall], with whom Lang is having an affair)[21] work amidst minimalist frigidity. Evocations of imprisonment and exile abound as *The Ghost* shimmers with the rumours of Blair's non-domicile tax status and carries the residual tensions of Polanski's own outcast status.[22]

The plot is as follows. Following the death of Lang's trusted aide and ghostwriter, Mike McAra, whose body is found washed up on the shore of Martha's Vineyard, a new writer (Ewan MacGregor) is contracted to 'ghost' Lang's memoirs. As the ghost-writer is about to leave the UK, news breaks that Lang is being investigated for war crimes, specifically for sanctioning the illegal use of British forces to seize four suspected al Qaeda terrorists in Pakistan and hand them over to the CIA for interrogation. He arrives to start work on the manuscript amidst the febrile siege-like atmosphere at the Rhinehart mansion, at whose gate camps a group of anti-war protestors, among them an angry father whose son was killed in 'one of Lang's illegal wars'. The father recalls actual peace campaigner Brian Haw, who featured in *The Trial of Tony Blair* and who, for almost a decade from June 2001, set up camp in Parliament Square in opposition to the Iraq War. Hidden in McAra's un-emptied room, the ghost-writer finds photographs from Lang's Cambridge days (which include Paul Emmett [Mark Wilkinson], a Harvard Professor and CIA agent) and a phone number, which he discovers to be that of Richard Rycart, embittered former Foreign Secretary and now outspoken critic of Lang's international policies, who bears more than a passing resemblance to Blair's Foreign Secretary, Robin Cook. While Adam Lang is away, the writer sleeps with his wife Ruth (Olivia Williams). He goes for a drive, opting to follow the pre-programmed satellite navigation which charts McAra's final journey and leads him to Emmett's house. He later meets Rycart, who explains Emmett is in the CIA. Lang tracks down the writer and picks him up in a 'Hatherton' private jet, aboard which the writer tells Lang what he has pieced together – that at Cambridge Emmett recruited him into the CIA and that McAra had betrayed him to Rycart, a revelation which hurts Lang more than anything else. At the airport, Lang is shot by the grieving father/protestor clad in full desert combat gear. The memoirs are published, but at the launch party the ghost-writer suddenly decides to go through McAra's original manuscript one last time in order to pursue a clue McAra had left Rycart – that the truth about Lang is hidden in the book's 'beginnings'. He sees that the first words of each chapter form the sentence: 'Langs Wife Ruth Was Recruited As A CIA Agent In America By Professor Paul Emmett of Harvard University'. The writer passes a note of this to Ruth, but as he leaves, he is run over in the street, the leaves of the manuscript fluttering in the wind. (The book has a slightly different coda in which the ghost-writer recounts a different final meeting with Lang and writes directly to the reader that, if we are reading this, 'it probably means I'm dead').

As with all of Robert Harris's 'approximations', the moments when thriller and reality collide are especially effective, when distanciation and proximity come together as a means of crystallising the critique of Blair. The greater a character's

involvement in the CIA-focused thriller plot of *The Ghost*, the least similar to –
but not necessarily the least critical of – their prototype they are. The CIA agent
Emmett with links to the fictional 'Hatherton Corporation', for instance, is not
discernibly based on a real person in the way Adam Lang is, although 'Hatherton'
recalls Halliburton, one of the world's largest oil field service companies of which
former US Vice President, Dick Cheney, was at one point CEO. The sinister implications of *The Ghost*'s CIA plot insinuate themselves into and colour the political
mimicry, even when there are no even covert connections (Ruth Lang, for example,
has very little in common with Cherie Blair beyond having been the cleverer and
more politicised future wife of a future Prime Minister). Olivia Williams plays Ruth
as a caged animal, ostensibly motiveless in her malign anger beyond jealousy (for
Amelia Bly) until, that is, we learn that it is she, not Adam, who is the CIA agent.
Just as some part of Tony Blair must have enjoyed being played by a former 007,
so Cherie Booth QC (Queen's Counsel) might have liked for once not being the
vacuous, vain, money- and celebrity-obsessed figure she so often is in the satirical
comedies about her husband.[23]

Elsewhere, proximity between real people and their 'ghostly' doubles becomes
more explicit and mischievous. With Rycart (Robert Pugh) who, along with the
United Nations is actively working to get Lang indicted for war crimes, Harris has
drawn a cartoon of the equally disillusioned Robin Cook, who, on 17 March 2003,
left the Labour front bench in opposition to the war against Iraq. Rycart lacks
Cook's eloquence, but his entrapment of Lang for his international crimes indirectly re-invokes Cook's impassioned resignation speech and his critique of Blair
for allowing the UK to be 'pushed into a war too quickly by an American administration with an agenda of its own'.[24] Cook's emphasis on the then UK government's subservience to the US adds depth to his cruder and more openly vengeful
fictional counterpart. Adam Lang is likewise a coarser, one-step-removed spectral
haunting of Blair, his biography peppered with both indirect and direct allusions
to Blair's: that Lang is an alumnus of Cambridge, Blair of Oxford; that Lang aspired
to acting, Blair to being a rock star or footballer; that Lang is pictured alongside
Emmett at Cambridge wearing a straw boater as Blair had been in one widely circulated photograph from his Oxford days. These petty allusions to Blair are essentially McGuffins, the masquerade for Harris's more profound venom, which he
reserves for Lang's shallow menace, his criminality and his subservience to the US.

The truth remains the phantom that haunts the fictional narrative, suppressed
by Lang but fatally unearthed by his two ghost writers; it would work as a thriller
without recourse to that background truth but makes far more sense once the
parallels are detected. The 'approximate' complexities, the sequence of echoes from
reality to fiction and *vice versa*, enrich our viewing experience as *The Ghost* becomes
the backdrop to an intricate game of disavowal and masquerade in which the
thriller narrative ostensibly represses explicit political mimicry while sporadically
permitting suggestive resonances of historical reality to percolate to the surface.
Harris comments that it is 'better to have small people in the midst of great events'
(Gilbey, 2010); the ghost-writer is the outsider looking in. The shadowy reiterations

of real events only ever leave reality partially hidden, the film's subcutaneous layer, barely camouflaged by the thriller's opaque 'skin'. The interweaving between the subject and its masquerade makes watching *The Ghost* a tensely synaesthetic experience. Synaesthesia is a condition whereby individuals experience certain sensations which relate directly to one sense or part of the body in or through another sense or part of the body, for example seeing a shape or colour when eating a particular food or being able to taste a particular place. Others experience 'mirror-touch synaesthesia', whereby they 'feel the same sensation another person feels', as in feeling pain at the sight of a fracture or tensing muscles in empathetic response to an actor running on screen (Dutton, 2015). A comparably synaesthetic transference occurs in *The Ghost*, between its two strata: generic thriller and political critique. As an evocative film that occupies a fraught liminal space between these domains, the sensibility and sensuousness of the metaphorically rich *mise-en-scène* is never merely a backdrop against which the fast-paced intrigues are enacted; rather, what occurs in one 'sense' (the visuals of the *mise-en-scène*) is felt in and transferred to another (the political sub-text and sometimes subliminal references to real events, principally the repercussions of the Iraq War).

When out for a walk, Ruth Lang likens being holed up with her husband to 'being married to Napoleon on St Helena'. Her exile is elemental. Dressed in dark hues, Ruth, the ghost-writer and her ever-present security chaperone (security is the film's other 'ghostly' presence) contrast with the pale sands, scrappy tufts of grass, choppy waters and brooding skies behind them, their hair and clothes perturbed by the wind. Encircled by the agitated ocean that has already washed up the body of Mike McAra, Rhinehart's villa, with its prison-like ratio of walls to windows, stands like a squat Martello lookout tower engaged in perennial battle with the forbidding landscape from which it is divided by a grim moat of deep gravel. Swirling winds, torrential rains and radioactive grey and clouded skies rail against its inhabitants as if the house or what it stands for has disturbed the island's elemental equilibrium. The futility of the fight against raging nature is captured in the repeated futile gesture of the male servant attempting in vain to clear the porch of leaves. Inside, the modernist slab of a house is pathologically inhospitable: a floating staircase, monochrome leather sofas and desks, vast but anonymous canvases hanging from its concrete walls. When transferring from his hotel room to the house on account of the media frenzy that has erupted following Rycart's public accusations, the ghost-writer (clutching his, in this setting, comically anomalous wheelie suitcase) remarks: 'this place is like Shangri-La in reverse'. The brutal terrain and elemental unrest impinge on the plot symbolically (the lashing rain leads the ghost-writer to seek shelter in Eli Wallach's porch, for example, where he learns more about McAra's death) and make sensory impressions that can only be fully understood as metaphorical critiques of Lang and, by association, Blair.

A sensory transference occurs when the ghost-writer sits down for the second time to interview Lang for the book. The scene begins just after Lang has taken a difficult phone call, which we subsequently discover was Rycart calling to inform him that his decision to speak about the handing over of terrorists to the

CIA was 'nothing personal'. Lang, arms outstretched above him, is standing against an uncharacteristically large, frameless, floor to ceiling window that looks out on the muted landscape beyond. The glass might silence it, but across the invisible expanse Lang merges with angered nature, his hands splayed, as if trying to tame his anger, his memories and the biblical skies. The interview begins badly as the writer becomes interested in Lang's experience of acting and the pleasure that comes from pretending to be 'somebody else and people actually applaud[ing] you for it'. Lang, dismissed by opponents for being 'a fucking actor', is not interested and resumes his pose and position at the window, literally on the edge between interiority and exteriority, between repressed and rising guilt. Inside the house Lang's entrapment is palpable: he is forever being managed, while his life – in the form of McAra's verbose manuscript – is literally kept under lock and key by an ever-attentive Amelia. Outside is threatening and Lang ventures there rarely; his preoccupation with security surfacing in his final speech aboard the Hatherton jet just before being shot:

LANG: Whatever I did I did because I believed it was right.
WRITER: Even supporting illegal kidnapping for torture?
LANG: You know what I'd do if I were in power again? I'd say, okay then, we'll have two queues at airports. One for flights where we'd done no background checks, infringed on no one's civil bloody liberties . . . and on the other flight, we'd do everything we possibly could to make it perfectly safe. And then we'd see which plane the Rycarts of this world would put their bloody kids on. And you can put that in the book!

Lang is imprisoned by his past, his mistakes, his platitudes and his fear. Framing *The Ghost* in terms of synaesthesia it is significant that, at the denouement of the thriller plot, with politics all but forgotten, there comes this allusion, as clear as anything, back to Blair that cuts through the layers of fiction, symbolism and abstraction: 'Whatever I did I did because I believed it was right'. Brosnan is not here *doing* Blair, his is not an imitation, but this moment nevertheless exemplifies Schechner's notion of performance as 'twice-behaved behavior' (1985: 36), as being both 'not' and 'not-not'.[25] Having seemed at first relatively unambiguous, the boundaries between different Blairs, different Langs have become less distinct: Brosnan as Lang is not Blair, but then again, he is not-not Blair; they are on the same continuum and so, within the parameters of *The Ghost* as a masquerade of Blair, he *is* Blair.

The film's yoking of distant fantasy with incisive historical references is especially effective as a critical tool; proximity in no way guarantees more direct access to the truth. The faking of the Cambridge photographs, for instance, is rudimentary and quite flamboyantly amateurish, as Brosnan and Wilkinson as Lang and Emmett are so obviously cut and pasted in and not inhabiting contiguous space at all. This is not Blair – or at least not the one we are interested in – these crude pictures proclaim, so look for him elsewhere. Significantly cleaner and less jarring as signposts to recognisable truths are the television news stories that punctuate the action. At Heathrow Airport bound for Martha's Vineyard, the ghost-writer is at a bar. Behind him Sky News with real newscaster, Anna Botting, can be heard announcing that Adam Lang is 'back in the news tonight'. The writer turns around. 'According to leaked documents', the real newscaster continues, 'Mr Lang authorised the illegal use of British special forces to seize four suspected al Qaeda terrorists in Pakistan and then hand them over for interrogation by the CIA'. A split screen image shows us both Botting and, on the left, Lang surrounded by troops in desert camouflage gear, an explicit visual allusion to Blair's visit (the first by a Western leader to Iraq since the war had begun) on 29 May 2003 to British troops in Basra. The faked archive image then takes up nearly the entire screen, by which point Lang is addressing the camera, rows of soldiers behind him, just like Blair had been. As the news item goes from fictive archive to fictional mimesis (Botting recounting the seizure and torture of the four suspected terrorists) the writer gets on the phone and, with the news report still running in the background (the word 'illegal' is audible) asks his agent: 'what have you gotten me into?' Like Lang, the criminal premise for the plot (Pakistan, the CIA, interrogation and torture) is both 'not' Blair's alleged war crimes and 'not-not' them; as later Rycart runs through, for the writer's benefit, a litany of decisions Lang made whilst Prime Minister that were directly 'in the interests of the USA', he opens with Iraq.

The Ghost is, for Harris, 'a record of disillusion' (Freedland, 2007), and as Jonathan Freedland then summarises:

> He [Harris], along with the folks behind Called to Account and The Trial of Tony Blair, is part of a section of the British liberal opinion that once had such high hopes for Blair and now feels badly let down, if not betrayed, chiefly by Blair's eager partnership with Bush.
>
> (Freedland, 2007)

The dual catalysts for this 'disillusion' are Blair's allegiance to the US and, concomitantly, the joint decision to wage war against Saddam Hussein's Iraq. 'Adam Lang is not Blair', Harris insists, but the real 'American in Downing Street' haunts the fictional text. And yet, for all this, Lang is 'not meant to be a lookalike. It's not like The Queen' but 'a story . . . midway . . . between reality and fiction, with the fiction drawing on reality and moulding the two' (Harris quoted in Palmer, 2010). Fiction is not only dominant in The Ghost, Harris is arguing, it influences our view of the realities on which it is based. The 'reverse uncanny' is especially effective in this instance at destabilising and rendering unhomely familiar perceptions of reality. The effect of seeing Blair through the 'filter' of Pierce Brosnan is both flattering and yet also uncanny; the thriller is emphatically 'not' lookalike mimicry, but neither can we discount it as pure fiction, so the film overall is likewise not-not about Iraq, New Labour and relations with the US, all of which helps defend fictionalisation against detractors who see the drama elements of drama documentary as 'a contamination' (Paget, 2013: 175) or the form of 'last resort' (Leslie Woodhead in Rosenthal, 2014: 17). Fiction affords writers great freedom and (overused term though it is) artistic license.

In setting out her idea of 'political mimesis' Jane Gaines cites anthropologist Michael Taussig when he talks of wanting to restore the notion of mimesis as a 'way of knowing' (Gaines, 1999b: 93). Gaines's idea of 'political mimesis' is quite specific, namely that certain scenes in a documentary elicit a physical response in those watching and make them 'want to do something *because of the conditions in the world of the audience*' (90); filmmakers use 'images of bodies in struggle *because they want audiences to carry on that same struggle*' (91). The reviewer from the *Socialist Worker* of John Keane's exhibition, 'Scratching the Surface, Joining the Dots', touches on something similar when they find that the paintings 'scream disdain for Blair' (Ruddick, 2012), even though Blair is, in some of the pictures, only just identifiable. After Taussig, Gaines is arguing for a 'body-first way of knowing . . . the power to produce compelling similarities – *in* one's body – through imitation' (Gaines, 1999b: 94). The visceral appeal of documentaries such as *Union Maids* or *Uprising of '34* is in part, for Gaines, that they 'work to rouse audiences' so the audience discovers 'the ability to "body back", to carry on the same struggle' (99–100).

Gaines's notion of an audience being able to 'body back' and 'carry on' a struggle offers a parallel for the mimicking actor who is also, in their interpretation of a role, a real body, is 'bodying back' that past and that body. The charge of this reciprocal 'bodying' is felt most acutely in the more politically motivated performances, when performance is also commentary. Broadening this out to consider history and politics more loosely, facts and their mimetic representation have a specific thrill – of 'being there'. And yet, indirect representations, performances or dramatizations can also influence, can also elicit strong responses and make audiences 'want to do something'. They are essentially bodily interventions into the situations they mimic, whether this be their imitation of mannerisms (Blair's choppy hands), personal style (Thatcher's bouffant hair) or the placement of people in familiar settings (Downing Street, Buckingham Palace).

The body in political mimicry, while both not and not-not the original it mimics, needs to be recognisable for the mimicry to work. In Alison Jackson's spoofed celebrity photos and videos, convincing look-alikes are placed in demeaning comic situations: Blair is put in a sauna with David Beckham or on all fours as George Bush uses him to mount his horse while, in a more recent series (for the 2016 New York exhibition, 'Truth is Dead'), President Donald Trump is staged taking a selfie with a trio of beauty queens in the Oval Office, admiring the assets of Miss Mexico as she lies, legs akimbo on his desk and getting finger extensions. The necessary collision that brings about 'approximation' is, in these instances, bodily. Even in the more positively affirmative and less political work of Peter Morgan, Blair's outburst to Alastair Campbell after he has criticised the Queen is a moment of bodily rupture, although the broader mimicry found in *The Trial of Tony Blair, A Very English Scandal* and *The Ghost* opens up even further that crucial space for commentary, debate and fantasy.

The body is central because these portraits of Blair and Thorpe are performances; but what is being performed? Firstly, of course, the past and the facts and individuals who inhabit it, but also, less tangibly, memories and fantasies of that past. Most examples of political mimesis contain archival reference points, direct indexical links to a historical moment or real person against which the performances and the memories can, in part, be judged, resulting in the political mimicry always being the 'body too much', always being in dialectical collision with its model, always being, therefore, an 'approximation'. Political mimicry is not only an approximate genre, it is a deeply equivocal one: reenacting facts that can often be verified through recourse to archive (and so, maybe, indicate how the 'body too much' has failed), while also signalling its detachment from that past by fictionalising it. There is an inherent duality to political mimicry's embodiment of the past which Alan Rosenthal touches on when he observes that 'the fact-based script, or docudrama, path is like no other. You have entered strange terrain, trodden before and yet still waiting to be explored' (2014: x). This is the favoured territory of 'approximation': the territory that is both 'homely' and 'unhomely', precisely the polarities embodied in political mimicry, as the actor is not and not-not the recognisable historical figure, both performing the past and performing memories (or fantasies) of that past. As Steven Lipkin argues, historical performance can also be historiography, 'a form of representing history, rather than . . . a representation of historical fact' (2011: 15). Political mimicry extends beyond performance, using mimesis 'approximately' to also make an intervention into and destabilise the history it imitates.

Notes

1 Flowers Gallery, Cork Street, London, 11 January–11 February 2012.
2 Blair also gave evidence 21 January 2011. https://webarchive.nationalarchives.gov.uk/20171123123237/www.iraqinquiry.org.uk/. Accessed 18 September 2019.
3 The full text at the start of *Loro* is translated as follows: 'This film stems from its authors' independent and free imagination; any reference to real people or events is wholly artistic and makes no claim to represent an objective truth. The authors took inspiration from news stories to create a narrative that brings together non-existent characters and real people in entirely invented contexts to create an original artistic work. No reference to people and/or events except those specifically identified as real is intended or should be inferred'.
4 As captured in the publication: Victoria Brittain, Nicolas Kent, Richard Norton-Taylor and Gillian Slovo, *The Tricycle: The Complete Tribunal Plays, 1994–2012*, London: Oberon Books, 2014.
5 Cf. www.youtube.com/watch?v=ft_rZ-BtqGQ. Accessed 15 September 2019.
6 Cf. Bruzzi, 2015.
7 Cf. the home page for Blythe's company, Recorded Delivery. www.recordeddelivery.net/about.html. Accessed 14 May 2019.
8 Discussion after 'Performing Documentary' Symposium, Goethe-Institut, London, November 2013.
9 An exception to this rule is Gabriel Range's *Death of a President* (2006) in which the real George W. Bush is also cut into the drama.
10 Cf. Sigmund Freud, 'The Uncanny', in *Art and Literature, Penguin Freud Library Vol. 14*, London: Penguin, 1992 [1919].
11 Janelle Reinelt's specific 'personal memory' related to a connection she experienced with the 1984 verbatim play, *Execution of Justice*, about the murder of Harvey Milk, as she was resident in North California at the time of his death.
12 The notion of the 'reverse uncanny' is developed further in the discussion of *Mad Men* and incidental events.
13 Cf. Campbell and Hagerty (2010: 126): 'We agreed that it was fine to be emotional and to call her the People's Princess; and Blair (2010: 139): 'The phrase "People's Princess"

now seems like something from another age. And corny. And over the top. And the rest of it. . . . Those few words scribbled on the back of an envelope probably had as much coverage as anything I ever did'.

14 Bill Nichols, Derek Paget and Belén Vidal among them.

15 At its start, *The Deal* reuses the words from the outset of *Butch Cassidy and the Sundance Kid*: 'Most of what follows is true'.

16 Cf. Comolli et al., 1971.

17 Cf. Derek Paget, 2013.

18 Cf. www.youtube.com/watch?v=Nub7UVR3Jmw. Accessed 25 May 2019.

19 Cf. Gavreil Rosenfeld, 'Why Do We Ask "What If?" Reflections on the Function of Alternative History', *History and Theory*, 41, December 2002, 90–103.

20 The famed Hugh Hudson-directed Labour PEB of 1987, however successful at creating a new informality, still maintained the distinction between Neil Kinnock's public and private selves.

21 Many have drawn parallels between Amelia Bly and Blair's confidante and friend from childhood, Anji Hunter, described by Blair in *A Journey* as 'my best friend' and in possession of 'perhaps the most naturally intuitive political instinct of anyone I ever met' (Blair, 2010: 21–22). Harris always strenuously denied that readers should infer that Blair and Hunter ever had an affair, though Blair does also recount in his memoirs how he, aged 16, 'tried climbing inside her sleeping bag at a party. . . (without success!)' (21).

22 Roman Polanski fled from the US legal system in 1978 (he was subsequently rearrested during the editing of *The Ghost*), after pleaded guilty to statutory rape before jumping bail to Paris.

23 The nadir is the implausibly ditsy Cherie Doon Mackichan plays in Alistair Beaton's *A Very Social Secretary* (2005), a satirical retelling of Labour Home Secretary, David Blunkett's affair with publisher, Kimberly Quinn and precursor to *The Trial of Tony Blair*.

24 Available to view on YouTube. www.youtube.com/watch?v=65ci6rZYVes. Accessed 30 May 2019.

25 Cf. Martin, 2006: 10 for a parsing of Schechner's ideas.

6

DOCUMENTARY RE-ENACTMENT

The 'model' approximation

Just as for Michel Foucault fetishism was the 'model perversion' which 'served as the guiding thread for analysing all the other deviations' (Foucault, 1990: 154), re-enactment is the 'model' 'approximation' which, as the reiteration of a past action, is defined by both its detachment and its proximity to reality. A re-enactment is a copy, a repetition of something that has already happened, which it resembles (usually closely, sometimes critically) but from which it remains distinct. It might even be so indistinguishable from the act it copies that it gets mistaken for it, but it will never *be* what it looks like. Beyond duplication, a re-enactment might also *transform* and *change* the action or event it mimics, and its frequently complex fragmentariness keeps in mind and incorporates knowledge of prior iterations: the original act and its enactment (in, for example, a documentary where the event is recounted for the first time). This book's underpinning notion of 'approximation' is rooted in a fascination with the real that is not quite real, the image that resembles and approximates but cannot ever be quite the same as the real. A re-enactment is always a repeated action: usually a *re*-experiencing or a *re*-opening of an already performed moment, but also, more contentiously, an acting out of a more speculative, hypothetical, maybe even merely imagined one (not each reconstruction of the same events in Errol Morris's *The Thin Blue Line*, for instance, can accurately represent what happened). 'Re-enactment' is both a generic category and a bodily performance – the active doing or performing on which rests that generic construction.

Although it has proved a resilient and popular documentary trope, as Jerome de Groot observes, 'Re-enactment often doesn't get a good press' (de Groot, 2011: 587). The use of re-enactment in documentary is widespread and comes in very different forms and visual styles, from the performance studies-influenced, Brechtian *mise-en-scène* of *The Last Days of the Ceausescus* or *The Arbor*, to the hyper stylisation of the reconstructions in *Standard Operating Procedure*, *The Jinx*, or *Dreams of a Life* (2011), to the use of animation in *The Missing Picture* or *Chicago 10*.

The use of 'dramatic reconstruction' to represent events for which archive does not exist is probably now its most common deployment. Most frequently viewed as a means (from *Shoah* [1985] to *The Act of Killing*) of accessing 'a traumatic history' (Caruth, 1995: 151), documentary re-enactment is also linked to notions of confession and first-person re-telling (as in *Stories We Tell* [2012]) or, quite separately, to 'living history', a use of historical re-enactment that has gained in currency and prominence and has, as Rebecca Schneider comments, become an intellectually respectable part of 'the twentieth-century academic "memory industry"' (2011: 2). Jeremy Deller's re-enactment of *The Battle of Orgreave* exemplifies the convergence of art and 'living history' and is discussed below.

Re-enactments presume there is value in remembering and repeating, although every reconstruction is also in part defined by the residual fear of getting stuck in the past. David Rieff posits the benefits of forgetting, of leaving the past behind, of 'mustering the courage, at least from time to time, to contemplate the ultimate meaninglessness of history' and 'to take on board the fact that sooner or later the past will recede in importance before it is lost entirely' (Rieff, 2016: 5, 9). The re-enactment, of course, brings with it the compulsion to remember and mitigates against the implied passivity of Rieff's characterisation of history as something that is done to us; the spur for the majority of re-enactments is the desire to more actively engage with, understand, bring into the present, change perceptions of and learn from that past. And yet, documentary re-enactments act out and are defined by contradictory impulses of wanting to revise and wanting to move on; remaining transfixed, Narcissus-like, by the alluring proximity to reality as André Bazin was when he declared 'The photographic image is the object itself' (1967: 14), but of also wanting to propose an alternative reality. Just as it counters Rieff's call to forget history, so re-enactment argues against Bazin's reductive claim that 'Every image is to be seen as an object and every object as an image' (1967: 13–14). But if, as Paula Rabinowitz suggests, all documentary is 'usually a reconstruction – a re-enactment of another time or place for a difference audience – a graphing of history, in and through the cinematic image and taped sound, onto the present' (Rabinowitz, 1993: 119–120), our relationship with memory and the photographic image is never stable or the image/object link fixed. As exemplified by the re-enactment, looking back will always entail a certain amount of moving on.

To conclude either that the image is the object or that all documentaries are re-enactments is to elide the potentially problematic issue of the conscious, active reconstruction of reality. In the late 1990s to early 2000s many found the overt performativity of docusoaps troublesome, for instance, when social actors such as *Driving School*'s Maureen Rees acted out their ordinary lives for and with the implicit acknowledgement of the camera. Scenes were scripted and typical scenarios (such as Maureen rousing her husband in the middle of the night to get him to help her prepare for her theory test) replayed specially for the camera. For a while, at least in the UK, each documentary reconstruction, however trivial, was signposted. This seemed (and was) unnecessary, for the pact between documentary and viewer was obvious. Fast forward a few years and the ingenuous 'acting' on *Driving School* has been supplanted by the hyper-performativity of the latest social experiment reality shows such as *Love Island*, in which participants act up disingenuously for the panoptic cameras 24 hours a day. Most documentaries in what John Corner has identified as the age of '"postdocumentary" culture' (Corner, 2002) are comfortable with the notion that being, let alone being in a documentary, is performative.

Re-enactment has proved itself to be a prominent feature of '"postdocumentary" culture', a conscious choice by many filmmakers to challenge received notions of how reality could be represented, to accept the performative dimension of all documentary and to feel comfortable with the relaxation of boundaries between 'documentary' and 'fiction'. Sarah Polley's *Stories We Tell* is an exemplary 'postdocumentary' film, an intimate autobiography that mixes a variety of documentary and non-documentary modes to recount the story of Polley's dead mother Diane and the discovery, following a 40-page email from her father, Michael, that she was the result of her mother Diane's love affair with another man. Re-enactment is the primary tool Polley deploys to re-tell her family's complicatedly entwined narrative using a multiplicity of personal and sometimes incompatible perspectives. From its release, *Stories We Tell* has proved tricky to categorise and Polley herself refers to it as 'a hybrid: something between a documentary and an experimental film' (Porton, 2013: 36). Alongside Clio Barnard (whose film *The Arbor* is discussed below) Polley embodies the revival of the experimental documentary tradition of Vertov, Vigo, Franju and Greenaway; she also recognises the freedom the documentary mode afforded her: that 'documentary allows life to happen and for you to change your direction' (36). Polley flouts (or questions) convention: her interviewees (in particular her siblings) regularly break 'the fourth wall', for example, and she does not signpost the distinctions between documentary and fictional material. *Stories We Tell* is only half 'about' the secret family history and Polley's search for her biological father; as identified by Michael Polley the documentary is really 'about', as he terms it 'the vagaries of truth and the unreliability of memory'. These 'vagaries' are enacted using a variety of tropes, from the most explicitly documentary elements (interviews, genuine grainy Super-8 home movie footage and Michael's studio recording of his lengthy account of the family's history) to the film's two especially idiosyncratic and genre-defying kinds of re-enactment: fake home movie footage in which family members are played by actors, and reconstructions in which Polley and other family members reenact encounters that were not filmed but have been described in interview.

Polley's radical reappraisal of truth and reality hinges on and is typified by the polarised perspectives of her two fathers: Michael, who is accepting of the 'vagaries of truth' (and of his daughter's biological parentage) and Harry, who holds more rigid views of who has the right to tell the story of that parentage. Harry's conceptualisation of 'truth' is as a series of concentric circles with the absent Diane at the epicentre. 'The only person who could provide the essence, the essentials of what took place' would have been Diane, (who died when Sarah was 11) Harry tells Sarah; 'you have to limit it to those who are involved in the events, directly involved', he continues, 'and the direct witnesses to the events are two, and one is not around'. In effect, his biological daughter's entire documentary unfolds gently but assuredly as an elaborate argument against such rigidity, as its many re-enactments take the investigation ever further from Harry's idea of where 'truth' resides. As articulated by Sarah's sister, Joanna, when pondering who Diane was:

> I don't think there was a what actually happened. . . . There were lots of perspectives form the very beginning. You don't ever get to an answer. You don't ever get to 'yeah, now we've figured it out . . . we know exactly the person she was'. I think those things are delusory.

It is through the fragmented structure of *Stories We Tell* and Polley's deployment of re-enactment that Joanna's idea that it is impossible to know 'what actually happened' emerge.

The idea behind the documentary's fracturedness was, as Polley explains, 'to construct something from the past while also calling that entire process of construction into question' (Porton, 2013: 39), a questioning that emerges most powerfully in the two most explicit forms of Super-8 re-enactment: fictional home movie footage using actors and the mute reconstructions in which interviewees play themselves. The fictionalised re-enactments explicitly fill in archival gaps: semi-public scenes and private, incidental moments that would seldom, if ever, have made it into even the most intrusive home movie. The fake home movie sequences often adopt the jerky, roaming, observational style familiar from *faux*-documentaries and closely shadow what interviewees are describing, for example, the camera panning across and zooming into a table of uncleared plates, crumbs and a full ashtray as Sarah's sister Susy recalls how, following Diane's death, Michael lived in 'a home of utter neglect'. Although Polley (and her brother John who helped her with casting) deliberately worked to cast actors who resembled the real people closely, she found herself 'amazed' that some viewers were 'fooled' by these re-enactments (Porton, 2013: 36).

Reflexive signposting ensures that the Super-8 re-enactments of conversations performed by Sarah and other relatives to the audio of interviews with them and others are, while formally intricate, not comparably confusing. In these mute sequences, participants mouth words (not always their own, nor often in sync) from the interviews they accompany. As narrated words and images slip in and out of step with each other and history brushes past the present, these re-enactments evoke Schneider's idea of the re-enactment's 'syncopated' temporality (Schneider, 2011: 1), of the temporal planes being both in step with each other but also reflective of perspectival difference. Two especially crucial scenes are rendered this way: Sarah's meeting with Harry in a café in Montreal at which she finds out that he is her biological father and its partner scene in which she visits Michael to inform him of her discovery. The sequence with Harry begins to the accompaniment of a silent cinema-style old piano and, rather as in a silent movie, voice and image undulate in and out of time with each other, making the infrequent moments of *synchronicity* doubly emphatic. The most vital revelations are approximately in synch, as when, in extreme close-up, Harry mouths 'no' to his own voice in interview recalling his response to Sarah asking him if he thought her biological father 'was

Geoff Bowen (sic)?'.[1] However, when Harry then recalls Sarah's consequent question ('do you know who it was?'), in a playful deployment of syncopation Harry is not, as we might anticipate, granted the satisfying, synchronous simplicity of mouthing and saying 'yes'; instead, accompanying an image of Harry is a montage of Sarah's siblings' voices recalling *their* memories of what Sarah said about Harry's revelation. At every turn, *Stories We Tell* uses re-enactment to draw attention to the splintering as well as the fusion of identity, time and memory.

The comparable sequence in which Sarah goes to tell Michael about Harry follows a similar pattern, although the words throughout are supplied by Michael from his scripted reading. Again, the dislocation between words and images and the delaying tactics of dramatic irony enact and accentuate paralleled disparities of knowledge: that Sarah has come to impart some momentous, potentially traumatic information, of which Michael, until he finally allows her time to speak, remains ignorant. As in the meeting with Harry, the re-enactment sidles in and out of time with the script. This re-enactment, however, is more formally complex with the insertion of a medley of faked archival shots from when Diane met Harry in Montreal, building to the moment of anagnorisis as Michael's ruminative words 'It took you quite a while to get to the moment of truth, if we can use that expression' are linked to this time genuine home movie footage of Diane kissing the cheek of the baby Sarah. Michael then re-enacts himself at this 'great moment of truth' as he finally comprehends that he is not her biological father, that that was 'Harry Gulkin?!', words that sound in perfect synchronicity with the image. However, it would be unwise to over-sentimentalise such moments of moving coalescence, for there is no consistent pattern to the synchronization. (Twice, for instance, Michael reads that the revelation that her biological father was Harry had rendered Sarah 'speechless' or 'quite stunned', descriptions that are totally *out of step* with the Super-8 images Sarah constructs to illustrate that moment, which instead show her to be talking and gesticulating animatedly.)

The 'approximate' status of *Stories We Tell* is the result of Polley's decision to construct the film's narrative around not only a variety of styles but also a 'cacophony of voices' (Porton, 2013: 39) between which the relationship is fluid and unpredictable. Just as it might seem clear, in line with this narrative structuring, that Polley adheres to the view that no single mode of re-enactment or rendition of the 'vagaries of truth' guarantees a more 'stable' or 'meaningful' version than any other, there comes (near the end) a merger between image and narration that, however fleetingly, adds credence to Harry's more restricted view of how to get at the story's 'truth'. In a piece of voiceover Polley speaks of the 'tsunami' Diane 'unleashed when she went', leaving her family 'still flailing in her wake, trying to put her together in the wreckage, and her slipping away from us, over and over again, just as we begin to see her face'. Polley's description of her mother going in and out of focus provides an apt metaphor for the molten and uncertain relationship to the truth acted out in *Stories We Tell,* and Sarah's words coincide with vibrantly authentic home movie footage of a family beach holiday by a huge expanse of calm sea, which culminates in a luminously expressive close-up of Diane's face sunbathing. In terms of Harry's concentric circles, this image of Diane – an unsullied burst of close-up, unadulterated genuineness – is ostensibly the truest, most authentic truth a documentary could muster. And yet, as Diane squints into the lens, oblivious to how this casual, inconsequential snapshot will later be subsumed into another, far more complex narrative, it seems to be more obvious than ever that, however spontaneous and real the image, however amplified or enhanced, it cannot, just by presenting itself to be looked at or by virtue of its own innate integrity, unlock *the truth*. Beyond the features of Diane's face, beyond her and the archive's function as raw and accidental record, what does this image, in and of itself, tell us? We may feel able, as the family saga unravels, to *read* more into the image and *understand* it better, but 'There's no art to find the mind's construction in the face' (*Macbeth* I.iv): we can never know if our deductions are correct or not.

As far as concerns Harry's concentric circles of truth: the *truest* form, the kernel, is unscripted piece of holiday home movie footage of Diane; the *falsest*, within the parameters of *Stories We Tell*, would thereby be the fake home movies. But Polley crafts a film in which the apparent continuum from one to another is not a continuum at all, but instead an unhelpfully circular argument in which the status of images is unhierarchical, exemplified by the multi-layeredness of each re-enactment or the relaxed way in which Polley flits from one type of performance or re-enactment to another, frequently within a single short sequence. Alongside which, there is Polley's own unpredictable treatment of ostensibly 'important' facts, for instance that, as we learn only relatively late in the film and in meagre detail, Diane had an unhappy first marriage (of which John and Susy are the progeny) that ended in divorce and as a consequence of which she made headlines for being the first woman in Canada to lose custody of her children. 'The vagaries of truth' trounce predictability after all, as re-enactment becomes the glue that holds the numerous and heterogeneous facts in Polley's story together, with the transformative power to capture 'how the story was changing as a result of us telling it and how the relationships were changing as a result of us . . . telling it' (Polley in Doucet, 2015: 99).

Predictably enough, *Stories We Tell* is not tied up neatly at the end. Instead, a sequence of uncertain status (it is probably a self-re-enactment, though it could be part authentic home movie) is cradled in the final, especially ambiguous, extract from Michael's account of the family story. A fly is filmed in close-up, silhouetted against a piercingly blue and big Torontonian sky. 'For that fly', he reads (to the strains of the silent movie piano) 'the word "why?" does not exist. Yes, Michael', he closes enigmatically, 'just accept the sentence: I will go on. I will go on'. The mute footage alongside the narration shows three of Michael's five children cavorting about with numerous grandchildren on a sun-drenched bed, no definite means of determining with certainty the status of the footage. *Stories We Tell* had opened with Michael citing Margaret Atwood's analysis that a story that has yet to be told is 'only a confusion'. By its end, Diane and Sarah's story may have been told, but it is still 'only a confusion' and the status of its truth and the tools used to represent it – archive and re-enactment – remain ambiguous. Re-enactment in this case complicates definitions of documentary; it is, as so often, an active choice on the director's part to make use of a form that problematises the stories it tells by juxtaposing multiple alternative perspectives. As Joanna says, it is 'delusory' to imagine we can ever definitively 'figure it out'.

Because it ostensibly sits in opposition to documentary's putative aim to represent reality as authentically and/or accurately as possible, re-enactment is often taken to be a sign of lack or failure. It is also, in its enduring appeal, illustrative of the realisation that such an aim is . . . unrealisable; that no image, no documentary, no piece of home movie footage will ever be interchangeable with what it captures. Instead, in a documentary such as Polley's, the discrepancies between the event and its representation are the magnificent tensions that underpin 'postdocumentary' documentary in the post-observational age, which signalled a return to as opposed to a rejection of re-enactment. Bill Nichols opens his influential essay on documentary re-enactment with the comment:

> Reenactments, the more or less authentic re-creation of prior events, provided a staple element of documentary representation until they were slain by the 'verité boys' of the 1960s . . . who proclaimed everything except what took place in front of the camera without rehearsal or prompting to be a fabrication, inauthentic.
>
> *(Nichols, 2008: 72)*

With its fixation on the unrehearsed, spontaneous action, *cinema verité* sought to bring about the redundancy of re-enactment. What was heralded as documentary's eureka moment (the potential, enabled by technological advances such as the arrival of portable sound equipment and lightweight cameras, to capture life without re-enactment) instead turned out to be its Icarus moment. Emile de Antonio, chronicler of 1960s and 1970s US politics via his 'collage junk' archival methods, argued that 'Only people without feelings or convictions could event think of making *cinema verité*', because the belief in pure observation was a 'childish assumption about the nature of film' (Rosenthal, 1978: 7). Technology could not de-subjectify the film-making process as the 'verité boys' believed; observation did not provide a window on the world as directors such as Pennebaker and the Maysles claimed. *Verité* was a sticking place for documentary because what it successfully 'proved' was the futility of documentary's putative quest to reproduce reality without bias or manipulation.[2]

Re-enactment offers one way to resolve the sense of 'failure', maintaining as it does its dual acknowledgement of the authenticity of facts and the value to documentary of reinterpreting them. The image is not 'truth', as Ellis reminds us, because 'photographic evidence was a bonus for documentaries rather than its basis. Truth was located before the images' (Ellis, 2012: 13). Or, as Errol Morris posits, 'believing is seeing, not the other way around' (Nubar, 2002: 108). Of the relationship between image and words Morris argues, for example, that:

> Truth is not guaranteed by style or presentation. It's not handed over on a tray like a Happy Meal. It's a quest, and . . . whatever truth is, it's a linguistic and not a visual thing. . . . To talk about a photograph being true or false is utterly

meaningless. Words give you a picture of the world and visuals take you into the mystery of what is out there and whether language has captured it or not.

(Nubar, 2002: 108)

Although not stating it explicitly, Morris, in his dismissal of the indexical truth of the photograph and his elevation of words over images as the means to solve 'the mystery', is here mounting a forceful validation of the re-enactment, a form he revived and redefined in the late 1980s. A documentary such as Carol Morley's *Dreams of a Life* explicitly employs dramatised re-enactments to solve the 'mystery' of a death – Joyce Vincent's – about which almost nothing is known. *Dreams of a Life* attempts to piece together Vincent's life and death, but she remains, quite literally, the haunting 'lost object' Nichols argues lies at the heart of each re-enactment, a subject 'reconstituted from available resources', but which ultimately remains an unreconstructible 'irretrievable moment' (Nichols, 2008: 74–75). Vincent's body was discovered early in 2006 in her flat above a shopping centre in Tottenham, North London by bailiffs who had come to serve a repossession order. She had died late in 2003 and was found in such a bad state of decomposition (her body had 'basically melted into the carpet' as one interviewee puts it) that she could only be identified by comparing her teeth to a holiday photograph. Vincent's death was surrounded by multiple 'unknowns', the most painful of which was that the authorities had not been notified by family, friends or colleagues of her disappearance. When her body was discovered, her television set was still on and next to her lay a pile of unlabelled wrapped Christmas presents. An inquest returned an open verdict, the cause of death unknown; it could have been asthma, possibly a peptic ulcer. One friend speculates that she had a 'hidden sadness in her life' or had had to escape from a violent boyfriend.

Dreams of a Life is a documentary built on speculation and offers a metaphor of sorts for re-enactment, its limits and its capabilities. A former friend of Vincent's (she had lost touch with all the friends Morley had traced via a plea for information she placed in a London newspaper) muses: 'In the 21st century you can still fall through the cracks'. Morley's re-enactments of Joyce's (Zawe Ashton) last hours are built around those fissures, offering up incomplete and colliding truths. There is an unsettling concreteness to the film's re-enactments – the depressing ugliness of Joyce's grubby kitchen, the garish blue of the plastic carrier bags she deposits on the worktop – 'unsettling' because, despite their detailedness, these re-enactments can only ever be hypothesis, fantasy or supposition, confirmation, it might seem, of the film's lack of 'evidence', of re-enactment being something a documentary filmmaker 'would *resort to*' in the absence of any 'cinematic record', as Spence and Navarro argue (2010: 215; my italics). And yet, the re-enactments in *Dreams of a Life* go far beyond being a spectral presence or record of absence: they give Joyce Vincent a life.

The focal point of Spence and Navarro's distrust of re-enactment is the elevated status in documentary studies granted to indexicality; as Jean-Luc Comolli and Jean Narboni asserted in 1971 'Clearly, the cinema "reproduces" reality: this is what a camera and film stock are for' (1971: 30). Concomitantly, Bazin was equally categorical in his belief that

> [P]ainting is, after all, an inferior way of making likenesses. . . . Only the photographic lens can give us the kind of image of the object that is capable of satisfying the deep need man has to substitute for it something more than *a mere approximation.*
>
> *(Bazin, 1967: 14; my italics)*

Much more recently, Nichols deduces that 'the re-enactment *forfeits* its indexical bond to the original event' (Nichols, 2008: 74; my italics). The underlying presupposition in all of these statements is that not just proximity but resemblance to reality remains the defining aspirations of photography or documentary, that lookalike-ness possesses, as Roland Barthes observes in *Camera Lucida,* 'an absolutely superior, somehow eternal value' (Barthes, 1981: 79). The photograph means 'I can never deny that *the thing has been there*' (76), Barthes argues, as 'From a phenomenological viewpoint . . . the power of authentication exceeds the power of representation' (89). Barthes, however, alights on the photograph's essential ambivalence when he also notes that the photograph marks the reality it represents as being 'already dead' (79).

That there is a difference between an event and its representation is unnegotiable, although there are potentially instances when it might be invisible. With the potential blurring of that difference comes the concomitant secondary issue of trust. It is an ethical obligation, Nichols intimates, not to elide the distinction between enactment and re-enactment, for if it 'goes unnoticed or unrecognized, the question of deceit arises' (Nichols, 2008: 73), as it did for some viewers of *Stories We Tell.* 'Viewers *must* recognise' he continues, 'a re-enactment as a re-enactment even if this recognition also *dooms* the re-enactment to its status as a *fictionalized* repetition of something that has already occurred' (73–74; my italics). Nichols' reservations and imperatives signal that re-enactment faces 'an impossible task', for it is 'to retrieve a lost object' and repeat 'what remains historically unique. A spectre haunts the text' (74).

Unlike philosopher R.G. Collingwood in his analysis of history, Nichols argues persistently for a clear hierarchy between the event and its re-enactment; the irretrievable event is in possession of a 'uniqueness' that the spectral copy is 'doomed' never to be able to emulate. Re-enactment here is trapped in an impossible 'catch-22' bind; its 'very syntax', Nichols argues, 'affirms the have-been-thereness of what can never, quite, be here again. Facts remain facts' (79). However, there is a residual tension throughout Nichols's article between the finality of such a declaration and the desire to permit re-enactment to 'foil the desire to preserve the past in the amber of an omniscient wholeness' (79). Ultimately, though, Nichols comes down on the side of historical fixity when he says, 'Reenactments produce an iterability for that which belongs to the singularity of historical occurrence' (79). The re-enactment is a ghostly uncanny copy whose role is to 'make good [the] loss' of the 'lost object'

(74) and revive an 'irretrievable moment' (75); the present it embodies does not enter into vital, dialectical engagement with the past of which it is a pallid echo.

The re-enactment finds itself in an *impasse* as the very status of repetition is perceived as problematic, a 'mere approximation' that can only reiterate, 'anathema to most documentarians', illustrative of 'what might be called *tabloid* interest in dramatic verisimilitude' (Rosenheim, 1996: 226). All re-enactments are repetitions, but as Blackson remarks, 'few repetitions become reenactments' (2007: 30). A film of a performance piece that tests the value of repetition is Milo Rau's *The Last Days of the Ceausescus*, a re-enactment of the trial of Romanian Communist dictator, Nicolae Ceausescu, and his wife, Elena, which premiered at the Odeon Theatre, Bucharest to mark the 20th anniversary of their execution by firing squad on 25 December 1989. The original trial was videoed (excerpts available online) and, for the film version, Rau inserts selections of archive footage which he then dovetails tightly with moments from the re-enactment. Repetition is not, Rau's work suggests, simply a neutral act, even if in cases when the re-enactment is mistaken for its original. As British playwright David Edgar remarked when talking about his 1974 documentary play about Watergate, *I Know What You Meant*, the words 'spoken on screen had actually been spoken in reality, and we had the transcripts to prove it'; in spite of this, the 'whole process' of making the play 'was bristling with impurities' and 'value judgements' (quoted in Megson, 2009: 197).

Arrested in the winter of 1989, which saw the demise of East European communism, Ceausescu and his wife were granted a short trial by kangaroo court. Proceedings were organised and presided over by defence minister, General Victor Stanculescu, and culminated in the Romanian dictator and his wife being found guilty of multiple charges including genocide and subversion of state power. *The Last Days of the Ceausescus* is, as introductory on-screen text explains, based on 'numerous conversations . . . with those involved in the overthrow and execution of the Ceausescus'. The film version is a collage of television news archive, interviews (with actors standing in for interviewees), images from inside the Odeon Theatre, scenes from the play as staged and sections of the play shot specially for the screen. The set where the makeshift tribunal takes place (the actual tribunal was held in an army barracks outside Bucharest) is a faithful replica of the actual room and the actors' costumes stick very close to the originals. As the re-enactment gets underway, two images are edited together into a completed sequence: rough quality video archive of Nicolae Ceausescu extending his right hand to rest it on his wife's, and an infinitely sharper segment of a reconstruction that, as he withdraws it, completes the gesture, albeit from a slightly different angle. A narrator surmises: 'original and copy, on stage at Bucharest's Odeon Theatre, it's hard to tell them apart'. Of course, it is relatively easy to 'tell them apart', and Rau does not attempt to disguise that; but what he is probing here is the value in having noted the similarity as well as the value in differentiating between the 'reality' of the original and the 'artificiality' of the copy. In terms similar to Peter Weiss's radically influential discussion of documentary theatre in the early 1970s,[3] Rau's narrator assures his audience that 'No gesture, no glance is made-up'. Which is true – except that it is a copy.

Focus on the value of explicit gestural mimicry is exemplified by Rau's re-enactment of the Ceausescus' arrest following Stanculescu's sentencing (the real Victor Stanculescu is looking on from the theatre's auditorium). Soldiers move to bind their hands and escort them out; their struggle is dramatized in frenetic, choppy close-ups. The short sequence showing Elena Ceausescu's wrists being bound is made up of dramatized shots and three short segments of archival footage, all of which segue in and out of each other, so a movement started in the archive is once again completed almost seamlessly by the reconstruction: 'original' history and its ghostly 'copy' interlocking like pieces of parquet. Anthropologist Michael Taussig defined mimesis as 'to get hold of something by means of its likeness' (1993: 21): a reiteration that is also an interpretation; an eloquent way to describe the active value of the kind of extreme gestural precision reproduced in the bind-ing of Elena Ceausescu's hands. Rau's mimesis is not copying for copying's sake, but a meditation on the intrinsic status and worth of the act of copying. A practi-tioner who has repeatedly incorporated re-enactment into his work, Rau, as part of another project (the 2014–2016 piece, *Reenactment: Probing a Theatrical Concept*), poses a series of questions about the 'dividing line between tautology and under-standing, between mere mass-media repetition and "cultural memory", between perfect imitation and critical reproduction'.[4] A primary motivation for this study of 'approximation' is the desire to understand what difference the act of duplication, reiteration, reprisal makes.

Judith Butler argued for drag to be understood as an imitative 'site of ambiva-lence', the sort of ambivalence offered by a layered reconstruction (as in Rau's work) in which, essentially (and ironically), enactment and re-enactment are, if not quite equivalents, then working in unison as alternative but parallel performative re-visionings of the same act. The assumed hierarchy between enactment and re-enactment – that iterations operate like a series of onion layers, taking us further and further from the core of truth – is disputed by the sort of openly contrapuntal renegotiation with history performed in a reconstructive sequence such as the one that acts out the demise of Elena Ceausescu. The manner in which Rau invites analysis of history and includes his audiences (both the theatre's diegetic audience and the viewers of the film) in his dialectical exchanges puts the emphasis on what knowledge and insights can be *gained* through re-enactment, not on what is irrevo-cably *lost* by it. 'Reenactments are clearly *a* view rather than *the* view from which the past yields up its truth' as Nichols identifies (2008: 79), but this partiality is shared by all documentary, all performative acts; as Dziga Vertov understood, reality starts to change the moment it is looked at.

So, what is the status and the comparable 'uniqueness' of the re-enactment? 'The problem posed by "lookalikeness" or iconicity', Jane Gaines (after Foucault) writes, 'is, of course, endemic to all mimetic technologies', and the indexical bond 'between the photographic image and the object in the real world to which the image refers' is fundamental to documentary (Gaines, 1999b: 5). But resemblance is no longer the exclusive, prize attribute of non-fiction, so, Gaines wonders, 'Can we at least say that documentary has an inside track on reality, that it has a something, even if it can no longer be said to have a "trace" of the real?' (6). Postmodern scepticism notwithstanding, it is, ironically, our collective, pervasive 'fascination with resemblances' (the 'cinema of taxidermy') and the 'possibility of seeing cinematic realism as an invitation to knowledge' (8) that liberates the re-enactment *per se* – if not the documentary as a whole. Gaines raises a hugely important piece of cinematic and documentary heritage when she touches on, *a propos* of Dziga Vertov, 'how much has been lost in the translation of *Kino Pravda* into cinema verité' (12). The attraction to a cinema of intellectual engagement that couched its 'fascination with resemblances' within a framework that acknowledged its own constructedness (the Soviet tradition) became marginalised once the Hollywood model became ubiquitous. The dominance of realist cinema – cinema that disavows the signs of its very modes of construction – leads more or less directly to the perceived 'failure' of mimetic re-enactment: if, as Nichols argues, the difference between the enactment and the re-enactment goes undeclared, then the re-enactment is fraudulent; if, conversely, the re-enactment foregrounds its constructedness (and concomitantly admits its artifice) then it moves too far from the authentic moment it recreates and fatally undermines the indexical bond. Which returns us to the syntactical paradox of the re-enactment as both witness to and perpetually absent from the moment it recreates.

Errol Morris's pioneering insight into the value of re-enactment has been to challenge the innate, assumed value of the indexical image – not because he does not believe in 'truth', as explained above, but because he does not believe it is guaranteed by a realist style. Radical and innovative in *The Thin Blue Line* or *Mr Death* and widely imitated in documentaries such as *Deep Water* (Osmond and Rothwell, 2006) *The Jinx* and *Out of Thin Air*,[5] Morris's style later arguably became, however influential, 'something of a cliché' (Austin, 2011: 350). In Morris's recent documentary feature, *Standard Operating Procedure*, a film about the Abu Ghraib photographs depicting the human rights atrocities perpetrated by US military and CIA personnel against Iraqi detainees, the re-enactments are shot by Martin Scorsese and Quentin Tarantino's cinematographer, Robert Richardson, in majestic ultra-slow motion at 1,000 frames per second. The problem some critics perceived with *Standard Operating Procedure* was the extreme incompatibility between the re-enactments' resplendent beauty and their sober, traumatic subject matter: perennially, perhaps, Morris's fatal flaw. Morris will have a considerable legacy; he invented the 'interrotron' and later the 'Megatron' – elaborate sets of lenses and mirrors which enable interviewees to look into the camera and at Morris at the same time – and his endgame has, in the past, been to successfully match style with seriousness of intent, and thereby to counteract the extravagancies of his re-enactments with weighty purpose. But in recent films the balance has tipped; however visually striking, his Academy Award-winning *The Fog of War* (2003) let Robert McNamara, the 'architect of the Vietnam War' off the hook,[6] while *Standard Operating Procedure* has attracted sustained criticism, even vitriol.

Paul Arthur charged Morris's re-enactments in *Standard Operating Procedure* with providing 'titillation through horror', arguing that 'to employ this rhetoric in a documentary about actual horror is obscene' (Arthur, 2008: 112). Arthur's subsequent accusation that 'aesthetic thrills' were offered as 'a substitute for specificity of meaning' (112) would have hurt Morris the most. Under the heading 'Feelings of Revulsion and the Limits of Academic Discourse', Bill Nichols, via *Jump Cut*, sent Morris an open letter in which he articulated his visceral response to *Standard Operating Procedure*. Nichols speaks of how trauma resists 'contextualization' and 'remains incomparable', accusing Morris of portraying 'traumatic events in an abstract, almost ethereal way that produces something like a traumatic effect in me' (Nichols, 2010).'We address the unspeakable and give it form', Nichols goes on, but clearly feels that, with *Standard Operating Procedure*, a line has been crossed and that the film transcends the 'limits of academic discourse' (2010).

At the other end of the spectrum from those of Rau's Elena Ceausescu sequence, Morris's re-enactments, while emblematic and figurative of the abuse and torture of Iraqi prisoners at the hands of US guards and interrogators, are not literal. Their collaborative juxtaposition with the interviewees around them is crucial. Nichols references but does not analyse in detail the re-enactment narrated by the words of Civil Interrogator Tim Dugan (who is extremely critical of the 'softening up' tactics adopted by the Ubu Ghraib Military Personnel). The re-enactment is representative and symbolic; it is not a detailed reconstruction and is heavily stylised. It begins with a backwards tracking shot down a prison corridor populated by the ghostly, half-exposed images of guards going about their routine business. When the camera reaches the corridor's end there is an edit to a chiaroscuro, canted shot of a detainee on a cell floor, crouching forward with, over his head, a pair of underpants, stained pinkish by blood, an image that is almost perfectly reflected in a puddle on the floor. The same image then appears closer and upside down, the inversion making it more expressionistic and elliptical, a repercussion of which is to muddy the brutality of what is being represented and described. This luxurious and unstable picture prompts, at the very least, ambivalent responses; the symmetrical composition, lush colouring and atmospheric soft lighting collide with, maybe also compromise, Dugan's account of the illegal interrogation methods.

Morris, of course, sees the style of his re-enactments in *Standard Operating Procedure* very differently to someone like Nichols, returning in one defence to the issue of how truth is guaranteed. 'People used to think that the truth should be shot badly'; but, as Morris continues, 'The truth is not guaranteed by natural lighting or a handheld camera' (quoted in Austin, 2011: 350). Instead, Morris talks of having wanted Robert Richardson 'to do the re-enactments so they would look unmistakably different from everything else, so there could be no question whether or not they were created by me' (350). Morris's choice of words is crucial here: he is not justifying his re-enactments on the grounds of their superlative, extravagant style, but rather in terms of what can be inferred from their cinematic style, that is: that they are authored, and cannot be mistaken for the realities of the film's other images – the photographs or the interviews.

Morris's re-enactments of torture ask complex, disconcerting questions about the appropriateness of the conjunction between visual flamboyance and traumatic subject matter;[7] they are arrestingly elegant and, pared down to an abstract level and could even be termed beautiful, which is in itself an obscene realisation. That they offer a critique of the outmoded view that 'the truth should be shot badly' or that they should stand out 'from everything else' are necessarily secondary considerations to their ethical, psychological impact. In the multitude of photographs documenting the systemic torture of prisoners at Abu Ghraib, Judith Butler found (after Arendt) the 'banalization of evil', a horror 'alarming only to those who were outside the scenes of war and imprisonment', not to those within it, who can be seen, like Sabrina Harman (interviewed extensively by Morris), smiling and giving the thumbs up to the camera. Butler also reminds us that 'the photo has no magical moral agency' (Butler, 2007: 963). The function of the re-enactments in *Standard Operating Procedure* is to fill in the background to those images. It is conceivable that, the discursive dialogue between the film's two image-based systems (the stylised, other-worldly re-enactments and the 'banal' photographs), is intended to compel audiences to look afresh at the photographs rather than become inured to the traumas they depict,[8] but their elegiac and dreamy qualities dissipate and deflect attention away from that. Atrocities test the limits of representation as Nichols argues, but especially on the big screen, *Standard Operating Procedure* creates a visual pleasure that is in itself traumatic.

One fundamental issue with Morris's re-enactments in *Standard Operating Procedure* is not their hyper-stylisation *per se* but that they offer a description as opposed to an analysis of the Abu Ghraib photographs. The re-enactments in both *The Last Days of the Ceausescus* and *Standard Operating Procedure* – though very different in terms of proximity to indexical images and style – 'act out' or repeat the scenes they represent; they do not in themselves attempt to 'work through' actions; instead, they repeat them. 'Acting out' and 'working through' are Freud's terms, and his essay 'Remembering, Repeating and Working Through' was an important starting point for my thinking on re-enactment. Written in 1914, Freud's thinking on the value of remembering and working through was likely coloured by the commencement of the 'terrible war' as he terms the conflict of 1914–1918 in his 1920 essay, 'Beyond the Pleasure Principle'. In the 1914 essay, his initial crucial observation is that 'acting out' occurs instead of remembering; that a patient who (often repeatedly and compulsively) 'acts out' a repressed memory does so because they do 'not *remember* anything at all of what he has forgotten and repressed' (Freud, 2006: 394). 'The greater the resistance', Freud adds, 'the more thoroughly remembering will be replaced by acting out (repetition)' (395); 'acting out' effectively becomes a barrier as well as an alternative to remembering.

Freud's psychoanalytic aim was to get his patients to the point of 'working through' their personal trauma, but a significant portion of documentary re-enactment sticks with 'acting out': 'living history' re-enactments, for instance, do not set out to change or tamper with historical fact, neither does *Shoah* (1985) in which Claude Lanzmann compels his interviewees to return to and reprise their experiences of the holocaust. Not all of them want to 'go back', as Polish envoy Jan Karski terms it, while others, such as hairdresser Abraham Bomba, Treblinka prisoner and hairdresser, do consent to reprising their actions for Lanzmann. *Shoah* raises the issue of the powerful psychological imperative *not* to 'work through' and the value of repeating actions in the present in order to ensure that traumatic events are not *condemned to* memory and history. Writing about Karski's resistance, Ivone Margulies notes how an 'Inability to recompose a narrative about the past yields a therapeutic impasse' (Margulies, 2019: 145–146), a reluctance to 'work through' which Dominick LaCapra frames as wanting to 'keep faith with' the original traumatic memory (LaCapra, 2001: 22).

As here, the most prevalent form of re-enactment in documentary is 'in-person re-enactment',[9] when the individual involved in the recalling of a past action had also been the person who performed that action in the past. In documentaries this 'acting out' often takes the literal form of 'walking through' past actions, as occurs, for instance, in Peter Greenaway's *Act of God* (1980), in which various interviewees describe and 'act out' their experiences of having been struck by lightning. Another archetypal example of in person 'acting out' and 'working through' is the interview with former miner, Michael Wilson, in Yvette Vanson's *Battle for Orgreave* (1985). Wilson literally 'acts out' the moment he was chased and beaten by riot police on the day of the eponymous 'battle' during the Miners' Strike of 1984–1985 by 'walking through' the event for the benefit of Vanson's following-the-subject camera.[10] Wilson, among the miners arrested on riot charges, recalls being chased by police who he soon realised 'were going to hit me'; he begins to both speak about and 'act out' how he 'turned and ran', before falling down and being beaten and kicked by police. With the camera in pursuit, Wilson rolls to the ground on or near the spot where he 'went down' and continues to retell his story from a prone position, the police brutality he describes being later corroborated by a black and white photograph showing him flanked by policemen and bleeding from the temple.[11] Wilson's bodily re-enactment performs multiple functions, from basic repetition to complex historical reassessment: it is a unique *enactment* as opposed to a faithful simulation of what happened to Wilson; it re-enacts an individual memory; and it re-enacts a representative historical moment. It is also underpinned, via the photograph at the end, by a strong indexical link to the events of 18 June 1984.

When I began thinking about re-enactment in documentary in relation to 'acting out', my assumption was that the aim of many if not all re-enactments would be to 'work through', to resolve and maybe conclude the complexities of the events being reiterated. Now, that seems less clear; a significant portion of factual re-enactment is actively concerned with 'acting out' as repetition acquires its own historical and therapeutic value. The viewer's role is crucial: the individual miner in Vanson's documentary, or the interviewees in Greenaway's *Act of God* stick to 'acting out' past actions and memories; as a result, it remains for the viewer to make sense of and 'work through' those individual events by putting them in context. At this juncture, 'acting out' becomes not just a symptom of the re-enactment of memory, but an 'approximation': a bringing together of multiple perspectives as a means of re-evaluating a past action. Specific to the documentary's 'acting out' is also that it is a *performance*, a performativity central to a film such as *The Last Days of the Ceausescus* or to T.R. Uthco and Ant Farm's *The Eternal Frame*, in which the obsessive 'compulsion to repeat' manifests itself in multiple site-specific re-enactments of President Kennedy's death. While *The Eternal Frame* mediates the mediarisation of images and events, it does not put forward a theory about 'who killed Kennedy'. Instead, its re-enactments are repetitive reruns of the assassination in front of interested spectators and the artists' cameras. Just before running back out onto Elm Street to re-join one of numerous reconstructions, artist Jody Proctor, playing a secret service agent, is being interviewed. 'Unfortunately, we fucked up on this one', he admits, as he starts to walk away. A voice comes from behind the camera with the suggestion that he embark upon the next re-enactment 'as if it hasn't happened yet'. 'As if he's still alive?', Proctor repeats, cheering up considerably. The conversation then continues, in strangely oblivious fashion, as if Kennedy is not dead. 'You don't expect anything to happen, do you?', the interviewer asks, to which the agent replies, before running towards the limousine to take part in yet another reprisal of that fatal drive on 22 November 1963: 'Well, we've always worried about Dallas. It's a tough city. It's a gun city. And, uh, there's a lot of kooks here. . . . I've gotta go now'. Here, comically enacted, is the obsessive present-ness and disavowal intrinsic to 'acting out', the sense, however ludicrous, that this time the re-enactment – even one as definitively familiar and in the past as the Kennedy assassination – could turn out differently. Once again, it is the viewer who 'works through' the conflicts between fantasy and reality exemplified by this ironic exchange. Bruce Conner gave as the reason for why his 1967 found footage film about the assassination, *Report*, had taken him three years to finish that: 'If the film was completed then he [Kennedy] was as dead as they made him' (Conner, 1969: 18). Repetition of traumatic events (which plays a significant part in *Report*) likewise keeps reality's finality at bay.

The realisation that maybe walking through ≠ working through, and hence not necessarily the psychological cure Freud anticipates, is a defining tension of re-enactment. Throughout 'Remembering, Repeating, and Working Through' Freud returns to the question of his patients' 'resistance' to 'working through', which 'may in practice become an arduous task', but nevertheless a 'phase of treatment that effects the biggest change' (2006: 400). It is specifically in this moment of resistance that, in the re-enactment, 'acting out' most commonly resides, as the 'arduous' task of turning compulsive repetition into 'a means of activating memory' (Freud, 2006: 398) – or, as in the case of *The Eternal Frame*, of activating disavowal – is undertaken. That both 'working through' and disavowal might be the *active* outcomes of re-enactment is explained most clearly by Freud in 'Beyond the Pleasure Principle', in which he discusses repetition and the desire to obliterate past events. 'Obliteration of past events' is the more prosaic translation offered for the German word *Ungeschehenmachen*, whose more poetic as well as literal translation is to 'render something un-happened'. But in 'rendering something unhappened', Freud detects a duality: that wanting to cancel out an unwanted memory 'as though it had never happened', leads in fact to both the memory and its erasure co-existing and having *happened* (Freud, 2003: 187). Just as re-enactments can never supplant the events they reconstruct – and remain, even as 'mere' repetitions, in tandem with the original events – so the event being rendered 'un-happened' is not simply buried under its re-enactment but instead comes to exist in dynamic dialogue with it. As Freud then determines, 'Anything that did not happen in the way the person wanted it to happen is obliterated by being subjected to repetition in a *different* way' (188). The repetitive but non-identical re-enactments of *The Eternal Frame*, for instance, illustrate this, as – far more cryptically – do the non-re-enactments of the attacks of '9/11' in James Marsh's *Man on Wire*. Throughout Marsh's documentary 'about' Philippe Petit's 1974 tightrope walk between the newly erected twin towers of New York's World Trade Center, we find ourselves compelled to remember obliquely an event that is not there, that has quite effectively, on a literal level, been rendered 'un-happened'. To remember obliquely is not the same as to forget; the past can be 'acted out' and 'worked through' in the present: replaced but not obliterated.

This liminal positioning of the re-enactment emerges most forcefully in relation to trauma; as Caruth writes: 'The ability to recover the past is . . . closely and paradoxically tied up, in trauma, with the inability to have access to it' (Caruth, 1995: 152). In both Rithy Panh's *S-21: The Khmer Rouge Killing Machine* and Joshua Oppenheimer's *The Act of Killing*, the accessibilities and inaccessibilities of memory and trauma emerge through re-enactments that follow perpetrators 'acting out' past actions and crimes. Panh, 'the cinematic voice of Cambodia' (Boyle, 2010: 156), escaped from labour camp at 14; *S-21* (the code name for Tuol Sleng, a Phnom Penh high school used as a prison in which an estimated 17,000 Cambodians were interrogated, tortured and executed) pays tribute to the fate of the 2 million Cambodians who perished in the mid-1970s under Pol Pot's brutal regime. In his desire 'to move beyond re-enactment to "re-live" the past' (158), Panh brings together survivors (Vann Nath and Chum Mey) and interrogators to the now derelict S-21 within an adversarial framework which Margulies likens to a tribunal (2019: 187). The re-enactments assume the roles of witness testimony, the most frequently cited being the extended re-enactment by former guard, Khieu 'Poev' Ches, of a typical night-time patrol.

The sequence, 'one of the most haunting reenactment scenes in contemporary cinema' (Margulies, 2019: 183), follows Poev as he 'acts out' a routine nocturnal patrol. For over two minutes of screen time, he walks up and down part of a prison corridor, performing the unlocking and locking of cell doors and barking orders and threats at imaginary prisoners. The scene starts as a series of performative acts, as the former guard performs the actions as he verbalises them ('I unlock the door. . . . I remove the blindfold, I go out'), increasingly becoming more involved as the invented scenarios become more elaborate (Poev, for example, imagines an inmate asking to urinate and brings another some rice soup) and his threats more insistent ('And you! Calm down! If I come back in, you're gonna get it!'). The notion of re-enactment as reiteration and demonstration is here replaced by a more proactive fantasy of *re-entering* the past. Acknowledging the liminal space and the literal boundaries between private and public domains, Panh's camera is present but not intrusively judgemental as it hovers in cell doorways or looks at Poev's self-absorbed re-enactments via the relative neutrality of the grilles on the cell windows.

S-2, like The Act of Killing, makes sense only as and through re-enactments, as the reprisal of past events *becomes* the means of reconciling with them. With *The Act of Killing,* Errol Morris (one of its executive producers) argued, director Joshua Oppenheimer 'reinvent[ed] what it means to make a documentary' (Morris, 2013). Over a number of years, Oppenheimer filmed with perpetrators of the Indonesian massacres of 1965–1966 (in which between 500,000 and 1 million people died at the hands of the military), having previously spent several years in Indonesia working with survivors and their descendants.[12] He convinced several perpetrators to stage re-enactments of their murders in the styles of the genre movies they enjoyed, using 'a wide range of performance styles from extreme Method Acting . . . to Brechtian distanciation' (King, H., 2013: 30). The film's protagonist is Anwar Congo, a cinephile who, in 1965, had been the leader of a death squad in the city of Medan.

Repeated actions abound in *The Act of Killing* and, like Poev in *S-21,* Anwar and the other perpetrator-performers 'appear so fully immersed in their roles that they seem to forget they are acting in a movie and instead relive the events viscerally', a disassociation with reality which, for Homay King, recalls Post-Traumatic Stress Disorder (King, H., 2013: 30–31). Anwar Congo compulsively repeats his past crimes in extraordinarily intense ways, without necessarily making the transition from 'acting out' to 'working through', although Oppenheimer believes he is 'drawn to the pain' of reenacting his memories as he tries to

> replace the miasmic, shapeless, unspeakable horror that visits him in his nightmares with these contained, concrete scenes. It's like he's trying to build up a cinematic-psychic scar tissue over his wound.
>
> *(Bradshaw, 2017)*

Anwar and his fellow perpetrators create the very present, the very actual *mise-en-scène* of horror. Of crucial consequence to how one interprets the highly wrought, performative re-enactments in *The Act of Killing* for which Anwar literally cakes himself in fake scar tissue and blood, is whether one understands these performances to be the result of *re*pression or *sup*pression – the unconscious or the conscious internment of trauma and guilt. Errol Morris likens the fact that the murderers of the mid-1960s have been able to bury their historic 'foul deeds' to 'The Murder of Gonzago', the play within a play in *Hamlet* with which the eponymous, grieving Danish prince hopes to 'catch the conscience of the king' – of Claudius, his regicidal stepfather. Oppenheimer, like Hamlet, challenges impunity through performance and, according to Morris, 'has the optimistic thought that the past is inside us and can be brought back to life' (Morris, 2013).

The twin sequences that exemplify this are the two scenes in which Anwar Congo returns to the rooftop on which he performed many acts of killing. Early in the film (and shooting process) Anwar demonstrates, on a willing friend, his specialist garrotting technique, which features in some later richly performative cinematic re-enactments and the memory of which audiences bring to the viewing of the much later return to the rooftop. Dressed in a dapper mustard-colour suit, Anwar ascends the stairs to the roof terrace. His jaw tightens as he surveys the scene and walks towards the point 'where we tortured and killed'. As with Poev in *S-21*, the fantasy swiftly becomes a bodily 'acting out' (in a way in which the more exposi-tional earlier rooftop scene had not been); in the second scene Anwar physically 'walks through' the site of torture and murder and, as his memories return, emits a series of terrible, apparently involuntary and spasmodic retches. He has made simi-lar reflex noises before – such as when playing the part of a victim of garrotting in the film noir re-enactment – and these guttural, *Alien*-like discharges potentially suggest a body in revolt at the mind's attempt to suppress guilt, a live trauma only partially tempered by the camera's still detachment. Unlike Panh's, Oppenheimer's camera does not follow Anwar but, considering Margulies' likening of *S-21* to a tri-bunal, is it judging him? Oppenheimer's distant, observing camera adopts a similar perspective to the conventionally neutral gaze of the camera at a trial.

The two visits to the rooftop mirror the witness's two court appearances and, as Anwar goes from examination to cross-examination as it were, he mimics the progression from innocence to confession Margulies detected in Huoy (one of the prison guards) in *S-21*. First time, we had been appalled at the alacrity with which Anwar acted out his crimes; this second time, we are looking for more, namely remorse or an awareness of guilt. Are Anwar's retches – like Robert Durst's burping in his final interview in *The Jinx* – an acknowledgement of his guilt through bod-ily revolt? Or are they convenient performative gestures into a 'convenient trough' (Cribb, 2013)? Like Poev and Durst, Anwar, through this second roof scene, enters into an unsettling dialogue of justification with himself ('why did I kill them? . . . My conscience told me they had to be killed'). The camera keeps its distance, but the microphone picks up every subterranean sound. Is the dry heaving 'the somatic evidence' of remorse Walker judges it to be (2013: 16), or is it, like the trough and the pristine garrotting wire and sack Anwar picks up from the roof terrace floor, *too* 'convenient'? The intensity is grotesque and extremely difficult to watch, and finally relief comes in the form of an edit to Anwar walking unsteadily down the stairs, halting for what seems like an age on the turn.

What should we take from this moment of stasis and does it help us read the prior re-enactment? We are left at the end of *The Act of Killing* having to read expression and gesture, having to infer or superimpose meaning and interpretation with no confirmation of their accuracy. To return to the parallels with the trial sce-nario, what is the status of the (meagre) evidence proffered? The exchange between Errol Morris and Joshua Oppenheimer about the retching scene is fascinating. Morris praises Oppenheimer for using re-enactment in a novel way:

> as a way of asking a question about an even deeper mystery, the mystery of who we are, the mystery of what is inside of us – but at the end of the film I actually do not know who this man is.
>
> *(Morris, 2013)*

He then both praises and queries Oppenheimer's method as he asks 'whether the vomiting is one more performance for himself and for us, or if it is the result of something real. Can we ever know?', to which Oppenheimer responds:

> It's both. . . . He's performing for my camera. . . . At the same time, he's performing in such a way that he allows the past to hit him with an unexpected force in that moment.
>
> *(Morris, 2013)*

Remembering Butler's observation that the photograph is neutral, is Oppenheimer here expecting the image to do too much? Traumatic this final reprisal of past actions certainly is, but what does it *reveal*? Morris is 'left in the end with a question', as he tells Oppenheimer, 'I know that there is a past for people, but do they ever deal with it, or do they just try to reinvent it or just make it up out of whole cloth?'. Morris dares to raise a hugely contentious, controversial issue, but one that every documentarist (or lawyer) must face: are my subjects reinventing themselves for the camera or telling me *the truth*? Re-enactment's greatest asset is its ability to enact doubt, enact the realisation that there are alternative ways of seeing things – history, emotions, events – and that all a filmmaker can do is *re*-enact the contradictions, doubts and choices. At the end of *The Thin Blue Line* or *The Jinx,* Morris and Jarecki respectively extract – by accident or design – confessions out of their interviewees. Oppenheimer never does, although maybe in the second rooftop scene, he gets close. To return to the exchange with Morris: Oppenheimer appears horrified by Morris's intimation that Anwar's dry vomiting could be just another self-reinvention, that it could be just *acting*, not even *acting out*. 'You're raising a very, very scary thought', he counters:

> if the final moment is maybe yet another moment of performance . . . and there's no connection to the past on that roof, then it's almost too chilling for me to contemplate what the whole movie is really saying.
>
> *(Morris, 2013)*

Re-enactment, the performative *acting out* of differing and alternate perspectives, will never ultimately reveal 'what the whole movie is saying'.

The inherent tension of the re-enactment's contradictory status – that it both offers the potential to 'act out' and 'work through' unresolved events while at the same time admitting by its very nature as a live, present performance that it will forever remain incomplete – recalls Jacques Lacan's conceptualisation of 'the mirror stage', the period in time when the infant recognises itself in the mirror, becomes fascinated with that image and returns to it many times. Finding itself 'still sunk in his motor incapacity and nursling dependence' (Lacan, 1977: 2), the infant identifies with the 'ideal-I' it has discovered in the mirror and mistakenly conflates the control and stability it sees in the reflection and its own 'fragmented body' (4). The re-enactment, in prizing open a past event (which had been similarly misrecognised as complete and secure), admits through this gesture the fragmentariness and incompleteness of historical knowledge. The first error, where re-enactment is concerned, is to misrecognise the re-enactment as the same as and/or trying to be the same as the other, the 'ideal-I'; they are two distinctive entities and performances. The second misrecognition stems from having overlooked the contextual nature of all historical enquiry and repressed the realisation that historical knowledge is the result of a dialogue between present and past – but not one between two fixed moments, for, as Collingwood realised, the 'present' from which we look back at 'the past' is perpetually shifting. Just as it is not a simple case of the child being able to say, 'that's me' to its reflected image, so it is never a simple case of being able to say 'that was then, this is now' where engagement with history is concerned.

Temporal relations are inherently variable and inconstant; furthermore, as Laura Mulvey wrote in the early years of the millennium about our 'new technological age', 'the opposition between the reality of inscription and the fictional time of representation begins to become more porous and fragile' (Mulvey, 2004: 146). Our new digital technology can assume the immediate, infinite and unproblematic accessibility of the past in images; the video memory bank is there to be plundered, and it is easier than ever to blend CGI and action or to create the illusion of archive, for example. The potential to tamper with, distort and copy historical images is open to all and the repercussions for the re-enactment are various; just as the opportunities to revisit the past and thereby re-enact it are infinite, so it has become much more difficult to forget and bury images, evidence and knowledge in ways that it used to be possible to do. At a time when images are shared on social media instantaneously with the events they depict, it would be virtually impossible to hush up something such as the Jeremy Thorpe scandal (discussed in Chapter 5). Re-enactments have always disturbed the schism between 'then' and 'now', and we 'now' expect to be able to access 'then' with ever greater facility. Having said this, the authentic moment does produce a *frisson* the re-enactment cannot: the final mute home movie images at the end of *Dreams of Life*, for instance, carry a weight the prior mute re-enactments do not, but this charge does not deliver understanding or knowledge. (Direct Cinema documentaries are full of 'unreadable' moments, such as the end of the Maysles Brothers' *Salesman* [1969] when, because the closing image is edited out of sequence, it becomes impossible to interpret Paul Brennan's expression).

For all of these historical reasons, re-enactment is often now no longer used simply out of necessity but has become a creative choice (looking back at early re-enactment, Brian Winston talks of the 'honest, straightforward' re-enactment of Joris Ivens, for instance, or of Humphrey Jennings' use of 'actors and sets to re-enact situations otherwise unfilmable' [Winston, 1999: 164, 168]). Ironically, as it becomes both easier and less necessary, re-enactment in documentary (and elsewhere) has become both more pervasive and more heterogeneous. Arguably, the way to understand this proliferation of re-enactment is as testament not to a desire to deceive, but rather to the realisation that returning to 'what really happened', to an original event is neither possible nor the re-enactment's intended goal. In this respect, validation for re-enactment comes from the most unlikely source of André Bazin, who admitted. That 'realism in art can only be achieved one way – through artifice' (Bazin, 1971: 26). If re-enactments only ever grant access to *a* truth rather than *the* truth, then arguably fictionalisation is as valid a route as any to reality.

The omnipresent and underpinning issue around which such debates are structured is the relation between iteration and reiteration, between an event and its re-enactment. In *Bodies that Matter*, Judith Butler returned to some of the common misinterpretations of her earlier agenda-setting discussion of drag in *Gender Trouble*. Firstly, she writes, 'there is no necessary relation between drag and subversion. . . . At best, it seems, drag is a site of a certain ambivalence' (Butler, 1993: 125). Secondly, she expands:

> To claim that all gender is like drag, or is drag, is to suggest that 'imitation' is at the heart of the *heterosexual* project and its gender binarism, that drag is not a secondary imitation that presupposes a prior and original gender, but that hegemonic heterosexuality is itself a constant and repeated effort to imitate its own idealizations.
>
> *(125)*

Butler's revisiting of her prior discussions of the relationship between drag and heterosexuality affords a helpful model for this discussion of documentary and re-enactment. There is a difference between enactment and re-enactment, albeit a mutable and unstable one; there is no predictable or consistent 'gulf between now and then' (Nichols, 2008: 77), nor is the identity of the original event ever stable. Thus far, and in line with the majority of documentary scholars, I have used 're-enactment' as a simple, all-encompassing noun that stands for the acting out of a past event. But 're-enactment', even just in what can reasonably be called 'documentary', takes on many guises – from the restaging of battles, theatrical performance, verbatim reconstruction, elliptical reconstruction – as the range of documentaries attests. The term 're-enactment' has no fixed identity. Like drag in relation to gender, the re-enactment is a 'site of ambivalence', where possibilities are opened up rather than made to fit into a neat binary opposition. In ways similar to re-enactment, drag is, Butler concludes, 'subversive to the extent that it reflects on the imitative structure by which hegemonic gender is itself produced and disputes heterosexuality's claim to naturalness and individuality' (Butler, 1993: 125): the re-enactment's very presence probes the status of the 'original' event and raises the spectre of the enactment's own imitative status.

In order to reach a more dialectically fluid understanding of re-enactment it is necessary to break down the hierarchy of facts – the belief that the past is authentic and more important, while the present is the copy and secondary. Binary understandings of 'then' and 'now' as intractable states does not allow for the complexities of the re-enactment as identified by philosopher R.G. Collingwood. 'The past is never a given fact which he [the historian] can apprehend empirically by perception . . . the historian is not an eyewitness of the facts he desires to know'

(Collingwood, 1994: 282). Writing in 1946, Collingwood radically reconceptualised re-enactment as a dynamic dialogue between past and present, not 'passive surrender', but 'a labour of active and critical thinking' for which the historian 'not only re-enacts past thought, he re-enacts it in the context of his own knowledge' (Collingwood, 1994: 215). Collingwood's were mental re-enactments, 'not spectacles to be watched, but experiences to be lived through in [the historian's] own mind' (Collingwood, 1994: 218); 'he did not envisage re-enacting the past emotionally and physically' (McCalman and Pickering, 2010: 4), although it is a short leap from his writing to the physical performativity of historical re-enactment. Though not experienced physically, re-enactment *is*, for Collingwood, experiential and as such 'betrays the inevitably affective quality of the *experience* of mental re-enactment, which becomes the grounds for the self-reflective historical thinking that it induces' (Landsberg, 2015: 10).

The re-enactment enlivens, it physically repeats history and past actions as it both *does* and *performs* (see Kahana, 2009: 2). The assumption may be that re-enactment invariably brings past events into the present; however, in querying the stability and veracity of original enactments, re-enactments also reflect back on and inflect history, a duality exemplified by a film such as Peter Watkins's *Culloden* (1964) in which re-enactment is mobilised explicitly and purposefully as *analysis*, as a means of interrogating history (the battle of 1746) and emphasising the dynamic dimension of the relationship between past and present. Re-enactment is therefore both intellectual and corporeal; the literal embodiment of prior events, a physicalisation of history exemplified by *Culloden*. An in-person re-enactment such as this exemplifies the place re-enactment plays in 'history's affective turn' (Agnew, 2007: 300). The re-enactment is capable of constructing the emotively as well as factually charged moment and bringing history 'to life', and so to engage with what Landsberg identifies as a 'profound popular desire to touch and be touched by history' (2015: 10), to feel it as do the participants (and viewers) of immersive historical series such as *The Edwardian Country House* or *The Trench*.[13]

Though not, as he himself puts it, 'a trained historian' (De Groot, 2012: 589), British artist Jeremy Deller, in his work, *The Battle of Orgreave*, 'brings to life', the pivotal confrontation of the 1984–1985 UK Miners' Strike at Orgreave coking plant, Rotherham, South Yorkshire, on 18 June 1984.[14] A piece of affective, living historical re-enactment, the resulting piece was as much a cultural as a historical artefact, a site-specific performance by former miners, policemen and historical reenactors in front of local residents with Deller as their '*animateur*' (Stuart Hall cited in De Groot, 2012: 588). 'Orgreave' for many is synonymous with this confrontation between an estimated 14,000–15,000 police and picketers and the re-enactment is as much about place and the social politics of place as it is 'about' 1984. An affective historical and political performance, the physicality of the re-enactment and its treatment of history and place are fundamental to the re-enactment's dynamic juxtaposition of 1984, 2001 and the ever-shifting 'now'. Around 800 participants were involved in Deller's live retelling, under the direction of experienced historical re-enactor Howard Giles. Taking part were 280 locals, including 200 former miners (mostly veterans of Orgreave), a small number of ex-policemen and ambulance crew and members of more than 20 historical re-enactment companies. Where the former coking plant stood was, by 2001, a hole in the ground, so the re-enactment took place (near the 17th anniversary) over the weekend of 16–17 June 2001 in a nearby field. All action was rehearsed and performed *in situ*: the Saturday was the rehearsal day and the re-enactment was staged in full on the Sunday. It culminated, as it had done on the day, in the familiar and heavily mediarised charge by mounted police over the railway bridge and into the Handsworth village, and was, according 'to many participants and audience alike . . . was like witnessing the real thing' (Giles, 2016).

Like other performance pieces that use re-enactment, such as Pierre Huyghe's *The Third Memory* (a re-enactment of Sidney Lumet's *Dog Day Afternoon*) or Elisabeth Subrin's *Shulie* (a shot by shot remake of *Shulie*, an unreleased 1967 documentary about the [then] unknown art student, Shulamith Firestone), *The Battle of Orgreave* blends history and art. Though the re-enactment itself was ephemeral, *The Battle of Orgreave's* 'multiple ontology' (Bishop, 2012: 32) includes Mike Figgis's Channel 4 documentary of the weekend's events,[15] the book *The English Civil War Part II*, in which are collated primarily sources such as interviews, and the Tate Gallery's archival installation: *The Battle of Orgreave Archive [An Injury to One is an Injury to All]*. While, as he explains in his Foreword to *The English Civil War, Part II*, Deller 'wanted the re-enactment of the Battle of Orgreave to become part of the lineage of decisive battles of English history' (that is: 'The English Civil War Part II'), he also, as an artist, was interested in something less ordered – the 'recreation of something that was essentially chaos' (Deller, 2001: 7). He repeats to Figgis's camera (with in his hand his own Super-8 camera) this idea of chaos when he admits to not being 'in charge anymore . . . in a real situation like this you'd be excited and a bit worried as well . . . this is as close as you can get really'. The inherent unruliness of the re-enactment emanates from the fact that the Battle of Orgreave as an event remains unresolved, a 'forgotten' and 'embarrassing moment in history for a lot of people', as Deller refers to it in the documentary. *The Battle of Orgreave* was not 'about healing wounds – it is going to take more than an art project to heal wounds';[16] neither was it 'meant to make people feel good about the strike or feel closure . . . it was meant to make people angry again. If anything, it was meant to act as a recreation of a crime' (De Groot, 2012: 592).

Drawing together Deller's observations here about the re-enactment, *The Battle of Orgreave* should be viewed as a hybrid project: part historical re-enactment, part cultural artefact; as Schneider identifies, despite the fact that the two frame 'history' in very different ways, the 'burgeoning of historical reenactment and "living history"' has nevertheless grown alongside the comparable 'practice of re-playing and re-doing a precedent event . . . in performance-based art' (Schneider, 2011: 2). Maybe because the two are not diametrically opposed, Schneider, the performance studies academic, found herself 'continually surprised by the complexities in the (re) actions I witnessed' when she started attending Civil War re-enactments, as the past performatively passes through, is understood through, the bodies of the reenactors (8). The 'living history' re-enactment directly acknowledges that 'history is made up of bodies' (Foster, 1995: 10); physical embodiment of a historical event, whether deep in the past or recent, offers a different, dynamic and participatory understanding of history, and the 'affective turn' has enabled the reanimation of history 'through physical and psychological experience' (Agnew, 2004: 330). For the veterans of Orgreave who participated on the day, the re-enactment ultimately brought 'it all back' as one of them tells Figgis: the camaraderie (one miner welcomed seeing former colleagues he had not seen 'for, well, over 17 year') as well as the anger (memories of how the strike led them to lose their jobs, their home and, in some cases, families).

The re-enactment sought to keep faith with the past through maintaining a close proximity to historical events. These two aspects to 'fidelity' are brought together as Howard Giles explains on camera:

> It's very important when you do this to make sure everything you do is as accurate as possible and that there's no spin either way. It's important that people don't forget what happened to *them*.

As the story of the Battle of Orgreave was, at the time, mis-told (as Giles acknowledges later in the documentary: 'at the time, of course, the reportage wasn't quite as accurate as it should have been, and we hope we can redress that balance'), living history's ideals of accuracy and meticulous planning supported Deller's motivation to use the re-enactment to set the records straight. Although 'living history' re-enactments assume the position that the events portrayed are finished and finite, that while possible to recreate them, they will remain unaltered by such performances, an equally crucial component of Deller's re-enactment is the need to explicitly acknowledge that histories of that day have *not* reached closure. *The Battle of Orgreave* is thereby informed by a dual outlook: the 'living history' notion of finite accuracy alongside the ethos of performativity and unfinished history. Though Giles's research identified three phases to the original 1984 battle (the friendlier early morning skirmishes, a more aggressive phase when the police advanced and forgot their putative objective of keeping the road open to Orgreave to enable lorries to get through, and the mounted chase through the town),[17] the re-enactment was divided into two distinct parts – before and after the police deployment, under the command of Assistant Chief Constable Tony Clement, of 42 horses-mounted officers intent on breaking up the large group of picketers. On this order hinged both the 'battle' and its historicisation. The first half of the re-enactment involved large numbers, while the post-charge scenes, centred on skirmishes on the streets of Handsworth, involved many fewer re-enactors and were filmed in close-up, so as to better show the individual battles – something that is 'very rare in a live re-enactment' (Giles, 2016).

Thinking of how, as Claire Bishop notes, Deller's own 'anxious thrill is inseparable from the work's overall meaning, since every one of Deller's choices had both a social and artistic resonance' (Bishop, 2012: 33), one of the greatest re-enactment challenges was maintaining the balance between order and disorder. 'Although they had to look unorganised', Giles explains, 'for safety and scripting reasons they had actually to be *highly* organised' (Giles, 2016). The rules for the day are indicative and included, for example, the decision to place all units on both sides under the command of experienced re-enactors,[18] and that only re-enactors could carry and throw the small number of stones available (about 12). Extras were also reminded that, if they got out of hand, they would forfeit their £60 fee. The trepidation with which many of the re-enactors approached the restaging becomes a recurrent refrain; one of them admits to feeling 'quite nervous. . . . It's a bit ultra-realistic today, so we'll see how it goes', whilst another comments that 'it's scary'. But herein lies the fundamental contradiction of even the most carefully stage-managed re-enactment: that this is *living* history and therefore inherently unstable for, as one re-enactor admits, not only could he envisage 'experienced re-enactors getting swept up in it' but 'getting swept up in it is probably part of the reason we do it'.

The potential to go against the *status quo* is integral to the *live* re-enactment. Giles stresses that *The Battle of Orgreave* was a 're-creation, not a refight', but as one former miner, about to enter the fray, jests: 'Fuck the 60 quid! We're going for it! . . . If they throw us off, they throw us off!'. This casual remark captures much of the complexity of Deller's re-enactment. On the one hand, it comes with serious political intent to discredit the establishment version of what happened at Orgreave, by, for example, making the charge by the mounted police so narratively pivotal, a choreographic decision in direct response to the BBC's infamous inversion of the events of the day in its evening's new bulletins, which had made it look as though the police charged the miners in response to missiles being thrown at them. The BBC did in 1991 apologise for having 'inadvertently reversed' the 'sequence of events', a 'mistake made in the haste of putting the news together'. But, with what has come to light since about the deployment at Orgreave of the Metropolitan Police and the army alongside the local police, or the 2012 revelations (in the light of the Hillsborough Report)[19] that South Yorkshire police evidence pertaining to Orgreave had been systematically altered,[20] it becomes harder to see this as an innocent mistake. Conversely, the living complexity of *The Battle of Orgreave* was that it also gave its participants and audiences a good day out and 'gathered people together to remember and replay a charged and disastrous event' against an atmosphere 'more akin to a village fête' (Bishop, 2012: 32), a feeling that comes out in the film and is, ironically, reinforced by an observation David Douglass, NUM (National Union of Mineworkers) Branch Secretary and Mining Historian, makes on camera about how the original 'battle' had effectively been orchestrated by the government:

> they had signs telling you where to go . . . they had arrows pointing you to where you should go. All you needed was a starter flag and a whistle to set us off. Then we could battle for three hours, go for dinner, have a pint and then do it again in the second half.

Orgreave the site was a battle ground before the miners or police even arrived. In response to this, Deller's *The Battle of Orgreave* is tonally complex: a performative recreation that is not just the uncanny recall of events long repressed, but the reawakening of the fantasy that, through live repetition, things could, in the imagination at least, turn out differently (as touched on when a miner alights upon the idea of forfeiting the £60 fee in return for being able to reverse the historical outcome).

Ken Wyatt, ambulanceman at Orgreave in 1984, addresses the participants in the re-enactment, welcoming the re-enactors to South Yorkshire and reminding them that 'Orgreave on that day – things never could be the same after that', that the events have been 'burnt into a folklore, they're burnt into our community memory and our consciousness'. Alongside the brass band and the crowds of locals forming, Wyatt is issuing a reminder that Orgreave was a local trauma and not just a national political event. As it gets underway, the re-enactment, carries with it many connotations, one of which is to return the 'event' to its primal, pre-mediatization, pre-politicisation, pre-folklore state. The return to the site is the symbolic enactment of this. The re-enactment's status as commemorative entertainment emerges most clearly in its physicality: the more light-hearted manoeuvres of the first, pre-mounted police, half of the day, as miners knock about a football and offer spirited renditions of 'I'd rather be a picket than a scab' and 'Here we go', that subsequently give way to violent and aggressive combat following the charge through the field that divides the pickets. As happened on the day, the pickets are chased into the village and the battle becomes more unruly, as both sides are crammed, several lines deep, into narrow streets. Against the backdrop of terraced houses and accompanied by the sound of hooves on tarmac, police beat picketers to the ground; the re-enactment ceases to look like a containable English Civil War reconstruction, and instead becomes once more the confluence of personal and public history. Ken Wyatt had signalled the importance of 'putting on a good show'; by the latter stages of the re-enactment, as horses charge through Sheffield streets, the 'show' has brought the re-enactment full circle and returned to, become inseperable from the indelible archive images 'burnt into' not just the community's but the nation's 'memory'.

There is a strong tradition of site-specific re-enactment in documentary, as both 'living history' reconstructions and proximity to a location bring additional resonance. Site-specific re-enactment is used in documentaries especially in relation to traumatic events: the Kennedy assassination in *The Eternal Frame*, or the torture of political prisoners in *S-21* and *The Act of Killing*. The return to a site of a notable event carries with it connotations of pilgrimage as well as 'dark' tourism; it is an act of tribute, not merely ghoulish fascination. The majority of living history re-enactments (by virtue of being restagings of pre-20th century events) do not have recourse to an extensive bank of video and film archive materials as the re-enactors involved in *The Battle of Orgreave* did. The status of Deller's work as 'approximation' resides partly on the site-specific re-enactment's evocation of familiar and readily available archival footage and documents. Deller was inspired to stage the re-enactment after seeing, as a boy, television images in which 'thousands of men were chased up a field by mounted police' (Deller, 2001: 7). All the archive of Orgreave continue to inform each re-viewing of Deller's subsequent re-enactment: the 'armies' on either side, several lines deep; miners scrambling down the railway verges to escape the encroaching police; photographer Lesley Bolton about to be struck by a mounted officer wielding a long truncheon; horses and miners encircling the 'Rock on Tommy' ice cream van. The archive retains a sense of place and time, and although it is dangerous to assume that any historical moment has been saved automatically into the collective national unconscious, Orgreave is etched on the minds of many of us old enough, like Deller, to have watched the news in 1984. As an event that has had a noteworthy cultural, social and political afterlife, the 'battle' possesses the hallmarks of a significant 20th-century 'flashbulb memory' that leaves a visual and cultural trace on the collective unconscious.[21]

Whereas archival footage can, through its indexicality, evoke an event, a site-specific re-enactment additionally offers audiences and participants the affective, immersive and participatory physicality of 'being there'. (Now only accessible vicariously via the Mike Figgis documentary in which the re-enactment does not appear in its entirety). By 'acting out' an event and replicating its liveness, the re-enacted performance embodies the rough inconclusiveness of history, replacing a straightforward binary opposition between past and present with a more undulating and meandering 'trialectic'. Edward Soja in *Thirdspace* encourages us to 'think differently about the meanings and significance of space' (Soja, 1996: 1) and to challenge the 'persistent over-privileging of the powers of the historical imagination' that has 'silenced or subsumed the potentially equivalent powers of critical spatial thought' (15). Just as Soja seeks to 'open up the spatial imagination' (96), so the trialectical relationship between event, enactment and multiple re-enactments of 'the battle of Orgreave' enables the opening up and the destabilisation of Orgreave (as place) and of the events of 1984. *The Battle of Orgreave* complicates and reformulates the term 'living history', as the overlapping domains of the film's past, present and future (1984, 2001 and the impermanent 'now') meet, disperse and re-inform each other. The re-enactment at its heart is characterised by a series of conflicting emotions and impulses; its version of 'living history' emphasises the uncontainability and mutability of 'living' and presents an approximate and dynamic jostling between past and multiple presents, that perpetually redefine and interact symbiotically with each other.

The sight of Deller and his re-enactors traipsing across a field on the outskirts of Rotherham metonymically evokes the events of 1984 while also bringing to mind the important physical underpinnings to Freud's notion of the 'uncanny effect' of *déjà vu*, produced 'when the distinction between imagination and reality is effaced' (1992: 367). 'Being there' is fundamental to both documentary and the uncanny and the site specificity of the whole *Battle of Orgreave* project is a significant determining element. A re-enactment such as Deller's is the meeting point between two different uncanny experiences: the conventional Freudian uncanny of finding oneself 'led back to what is known of old and long familiar' (340) and a more contemporary recall or a 'reverse uncanny' (discussed at various different junctures in this book), whereby the return to an iconic site recalls familiar, collated mediarised images of what happened at that location as opposed to the location itself. Orgreave is an actual site, not merely a site of memory and history to be, in perpetuity, associated with 1984.

In 2014 I visited Orgreave to experience both the reverse uncanny return to the buried site of Orgreave's mediarised political history and to witness the regeneration (in the form of the transformation of the former Orgreave plant by Rotherham Borough Council) such a burial has prompted. Having previously been occupied by the British Steel coking plant and two underground collieries (Orgreave Colliery closed in 1981 and the coking ovens in 1990), the site had since remained bare. Since 2004, the top 100-acre portion of the barren Orgreave plot has been used to accommodate Waverley Advanced Manufacturing Park, and until as recently as April 2014, the Google satellite image looked like this:

FIGURE 6.1 The site of Orgreave coking plant on Google Earth until 2014.
(maps.google.co.uk/maps/ms?msa=0&msid=209591532897603650948.0
004b4d6bb54299313294&dg=feature -- Orgreave vew - Google Maps)

FIGURE 6.2 'The Edge' Barratt Homes Development, taken from Highfield Spring

By 10 April 2014, however, the regeneration of the lower portions of the site was already well underway, with the construction of new developments of affordable housing, 'The Banks' and 'The Edge', along with several new roads. Public open spaces are planned, incorporating the existing Lake Waverley.

Superimposed onto the fraught, blighted memory site, the new development makes no mention of mining, steel work or any of the industry that, in still recent history, used to bind together the communities from the more established villages around 'Waverley'. 'The Edge' is an apt name for the Barratt development, for there are edges or boundaries everywhere: between the various developed sites; between the roads and railways that encircle it; between the architectural style of this complex and that of the former mining villages the other sides of the arterial roads. The 'edge' that is missing is the 'uncanny' one between current and past occupancy of the kidney-shaped expanse of land.

It remains possible to chart the route (familiar from archive and the re-enactment) of the Battle of Orgreave, from coking plant site to Highfield Lane, over the railway line towards Handsworth and past the City of Sheffield road sign at the junction with Orgreave Lane, despite there being nothing, beyond memories and these archival images, that officially marks its forgotten history. As I orientated myself using my Google satellite image, I became aware that I had visited Orgreave, quite fortuitously, at a charged but privileged moment: the landscape was changing and the coke plant being erased and replaced by housing, but Google had not yet caught up. I experienced both living and dead history, *heimlich* and *unheimlich* memories entwined, as some sites remained familiar while others had disappeared. The visceral impact of 'walking through' the 'Battle of Orgreave' was tempered by an awareness of displacement: the railway bank down which terrified miners had run is recognisable, whereas the old Asda store (to whose car park some picketers retreated in 1984 and which features in the film, *The Full Monty*) has been relocated. Just as Deller had to re-enact the first stage of the 'battle' on a field nearby the one in which the battle actually took place, the 30th anniversary commemorations took place at nearby Catcliffe Recreational Ground. In terms of the uncanny and its potential reversal, I re-entered a space of archival memory, trying to fit the contemporary Orgreave and Handsworth into places that exist overwhelmingly in the imaginary as iconic mediated memory sites. Unlike a visit on any day of the year to Dealey Plaza in Dallas, however, I was not one of many pilgrims and am pretty sure I was the only person attempting to establish where the 'Rock on Tommy' ice cream van was parked in relation to the City of Sheffield road sign along Highfield Lane. And although the 'battle' is regularly commemorated, there is no blue plaque to mark the site of the Battle of Orgreave as there is now, for instance, on the front of playwright Andrea Dunbar's former home on the Buttershaw Estate. (Dunbar is the subject of *The Arbor*, discussed below). Time around Orgreave has marched on. 'Orgreave' is a complex, mutable trialectic space inhabiting the 'permanent now'.[22]

This chapter comes from the standpoint of believing in re-enactment as an effective as well as affective documentary trope; effective at representing reality and offering insights into 'what really happened'. Returning to notions of performativity, I want to suggest here that it is not a question of supplanting one truth for another, of believing that any single re-enactment has unlocked the truth of the

FIGURE 6.3   A Google Earth image of the Orgreave site in 2020. (https://www.google.
com/maps/place/Orgreave/@53.3758562,-1.3780836,5114m/data=!3m
1!1e3!4m5!3m4!1s0x48799d8f5fe65a63:0x50cf99eed6ceda0!8m2!3d53.38
01404!4d-1.3634867, accessed 14 April 2020)

event(s) recreated, of thereby reaching a point when an event in the past can be
closed to critical enquiry or found to be solved. The very act of *re*-enacting through
the dynamics of performance challenges the binary oppositions between past and
present, between fact and interpretation, between differing interpretations of the
same event. In her analysis of theatrical re-enactment Rebecca Schneider adopts
and adapts from Gertrude Stein the idea of 'syncopated time'. Returning to the
persistent binary of 'then' and 'now' Schneider writes:

> In the syncopated time of re-enactment, where *then* and *now* punctuate each
> other, reenactors in art and war romance and/or battle an 'other' time and try
> to bring that time – that prior moment – to the very fingertips of the present.
>
> *(Schneider, 2011: 2)*

This notion of 'syncopated time' – in time with, but off the beat – captures the
sense of not just the unpredictability of the temporal relationship between 'then'
and 'now' but of the dynamic interaction between the two altering the event in 'an
"other" time'. As Schneider goes on to say, the distinct temporal domains that comprise the re-enactment 'interinanimate' or mutually animate each other:[23] they alter
each other's identity, *render each other ambivalent* through being intertwined in, for
example, a living history re-enactment in which those who 'cross-temporal dress'
pass between 'now' to 'then' (Schneider, 2011: 9).

To repeat is never simply to be, as a re-enactment is not quite the past action it mimics; but then neither, as Richard Schechner would put it, is it not-not the past action, for the bodily re-enactment is performed in what Schneider refers to as 'again-time' (2011: 8). Re-enactment is a way to effect an affective engagement with the past in keeping with (as scholars such as Agnew, Schneider, Landsberg and de Groot have noted) developments in re-enactment this millennium. In Vanessa Agnew's estimation, re-enactment is a form of 'affective history – i.e. historical representation that both takes affect as its object and attempts to elicit affect' (2007: 301); it is an innately physical form of historiography, one that foregrounds the roles of performance and performativity, injects dynamism into historical reconstruction but also emphasises its ephemeralness through corporeality.

In Clio Barnard's *The Arbor*, re-enactment becomes transformative through the bodily re-inhabiting and rehabilitation of history, more specifically the story of British playwright Andrea Dunbar. As Adrienne Rich advocated in 1971 when contemplating the masculinity of the literary canon, revisioning is 'the act of looking back, of seeing with fresh eyes' (Rich, A., 1971: 35), which is what Barnard achieves, both in terms of the retelling of Dunbar's story and in terms of stretching definitions of 'documentary' through re-enactment. Andrea Dunbar wrote the play 'The Arbor' in 1977 aged 15 as part of her Certificate of Secondary Education English coursework. Like her later writings, it is largely autobiographical, set on Bradford's Buttershaw Estate where she grew up, and portrays aspects of her life such as alcoholism, teenage pregnancies, racial and familial tensions. Dunbar was discovered by Max Stafford-Clark, Artistic Director of London's Royal Court Theatre, where 'The Arbor' premiered in 1980; she went on to write *Rita, Sue and Bob Too* in 1982 (later made into a film directed by Alan Clarke) and *Shirley* (1986), but died in 1990, aged just 29, of a brain haemorrhage, leaving behind three children: Lorraine, Lisa and Andrew.

In ways not dissimilar to Sarah Polley's *Stories We Tell*, *The Arbor* is a hybrid film that expands notions of documentary. Barnard recalls how, for example, some people were 'annoyed' and 'felt cheated in some way' (Brooks, X., 2010) when she won the Best New Documentary Filmmaker award at the 2010 Tribeca Film Festival, because they did not consider *The Arbor* to be a documentary. Barnard's beliefs that authenticity is 'a futile aspiration' and that the representation of reality 'is always going to be mediated' (Lim, 2011) find their expression in *The Arbor*, whose hybridity refuses to 'smooth out the tensions' of representation and instead draws attention to the 'negotiation' between reality and fiction (Brooks, X., 2010) through the juxtaposition of multiple elements. As 1980s television archival material (a BBC2 *Arena* documentary and local BBC news reports), site-specific performances from the play 'The Arbor' and, most experimentally, lip-synching by actors to interviews Barnard undertook with Dunbar's family and friends are interwoven, *The Arbor* mediates between documentary and fiction, between history and the present. Most of *The Arbor* is 'acted', although its 'authentic' core – in the form of the words and voices of interviewees such as Andrea's daughters, Lorraine and Lisa – remains intense, as it is through the collisions between elements that Barnard accentuates the fluidity and permeability of generic boundaries. *The Arbor* might be dominated by performance, but there is in it little *pretence*; it opens, for instance, with a bald statement about how the lip-synching is to be used: 'This is a true story filmed with actors lip-synching to the voices of the people whose story it tells'. Ironically, however, this assertion is immediately juxtaposed with a short opening sequence of two dogs running through long grass that, in its elliptical, non-narrative vividness, could easily be the prelude to a fictional feature film. Just as 'The Arbor' was, in the words of Stafford-Clark, a 'a misleading title' for Andrea Dunbar's singularly unpastoral play,[24] so we, to an extent, find ourselves 'misled' by the vibrancy in Barnard's film, until it begins to emerge obliquely that the film's colourfulness is in itself a political statement that counters the gritty, frequently monochrome conventions governing the ways in which, as Barnard sees it, the demographic on whom the film is focused (working class council estate residents) has traditionally been represented. The 'particular visual style' which is thought to be 'somehow more authentic' (Lim, 2011) is still represented in *The Arbor*, but by the bleak 1980s television archive of teenage mothers pushing flimsy buggies through melting snow and past grey, lichen-smeared stone walls, for instance.

The technically arduous, 'nearly Cubist structural device' (Thomson, 2011) of lip-synching is as energetic and contrapuntal to the film's use of colour, bringing to *The Arbor* a subversive synchrony which, by perpetually embodying the coexistence of, as well as dislocation between, past and present, just as persistently forefronts the issue of there being multiple routes to representing 'reality' or 'history'. As a technique with a rich cultural heritage, from verbatim theatre to teenage girls mouthing along to songs and making their own music videos on TikTok, lip-synching (which Barnard had used before in her short 1998 film, *Random Acts of Intimacy*) severs the ties between voice and image before then (almost) suturing them back together. One truism the lip-synching exposes and confronts is the presumed hierarchy, in documentary, between image and sound: that the latter remains subservient to the former as a means of capturing reality. In *The Arbor*, it is *sound* rather than image (including the hesitations and stumbles of natural speech) that brings the solid link to documentary truth. As a way to enhance this realization, much about the film's lip-synching is artificial and challenging to conventional notions of documentary, as actors deliver monologues that break the 'fourth wall', for example, a technique established in the first narrative scene, which opens with a head and shoulders shot of Lorraine (played by Manjinder Virk) looking directly into the camera. Framed against a gloomy interior space, Virk lip-synchs the words: 'I've got loads. . . . I've got loads of childhood memories, but none of them are really good. Umm, I don't think you remember the good stuff'. The inferences from this ostensibly undramatic opening are many: having been told at the outset that the actors will lip-synch to the voices of the interviewees, watching *The Arbor* will always be alienating, always accompanied by the awareness of a largely imperceptible (but known) disassociation between image and sound that destabilises the entire viewing experience. The residual fear is that the lip-synching in *The Arbor* will bring with it an attenuation of the words' residual power and clarity; instead, the deflection of our attention from *what* is being said onto *how* it is being relayed has the contrary effect of inculcating active listening. Alongside its affective and epistemological connotations, the technicalities of this 'nearly Cubist structural device' are also interesting, as the actors all approached the task of lip-synching slightly differently. Virk's relatively flat delivery that blurs the individual words and sounds is very different from, for instance, Christine Bottomley's as her sister Lisa, but this corresponds directly to the latter's more animated, guttural and varied vocal range; while the marked series of twitches and ticks with which Danny Webb embellishes his portrayal of Max Stafford-Clark potentially serve as a cryptic, potentially unflattering meta-commentary on the director himself. In turn, it sounds as if the non-immersive distanciation that characterises *The Arbor* as viewing experience was matched by the atmosphere on set. The actors, as Clio Barnard explains, 'had to be very present – never thinking ahead or they would trip up' (Barnard in Wood, 2011); they were fitted with earpieces while sound designer, Tim Barker, operated a playback system only audible to them, Barker and Barnard, making for 'a very strange … mostly silent' set (Barnard in Falk, 2010).

Though she works the synching the other way around (in that the audible voices are the actors' who have the interviewees' voices playing in their ears), playwright Alecky Blythe frames the value of the technique as making it possible to arrive at a less 'performed' truth.[25] To Blythe's mind, 'once actors have memorised their lines, they stop listening to how they were actually spoken in the first place'; 'an actor's instinct is to perform: to heighten, to try and make their lines more "interesting"', she continues, which potentially negates the power of the un-performed, for 'everyday speech is often more mundane and "everyday" than anyone dares to invent' (Hammond and Steward, 2008: 81–82). Blythe's reasoning has explicit implications for *The Arbor* in which the superficially extreme artifice of the re-enactments yields an unlikely alternative, multifaceted authenticity, exemplified by a surreal re-enactment near the beginning in which Lorraine and Lisa share conflicting versions of a shared childhood memory of setting their bed on fire.

FIGURE 6.4 Lorraine and Lisa recount the bedroom fire in *The Arbor* (Clio Barnard, 2010)

The two sisters' memories of the fire, who started it and who was then to blame for them not being able to get out of the bedroom, are muddled and contradictory; Lorraine says she lit the fire in order to keep herself and her siblings warm, while Lisa then admits: 'but I think, I think, I don't know if . . . I think it were actually me' that made it impossible to get out after she had made the door handle fall out. Confusion over the truth is accentuated by the way in which the conflicting accounts are rendered; the 'authentic' voices of the two Dunbar sisters are delivered, as elsewhere, in the form of monologues directly to camera, though the staging is intensely Brechtian, as Virk and Bottomley do not interact with each other and look down as the other is speaking. The background set is an archly minimalist replica of their childhood bedroom, the bed on fire occupying a space contiguous and yet kept apart from the actors by the use of a shallow depth of field. The various layers of the re-enactment (speech, synching, adult space, childhood space, foreground, background, contradictory memories) cross temporalities, spaces and subjectivities; it is the voices as opposed to the images that retain the traces of the real and become the forces of continuity and guarantors of reality.

As with the lip-synching, the closely autobiographical content of Andrea Dunbar's plays blurred the boundaries between the real and the fictional; as Dunbar explains in an extract from the *Arena* documentary: 'You write what's said, you don't lie'. The truth that is artificially conceived is no less 'truthful', Dunbar seems to be arguing, a paradoxical realisation most clearly realised in Barnard's *The Arbor* in the site-specific re-enactments of scenes from Dunbar's playscript of 'The Arbor' on the grass adjacent to Brafferton Arbor, watched by an assembled crowd of residents, actors and (uncredited) family members.[26] Alienating in their anti-realism (the scenes are announced, for example, by Natalie Gavin playing 'The Girl'[27] speaking directly to camera before segueing seamlessly into character) these performances nevertheless provide an alternative indexicality. The intensity of the performances' layered constructedness is exemplified by the pivotal Act 2 Scene 2 ('the Girl'), in which the Dunbars and Yousaf (Andrea's partner and Lorraine's father) are watching television soon after the death of her 11-year-old brother. Her father (played by Danny Webb again) is drinking, and a row soon escalates. As it does so, the play's space becomes demarcated from Brafferton Arbor by the use of closer, rougher camerawork that contrasts with the wider, more stable cut-aways to the surrounding audience. The reflexivity continues as the performance is intercut with Virk as Lorraine reading a book (which we can assume is the playscript for 'The Arbor') and offering a meta-commentary on the fictionalised scene. When her fictional father Yousaf says, for instance, 'I didn't ask to be a Paki', Lorraine (who is throughout far more critical of and bitter towards her mother than Lisa) chimes in that 'I didn't ask to be conceived'.

The slippage between planes of reality recurs as the scene concludes with the girl's brother's arrest. As the actor who plays the brother in the play is escorted away by a policeman, he walks into the audience and brushing past Jonathan Jaynes who plays David Dunbar in the film. Jaynes then looks to camera and lip-synchs David's actual memories of that night, before Kathryn Pogson as Pamela, Andrea's sister (as if she too has just watched a piece or archive as opposed to a play), mouths Pamela's recollection of how this had been the night 'Andrea moved out . . . and went to live with Yousaf, Lorraine's dad'. As multiple elisions and interconnections occur, drama and re-enactment here explicitly blend into each other to become alternative indexicalities. Though unidentified, the real Pamela (who still occupies the house next door to the Andrea's former home) is watching the filming of the play, alongside both her actor-double and Dunbar's son, Andrew, who remarked that the filming was 'freaking me out a bit . . . like watching my childhood played back' (Hickling, 2010).

The Arbor is a ballet of refractions, every element altered by its encounters and collisions with others as re-enactment becomes just another reality, or just another fiction. Its hybridity culminates in the documentary's short concluding sequence. Built on interrelated contingencies, the finale revolves around one last fragment of archive in which Andrea swaddles baby Lorraine and takes her on a train. Andrea's affection for her eldest child is palpable but also destabilising as she, a mother hitherto described by Lorraine as more interested in going down to the pub or writing than looking after her children, remarks: 'if they were taken away from you, you'd miss 'em and want 'em back . . . I don't think they're that much trouble . . . maybe it's just Lorraine because she's a good baby'. This image of a loving and attentive teenage Andrea arrives on the back of two short scenes with Lorraine. In the first, Andrea Dunbar's eldest child criticises her mother's autobiographical writings for being 'disgusting', while in the second, she is seen emerging from prison having served her sentence for the manslaughter of her son Harris from methadone poisoning. Lorraine Dunbar has, more or less explicitly throughout *The Arbor*, blamed her mother's lifestyle and choices for her own tragedies.

The emotional charge then of Andrea talking so fondly of Lorraine at the end garners its strength from its simplicity and from being so utterly unexpected and contradictory. The grainy 16mm footage of Dunbar and Lorraine gives a fleeting glimpse of the return of the convoluted authenticity of archive and with it the potential *unreality* of re-enactment or drama. However, by this final stage of *The Arbor*, so much *performance* has taken place around the portions of archival footage that we have become acutely aware of the performativity of the indexical image as well. And here, as we observe Andrea folding up her buggy and then looking out of the train window with Lorraine on her knee, we become acutely aware that this documentary scene is also a performance, the repetition of an everyday gesture and the sort of enactment, therefore, that features automatically, almost unconsciously, in so many documentaries. *The Arbor* closes with a chain of three travelling shots is which the film's many layers of re-enactment find one final elliptical expression; smoothly sutured together to form one continuous cinematic and narrative move are the view from the train window, a tracking shot dissecting the Buttershaw Estate from the 1980s archive and a final track along Brafferton Arbor today, cruising past the grass, the new houses and the street's road sign as temporal and indexical planes converge and diverge with equal force.

A re-enactment follows on from, recalls and comments upon reality, but it is always essentially a rupture or series of ruptures. In its very form, the re-enactment problematizes the notion of completeness and questions the realistic possibility of working something through to a neat conclusion. Its residual unfinishedness – characterised as formal layers and temporal levels – signals the fact that re-enactments are never finished or representative of actions that are 'done with', but are, instead, perennially open to change, to modifications in light of and in relation to later events, arguments and discoveries. As his re-staging of the Battle of Orgreave gets underway, Jeremy Deller confesses to Mike Figgis's documentary camera that he is no longer in control, a potentially apt metaphor for all re-enactments that fits alongside the haphazardness of the psychodynamic process: re-enactments are best characterised as studies in the randomness and fragility of memory and remembering – as relinquishing control in order to potentially pave the way to 'working through'

Logically, the ultimate test to gauge if a re-enactment has 'worked through' as well as 'walked through' the event copied, is to see if it reveals 'what really happened'. Errol Morris has argued that re-enactments 'helps us look beyond the surface of images to something hidden, something deeper – something that better captures *what really happened*' (Morris, 2008; my italics). So how might a re-enactment be capable of capturing 'what really happened' better (Morris presumably means) than the enactment? In *The Thin Blue Line* Morris recreated the conflicting eye-witness accounts to the same crime of five prosecution witnesses; testament, consequently, to the realisation that a *prior enactment* (the testimony, for example) only ever grants *a* view, not *the* view. Conversely, the re-enactment, by virtue of being different from the enactment, *acts out* the awareness that there is always at least more than one way of looking at an event. So, what do re-enactments add besides ambiguity and complexity? The example of the re-enactment that mimics quite precisely the enactment (such as the binding of Elena Ceausescu's hands), superficially at least, does not add any new knowledge. What it does do, however, is present the argument for there being other, maybe multiple versions of an event, which might corroborate, conflict with or problematise entirely the version portrayed in a previous enactment. Just as filmmakers and Freud admit that the unstable stage of 'acting out' is the moment of maximum complexity and insight, so re-enactments are at their most powerful, exciting and radical when 'rendering something un-happened' but not resolved. Re-enactments perform the realisation that if discovery of 'what really happened' follows, it is purely by luck; their radicalism stems not from any new *information* that might result from them, but from their mere presence, for it is their repetitive presence which indicates that there is no such thing as a fixed and stable truth.

Michel Foucault explains that fetishism is, in his estimation, the 'model perversion' because it most clearly enacts the individual's 'fastening to an object' – the basis for all 'perversions' – that has historically 'served as the guiding thread for analysing all other deviations' (1990: 154). In comparable ways, re-enactments quintessentially exemplify the layerings perceptible across 'approximation', the acknowledgement that 'truth' is accessible from multiple, often contradictory routes, and that proximity is not necessarily a more direct channel through which to access that 'truth' than detachment. The mathematical symbol for 'approximation' is $\approx$, an evocative (at least for someone who knows very little about mathematics) representation of 'not quite equal'. A glance at other definitions of 'approximation' indicate 'a value or quantity that is not quite correct', a 'process of drawing together' or 'the quality or state of being close or near', all of which could vaguely describe the re-enactment, which is likewise 'not quite correct', and capable of drawing different temporalities, different versions of its truth 'together'.

Notes

1 The incorrect assumption amongst friends and family prior to the meeting with Harry was that actor Geoffrey Bowes (also interviewed for *Stories We Tell*) was Sarah's biological father.
2 Cf. Stella Bruzzi, *New Documentary*, 73–80 in 2006 for an earlier discussion of these problems.
3 Cf. Weiss, 1971.
4 http://international-institute.de/en/4350-2/. Accessed 12 September 2019.
5 For some further discussion of the latter two, please see the chapter on documentary and law.
6 Cf. Stella Bruzzi, *New Documentary*, 2006 for a longer discussion of *The Fog of War*.
7 As Julie Lesage comments, many found Morris's 'visual and musical "embellishments" not appropriate for such a serious topic' (Lesage, 2009).
8 As Claude Lanzmann argued we had become to archival images of the Holocaust.
9 Cf. Ivone Margulies, *In Person: Re-Enactment in Postwar and Contemporary Cinema*, Oxford and New York: Oxford University Press, 2019.
10 Later discussed in more detail in relation to Jeremy Deller's *The Battle of Orgreave*.
11 In fact, Wilson concludes this interview with the accusation 'you're not policemen. Policemen don't act like that', corroborating the belief that the army had joined forces with regular constabularies to defeat the miners that day.
12 Following the global success of *The Act of Killing,* many survivors and families of victims of the genocide decided to break their silence and appear in Oppenheimer's subsequent companion film, *The Look of Silence* (2014).
13 Cf. Gray and Bell (2013), Chapter 4, 'Reenactment: Engagement, Experience and Empathy'.
14 The so called 'Battle of Orgreave' was the most notorious of many clashes between picketing miners and police during the year-long strike, which ended in defeat for the National Union of Mineworkers and was officially declared over on 3 May 1985, at which point 85 percent of the workforce returned to work. Orgreave became a focal battleground and many consider the 'battle' to have been the strike's 'turning point' (This is how Bill King, serving in the Bedfordshire police during the strike, referred to the Battle of Orgreave on Radio 4's *The Reunion:The Miners' Strike*, 11 April 2014 (cf. www.bbc.co.uk/programmes/b03zxmyt. Accessed 28 August 2019). The first clashes at Orgreave were 29 May 1984, when an estimated 6,500 picketers confronted 2,500 police, under the command of Tony Clement, Assistant Chief Constable at South Yorkshire Police. On 30 May National Union of Mineworkers President, Arthur Scargill, was arrested. When it came to 18 June, around 6,000 picketers stood against some 8,000 police, from Clement's force and the Metropolitan Police. As more recently released cabinet papers reveal, Prime Minister Margaret Thatcher, fearing that the country would 'grind to a halt', had been 'secretly preparing to use troops and declare a state of emergency at the height of the miners' strike' (Travis, 2014), and many, such as Tony Benn MP, who was interviewed for Figgis's film, believed they were deployed at Orgreave. As Conservative minister Kenneth Clarke commented on Radio 4's *The Reunion*, although industrial disputes

were relatively commonplace in the UK in the 1970s and 1980s, the miners' strike was a prolonged war of attrition between polarised political and ideological opposites.

15 Available to buy via Artangel but also to view on YouTube, Figgis's documentary cuts together segments from the re-enactment, rehearsal and preparations with more standard interviews with the politician Tony Benn MP, ex-miners and union members, as well as archival footage and photographs from the day. It is an excellent record to have, although it is explicitly partisan in a way the re-enactment was only implicitly so.

16 Deller in the documentary.

17 As explained in Deller, 2001: 16.

18 Philipp Elliot-Wright of *The Southern Skirmish Association (American Civil War Re-enactors)* commanded the ordinary police lines, while Jonathan Taylor of *The English Civil War Society* and Alan Larsen of *The Troop* led the mounted contingent. Local ex-policeman Mac McLoughlin, who served at Orgreave on 18 June 1984 (and is interviewed extensively for *The Battle of Orgreave*) volunteered to help and 'very soon found himself as official technical advisor to the police side'. He also took a more active role, accompanying the short-shield snatch squads in action. www.historicalfilmservices.com/orgreave%20article2.htm.

19 The Report found evidence that the same South Yorkshire police had, in the wake of the Hillsborough stadium disaster of 15 April 1989, systematically altered and fabricated evidence. 'The Report of the Hillsborough Independent Panel' (2012) at www.gov.ac.uk/government/publications/the-report-of-the-hillsborough-independent-panel. Accessed 14 February 2020.

20 As demonstrated, for example, by the fact that numerous police statements from 1984 began with exactly the same words: 'As we stood there in the line a continuous stream of missiles came from the pickets into the police line'.

21 Cf. Emily Godbey, 'Making Memories: Tragic Tourism's Visual Traces', in Anne Teresa Demo and Bradford Vivian (eds.) *Rhetoric, Remembrance, and Visual Form: Sighting Memory*, London and New York Routledge, 2012.

22 Will Self, 'The Novel Is Dead (This Time It's for Real)', *The Guardian*, Friday 2 May 2014. www.theguardian.com/books/2014/may/02/will-self-novel-dead-literary-fiction. Accessed 12 May 2014.

23 The word 'interinanimation' is first used by John Donne in the poem *The Ecstasy*.

24 Taken from *Taking Stock: The Theatre of Max Stafford-Clark* by Philip Roberts and Max Stafford-Clark, reproduced by permission of Nick Hern Books, c/o Artangel. www.artangel.org.uk/the-arbor/the-arbor-was-a-misleading-title/. Accessed 3 July 2019.

25 Cf. Taylor, Lib 2015 for a comparative discussion of the ways in which Blythe and Barnard deploy lip-synching.

26 Another theatrical re-enactment such as Peter Watkins' *La Commune* adopts a similarly spartan *mise-en-scene*.

27 At one point explicitly named – after the enacted car crash – as Andrea Dunbar.

BIBLIOGRAPHY

Agnew, Vanessa (2004) 'Introduction: What Is Re-Enactment?' *Criticism*, 46, 327–339.

——— (2007) 'History's Affective Turn: Historical Reenactment and Its Work in the Present', *Rethinking History: The Journal of Theory and Practice*, 11:3, 299–312.

Amis, Martin (2008) *The Second Plane*, London: Jonathan Cape.

Anderson, Lindsay (1971) *Documentary Explorations: Fifteen Interviews with Filmmakers* (ed. G. Roy Levin), New York: Doubleday and Co.

Angell, Elizabeth (2019) 'The Strange True Story of *AVES*', *Town and Country Magazine*, 4 January. www.townandcountrymag.com/society/tradition/a21999992/a-very-english-scandal-jeremy-thorpe-norman-scott-true-story/. Accessed 13 May 2019.

'Art of the Title' (2007) *Mad Men*. www.artofthetitle.com/title/mad-men/. Accessed 6 April 2017.

Arthur, Paul (2008) 'The Horror', *Artforum International*, 46:8, 112.

Asimow, Michael and Mader, Shannon (eds.) (2013) *Law and Popular Culture: A Course Book*, 2nd ed., New York and Oxford: Peter Lang.

Austin, Thomas (2011) '*Standard Operating Procedure*: The "Mystery of Photography" and the Politics of Pity', *Screen*, 52:3, Autumn, 342–357.

Bagli, Charles V. (2019) 'As Durst Murder Case Goes Forward, HBO's Film Will also Be on Trial', *The New York Times*, 24 April. www.nytimes.com/2019/04/24/arts/television/robert-durst-the-jinx.html?rref=collection%2Ftimestopic%2FDurst%2C%20Robert%20A.&action=click&contentCollection=timestopics&region=stream&module=stream_unit&version=latest&contentPlacement=1&pgtype=collection. Accessed 28 April 2019.

Bailey, Matthew (2011) 'The Uses and Abuses of British Political Fiction or How I Learned to Stop Worrying and Love Malcolm Tucker', *Parliamentary Affairs*, 64:2, April, 281–295.

Ballard, Samuel (2011) 'Ones to Watch – Manjinder Virk', *Clash*, 6 April. www.clashmusic.com/features/ones-to-watch-manjinder-virk. Accessed 5 July.

Baron, Jaimie (2014) *The Archive Effect: Found Footage and the Audiovisual Experience of History*, London and New York: Routledge.

Barthes, Roland (1975 [1973]) *The Pleasure of the Text* (trans. Richard Miller), London: Cape.

——— (1981) *Camera Lucida: Reflections on Photography*, New York: Hill and Wang.

Baudrillard, Jean (1988 [1996]) 'Simulacra and Simulations', in Mark Poster (ed.) *Jean Baudrillard: Selected Writings*, London: Polity Press.

——— (2002) *The Spirit of Terrorism* (trans. Chris Turner), new ed., London and New York: Verso.

Bazin, André (1967) 'The Ontology of the Photographic Image', in Hugh Gray (trans.) *What Is Cinema?* Berkeley and Los Angeles: University of California Press.

——— (1971) 'An Aesthetic of Reality', in Hugh Gray (trans.) *What Is Cinema? Volume II*, Berkeley and Los Angeles: University of California Press.

BBC News (2011) 'BAFTA Introduces New "Constructed Reality" Award', 9 November. www.bbc.co.uk/news/entertainment-arts-15652404. Accessed 7 March 2017.

Beail, Linda (2015) 'Invisible Men: The Politics and Presence of Racial and Ethnic "Others" in *Mad Men*', in Linda Beail and Lily J. Goren (eds.) *Mad Men and Politics: Nostalgia and the Remaking of Modern America*, New York and London: Bloomsbury Academic.

Beail, Linda and Goren, Lily J. (2015) '*Mad Men* and Politics: Nostalgia and the Remaking of Modern America', in *Mad Men and Politics: Nostalgia and the Remaking of Modern America*, New York and London: Bloomsbury Academic.

Beck, John (2005) 'Visual Violence in History and Art: Zapruder, Warhol and the Accident of Images', in David Holloway and John Beck (eds.) *American Visual Cultures*, London and New York: Continuum.

Bishop, Claire (2012) *Artificial Hells: Participatory Art and the Politics of Spectatorship*, London: Verso.

Blackson, Robert (2007) 'Once More . . . with Feeling: Reenactment in Contemporary Art and Culture', *Art Journal*, 66:1, Spring, 28–40.

Blair, Tony (2010) *A Journey*, London: Arrow Books.

Bloom, Livia (ed.) (2010) *Errol Morris: Interviews*, Jackson: University Press of Mississippi.

Bolter, Jay David (2005) 'Preface', in Geoff King (ed.) *The Spectacle of the Real: From Hollywood to Reality TV and Beyond*, Bristol and Portland: Intellect Books.

Bordwell, David (2007) 'Unsteadicam Chronicles'. www.davidbordwell.net/blog/2007/08/17/unsteadicam-chronicles/. Accessed 2 December 2013.

Borradori, Giovanni (2003) *Philosophy in a Time of Terror: Dialogues with Jurgen Habermas and Jacques Derrida*, Chicago: University of Chicago Press.

Boyle, Deirdre (2010) 'Trauma, Memory, Documentary: Re-Enactment in Two Films by Rithy Panh (Cambodia) and Garin Nugrohu (Indonesia)', in Bhashar Sarkar and Janet Walker (eds.) *Documentary Testimonies: Global Archives of Suffering*, London and New York: Routledge.

Bradshaw, Nick (2017) 'Build My Gallows High: Joshua Oppenheimer on *The Act of Killing*', *Sight and Sound*, July 2013 (revised 5 June 2017). www.bfi.org.uk/news-opinion/sight-sound-magazine/interviews/build-my-gallows-high-joshua-oppenheimer-act-killing. Accessed 17 July 2019.

Bradshaw, Peter (2011) '9/11 Films: How Did Hollywood Handle the Tragedy?' *The Guardian Film Blog*. www.theguardian.com/film/filmblog/2011/sep/08/9-11-films-hollywood-handle. Accessed 27 November 2013.

Brewer, John (2010) 'Reenactment and Neo-Realism', in Iain McCalman and Paul A. Pickering (eds.) *Historical Reenactment: From Realism to the Affective Turn*, London: Palgrave Macmillan.

Brody, Richard (2015) 'Why Reenactments Never Work', *The New Yorker*, 20 March. www.newyorker.com/culture/richard-brody/just-say-no-to-reenactments-jinx-robert-durst. Accessed 15 April 2019.

Brooks, Peter (1996) 'Law as Narrative', in Peter Brooks and Paul Gewirtz (eds.) *Law's Stories: Narrative and Rhetoric in the Law*, New Haven and London: Yale University Press.

Brooks, Peter and Gewirtz, Paul (1996) 'Narrative and Rhetoric in the Law', in Peter Brooks and Paul Gewirtz (eds.) *Law's Stories: Narrative and Rhetoric in the Law*, New Haven and London: Yale University Press.

Brooks, Xan (2010) 'Can "Fake" Documentaries Still Tell the Truth?' *The Guardian*, 30 September. www.theguardian.com/film/2010/sep/30/fake-documentaries-the-arbor. Accessed 2 July 2019.

Broomfield, Nick (1993) 'Heroes and Villains: Pier Paolo Pasolini', *The Independent Magazine*, 6 February, 46.

Brown, Mark (2012) 'This Week's Art Diary', *The Guardian*, Tuesday 10 January. www. guardian.co.uk/culture/2012/jan/10/arts-diary-tony-blair-theatre-libraries. Accessed 1 June 2019.

Bruzzi, Stella (2006) *New Documentary*, London and New York: Routledge.

——— (2015) '"It Won't Be Iraq They'll Remember Me for, Will It?" Tony Blair and the War on Terror', in Stephen Lacey and Derek Paget (eds.) *The War on Terror: Post-9/11 Television Drama, Docudrama and Documentary*, Cardiff: University of Wales Press.

——— (2016a) 'Narrative, "Evidence Vérité", and the Different Truths of the Modern Trial Documentary', in Erika Balsom and Hila Peleg (eds.) *Documentary Across Disciplines*, Cambridge, MA: MIT Press.

——— (2016b) 'Making a Genre: The Case of the Contemporary True Crime Documentary', *Law and Humanities*, 10:2, 249–280.

Bunzl, Martin (2004) 'Counterfactual History: A User's Guide', *American Historical Review*, 109:3, June, 845–858.

Burgoyne, Robert (2008) *The Hollywood Historical Film*, Oxford: Blackwell Publishing.

——— (2010) *Film Nation: Hollywood Looks at US History* (revised edition), Minneapolis: University of Minnesota Press.

Butler, Judith (1993) *Bodies that Matter: On the Discursive Limits of "Sex"*, London and New York: Routledge.

——— (2004) *Precarious Life: The Powers of Mourning and Violence*, London and New York: Verso.

——— (2007) 'Torture and the Ethics of Photography', *Environment and Planning D: Society and Space*, 25, 951–966.

——— (2010) *Frames of War: When Is Life Grievable?* London and New York: Verso.

Cameron, Allan (2012) 'History in Real Time: National Trauma and Narrative Synchrony in *United 93* and *Out of the Blue*', *Quarterly Review of Film and Video*, 29:4, July, 365–376.

Campbell, Alastair and Hagerty, Bill (eds.) (2010) *The Alastair Campbell Diaries, Volume One: Prelude to Power, 1994–1997*, London: Arrow Books.

Cantrell, Tom and Luckhurst, Mary (eds.) (2010) *Playing for Real: Actors on Playing Real People*, London: Palgrave Macmillan.

——— (2013) *Acting in Documentary Theatre*, London: Palgrave Macmillan.

Carr, Edward Hallett (1961) *What Is History?* New York: Random House.

Carroll, Hamilton (2011) 'September 11 as Heist', *Journal of American Studies*, 45:4, November, 835–851.

Caruth, Cathy (1995) *Trauma: Explorations in Memory*, Baltimore: Johns Hopkins University Press.

Chomsky, Noam (2011) *9–11: Was There an Alternative?* New York: Seven Stories Press.

Christiansen, Christian (2009) 'Guest Editor's Note: Documentary Films After 9/11', *Studies in Documentary Film*, 3:3, 197—198.

Clover, Carol (2000a) 'Law and Order in Popular Culture', in Austin Sarat and Thomas R. Kearns (eds.) *Law in the Domains of Culture*, Ann Arbor: University of Michigan Press.

——— (2000b) 'Judging Audiences: The Case of the Trial Movie', in Linda Williams and Christine Gledhill (eds.) *Reinventing Film Studies*, London: Arnold.

Coe, Jonathan (2018) *Middle England*, kindle ed., London: Viking Press.

Collingwood, R. G. (1994 [1946]) *The Idea of History*, revised ed., Oxford: Oxford University Press.

Comolli, Jean-Louis (1978) 'Historical Fiction: A Body Too Much', *Screen* 19:2, 41–53.

Comolli, Jean-Luc and Narboni, Jean (1971) 'Cinema/Ideology/Criticism', *Screen*, 12:1, 27–38.

Conner, Bruce (1969) 'Bruce Conner Interview', *Film Comment*, 5:4, Winter.

Conrad, Peter (2007) 'OK Tony, It's a Wrap', *The Observer*, 14 January. Accessed 12 February 2020.

Corner, John (2002) 'Performing the Real: Documentary Diversions', *Television and New Media*, 3:3, 255–269.

—— (2007) 'Documentary Expression and the Physicality of the Referent: Observations on Writing, Painting and Photography', *Studies in Documentary Film*, 1:1, 5–19.

Correia, Alice (2012) 'Interpreting Jeremy Deller's *The Battle of Orgreave*', in Joram Ten Brink and Joshua Oppenheimer (eds.) *Killer Images: Documentary Film, Memory and the Performance of Violence*, London and New York: Wallflower Press.

Cowie, Elizabeth (1992 [1984]) 'Fantasia', in Elizabeth Cowie and Parveen Adams (eds.) *M/F: The Woman in Question*, Cambridge, MA: MIT Press.

Cribb, Robert (2013) 'An Act of Manipulation?' *Inside Indonesia*, 20 April. www.insideindonesia.org/review-an-act-of-manipulation. Accessed 18 July 2019.

Croft, Stuart (2006) *Culture, Crisis and America's War on Terror*, Cambridge: Cambridge University Press.

Crowdus, Gary and Georgakas, Dan (1988) 'History Is the Theme of All My Films: An Interview with Emile de Antonio', in Alan Rosenthal (ed.) *New Challenges for Documentary*, Berkeley and Los Angeles: University of California Press.

Cuevas, Efrén (2013) 'Home Movies as Personal Archives in Autobiographical Documentaries', *Studies in Documentary Film*, 7:1, 17–29.

De Antonio, Emile (1982) '*In the King of Prussia*: Emile de Antonio Interviews Himself', *Film Quarterly*, 36:1, Fall, 28–32.

De Groot, Jerome (2011) 'Affect and Empathy: Re-Enactment and Performance as/in History', *Rethinking History*, 15:4, 587–599.

—— (2012) '"I Am Not a Trained Historian: I Improvise". Jeremy Deller Interviewed by Jerome de Groot', *Rethinking History*, 16:4, 587–595.

—— (2016) *Remaking History: The Past in Contemporary Historical Fictions*, London and New York: Routledge.

DeLillo, Don (1988) *Libra*, Harmondsworth: Penguin.

—— (2001) 'In the Ruins of the Future: Reflections on Terror and Loss in the Shadow of September', *Harper's Magazine*, December, 33–40.

—— (2007) *Falling Man*, London: Picador.

Deller, Jeremy (2001) *The English Civil War Part II: Personal Accounts of the 1984–5 Miners' Strike*, London: Artangel.

Derbyshire, Harry and Hodson, Loveday (2008) 'Performing Injustice: Human Rights and Verbatim Theatre', *Law and Humanities*, 2:2, 191–211.

Derrida, Jacques (1995) 'Archive Fever', *Diacritics*, 25:2, Summer, 9–63 (Also Translated by Eric Prenowitz).

Dershowitz, Alan (1996) 'Life Is Not a Dramatic Narrative', in Peter Brooks and Paul Gewirtz (eds.) *Law's Stories: Narrative and Rhetoric in the Law*, New Haven and London: Yale University Press.

Dixon, Wheeler Winston (2004) 'Introduction: Something Lost – Film After 9/11', in Wheeler Winston Dixon (ed.) *Film and Television After 9/11*, Carbondale: Southern Illinois University Press, 1–28.

Doane, Mary Ann (1990) 'Information, Crisis, Catastrophe', in Patricia Mellencamp (ed.) *Logics of Television: Essays in Cultural Criticism*, Indianapolis: Indiana University Press.

—— (2002) *The Emergence of Cinematic Time: Modernity, Contingency, the Archive*, Cambridge, MA and London: Harvard University Press.

Donaldson, Arnold I. (1991) 'Carlo Ginzburg and the Renewal of Historiography', in James Chandler, Arnold I. Davidson and Harry Harootunian (eds.) *Questions of Evidence: Proof, Practice and Persuasion Across Disciplines*, Chicago: Chicago University Press.

Doucet, Andrea (2015) 'Ontological Narrativity and the Performativity of the *Stories We Tell*', *Visual Studies*, 30:1, 98–100.

Druick, Zoë (2008) 'The Courtroom and the Closet in *The Thin Blue Line* and *Capturing the Friedmans*', *Screen*, 49:4, Winter, 440–449.

Dutton, Jack (2015) 'The Surprising World of Synaesthesia', *The Psychologist*, 28, February, 106–109. https://thepsychologist.bps.org.uk/volume-28/february-2015/surprising-world-synaesthesia. Accessed 31 May 2019.

Eco, Umberto (1985) 'Strategies of Lying', in Marshall Blonsky (ed.) *On Signs*, Baltimore, MD: Johns Hopkins University Press.

Edemariam, Aida (2007) 'I Think Tony Blair Would See the Joke', *The Guardian*, 27 September. www.theguardian.com/politics/2007/sep/27/books.generalfiction. Accessed 29 May 2019.

Eisenberg, Eric (2010) 'Interview: Paul Greengrass Explains the Shaky Cam'. www.cinemablend.com/new/Interview-Paul-Greengrass-Explains-Shaky-Cam-17539.html. Accessed 3 September 2019.

Ellis, John (2012) *Documentary: Witness and Self-Revelation*, London and New York: Routledge.

Falk, Quentin (2010) 'Clio Barnard: Interview', *Guru*, October. http://guru.bafta.org/clio-barnard-interview. Accessed 5 July 2019.

Faludi, Susan (2007) *The Terror Dream: Fear and Fantasy in Post-9/11 America*, New York: Metropolitan Books.

Farquarson, Alex (2001) 'Jeremy Deller: *The Battle of Orgreave*', *Frieze*, 9 September. https://frieze.com/article/jeremy-deller. Accessed 10 July 2019.

Felman, Shoshana (1992) 'The Return of the Voice: Claude Lanzmann's *Shoah*', in Shoshana Felman and Dori Laub (eds.) *Testimony: Crises of Witnessing in Literature, Psychoanalysis, and History*, New York and London: Routledge.

—— (2002) *The Juridical Unconscious: Trials and Traumas in the Twentieth Century*, Cambridge, MA: Harvard University Press.

Feuer, Jane (1983) 'The Concept of Live Television: Ontology as Ideology', in E. Ann Kaplan (ed.) *Regarding Television: Critical Approaches*, Frederick, MD: University Publications of America.

Fielding, Steven (2011a) 'Fiction and British Politics: Towards an Imagined Political Capital?' *Parliamentary Affairs*, 64:2, 223–232.

—— (chair) (2011b) 'Practitioners – Roundtable: Why Do Dramatists Write About Politics?' *Parliamentary Affairs*, 64:2, 341–353.

—— (2014) *A State of Play: British Politics on Screen, Stage and Page – From Anthony Trollope to the Thick of It*, London: Bloomsbury Academic.

Fiske, John and Glynne, Kevin (1995) 'Trials of the Postmodern', *Cultural Studies*, 9:3, 501–521.

Foot, John (2009) *Italy's Divided Memory*, London: Palgrave Macmillan.

Forster, Edward Morgan (2005 [1927]) *Aspects of the Novel*, London: Penguin.

Foster, Susan Leigh (1995) 'An Introduction to Moving Bodies: Choreographing History', in *Choreographing History*, Bloomington and Indianapolis: Indiana University Press.

Foucault, Michel (1977 [1975]) *Discipline and Punish: The Birth of the Prison*, New York: Vintage Books.

———— (1990 [1978]) *The History of Sexuality: Volume 1*, New York: Random House.

———— (2002 [1969]) *The Archaeology of Knowledge*, London and New York: Routledge.

Freedland, Jonathan (2007) 'Yes, Minister', *The New York Times*, 4 November. www.nytimes. com/2007/11/04/books/review/Freedland-t.html. Accessed 7 May 2019.

Freud, Sigmund (1992 [1919]) 'The Uncanny', in *Art and Literature, Penguin Freud Library Vol. 14*, London: Penguin.

———— (1993 [1926]) 'Inhibitions, Symptoms and Anxiety', in *On Psychopathology, Penguin Freud Library Vol. 10*, London: Penguin.

———— (2003 [1920]) 'Beyond the Pleasure Principle', in *Beyond the Pleasure Principle and Other Writings*, London: Penguin.

———— (2006 [1914]) 'Remembering, Repeating and Working Through', in Adam Phillips (ed.) *The Penguin Freud Reader*, London: Penguin.

Frew, Elspeth and White, Leanne (2013) 'Exploring Dark Tourism and Place Identity', in Leanne White and Elspeth Frew (eds.) *Dark Tourism and Place Identity: Managing and Interpreting Dark Places*, London and New York: Routledge, 1–10.

Fuhs, Kristen (2012) 'Re-Imagining the Nonfiction Criminal Narrative: Documentary Reenactment as Political Agency', *Concentric: Literary and Cultural Studies*, 38:1, March, 51–78.

———— (2014) 'The Legal Trial and/in Documentary Film', *Cultural Studies*, 28:5–6, 781–801.

Fukuyama, Francis (1989) 'The End of History?' *The National Interest*, Summer. www.embl. de/aboutus/science_society/discussion/discussion_2006/ref1-22june06.pdf. Accessed 13 April 2017.

———— (1992) *The End of History and the Last Man Standing*, New York: Free Press.

Gaakeer, Jeanne, Herz, Ruth, Kee, Joan, Mulcahy, Linda, Pilcher, Jeremy, Gary, Watt and Young, Carey (2018) 'Carey Young's *Palais de Justice*', *Law and Humanities*, 12:2, 278–310.

Gaines, Jane M. (1999a) 'Introduction: "The Real Returns"', in Jane M. Gaines and Michael Renov (eds.) *Collecting Visible Evidence*, Minneapolis: University of Minnesota Press.

———— (1999b) 'Political Mimesis', in Jane Gaines and Michael Renov (eds.) *Collecting Visible Evidence*, Minneapolis: University of Minnesota Press.

Gewirtz, Paul (1995–1996) 'Victims and Voyeurs at the Criminal Trial', *Northwestern University Law Review*, 90, 863–897.

———— (1996) 'Narrative and Rhetoric in the Law', in Peter Brooks and Pual Gewirtz (eds.) *Law's Stories: Narrative and Rhetoric in the Law*, New Haven: Yale University Press.

Gilbey, Ryan (2010) 'Robert Harris: "I Used to Love Politics. Not Now"', *The Guardian*, 3 April. www.theguardian.com/theguardian/2010/apr/03/robert-harris-interview. Accessed 25 May 2019.

Giles, Howard (2016) 'Recreating the Battle of Orgreave – the 2001 Re-Enactment'. www. battleoforgreave.com/recreating-the-battle-of-orgreave. Accessed 10 July 2019.

Ginzburg, Carlo (1991) 'Checking the Evidence: The Judge and the Historian', in James Chandler, Arnold I. Davidson and Harry Harootunian (eds.) *Questions of Evidence: Proof, Practice and Persuasion Across Disciplines*, Chicago: Chicago University Press.

Godbey, Emily (2012) 'Making Memories: Tragic Tourism's Visual Traces', in Anne Teresa Demo and Bradford Vivian (eds.) *Rhetoric, Remembrance, and Visual Form: Sighting Memory*, London and New York Routledge.

Goodlad, Lauren M., Kaganovksy, Lilya and Rushing, Robert A. (2013) 'Introduction', in Lauren M. Goodlad, Lilya Kaganovsky and Robert A. Rushing (eds.) *Mad Men, Mad World: Sex, Politics, Style and the 1960s*, Durham and London: Duke University Press.

Gray, Ann and Bell, Erin (2013) *History on Television*, London and New York: Routledge.

Greenfield, Steve, Osborn, Guy and Robson, Peter (eds.) (2010) *Film and the Law: The Cinema of Justice*, 2nd ed., London: Hart Publishing.

Greengrass, Paul (2006) *United 93: Screenplay and Commentary*, London: Nick Hern Books.

Greif, Mark (2008) 'You'll Love the Way It Makes You Feel', *London Review of Books*, 30:20, 23 October. www.lrb.co.uk/v30/n20/mark-greif/youll-love-the-way-it-makes-you-feel. Accessed 25 July 2019.

Hammond, Will and Steward, Dan (eds.) (2008) *Verbatim: Contemporary Documentary Theatre*, electronic ed., London: Oberon Books.

Harris, Robert (2008) *The Ghost*, London: Arrow Books.

Hickling, Alfred (2010) 'Back to Bradford: Andrea Dunbar Remembered on Film', *The Guardian*, 12 April. www.theguardian.com/film/2010/apr/12/theatre. Accessed 2 July 2019.

Hirsch, Marianne (1997) *Family Frames: Photography, Narrative and Postmemory*, Cambridge, MA: Harvard University Press.

Hoberman, J. (2001) 'All as It Had Been', *The Village Voice*, 4 December. www.villagevoice.com/film/all-as-it-had-been-6396381. Accessed 3 April 2017.

Holdsworth, Amy (2010) 'Televisual Memory', *Screen*, 51:2, Summer, 129—142.

Hutcheon, Linda (1988) *A Poetics of Postmodernism: History, Theory, Fiction*, London: Routledge.

Institute for Global Change (2016) 'Responding to the Publication of the Chilcot Report'. https://institute.global/news/statement-tony-blair-chilcot-report. Accessed 29 March 2019.

Isaacs, Jeremy (2004) 'All Our Yesterdays', in David Cannadine (ed.) *History and the Media*, London: Palgrave Macmillan.

Jameson, Fredric (1984) 'Periodizing the 60s', *Social Text*, 9–10, Spring–Summer, 178–209.

———— (1991) *Postmodernism: Or, the Cultural Logic of Late Capitalism*, London: Verso.

Johnson, Beth (2016) 'Art Cinema and *The Arbor*: Tape-Recorded Testimony, Film Art and Feminism', *Journal of British Film and Television*, 13:2, 278–291.

Jordan, Justine (2019) 'Life Is a Much Chancier Thing That We Imagine: We're Never Very Far from the Edge', *The Guardian Review*, 11 May, 20–23.

Kahana, Jonathan (2009) 'Introduction: What Now? Presenting Reenactment', *Framework*, 50:1–2, Spring, Fall, 46–60.

Keane, John (2015) 'Speaking Power to Truth: John Keane in Conversation with Mark Lawson at Flowers Gallery, Cork Street'. www.johnkeaneart.com/index.php/welcome/cat/130/2/2. Accessed 2 June 2019.

Kellner, Douglas (2005) 'Media Culture and the Triumph of the Spectacle', in Geoff King (ed.) *The Spectacle of the Real: From Hollywood to Reality TV and Beyond*, Chicago: University of Chicago Press.

Kettle, Martin (2018) '"Hugh Grant Is Uncanny": Liberals Glued to *A Very English Scandal*', *The Guardian*, 2 June. www.theguardian.com/tv-and-radio/2018/jun/02/hugh-grant-is-uncanny-liberals-glued-to-a-very-english-scandal-jeremy-thorpe. Accessed 14 May 2019.

King, Geoff (2005) '"Just Like a Movie?" 9/11 and Hollywood Spectacle', in Geoff King (ed.) *The Spectacle of the Real: From Hollywood to Reality TV and Beyond*, Bristol and Portland: Intellect Books.

King, Homay (2013) 'Repetition and Fantasy in *The Act of Killing*', *Film Quarterly*, 67:2, Winter, 30–36.

King, Stephen (2011) *11.22.63*, kindle ed., London: Hodder & Stoughton.

Kirchengast, Tyrone (2010) *The Criminal Trial in Law and Discourse*, London: Palgrave Macmillan.

Kitamura, Katie (2010) '"Recreating Chaos": Jeremy Deller's *The Battle of Orgreave*', in Iain McCalman and Paul A. Pickering (eds.) *Historical Reenactment: From Realism to the Affective Turn*, London: Palgrave Macmillan.

Knight, Peter (2007) *The Kennedy Assassination*, Edinburgh: Edinburgh University Press.

Kozinski, Alex (2006) 'Foreword', in Paul Bergman and Michael Asimow (eds.) *Reel Justice: The Courtroom Goes to the Movies*, revised ed., Riverside, NJ: Andrews McMeel Publishing.

Kroes, Rob (2011) 'The Ascent of the Falling Man: Establishing a Picture's Iconicity', *Journal of American Studies*, 45:4, November, 1–10.

Lacan, Jacques (1977 [1949]) 'The Mirror Stage as Formative of the Function of the I as Revealed in Psychoanalytic Experience', in *Écrits: A Selection*, London: Routledge.

LaCapra, Dominick (2001) *Writing History, Writing Trauma*, Baltimore, MD and London: Johns Hopkins University Press.

Landsberg, Alison (2015) *Engaging the Past: Mass Culture and the Production of Historical Knowledge*, New York: Columbia University Press.

Lang, Clarence (2013) 'Representing the *Mad* Margins of the Early 1960s', in Lauren M. Goodlad, Lilya Kaganovsky and Robert A. Rushing (eds.) *Mad Men, Mad World: Sex, Politics, Style and the 1960s*, Durham and London: Duke University Press.

Lasch, Christopher (1983) 'The Life of Kennedy's Death', *Harper's*, October, 32–40.

Lawson, Mark (2005) 'A Drama Out of a Crisis', *The Guardian*, 14 March. www.theguardian.com/media/2005/mar/14/television.broadcasting. Accessed 7 May 2019.

Lennon, John and Foley, Malcolm (2000) *Dark Tourism*, London and New York: Continuum.

Lesage, Julie (2009) 'Torture Documentaries', *Jump Cut*, 51, Spring. www.ejumpcut.org/archive/jc51.2009/TortureDocumentaries/. Accessed 16 July 2019.

Lévi Strauss, Claude (1962) *The Savage Mind*, Chicago: University of Chicago Press.

Levine, Caroline (2013) 'The Shock of the Banal: *Mad Men*'s Progressive Realism', in Lauren M. Goodlad, Lilya Kaganovsky and Robert A. Rushing (eds.) *Mad Men, Mad World: Sex, Politics, Style and the 1960s*, Durham and London: Duke University Press.

Lewallen, Constance (2004) 'Interview with Ant Farm: Constance M. Lewallen in Conversation with Chip Lord, Doug Michels and Curtis Schreier', in Constance M. Lewallen and Steve Seid (eds.) *Ant Farm: 1968–1978*, Berkeley and Los Angeles: University of California Press.

Lim, Denis (2011) 'Lip-Syncing the Realities of Life', *The New York Times*, 22 April. www.nytimes.com/2011/04/24/movies/the-arbor-revisits-the-troubled-life-of-andrea-dunbar.html?_r=0. Accessed 3 July 2019.

Lipkin, Steven N. (2011) *Docudrama Performs the Past: Arenas of Arguments in Films Based on True Stories*, Newcastle: Cambridge Scholars.

Lockwood, Dean (2005) 'Tetralogy of the Spectacle', in Geoff King (ed.) *The Spectacle of the Real: From Hollywood to Reality TV and Beyond*, Bristol and Portland: Intellect Books.

Lubin, David M. (2003) *Shooting Kennedy: JFK and the Culture of Images*, Berkeley and Los Angeles: University of California Press.

Lukács, Georg (1981 [1962]) *The Historical Novel*, Harmondsworth: Penguin.

Mackay, Ruth (2011) '"Going Backwards in Time to Talk About the Present": *Man on Wire* and Verticality After 9/11', *Comparative American Studies*, 9:1, March, 3–20.

Mailer, Norman (1967) *The Leading Man: A Review of JFK – The Man and the Myth'*, *Cannibals and Christians*, London: Andre Deutsch, 165–171.

Margulies, Ivone (2019) *In Person: Re-Enactment in Postwar and Contemporary Cinema*, Oxford and New York: Oxford University Press.

Martin, Carol (2006) 'Bodies of Evidence', *TDR/The Drama Review*, Fall, 50:3, 8—15.

McCalman, Iain and Pickering, Paul A. (eds.) (2010) *Historical Reenactment: From Realism to the Affective Turn*, London: Palgrave Macmillan.

McSweeney, Terence (2014) *The 'War on Terror' and American Film: 9/11 Frames Per Second*, Edinburgh: Edinburgh University Press.

Meek, Allen (2010) *Trauma and Media: Theories, Histories and Images*, London and New York: Routledge.

Megson, Chris (2009) '*Half the Picture*: "A Certain Frisson" at the Tricycle Theatre', in Alison Forsyth and Chris Megson (eds.) *Get Real: Documentary Theatre Past and Present*, London: Palgrave Macmillan.

Mellencamp, Patricia (1990) 'TV Time and Catastrophe, or *Beyond the Pleasure Principle* of Television', in Patricia Mellencamp (ed.) *Logics of Television: Essays in Cultural Criticism*, Indianapolis and London: Indiana University Press, BFI Publishing.

Mnookin, Jennifer (2005) 'Reproducing a Trial: Evidence and Its Assessment in *Paradise Lost*', in Austin Sarat, Lawrence Douglas and Martha Merrill (eds.) *Law on Screen*, Stanford: Stanford University Press.

——— (2014) '*Semi-Legibility* and Visual Evidence: An Initial Exploration', *Law, Culture and Humanities*, 10:1, 43–65.

Moretti, Franco (1983) *Signs Taken for Wonders: Essays in the Sociology of Literary Forms* (trans. Susan Fischer, David Forgacs and David Miller), London: Verso.

Morris, Errol (2008) 'Play It Again, Sam Re-Enactments, Part One', *The New York Times*, 3 April. https://opinionator.blogs.nytimes.com/2008/04/03/play-it-again-sam-re-enactments-part-one/. Accessed 24 June 2019.

——— (2013) 'The Murders of Gonzago', *Slate*, 10 July. www.slate.com/articles/arts/history/2013/07/the_act_of_killing_essay_how_indonesia_s_mass_killings_could_have_slowed.html?via=gdpr-consent. Accessed 17 July 2019.

Mulvey, Laura (1975) 'Visual Pleasure and Narrative Cinema', *Screen*, 16:3, Autumn, 6–18.

——— (2004) 'Passing Time: Reflections on Cinema from a New Technological Age', *Screen*, 45:2, 142–155.

Muntean, Nick (2010) '"It Was Just Like a Movie": Trauma, Memory and the Mediation of 9/11', *Journal of Popular Film and Television*, 37:2, 50–59.

Musser, Charles (1995–1996) 'Film Truth, Documentary, and the Law: Justice at the Margins', *San Francisco Law Review*, 30, 963–984.

Nichols, Bill (1991) *Representing Reality: Issues and Concepts in Documentary*, Bloomington and Indianapolis: Indiana University Press.

——— (2008) 'Documentary Reenactment and the Fantasmic Subject', *Critical Inquiry*, 35, Autumn, 72–89.

——— (2010) 'Feelings of Revulsion and the Limits of Academic Discourse', *Jump Cut*. www.ejumpcut.org/archive/jc52.2010/sopNichols/index.html. Accessed 16 July 2019.

Nubar, Alexanian (2002 [2010]) 'Truth Is a Linguistic Thing', in Livia Bloom (ed.) *Errol Morris: Interviews*, Jackson: University Press of Mississippi.

O'Leary, Alan (2011) *Tragedia all'Italiana: Italian Cinema and Italian Terrorisms, 1970–2010*, Oxford: Peter Lang.

Ono, Kent (2013) '*Mad Men's* Postracial Figuration of a Racial Past', in Lauren M. Goodlad, Lilya Kaganovksy and Robert A. Rushing (eds.) *Mad Men, Mad World: Sex, Politics, Style and the 1960s*, Durham and London: Duke University Press.

Øyvind, Vågnes (2011) *Zaprudered: The Kennedy Assassination Film in Visual Culture*, Austin TX: University of Texas Press.

Paget, Derek (2007) 'Acting with Facts': Actors Performing the Real in British Theatre and Television Since 1990: A Preliminary Report on a New Research Project', *Studies in Documentary Film*, 1:2, 165–176.

——— (2013) 'Making Mischief: Peter Kosminsky, Stephen Frears and British Television Docudrama', *Journal of British Cinema and Television*, 10:1, 171–186.

Palmer, Martyn (2010) 'Robert Harris: Tony Blair Might as Well Have Been an American in Downing Street', 27 March. www.opendemocracy.net/en/opendemocracyuk/robert-harris-on-tony-blair-and-new-film-of-ghost/. Accessed 29 March 2019.

Pasolini, Pier Paolo (1980 [1967]) 'Observations on the Long Take', *October*, 13, Summer, 3–6.

Plunkett, John (2007) 'That Joke isn't Funny Anymore', *The Guardian*, 9 January. www.the-guardian.com/media/2007/jan/09/channel4.broadcasting. Accessed 25 May 2019.

Polan, Dana (2013) 'Maddening Times: *Mad Men* in Its History', in Lauren M. Goodlad, Lilya Kaganovksy, and Robert A. Rushing (eds.) *Mad Men, Mad World: Sex, Politics, Style and the 1960s*, Durham and London: Duke University Press.

Porton, Richard (2013) 'Family Viewing: An Interview with Sarah Polley', *Cineaste*, 38:3, Summer, 36–40.

Prince, Stephen (2009) *Firestorm: American Film in the Age of Terrorism*, New York: Columbia University Press.

Rabinowitz, Paula (1993) 'Wreckage Upon Wreckage: History, Documentary and the Ruins of Memory', *History and Theory*, 32:2, May, 119–137.

——— (1994) *They Must Be Represented: The Politics of Documentary*, London: Verso.

Rapold, Nicolas (2011) 'The Arbor', *Film Comment*, 47:2, March–April, 68–69.

Rascaroli, L. (2013) 'A Common European Home? Filming the Urban Thirdspace in Marc Isaacs's Lift (2001)', *Studies in Documentary Film*, 7:1, 3–15.

Reinelt, Janelle (2009) 'The Promise of Documentary', in Alison Forsyth and Chris Megson (eds.) *Get Real: Documentary Theatre Past and Present*, London: Palgrave Macmillan.

Rich, Adrienne (1971) 'When We Dead Awaken: Writing as Re-Vision', in *On Lies, Secrets, and Silence: Selected Prose, 1966–1978*, New York: W. W. Norton and Company.

Rich, B. Ruby (2004) 'After the Fall: Cinema Studies Post-9/11', *Cinema Journal*, 43:2, Winter, 109–115.

Rieff, David (2016) *In Praise of Forgetting: Historical Memories and Its Ironies*, New Haven and London: Yale University Press.

Rodney, Leo (2005) 'Real Time, Catastrophe, Spectacle: Reality and Fantasy in Live Media', in Geoff King (ed.) *The Spectacle of the Real: From Hollywood to Reality TV and Beyond*, Bristol and Portland: Intellect Books.

Roiphe, Katie (2010) 'The Allure of Messy Lives', *The New York Times*, 30 July. www.nytimes.com/2010/08/01/fashion/01Cultural.html?pagewanted=all&_r=0. Accessed 9 July 2014.

Rosenfeld, Gavriel D. (2005) *The World Hitler Never Made: Alternate History and the Memory of Nazism*, Cambridge: Cambridge University Press.

Rosenheck, Mabel (2013) 'Swing Skirts and Swinging Singles: *Mad Men*, Fashion and Cultural Memory', in Lauren M. Goodlad, Lilya Kaganovsky and Robert A. Rushing (eds.) *Man Men, Mad World: Sex, Politics, Style and the 1960s*, Durham and London: Duke University Press, 161–180.

Rosenheim, Shawn (1996) 'Interrotroning History: Errol Morris and the Documentary of the Future', in Vivian Sobchack (ed.) *The Persistence of History: Cinema, Television, and the Modernist Event*, London and New York: Routledge.

Rosenstone, Robert (1988) 'History in Images/History in Words: Reflections on the Possibility of Really Putting History onto Film', *American Historical Review*, 93:5, December, 1173–1185.

——— (2012) *History on Film/Film on History*, London and New York: Routledge.

Rosenthal, Alan (1978) 'Emile de Antonio: An Interview', *Film Quarterly*, 31:1, Fall, 4–17.

——— (2014) *From Chariots of Fire to The King's Speech: Writing Biopics and Docudramas*, Carbondale: Southern Illinois University Press.

Ruddick, Siân (2012) 'John Keane Captures Blair's Lies and Iraq's Horrors on Canvas', *The Socialist Worker*, 2288, 4 February. https://socialistworker.co.uk/art/26888/John+Keane+captures+Blairs+lies+and+Iraqs+horrors+on+canvas. Accessed 1 June 2019.

Russell, Catherine (1999) *Experimental Ethnography: The Work of Film in the Age of Video*, Durham: Duke University Press.

Scannell, Paddy (2004) 'Broadcasting Historiography and Historicality', *Screen*, 45:2, 130–141.

Schama, Simon (2004) 'Television and the Trouble with History', in David Cannadine (ed.) *History and the Media*, London: Palgrave Macmillan.

Schechner, Richard (1985) *Between Theatre and Anthropology*, Philadelphia: University of Pennsylvania Press.

——— (2014) *Performed Imaginaries*, London and New York: Routledge.

Schneider, Rebecca (2011) *Performing Remains: Art and War in Times of Theatrical Reenactment*, London and New York: Routledge.

Schulz, Kathryn (2016) 'Dead Certainty: How *Making a Murderer* Goes Wrong', *The New Yorker*, 17 January. www.newyorker.com/magazine/2016/01/25/dead-certainty. Accessed 10 April 2019.

Sciascia, Leonardo (2002 [1987]) *The Moro Affair*, London: Granta Books.

Seid, Steve (2004) 'Tunneling Through the Wasteland: Ant Farm Video', in Constance M. Lewallen and Steve Seid (eds.) *Ant Farm: 1968–1978*, Berkeley and Los Angeles: University of California Press.

Sharpley, Richard and Stone, Philip R. (eds.) (2009) *The Darker Side of Travel: The Theory and Practice of Dark Tourism*, Bristol, Buffalo and Toronto: Channel View Publications.

Sherwin, Richard K. (2011) *Visualizing Law in the Age of the Digital Baroque: Arabesques and Entanglements*, London and New York: Routledge.

Shivas, Mark (1963) 'Interviews: Richard Leacock', *Movie*, 8, April.

Silbey, Jessica (2007) 'A History of Representations of Justice: Coincident Preoccupations of Law and Film', in Antoine Masson and Kevin O'Connor (eds.) *Representations of Justice*, Oxford: Peter Lang.

——— (2009–2010) '*Evidence Verité* and the Law of Film', *Cardozo Law Review*, 31, 1257–1299.

——— (2012–13) 'Images in/of Law', *New York Law School Law Review*, 57, 171–183.

Simon, Art (1996) *Dangerous Knowledge: The JFK Assassination in Art and Film*, Philadelphia: Temple University Press.

Sjöberg, Patrik (2001) *The World in Pieces: A Study of Compilation Film*, Stockholm: Aura Förlag.

Slyce, John (2003) 'Jeremy Deller: Fables of the Reconstruction', *Flash Art International*, 36:228, 74–77.

Smith, Damon (2011) 'Clio Barnard: *The Arbor*', *Filmmaker*, 27 April. https://filmmaker-magazine.com/23471-clio-barnard-the-arbor/#.XR6GyS_My-o. Accessed 5 July 2019.

Smith, Gavin (2006) 'Mission Statement', *Film Comment*, 42:3, May–June, 24–28.

Sobchack, Vivian (1996) 'Introduction: History Happens', in Vivien Sobchack (ed.) *The Persistence of History: Cinema, Television, and the Modern Event*, London and New York: Routledge.

——— (1999) 'Towards a Phenomenology of Nonfictional Film Experience', in Jane M. Gaines and Michael Renov (eds.) *Collecting Visible Evidence*, Minneapolis: University of Minnesota Press.

——— (2004) *Carnal Thoughts: Embodiment and Moving Image Culture*, Berkeley and Los Angeles: University of California Press.

Soja, Edward W. (1996) *Thirdspace: Journeys to Los Angeles and Other Real-and-Imagined Places*, Oxford: Blackwell.

Sontag, Susan (2001) 'Talk of the Town: Tuesday, and After', *New Yorker*, 24 September. www.newyorker.com/magazine/2001/09/24/tuesday-and-after-talk-of-the-town. Accessed 5 April 2017.

——— (2003) *Regarding the Pain of Others*, London: Penguin.

——— (2007) *At the Same Time*, London: Penguin.

Spence, Louise (2004) 'Teaching 9/11 and Why I'm Not Doing It Anymore', *Cinema Journal*, 43:2, Winter, 100–105.

Spence, Louise and Navarro, Vinicius (2010) *Crafting Truth: Documentary Form and Meaning*, New Brunswick: Rutgers University Press.

Spigel, Lynn (1988) 'Installing the Television Set: Popular Discourses on Television and Domestic Space, 1948–1955', *Camera Obscura*, 6:1, 16, 9–46.

——— (2004) 'Entertainment Wars: Television Culture After 9/11', *American Quarterly*, 56:2, June, 235–270.

Stamelman, Richard (2003) 'September 11: Between Memory and History', in Judith Greenberg (ed.) *Trauma at Home: After 9/11*, Lincoln: University of Nebraska Press.

Stanley, Alessandra (2010) 'Back to Work for *Mad Men*', *The New York Times*, 16 July. www.nytimes.com/2010/07/18/arts/television/18mad.html?_r=0. Accessed 26 May 2014.

Steedman, Carolyn (2001) *Dust*, Manchester: Manchester University Press.

Stewart, Michael and Butt, Richard (2011) 'We Had It Coming: Hypothetical Docudrama as Contested Form and Multiple Fantasy', *Critical Studies in Television*, 6:1, 72–88.

Storr, Robert (2010) *September: A History Painting by Gerhard Richter*, London: Tate Publishing.

Street, John (2003) 'The Celebrity Politician: Political Style and Popular Culture', in John Corner and Dick Pels (eds.) *Media and the Restyling of Politics*, London: Sage Publications.

Sturken, Marita (1997) *Tangled Memories: The Vietnam War, the AIDS Epidemic, and the Politics of Remembering*, Berkeley and Los Angeles: University of California Press.

——— (2007) *Tourists of History: Memory, Kitsch, and Consumerism from Oklahoma City to Ground Zero*, Durham: Duke University Press.

Suárez, Juan A. (2004) 'City Films, Modern Spatiality, and the End of the World Trade Center', in Wheeler Winston Dixon (ed.) *Film and Television After 9/11*, Carbondale: Southern Illinois University Press.

Taussig, Michael (1993) *Mimesis and Alterity: A Particular History of the Senses*, London and New York: Routledge.

Taylor, Lib (2013) 'Voice, Body and the Transmission of the Real in Documentary Theatre', *Contemporary Theatre Review*, 23:3, 368–379.

Ten Brink, Joram (2012) 'Re-Enactment, the History of Violence and Documentary Film', in Joram Ten Brink and Joshua Oppenheimer (eds.) *Killer Images: Documentary Film, Memory and the Performance of Violence*, London and New York: Wallflower Press.

Thiess, Derek (2014) *Relativism, Alternate History, and the Forgetful Reader: Reading Science Fiction*, London: Lexington.

Thomson, David (2011) 'David Thomson on Films: "The Arbor"', *The New Republic*, 20 May. https://newrepublic.com/article/88732/the-arbor-clio-barnard-andrea-dunbar-playwright. Accessed 6 July 2019.

Travis, Alan (2014) 'Thatcher Had Secret Plan to Use Army at Height of Miners' Strike', *The Guardian*, 3 January. www.theguardian.com/politics/2014/jan/03/margaret-thatcher-secret-plan-army-miners-strike. Accessed 12 July 2019.

Tuchman, Mitch (1978) 'Kennedy Death Films', *Take One*, 6:6, May, 18–22.

Turpin, Ruby (2012) 'Is the *Mad Men* Season 5 Poster in Bad Taste?' *Starcasm*, 28 January. http://starcasm.net/archives/141151. Accessed 6 April 2017.

Varon, Jeremy (2013) 'History Gets in Your Eyes: *Mad Men*, Misrecognition, and the Masculine Mystique', in Lauren M. Goodlad, Lilya Kaganovsky and Robert A. Rushing (eds.) *Man Men, Mad World: Sex, Politics, Style and the 1960s*, Durham and London: Duke University Press, 257–278.

Vaughan, Dai (1999) *For Documentary: Twelve Essays*, Berkeley and Los Angeles: University of California Press.

Vidal, Belén (2014) 'Morgan/Sheen: The Compressed Frame of Impersonation', in Tom Brown and Belén Vidal (eds.) *The Biopic in Contemporary Film Culture*, New York and London: Routledge.

Walker, Janet (2013) 'The Act of Killing and the Production of a Crime Scene', Film Quarterly, 67:2, Winter, 14–20.

Wallace, Richard (2018) Mockumentary Comedy: Performing Authenticity, London: Palgrave Macmillan.

Watt, Nicholas (2010) 'Tony Blair Hopes to Silence "Cheeky" Author Who Mocked Him in The Ghost', The Guardian, 1 September. www.theguardian.com/politics/wintour-and-watt/2010/sep/01/tonyblair-pierce-brosnan. Accessed 30 May 2019.

Waugh, Thomas (1976) 'Beyond Verité: Emile de Antonio and the New Documentary of the 70s', Jump Cut, 10–11. www.ejumpcut.org/archive/onlinessays/JC10-11folder/EmileDeAntonio.html. Accessed 30 August 2019.

Weber, Cynthia (2006) Imagining America at War: Morality, Politics, and Film, London and New York: Routledge.

Weiner, Bernard and de Antonio, Emile (1971) 'Radical Scavenging: An Interview with Emile de Antonio', Film Quarterly, 25:1, Autumn, 3–15.

Weiss, Peter (1971) 'The Material and the Models', Theatre Quarterly, 1:1, January–March, 41–45.

Westwell, Guy (2011) 'Regarding the Pain of Others: Scenarios of Obligation in Post-9/11 US Cinema', Journal of American Studies, 45:4, 815–834.

―――― (2014) Parallel Lines: Post-9/11 American Cinema, London: Wallflower Press.

White, Hayden (1980) 'The Value of Narrativity in the Representation of Reality', Critical Inquiry, 7:1, Autumn, 5–27.

―――― (1987) The Content of the Form: Narrative Discourse and Historical Representation, Baltimore, MD: Johns Hopkins University Press.

―――― (1988) 'Historiography and Historiophoty', American Historical Review, 93:5, December, 1193–1199.

―――― (1996) 'The Modernist Event', in Vivian Sobchack (ed.) The Persistence of History: Cinema, Television and the Modern Event, London and New York: Routledge.

White, Theodore (1963) 'For President Kennedy: An Epilogue', Life Magazine, 6 December. https://timedotcom.files.wordpress.com/2016/12/jfk-epilogue.jpg. Accessed 1 September 2019.

Whitfield, John (2006) 'From Microscope to Multiplex', Nature, 44:22, June, 922–925.

Winston, Brian (1999) '"Honest, Straightforward Re-Enactment": The Staging of Reality', in Kees Bakker (ed.) Joris Ivens and the Documentary Context, Amsterdam: University of Amsterdam Press.

―――― (2008) Claiming the Real: Documentary: Grierson and Beyond, London: BFI Publishing, Palgrave Macmillan.

―――― (2013) 'Introduction: The Documentary Film', in Brian Winston (ed.) Brain The Documentary Film Book, London: BFI Publishing, Palgrave Macmillan, 1–29.

Wollen, Peter (1989) 'Cinema/Americanism/the Robot', New Formations, 8, Summer, 7–34.

Wood, Jason (2011) 'The Arbor: Interview with Clio Barnard', Electric Sheep: A Deviant View of Cinema, 2 March. www.electricsheepmagazine.co.uk/2011/03/02/the-arbor-interview-with-clio-barnard/. Accessed 5 July 2019.

Žižek, Slavoj (2002) Welcome to the Desert of the Real! Five Essays on September 11 and Related Dates, London: Verso.

Zutter, Natalie (2012) 'Mad Men's Season 5 Poster Criticized for Looking Like Tragic 9/11 Photograph'. www.crushable.com/2012/01/17/entertainment/mad-men-season-5-poster-march-25/. Accessed 27 November 2013.

INDEX